To my 'A-Team'

KU-655-800

REAGAN AND THATCHER

The Difficult Relationship

Richard Aldous

LIBRARIES NI
WITHDRAWN FROM STOCK

HUTCHINSON
LONDON

Published by Hutchinson 2012

2 4 6 8 10 9 7 5 3 1

Copyright © Richard Aldous 2012

Richard Aldous has asserted his right under the Copyright, Designs and Patents Act 1988 to be identified as the author of this work

This book is a work of non-fiction.

This book is sold subject to the condition that it shall not, by way of trade or otherwise, be lent, resold, hired out, or otherwise circulated without the publisher's prior consent in any form of binding or cover other than that in which it is published and without a similar condition, including this condition, being imposed on the subsequent purchaser.

LIBRARIES NI

C701022665

RONDO 09/03/2012

327.73041090 £ 14.99

RTC

First published in Great Britain in 2012 by Hutchinson

Random House, 20 Vauxhall Bridge Road, London SW1V 2SA

www.randomhousebooks.co.uk

Addresses for companies within The Random House Group Limited can be found at: www.randomhouse.co.uk/offices.htm

The Random House Group Limited Reg. No. 954009

A CIP catalogue record for this book is available from the British Library

ISBN 9780091926083

The Random House Group Limited supports The Forest Stewardship Council (FSC®), the leading international forest certification organisation. Our books carrying the FSC label are printed on FSC® certified paper. FSC is the only forest certification scheme endorsed by the leading environmental organisations, including Greenpeace. Our paper procurement policy can be found at www.randomhouse.co.uk/environment

FSC www.fsc.org MIX Paper from responsible sources FSC® C016897

Typeset in Bembo by Palimpsest Book Production Limited, Falkirk, Stirlingshire

Printed and bound in Great Britain by Clays Ltd, St Ives plc

Contents

Prologue

President Reagan's state funeral. 11 June 2004. Margaret Thatcher sat expressionless as her pre-recorded words rang around the National Cathedral in Washington, DC. Beside her was the man she had famously introduced onto the world stage with the words, 'I can do business with Mr Gorbachev.' Immediately in front sat Ronald Reagan's widow, Nancy, who had invited the former prime minister to speak and later to accompany her on the Air Force jet to California for the interment. The incumbent president, George W. Bush, watched intently, knowing that his own eulogy would be judged against the standard set by the 'Iron Lady'. Few questioned Thatcher's place in this gathering as an equal. Her tribute to the former president – videotaped because doctors advised against a live oration – was both affectionate and uplifting. She brimmed with evident pride at the friendship they had enjoyed and their shared role in changing the world.

'We have lost a great president, a great American, and a great man,' she delivered in her familiar breathy tones. 'I have lost a dear friend . . . Others prophesied the decline of the West. He inspired America and his allies with renewed faith in their mission of freedom.'[1]

Speaking afterwards to CNN, Harold Evans, the eminent commentator and former *Sunday Times* editor, judged that 'Churchill and Roosevelt had a relationship; I think the relationship between Thatcher and President Reagan was closer even than Churchill and Roosevelt.'

Reagan and Thatcher would have been delighted with Evans's assessment. It was a view they had consciously attempted to foster during their shared time in office. Each had vigorously asserted it in their memoirs and reminiscences. But their presentation masked the reality of a complex, even fractious alliance.

Reconstructing this competitive relationship is possible through the comprehensive primary material that is now available in public and private archives. Historians no longer have to rely just on anecdotal material or even the excellent published memoirs of the period. Instead, the cut and thrust of vigorous debates on key strategic differences comes alive in recently declassified documents. Tens of thousands of pages of official documents relating to Ronald Reagan and Margaret Thatcher have been made available on both sides of the Atlantic. Reagan's diaries are in the public domain. Papers from Margaret Thatcher's private archive have been opened. Added to these written sources are the extensive oral history projects that have recorded and interrogated the recollections of key figures within each administration.[2] In every sense the Reagan–Thatcher era is now history.

Even Margaret Thatcher herself has, over time, been prepared to let down the guard a little about her relationship with the president. Visiting Chequers in 2008, she confided to the prime minister's wife, Sarah Brown, the secret of her relationship with Reagan. 'It all worked,' Lady Thatcher suggested, 'because he was more afraid of me than I was of him.'[3]

Sir Nicholas Henderson, Thatcher's ambassador to Washington when Reagan was elected, would not have been surprised at this less-than-flattering analysis. In a chance encounter with a former Labour cabinet minister, Tony Benn, in the 1990s, Henderson was asked whether he had ever known anything really secret.

After considering for a few moments, the ambassador replied, 'If I reported to you what Mrs Thatcher really thought about President Reagan, it would damage Anglo-American relations.'[4]

What follows is the story of that difficult relationship.

1

Churchill, Jefferson and Jesus

'Nervous.' It was not a word often associated with Margaret Thatcher, but that was how Nicholas Henderson found the prime minister in Downing Street on 18 February 1981. It was exactly a week before Thatcher's first visit to meet the recently inaugurated fortieth president of the United States, Ronald Wilson Reagan. 'Mrs T told me that she was a little worried by her forthcoming visit to Washington,' Henderson wrote in his diary afterwards. 'She did not quite see how it would go. She admitted being nervous about it.' Thatcher was taken aback when the ambassador mentioned that the toasts at dinner would be televised. She fretted about the allusions to the past that she would use – 'I shall want all the best historical advice I can get!' And when they discussed what gifts she might present to the Reagans, the PM rushed from the room to retrieve the exquisite Halcyon boxes that she thought might be suitable. Thatcher's nerves and uncharacteristic giddiness were not the only surprise. 'It was noticeable how little we talked about the substance of her discussions with Reagan,' the ambassador noted. What mattered, he concluded, was that she wanted to see the president alone.[1]

It was a point the new American administration could hardly have failed to miss. 'The Prime Minister wants, above all, to build upon her relationship with you,' the new US secretary of state, Al Haig, told the president that same day, 'and to have her visit perceived as a very strong reaffirmation of the "Special Relationship".'

No sooner had the Reagan transition team arrived in Washington following an election victory in November 1980 than Henderson had begun an elegant but relentless diplomatic offensive to secure an early invitation for Thatcher to the White House. There was no better man for the task. 'Nico' Henderson was a charming character whose rumpled appearance masked shrewd political instincts. He had shot to notoriety in 1979 when his valedictory dispatch as ambassador to Paris, which had been scathing about the mentality of failure in British foreign policy, had found its way into the hands of the *Economist* magazine. Thatcher had been impressed enough with his biting assessment, which matched her own, to bring Henderson out of retirement and send him to Washington.[2]

Henderson's patrician blend of good-humoured eccentricity combined with a reputation for knowing how to play the game made him a prized guest on the Washington social circuit. He exploited those connections ruthlessly on behalf of his country in a way not seen since the days of David Ormsby-Gore, friend of JFK and Britain's representative at 'Camelot'. In early December 1980, Henderson attended a dinner for the Reagans organised by Katharine Graham, the formidable owner of *The Washington Post*. The Hendersons had spent the Thanksgiving weekend with Graham and her family on Martha's Vineyard, where the ambassador had encouraged her to host a dinner for the president-elect. Only when everything was in place did she phone Henderson to say that her friend Henry Kissinger, the former secretary of state, had advised her it would be most improper for an ambassador to attend. It took all the fancy footwork at Henderson's disposal to make sure he stayed on the guest list.[3]

Once in the door, Henderson made the most of his chance. He buttonholed Ed Meese, the campaign chief of staff and 'one of the most powerful men in the Reagan entourage', to raise the subject of an early Thatcher visit to the White House. Meese, who had met Thatcher previously and liked her, told Henderson that the prime minister would be among the first allies that the new president wanted to receive. Meese promised to talk to Richard Allen, the incoming national security adviser. Allen was another admirer of Thatcher, having met her when accompanying Reagan on a visit to London in 1978 and at a subsequent talk in Downing Street. Shortly after Meese had promised to speak to Allen, a formal invitation was issued to visit the White House.[4]

Henderson even managed to take advantage of the new administration's inexperience by securing an acceptance by the president to attend a dinner at the British Embassy in DC. The staff in the Protocol Department at the State Department were furious, saying that this would spark a diplomatic incident, because the president would not be accepting invitations from other embassies. Allen tried to pressure Henderson into cancelling the dinner, but in the end accepted that it was a *fait accompli*. The ambassador decided not 'to reveal to Number 10 how nearly it came to vanishing point.' In fact, he did not even tell his wife, who was already making the arrangements. But the slip by the incoming administration was one more small way in which Thatcher and the British were able from the outset to point to a relationship that was just that little bit 'special'. In any event, Haig told the president, it fitted with the first stated objective of the visit for the new administration: 'to demonstrate publicly and privately that Thatcher is the major western leader most attuned to your views.'[5]

At 3.45 pm on Wednesday, 25 February 1981, Thatcher took off in an RAF VC-10 bound for Washington. Although still somewhat nervous, she was 'delighted . . . that the new president wished me to be the first foreign head of government to visit the United States after he took office.' Not quite, as it turned out. The myth would quickly take hold that Thatcher was the first leader through the doors of the White House in 1981. In fact, Prime Minister Seaga of Jamaica and President Chun of South Korea beat her to it as official visitors, and there had been several other private meetings. But irrespective of whether she was first, Thatcher understood that she had been given an early opportunity, as she wrote to Reagan, for 'renewing our friendship' and 'consolidating the close relationship between our two countries.'[6]

This attitude was a contrast to the early days of Thatcher's relationship with Reagan's predecessor, Jimmy Carter, in 1979.

Right from the beginning, there had been speculation in London and Washington that the Carter administration had wanted Thatcher to lose the general election. The president had previously developed a relationship with the Labour prime minister, Jim Callaghan. Thatcher on the other hand he found to be a 'not unattractive woman' but 'overbearing' when they had met in 1977. Writing days after her election in May 1979, national security adviser Zbigniew Brzezinski admitted to Carter that 'it will take patience to deal with Mrs Thatcher's hard driving nature and her tendency to hector', but he encouraged the president to believe 'we can work with her'. In particular, he noted astutely, 'she will benefit greatly from the fact and the feeling of your personal attention.'[7]

Although Thatcher came to feel a certain regard for Carter on a personal level – 'It was impossible not to like Jimmy Carter' – her later assessment of his presidency was negative. He was 'unsure' on economics. He was 'inclined to drift'. In foreign policy he often found himself 'surprised and embarrassed'. In general, Thatcher concluded, Carter had no vision of America's future.[8]

Yet whatever her views afterwards, at the time she did her best to get along with Carter and to strengthen transatlantic ties. Early telephone conversations and encounters at summit meetings were usually stilted and lacking in either personal warmth or political understanding. 'Thatcher is a tough lady,' Carter complained in his diary at the Tokyo G-7 summit in June 1979, 'highly opinionated, strong-willed, cannot admit that she doesn't know anything.' Only latterly did the relationship warm up as the president came to welcome Thatcher's toughness. At the end of 1979, with Carter mired in the Iran hostage crisis, Thatcher made a morale-boosting visit to Washington. 'A member of the White House said privately afterwards that the discussion there had been the best he had ever attended,' Henderson reported. By the end of the visit there was no doubting 'the president's inner conviction that Britain, through its prime minister, is his soundest international partner.' Shortly afterwards, in a telephone conversation, Carter told Thatcher that he spoke to other allies only 'after I've got to talk to you'. By 1980, he was telling her how much 'Americans admire the leadership that the United Kingdom and you personally are showing,' and expressing his own 'deep personal appreciation' for her support.[9]

It had been a long haul, but that ability to work with Carter, a man she did not respect politically, and to become his 'soundest international partner', showed the extent to which Margaret Thatcher was able to set aside any lack of political empathy to ensure that the transatlantic relationship flourished. As a young MP in the late 1950s and early 1960s, she had watched and learnt from the prime minister, Harold Macmillan, that 'appearance did seem to count for a lot' in foreign affairs. Cementing friendships with US presidents and delivering put-downs to America's political opponents would become as much a signature of Thatcher's foreign policy as it was for Macmillan, although she rarely attempted his wit. But just as Macmillan had worked on his relationship with Kennedy, whom he had feared would regard him as an irrelevant relic of an earlier century, so too Thatcher nurtured her ties with Carter, even though there seemed little basis for friendship or ideological sympathy. Perhaps their shared non-conformist background had helped. Carter was a devout Baptist; Thatcher had been raised a strict Methodist (as was Carter's vice-president, Walter Mondale). They may not have prayed together, as George W. Bush and Tony Blair were later rumoured to have done, and neither did they discuss faith or religion. But they did share a certain view of the world that gave them at least some point of connection. In May 1979, Margaret Thatcher had crossed the threshold of No. 10 quoting St Francis of Assisi. It is not difficult to imagine that Jimmy Carter too was a man who believed that 'Where there is error, may we bring truth'.[10]

Thatcher's success in keeping the Anglo-American relationship on an even keel was to a significant degree institutional, not personal – a testament to the strength of the Atlantic Alliance. The underlying structure of that alliance had remained more or less in place since its inception during the Second World War. Historians have identified three fundamentals as its touchstones since the 1940s: consultation; intelligence; and nuclear weapons. Officials in each government easily and naturally consulted their opposite numbers to get a sense of their thinking. More often than not this was informal, even social. Their interactions enabled both sides to get a feel for policy options and the rationale behind proposals, which in turn allowed each to influence the decision making of the other. This was particularly important in Washington, where policy making was so diffuse. Consultation did not necessarily mean consensus. Often it could result simply in an agreement to disagree. But it did mean there were few surprises.

Difficulties when they arose, such as the Suez crisis in 1956, were often as much about a failure to consult – and warn – as any irreconcilable or intractable policy differences. Intelligence was a central feature of that process of consultation. The two countries had cooperated to an unprecedented degree during the Second World War, and continued to do so throughout most of the cold war. There were occasional breakdowns in trust, not least surrounding the 'Cambridge Five' Soviet spy ring within British intelligence throughout the 1940s, 1950s and 1960s – Thatcher unmasked one of the five, Sir Anthony Blunt, shortly after becoming prime minister. Personnel from intelligence-gathering operations in Britain (GCHQ) and America (NSA) naturally pooled resources, which fed into more general defence cooperation, often including nuclear technology. From 1958 onwards America had given Britain unique access to its nuclear weapons systems – successively Skybolt, Polaris and Trident. Britain in return gave the United States the right to use several of its key strategic bases.[11]

Yet personal chemistry, or the lack of it, between the principal actors could often be a catastrophically destabilising element in the Anglo-American relationship. This feature, some might even say weakness, was built into the alliance since its inception.

Modern relations between Britain and the United States have a distinctive language and etiquette that is rooted in the wartime alliance and the first meeting between Churchill and Roosevelt in August 1941 at Placentia Bay, Newfoundland. Its tone is one of shared culture, history and struggle burnished in fighting a global war together. For shorthand, it is sometimes referred to by both sides in Churchillian terms as the 'special relationship'. 'It is my deepest conviction,' Churchill had written in 1944, coining the phrase, 'that unless Britain and the United States are joined in a special relationship another destructive war will come to pass.' Rather like the rules of cricket or baseball, the terms of that relationship have a quaint and archaic quality that obscures the reality of a fast and often adversarial conflict.

Churchill claimed this incomparable partnership between Britain and America was based on two unique friendships: that between the two countries as 'English-speaking peoples', and the close personal association he enjoyed with President Franklin D. Roosevelt. Subsequent prime ministers, not least Margaret Thatcher, would often evoke that Churchillian theme of national and personal solidarity. During her last visit to the Reagan White House in 1988, Thatcher would proudly declare that 'Together, we have been able to demonstrate the truth of Winston Churchill's words about our two peoples when he said this: "As long as our people act in absolute faith and honour to each other and to all other nations, they need fear none and they need fear nothing!"' President Reagan, she continued, had been 'more than a staunch ally and wise counsellor. You have also been a wonderful friend to me and my country.'[12]

Throughout the 1980s both Thatcher and Reagan would echo the evangelising Churchillian language of a 'special relationship'. They did so at a time when interpretations of the founding partnership between Churchill and Roosevelt were undergoing a fundamental revision towards something altogether more 'functional'.[13] A series of scholarly books published around the time of Thatcher's and Reagan's election victories demonstrated how the FDR-Churchill relationship had been both 'remarkably close and yet particularly strained'.[14] The wartime alliance itself had been one in which 'competition [was] the persistent counterpoint to the melody of cooperation' as 'Britain and America manoeuvred for advantage and pre-eminence'.[15] Indeed, one American historian has argued that 'Franklin Roosevelt was the most Anglophobic American president of the twentieth century, and despite [British] resistance he managed, as John Maynard Keynes put it, to "pick out the eyes of the British Empire" during World War II.'[16] Competitive cooperation would remain at the heart of the Anglo-American relationship in the decades that followed as their geopolitical interests overlapped or diverged.[17]

Rapport between the principal actors did often help to smooth the way at difficult moments. John F. Kennedy never forgot Macmillan's fellow-feeling at their first meeting, when the prime minister took him off for whisky and sandwiches after recent humiliation at the hands of the Soviet leader, Nikita Khrushchev. 'Kennedy, with his own fondness for the British political style,' later wrote presidential aide Arthur Schlesinger, Jr, 'liked Macmillan's patrician approach to politics, his impatience with official ritual, his insouciance with professionals, his pose of nonchalance, even when most deeply committed.' That personal regard could bring concrete results for Britain: when the United States scrapped the Skybolt missile system, Macmillan insisted in a one-to-one meeting with the president that he wanted Polaris instead. Kennedy, aware that the issue was 'political dynamite' for Macmillan, ignored the objections of his own officials and gave the prime minister what he wanted. As the official US report into the decision later concluded, 'it was a case of "king to king", and it infuriated the court.'

At other times, poor personal chemistry could have the opposite effect. Lyndon Johnson thought Macmillan's successor, Harold Wilson, was 'a little creep' and 'too clever by half'. Matters were not helped by the height disparity between the two men, which made Wilson feel physically humiliated. Their personal discomfort was more than matched by that of Edward Heath and Richard Nixon, who despite similar backgrounds and political ideals, took personal awkwardness between presidents and prime ministers to new and excruciating levels. Taken together, these two premierships resulted in disillusion on both sides and the longest sustained disharmony in the history of the Anglo-American relationship.[18]

For Margaret Thatcher, the Atlantic Alliance was a first principle of foreign policy. 'There is a union of mind and purpose between our peoples which is remarkable and which makes our relationship truly a remarkable one,' she would declare at a Washington banquet in 1985 to mark 200 years of diplomatic relations between Great Britain and the United States: 'It is special. It just is, and that's that.' Throughout her period in office, the alliance would prosper in a number of traditional ways. The nuclear relationship would be renewed by a deal on Trident, thereby reconfirming

Britain's status as the only ally to have access to US nuclear technology. The global division of labour in intelligence gathering, established in 1946–7, would continue to work effectively. The enduring association between the two navies would effortlessly kick into gear during the Falklands crisis. It was cooperation that reflected the strength of the institutional underpinnings of the alliance.

Yet while Anglo-American defence and diplomatic ties continued to traverse the ups and downs of competitive cooperation with skill and judgement, Thatcher time and again over the next eight years would find herself in conflict with a president who, despite her protestations to the contrary, she often viewed as much as a hindrance as a help to British foreign policy.

Concerns about Reagan would come later. At the outset, there was only admiration. The two had first met on 9 April 1975, just a few months after she had been elected as leader of the Conservative Party. Reagan, the recently retired governor of California and now presidential aspirant, was touring Europe to beef up his foreign policy credentials in preparation for a run at the presidency in 1976. In Britain, he found it hard to get in to see anyone. The prime minister, Harold Wilson, refused to see him on the bizarre grounds that the last time he had entertained a presidential candidate – George Wallace – at No. 10, the man had thrown up over the prime minister's desk. Jim Callaghan, the foreign secretary, cancelled saying he had to attend Splott Fair, a local event in his constituency.[19]

In the end, it was the junior Foreign Office minister, Roy Hattersley, who received him. 'Ex-governor Reagan arrived surrounded by muscular men in dark glasses – enough to stand guard at each of the Old India Office's imposing twin doors and the rather less spectacular pair that led to my private lavatory and the drinks cupboard,' Hattersley later recalled. While Reagan espoused his view that all unemployment was voluntary, 'the usually well mannered young men from the Foreign Office who sat beside me made choking noises.' At the end of the visit, Reagan fished out a bunch of 'Spirit of California' medals in gold, silver and bronze from his coat pocket. Hattersley was presented with silver; presumably the foreign secretary would have been given gold. It had all been perfectly cordial, but it was just one of dozens of similar meetings that a junior minister would take in any given week 'as a matter of courtesy rather than in order to do any serious business.'[20]

If Reagan had been something of a joke for Hattersley and his officials at the Foreign Office – many of whom had the same attitude towards Margaret Thatcher – then he was given a much more enthusiastic and admiring welcome from the new leader of the Conservative Party. There had been much talk about the governor of California among British Conservatives going back to the 1960s. Reagan's election in 1967 on a radical right-wing ticket had coincided with the popularity of free market economics in the Tory Party. Following a Conservative victory at the polls in 1970, 'the Governor' was a regular feature in private conversation, 'his identity and importance fully recognised,' said the journalist Hugo Young, 'without any need to mention his name.'[21]

The Conservative leader Edward Heath's move to the right proved short-lived, and so 'the Governor' faded from view in Britain. But Margaret Thatcher remembered him, and in 1975, having deposed Heath as leader, was keen to meet a man she hoped could be an intellectual soul mate. In particular, she remembered how her husband, Denis, had been impressed by a 'remarkable' speech Reagan delivered to the Institute of Directors at the Royal Albert Hall in 1969. 'In almost three years in government,' Reagan had declared, 'I have learned at first hand how savage can be resistance [within government] to any attempt to reduce the size and power of government. I have also learned that the size and power of government can be reduced – and the reduction will be hailed by the people, for men want to be free.' Margaret Thatcher later recalled, 'In a way he had the advantage of me, because he was able to say: "This is what I believe! This is what I have done!".'[22] Re-reading the speech in preparation for meeting Reagan, it seemed like a clarion call.

The introduction on 9 April 1975 had been set up by Justin Dart, the chairman of a Los Angeles pharmaceutical company and a member of Reagan's Californian 'kitchen cabinet', who was also an acquaintance of Denis Thatcher. Dart was known as 'Johnny

Appleseed' among the American business community for his 'Sunbelt evangelical' passion. It was an intensity that he recognised in Margaret Thatcher, whom he advised Reagan to find time to see in London. When they met in Thatcher's cramped rooms in Westminster, overlooking the parking pool where government drivers milled around smoking and chatting, there was an obvious and immediate rapport. They had planned to take only a few minutes together for a courtesy 'meet and greet'. In the end they spent closer to ninety minutes talking. 'They fell into conversation as if they'd been friends for years,' remembered Reagan's campaign adviser, Peter Hannaford, who was present. 'They were peas in a pod. The chemistry was perfect, and on policy they saw eye to eye.' Hovering in the background afterwards, straight out of central casting, was young Winston Churchill – Conservative MP and grandson of the great man himself – whom Thatcher liked to trot out for visiting Americans as a dynastic reminder of the 'special relationship'.[23]

Reagan recalled of this first meeting with Thatcher that 'I liked her immediately.' That same evening, attending a reception, he declared to a fellow guest – an Englishman – that he thought Thatcher would make 'a magnificent prime minister'. When the guest (no doubt transformed over the years in Reagan's frequent retelling into the worst Hollywood version of a peppery English m'lord) spluttered, 'My dear fellow, a WOMAN prime minister', the governor gently reminded him that 'England once had a queen named Victoria who did rather well.' It was a point the great nineteenth-century Conservative prime minister, Benjamin Disraeli, had often liked to make in support of women's suffrage.[24]

Back in California later that month, Reagan was quick to write to Thatcher to express his thanks and to invite her to visit. 'You were very kind and I was grateful,' he wrote. 'If you can, Mrs Reagan and I would like very much to return your hospitality. In the meantime please know you have an enthusiastic supporter out here in the "colonies".' Shortly afterwards Reagan told the historian Robert Conquest that he had 'the highest respect' for Thatcher. Importantly, the trip established informal links between the two offices. 'It began a correspondence with Thatcher and her staff that went on until he became president,' recalled

Hannaford, who also held meetings in London with senior Tories such as Sir Geoffrey Howe and Keith Joseph.[25]

Reagan met Thatcher for the second time during another visit to London in November 1978. Although the governor had lost the Republican nomination in 1976, his speech at the nominating convention had electrified the party's base. Now he seemed a genuine contender for the election of 1980. The Labour government afforded this potential presidential candidate more official recognition by arranging a meeting with David Owen, the new foreign secretary. Reagan was there to beef up his foreign policy credentials, but Hollywood glamour was never far away. Following the meeting, as the two men left Owen's office together, there was a touching breach of protocol when a Foreign Office tea lady approached and asked if this was 'Mr Ronald Reagan from Hollywood?' Then from behind the elegant pillars, with the bemused foreign secretary looking on, more and more of her colleagues appeared, all of whom had seen Reagan's films and wanted to know the gossip from *Kings Row*. If politics is 'just show business for ugly people', Reagan had the fans wherever he went to prove this was never the case for him.

The impromptu stop with the tea ladies of the Foreign Office made Reagan late for his meeting with Thatcher. Uncharacteristically, she seems not to have minded. By this time, the leader of the opposition had moved into better accommodation with a view onto the famous New Palace Yard. The two chatted animatedly for well over an hour in a conversation that covered a broad range of issues, including the cold war and a substantial exchange on privatisation. Establishing a pattern that would remain over the course of their relationship, Reagan was anecdotal, Thatcher policy-driven and analytical. Yet there was a clear rapport, one that was strengthened for Reagan by the obvious seriousness and respect with which Thatcher treated him and his ideas. The visit to Owen had been perfunctory. The American ambassador to London, Kingman Brewster, had refused to see him. Yet here was the Conservative leader, six months away as it turned out from becoming prime minister, paying Reagan the compliment of taking him seriously. 'Wonderful meeting with her and started a beautiful intellectual romance,' recalled Richard Allen, who had accompanied the governor.[26]

For Thatcher, the enthusiasm was much the same. 'When we met in person I was immediately won over by his charm, sense of humour and directness,' she recalled. 'In the succeeding years I read his speeches, advocating tax cuts as the root to wealth creation and stronger defences as an alternative to *detente*. I also read many of his fortnightly broadcasts to the people of California, which his press secretary sent over regularly for me. I agreed with them all.'[27]

Thatcher's words, written in retirement, may seem like the kind of warm glow required for a relationship that she had consistently presented as 'special' for well over a decade. Certainly she had been pleased Reagan made the effort to see her, not least in 1978 when it was still generally thought, before the industrial 'winter of discontent' engulfed the Labour government, that she would lose the forthcoming general election. A visit from a potential presidential candidate might help her own foreign policy credibility. But Thatcher's private papers confirm that at this early stage she was also genuinely interested in Reagan's ideas. For example, she marked up a wide-ranging speech on global affairs that Reagan sent her after his second visit. Those markings suggest a particular engagement with his ideas on free trade and the cold war. On trade, Thatcher noted Reagan's support for free trade balanced with his view that 'we cannot tolerate gross discrimination against US products abroad and still allow others virtually unrestricted access to our own markets . . . Reciprocity will be the governing feature of our policies.' On the cold war, she noted his assessment that 'If the present trends continue, the United States will be in a role of permanent military inferiority vis-a-vis the Soviet Union.' One consequence of that, Thatcher marked up, would be that the Soviets 'will intimidate, "Finlandize", and ultimately neutralize Western Europe.'[28]

Reagan included in this speech a line from Winston Churchill that 'When great forces are on the move in the world we learn we are spirits not animals.' Such Churchillian rhetoric would become a consistent and well-choreographed feature of Reagan and Thatcher's shared public performances. Less remarked upon is the shared religious sensibility that helped reinforce their mission. Reagan by the late 1970s was already the darling of evangelical conservatives who rallied at mass events such as 'Washington for Jesus'. Influential pastors including Tim LaHaye, author of the bestselling *Battle for the Mind*, would paint the next presidential election as an epic battle pitting faith against secular humanism – 'man's attempt to solve his problems independently of God.' Reagan was their candidate, running on a message of free market and religious conservatism. 'All the complex questions facing us at home and abroad,' he said of the Bible, 'have their answer in that single book.' Reagan, although 'born-again' in the 1960s, had learnt that lesson at his devout mother's knee. His childhood had centred on life in the mainstream Protestant Christian Church (the Disciples of Christ). The local minister had been like a father, helping Reagan get into Eureka College and even teaching him to drive. Eureka was a Disciples college, and later in his radio days and when he arrived in Hollywood, Reagan's closest friends were Disciples. It was not always widely understood when Ronald Reagan ran for president in 1980 on a message of 'Jefferson and Jesus' that his allegiance to Christ was more deeply rooted than his admiration for the third president.[29]

The British, by and large, prefer to keep religion out of politics ('We don't do God,' Tony Blair's press secretary famously observed). Yet Margaret Thatcher's background made it easy, even more than with Carter, to relate to the religious ethos and language of Reaganism, and its intermingling of God and Conservatism. 'Our lives revolved around Methodism,' Thatcher would write of her childhood. She had been brought up not just as a Methodist, but specifically as a Methodist in the Wesleyan tradition. Non-conformity in Britain had often been associated with liberalism and the left – most famously Gladstone in the nineteenth century – but Wesleyans by the inter-war years tended to be politically and socially conservative. Individual responsibility was the central message that was drummed into her by her father at home and when he preached from the pulpit. Listening twice every Sunday from the front pews ensured that the theology and language of Wesleyanism became an integral part of who she was. 'We were taught what was right and wrong in very considerable detail,' she reflected.[30]

Finkin Street Wesleyan Church in Grantham may have seemed a world away from the 'Sunbelt evangelicalism' of southern California that Reagan now represented. But at a fundamental level, it gave Thatcher a moral intensity and language – framing arguments in terms of 'right and wrong' – that Reagan recognised and understood from his own upbringing.

2

Thinking the Unthinkable

For Margaret Thatcher much of the early attraction in meeting Ronald Reagan had been the recognition that here was a politician who 'had been dismissed by much of the American political elite as . . . [someone] who could not be taken seriously.' That was something Thatcher well understood, because her own treatment by the British political elite, even now that she was leader of the Conservative Party, had been similar. Her background and gender made it difficult for many, perhaps most, Conservatives to take her seriously as a politician.[1]

Thatcher had grown up in Grantham in Lincolnshire, a place once described by its former town clerk as 'a narrow town, built on a narrow street and inhabited by narrow people.' *The Sun* would later call it 'the most boring town in Britain.'[2] Yet it is a place with a rich history, as a medieval market town with a church that boasts one of the tallest spires in England. Kings stopped here when travelling to the north. Richard III signed Buckingham's death warrant in the Angel Hotel. Later, when the railway came (routed through Grantham rather than Stamford because the Marquess of Exeter did not want his local town sullied by such a vulgarity), John Ruskin would always doff his cap from the train at the magnificent church spire. At the time that Margaret Thatcher was born there in 1925, the countryside around Grantham and the nearby town of Melton Mowbray had become the most fashionable retreat in England. The Prince of Wales hunted there – and where the prince went, society followed. Each day hundreds of royal watchers would turn out to watch the hunt hoping to catch sight of the prince. Just fifteen miles down the road from the Grantham of Margaret Thatcher's youth was the pleasure ground of the 'fast set' of English privileged society and everything that came with it: money, titles, grand houses, gossip, intrigue and sex.

As close as it was in physical proximity, it was a world that could not have been further away from that of young Margaret Beatrice Roberts, whose family ran a local grocer's shop. In later life, Thatcher would construct a myth around the importance of her Grantham upbringing. But the simple facts are these: she left when she was eighteen to go to university and thereafter she went back as little as she could. Her father, Alfred, a local alderman, had in his youth been an old-fashioned liberal in the Gladstonian tradition, who latterly became a Conservative. He instilled in her a strong work ethic, informed by Wesleyanism, and a sense of civic duty exercised through political life. There does not seem to have been much time for fun. They listened to *The Brains Trust* and radio talks by J. B. Priestley. 'I would have liked some things to be different,' she remarked wistfully in later life. 'For instance, on Saturday nights some of the girls at my school would go to dances or parties. It sounded very nice. But my sister and I didn't go dancing.'[3] Life for Miss Roberts was not about frivolity, it was about hard work. And in her case, this meant working hard in order to escape.

As for so many of her generation and class, the route for that escape was Oxbridge. A scholarship to Somerville College, Oxford, in 1943 was Margaret Roberts's first step into the world of the establishment. And it began a pattern that would consistently be repeated throughout her career: getting ahead while all the time being subjected to snobbish put-downs and underestimations as something of a second-rater. 'If I had been told that the first woman prime minister would be one of us, I would not have put Margaret among my first six guesses,' remembered one Somerville contemporary. 'This was because most of us found her boring and I think it did not occur to any of us in those heady days that anyone who was boring could possibly reach high places.' The verdict of her left-wing college principal, Janet Vaughan, was even more dismissive. 'We used to entertain a good deal at the weekends, but she didn't get invited,' Vaughan noted. 'She had nothing to contribute, you see.'[4]

Such pointless snobbery, most likely unendurable for Thatcher, sowed the seeds of her hatred of the liberal establishment. Yet she ploughed on, making her mark by becoming only the second woman president of the Oxford University Conservative Association. This was not as prestigious as becoming president of the Oxford Union, from which women were barred, but it would be an important card to play with the Conservative central office and local constituency associations when later she started looking for seats to contest.

Thatcher fought a good losing campaign in the safe Labour seat of Dartford at the general election in 1950 and again in 1951. As the youngest ever female candidate she attracted a great deal of media attention and confidently expected to find a safe Conservative seat for the next election. But she endured endless rebuffs, this time from the establishment in her own party, as less able candidates were selected ahead of her. In the end she failed to get selected for the 1955 election. A constituency had the right to whoever they wanted, Thatcher contended. 'What I resented, however, was that beneath some of the criticism I detected a feeling that the House of Commons was not really the right place for a woman anyway.' When finally she was elected for the safe seat of Finchley in the Macmillan landslide of 1959, the retiring Conservative MP, Sir John Crowder, did not hesitate to express his disgust at having 'a woman, for God's sake' succeed him.[5]

Being a woman in the Conservative parliamentary party in the late 1950s and throughout the 1960s was not easy, but it came with one distinct advantage: being such a rarity – one of just seven Conservative female MPs by 1966, as against 246 men – and a talented one at that, meant promotion followed quickly. Thatcher soon became, in her own words, the 'statutory woman' on the Tory front bench.[6]

Harold Macmillan made her parliamentary secretary at the Ministry of Pensions, among the least glamorous postings in government. Her minister, John Boyd-Carpenter, was initially scornful, but quickly came to respect her capabilities. 'Here was a good-looking young woman and [Macmillan] was obviously, I thought, trying to brighten up the image of his government,' he recalled. 'I couldn't have been more wrong, because once she got there she very quickly showed a grip on the highly technical matter of social security – and it's an extraordinarily technical, complex subject – and a capacity for hard work which she's shown ever since, and which quite startled the civil servants and certainly startled me.' Some found it harder to adapt than others. The permanent secretary, Sir Eric Bowyer, complained that Thatcher would 'turn up looking as if she had spent the whole morning with the coiffure and the whole afternoon with the couturier.' He was the latest but not the last in a succession of establishment figures to look down his nose at Thatcher. She would not easily forget it: Whitehall mandarins were added to a list that included Oxford dons and Conservative Party grandees who would be made to regret underestimating her ability and capacity for retribution.

In 1967, and no longer in government, a new Conservative leader, Edward Heath, promoted Thatcher to the opposition shadow cabinet, first to cover the Fuel brief, then Transport, and finally Education. This was not done without reservations. When a senior Tory MP recommended Thatcher, Heath had replied, after a characteristic long pause, 'Yes, Willie [Whitelaw] agrees that she's much the most able, but he says once she's there, we'll never be able to get rid of her.'[7]

In the end, she got rid of him. In 1975, following three general election defeats out of four, the Conservatives dumped Heath in favour of Thatcher. There was both luck and brilliant political strategy behind her surprise elevation – she had the courage to challenge Heath while others dithered and her campaign was run with 'black ops' efficiency by Airey Neave, who famously had escaped from the Colditz prisoner-of-war camp in Germany during the Second World War. But underpinning everything was a ferment in conservative ideas that was transforming the political landscape in Britain and America. This was the intellectual revolution that would define the age of Reagan and Thatcher.

In Britain, the crucial change agent in this was Keith Joseph and the think tank he established in 1974, the Centre for Policy

Studies (CPS). Margaret Thatcher, who revered Joseph and later dedicated a volume of her autobiography to his memory, became the inaugural deputy chairman of CPS. The rationale for the new centre was rooted in a shared critique of the Conservative government of which both Thatcher and Joseph had been members between 1970 and 1974. This administration had come to power committed to free market ideas and economic liberalism, but it had been knocked off course by an inability to generate popular and elite support. The task in 1975, declared Alfred Sherman, a co-founder of the CPS, was 'to win over opinion-forming and policy-circles to an understanding of cause and effect in social affairs with practical reference to the role of the market and the counter-productive nature of much of the post-war intervention.' If the CPS could build a new consensus around the primacy of free markets, this would help sustain a Conservative government when inevitable political difficulties hit and allow them to implement what they knew to be right.

The CPS was a think tank made for Margaret Thatcher. It is often observed, wrongly, that Thatcher was not interested in ideas. Certainly she was not an intellectual. Yet throughout her time as leader of the Conservative Party and as prime minister, Thatcher consistently showed a respect for and deep interest in the ideas of academics, intellectuals and policy centres, perhaps more so than any other prime minister of the modern age. She consistently brought academics into the heart of government, often to the fury of cabinet ministers. 'She was extraordinarily interested in ideas, new ideas,' recalled John Coles, her private secretary between 1981 and 1984. This serious engagement existed because Thatcher believed that politics was a battle of ideas. For her, power was never simply a question of managerialism. She believed that socialism and the 'post-war consensus' on full employment, a mixed economy and the welfare state could only be challenged by ideas that were better articulated.[8]

Thatcher was helped along in this effort by the prevailing sense of failure and despair that dominated British national life in the 1970s – a decade that would be characterised as a 'winter of discontent'. Economic and financial performance were disastrous, with record budget deficits necessitating a humiliating request for an IMF bailout. Inflation and interest rates were in double digits. Sterling was in crisis. Trades unions were out of control. The empire was gone. Public services and utilities were generally incompetent and expensive, led by the National Health Service with its dirty hospitals and long waiting lists. Lying behind this failure was a sense that the ideas which had dominated political life since the Second World War were now bankrupt. When the Labour prime minister, James Callaghan, told his party conference in 1976 that 'You cannot now, if you ever could, spend your way out of a recession', it seemed to signal the end of the Keynesian era. The question then became who would replace Keynes as the totemic figure in the realm of political ideas.[9]

Thatcher was never afraid to put the answer to that question on the table, often literally. A colleague in her first shadow cabinet in 1975 presented a paper arguing that the Conservative Party would win back public support by reverting to Macmillan's 'middle way'. Before he had finished speaking, Thatcher reached into her briefcase and took out a copy of *The Constitution of Liberty* by the Viennese economist F. A. Hayek. Interrupting the proponent of 'the middle way', she held up the book for everyone to see. '*This* is what we believe,' Thatcher declared, slamming the text down hard on the table.[10]

Only the previous year Hayek had shared the Nobel Prize in Economics. He had been a bestselling author in Britain and America during the 1940s, selling hundreds of thousands of copies of *The Road to Serfdom,* including one to the young Margaret Roberts. His view that every move towards big government had bad consequences would provide the intellectual underpinning to the Reagan–Thatcher era. Hayek argued that all the important knowledge in a modern economy was essentially local in character. Central planners and regulators could not know what was going on at the micro level. A 'market' economy always led to better choices than a heavily planned one, because the market allocated resources through the decentralised decisions of individual buyers and sellers based on particular circumstances. The market therefore provided a form of 'spontaneous order' that was infinitely more nuanced than a planned society. Government planning could simply never know enough. Instead, the role of government was to create laws that would be applied equally and fairly to enable individual transactions to occur. Hayek's view of equality in the marketplace could often lead him in unexpected directions, as the conservative political economist Francis Fukuyama has pointed out. 'It may surprise some of Hayek's new followers to learn,' he says of recent Tea Party enthusiasm for Hayek, 'that *The Constitution of Liberty* argues that the government may need to provide health insurance and even make it compulsory.'[11]

Thatcher later recalled that Hayek had been 'right at the top of the reading list given me by Keith Joseph' in the mid-1970s. In 1975 she had made him set reading for the shadow cabinet. Yet Hayek himself had always recognised that progress comes through action, moving from 'ideas' to 'practice'. That was why his followers in the 1970s invested so much in think tanks like the CPS, the Adam Smith Institute and the Institute of Economic Affairs, seeing them as central to the intellectual vigour of conservative leadership. Thatcher herself may not have been an original political thinker in the purest sense. Yet, argued Sherman, 'She is a consumer of ideas, she uses them, applies them. This is not unique, but rare, particularly in a Britain which in the last hundred years simply has developed an anti-intellectual tradition and a philistinism. It didn't used to be so. In the Victorian age politicians were people of ideas: Disraeli, Gladstone, Peel, Salisbury. The philistinism is a fairly recent development – it coincides with Britain's decline.'[12]

Think tanks such as the CPS claimed a mandate to blaze a trail for new ideas, to 'think the unthinkable'. Margaret Thatcher's great ability, like Ronald Reagan's, was to give those ideas political clarity. She was able to grasp complex economic issues, make them her own, and then communicate them in a way that was crisp and instilled with a distinctly Gladstonian virtue. 'I think that she's sensed some of the kinds of moral considerations in politics that underlie people's political and economic attitudes,' assessed Peter Shore, a Labour minister in the mid-1970s, 'and I think [she] articulated right-wing moral convictions in a more formidable and more committed way than any leader of the right in post-war Britain.'[13]

That ability to articulate a new way of thinking with both

conviction and clarity was something that had an impact in the United States as well as Britain. When Thatcher, newly elected as prime minister, spoke to a meeting of the US Congress held in the Senate in December 1979, she electrified her audience with the incisiveness of her answers. Even the minutes of the meeting capture something of this. Asked about the economy, she replied that 'her strategy was to reduce the role of the state in favour of that of the citizen, firstly [by] reducing public spending, which was difficult but necessary, and secondly by starting to give incentives to individuals. Britain had become a wealth-distributing rather than wealth-creating society. It had to be remembered that governments did not create wealth; people did.'[14]

Afterwards, Republican senators and congressmen flocked around her. The next day, after speaking at a Foreign Policy Association luncheon, an admirer slipped her a note: 'Would you accept the Republican nomination for president in 1980?'

Thatcher was pleased enough to keep it among her private papers.[15]

The American right were attracted to Margaret Thatcher's precision and her conviction. But they were also drawn to her electoral success. On 4 May 1979, she 'kissed hands' at Buckingham Palace to become Britain's first woman prime minister, just over half a century after the introduction of equal suffrage. Asked how it felt to to be a woman prime minister, she quipped, 'I don't know: I've never experienced the alternative.' The election campaign had been as much about a lack of confidence in Labour as any popular enthusiasm for Thatcher. Yet the outgoing prime minister, James Callaghan, recognised that her election was more than just a simple changing of the guard. 'You know, there are times, perhaps once every 30 years, when there is a sea-change in politics,' he shrewdly observed to his political adviser, Bernard Donoughue. 'It then does not matter what you say or what you do. There is a shift in what the public wants and what it approves of. I suspect there is now such a sea-change – and it is for Mrs Thatcher.'[16]

That change was not just a British phenomenon; it was part of a transatlantic revolution in politics and ideas. What the CPS did in Britain, the Heritage Foundation – the free market think tank set up in Washington, DC, in 1973 – did in America. The fact that the CPS and the Heritage Foundation were founded within a year of each other underlines just how closely intertwined were the intellectual and political development of economic liberalism in Britain and the United States. The CPS, Adam Smith Institute and the Institute of Economic Affairs in Britain worked closely with American counterparts such as Heritage and the American Enterprise Institute (AEI). Staff and ideas traversed the Atlantic easily and frequently. And they all worshipped at the altar of the Mont Pelerin Society, founded by Hayek in 1947 with Milton Friedman and Karl Popper.[17]

As in Britain, the American think tanks set about 'trail-blazing' for ideas that would shift public debate and prepare the way for a Republican victory in 1980. The Heritage Foundation, for example, commissioned a vast research project that produced *Mandate for Leadership*, a 3,000-page programme for change that gave the new think tank national exposure and immediate intellectual kudos. Policy analysts from Heritage and AEI would eventually take up key positions in the Reagan administration in 1981.

Yet in the end it was a think tank in California, not Washington, that helped produce a 'Thatcher' for the American right. The Hoover Institution for War, Revolution and Peace had been founded at Stanford University in 1919 through a donation by the zinc millionaire and future US president, Herbert Hoover. From the 1960s onwards, under its director Glenn Campbell, the institution built up a high-profile research staff and programme of visiting fellows, which included Milton Friedman.

Among those who joined the Hoover Institution in the early 1970s was Martin Anderson, who had been director of research for Nixon's successful presidential campaign in 1968. Anderson developed a close relationship with the governor of California, Ronald Reagan, and brought him inside the orbit of the Hoover Institution. Anderson was the senior policy adviser for Reagan's run for the White House in both 1976 and 1980. He would follow Reagan into the White House in 1981 as head of the Office of Policy Development, bringing scores of others with him from the Hoover Institution. Before he was president, Reagan became Hoover's third honorary fellow, alongside Aleksandr Solzhenitsyn and Hayek. It was the Hoover Institution that gave Reagan the grounding in 'Jefferson' to add to his Sunbelt evangelical 'Jesus'.[18]

The governor was less overtly interested in ideas than Thatcher, but he was a keen and constant bookworm. 'The one thing that people miss, he was a great book reader,' recalled Kenneth Adelman, head of the Arms Control and Disarmament Agency. Nancy Reagan remembered the 'small library' that her husband carried in his suitcase during a short-lived career as a nightclub entertainer in the fifties; the owner of the famous Last Frontier Hotel expressed himself astonished (and presumably worried) that an entertainer should be such a serious reader. A consultant during Reagan's run for California governor in 1966 was surprised that the candidate's 'library is stacked with books on political philosophy'. Reagan also had excellent recall for what he had read. David Gergen, a White House staffer, believed most people underestimated the president's 'steel-trap mind'. Reagan, he noted, read slowly but deeply, 'possibly because like the actor he had been, the president tended to memorize what he had read'.[19]

Reagan, like Thatcher, put a high premium on academic counsel and was never afraid to surround himself with strong and intellectually confident advisers. Even political opponents admired this. Robert Strauss, chairman of the Democratic National Committee in the mid-seventies, later noted that Reagan's staff was 'simply spectacular. It's the best White House staff I've ever seen.' Where President Carter often appeared uncomfortable and challenged by brilliance in others, Reagan thrived on it. Howard Baker, Reagan's chief of staff in 1987–8, found it one of the pleasures of working for him. 'He had strong views on political matters,' Baker noted. 'He coupled that with a willingness . . . to have strong people around him and to listen to them . . . He was not afraid of strong people.'[20]

While many mistakenly thought Reagan not particularly smart, Baker believed otherwise: 'He's quick and insightful. He was a quick study. By the way, the least deserved thing about the Reagan legacy is that he wasn't bright. He was very bright, very quick . . . The dimensions of the Reagan political personality have not yet been fully explored.'[21]

Throughout his political career Reagan never seemed bothered about needing to be the smartest guy in the room and was relaxed about listening more than he spoke. That often caused him to be underestimated, despite an impressive roster of political triumphs: the defeat of an incumbent governor in California in 1966, the near-defeat of an incumbent president for the Republican nomination ten years later, and the defeat of an incumbent president in 1980. 'Ronald Reagan accomplished so much with such apparent ease that the casual observer assumes he had nothing to do with it,' Martin Anderson observed.[22]

Like Thatcher, Reagan had the ability to articulate the message of the 'New Right' with more clarity than any of his rivals. That had been apparent from the day in October 1964 when he stepped onto the national political stage to give a TV address on behalf of Republican presidential nominee Barry Goldwater. It became known in Reagan folklore simply as 'The Speech'. Overnight it turned a B-movie star into a political contender.

The broadcast included many themes that would later become familiar Reagan favourites. 'I have spent my whole life as a Democrat,' Reagan began: 'I recently have seen fit to follow another course.' Many lines were delivered with breezy humour. He gently mocked those he accused of destroying the party he had grown up supporting. 'The trouble with our liberal friends is not that they're ignorant,' Reagan suggested, 'it's just that they know so much that isn't so.' There were similar sideswipes at Washington. 'No government ever voluntarily reduces itself in size,' he explained: 'So governments' programs, once launched, never disappear. Actually, a government bureau is the nearest thing to eternal life we'll ever see on this earth.'

At the end of Reagan's address he called on America to win the cold war:

> Every lesson of history tells us that the greater risk lies in appeasement, and this is the specter our well-meaning liberal friends refuse to face – that their policy of accommodation is appeasement, and it gives no choice between peace and

war, only between fight or surrender. If we continue to accommodate, continue to back and retreat, eventually we have to face the final demand – the ultimatum. And what then – when Nikita Khrushchev has told his people he knows what our answer will be? He has told them that we're retreating under the pressure of the Cold War, and someday when the time comes to deliver the final ultimatum, our surrender will be voluntary, because by that time we will have been weakened from within spiritually, morally, and economically. He believes this because from our side he's heard voices pleading for 'peace at any price' or 'better Red than dead,' or as one commentator put it, he'd rather 'live on his knees than die on his feet.' And therein lies the road to war, because those voices don't speak for the rest of us.[23]

The Speech was an immediate national sensation. It was estimated that the TV address raised $8 million for the Goldwater campaign nationally, not counting the places where it was rebroadcast to support local races. These results exceeded any previous campaign fund-raising event. More importantly, The Speech gave a fillip to Goldwater conservatives who already knew their candidate was headed towards defeat. Now here was a new national voice that might help galvanise them again. He had articulated and personalised an intellectual and political journey made by a New Deal Democrat to conservatism. He had glamour and fame. And he represented a 'Sunbelt' philosophy that was a clear departure from the eastern liberalism of those Rockefeller Republicans who had done so much to undermine the Goldwater cause.[24]

Overnight Ronald Reagan had become a hero of the American New Right.

While Margaret Thatcher had been raised in settled lower-middle-class respectability above her father's grocer's shop in Grantham, Ronald Reagan's upbringing had been an altogether harder experience. For all the glamour and Hollywood veneer that Reagan brought to politics, he was a boy who had grown up, in his own words, at a time and in a place where 'it seemed as if there was no hope.' Part of his later appeal to the so-called

'Reagan Democrats' stemmed from the fact that underneath the trappings of fame and wealth, Reagan understood real poverty and helplessness. And he seemed the epitome of the American dream. 'I don't think you can go back through forty-three presidents and find a president of the United States who came from as much poverty as Reagan,' observed Stuart Spencer, a later campaign adviser. 'Income-wise, dysfunctional families . . . this guy came from an alcoholic family, no money, no nothing.'[25]

Caspar Weinberger, an early Reagan loyalist and later secretary of defense, made a similar point. 'It's quite a revelation to go through one of his boyhood homes in Illinois,' he noted. 'These were very, very humble circumstances. And he emerged from that – to a very considerable extent by his own study, his own capabilities, and his own convictions – and became one of the most important persons in the world. It's a pretty good example of what can happen in America.'[26]

Reagan was born in Tampico, Illinois, in 1911, the son of an alcoholic father and a deeply religious mother.[27] It was from his mother that he inherited his distinctive mellow vocal tones, and the trick during moments of tension or conflict of almost whispering to convey intimacy and trust. After moving around from place to place, the family eventually settled in Dixon, Illinois, which Reagan always later regarded as his home town. A handsome and popular 'jock', he became football captain and president of his class at high school, and later president of the student body at Eureka College, Illinois. Reagan always said that growing up in a small town was an excellent foundation for anybody who wanted to go into politics. 'You discover that, despite their differences, most people have a lot in common,' he explained.[28]

After graduating from college, Reagan worked as a radio sportscaster in Des Moines. It was here that he polished his speaking style in the manner of his political hero, Franklin D. Roosevelt, whose 'fireside chats' he so admired. Although Reagan would eventually reject FDR's political legacy – the social democratic policies forged in the Depression – he never lost that deep respect for the man himself as a leader and a communicator. Sportscasting also taught Reagan to conjure images from the air to thrill and entertain an audience. A line on the Western Union ticker tape such as 'single to center' or 'foul ball' transmitted back to Reagan in the studio in Des Moines would produce a couple of minutes of dramatic commentary as though he were at Wrigley Field himself watching the Chicago Cubs in the flesh.[29]

But Reagan had his eye on greater things than commentary. He took his Hollywood screen test in 1937 at the age of twenty-six and was soon on his way to California. Within a year and a half he had made thirteen movies for Warner Bros., becoming, he later joked, 'the Errol Flynn of the B pictures'. Between 1937 and 1953, he would appear in fifty-three films, including the 'A'-movies *Kings Row* and *Knute Rockne – All American* (in which he delivered his most famous line: ask them to go in there and 'win just one for the Gipper'). A popular figure in Hollywood with fellow actors, Reagan got his first taste of hands-on politics between 1947 and 1952 when he served his first of two terms as leader of the actors' union, the Screen Actors Guild (SAG). During the McCarthy era he became convinced that Communists were attempting 'to take over the motion picture business', including his union. Determined to make the Screen Actors Guild into a bastion of anti-Communism, he covertly handed names to the FBI of those he suspected of being Communists. Reagan is the only US president to have served as a union leader, and it would give him authority and self-assurance in bargaining. His secretary of state, George Shultz, recognised those qualities in the president's 'self-confident' demeanour before the first Soviet summit with Mikhail Gorbachev. 'Reagan saw himself as an experienced negotiator,' he observed, 'going back to his days as president of the Screen Actors Guild.'[30]

By 1954, with his Hollywood career on the wane, Reagan was forced to take what seemed like a humiliating step down to become a spokesman for General Electric. Many now see it as the making of him as a conservative and a political figure. He served as host of GE's popular Sunday night TV show and spent the rest of his time as a travelling ambassador, visiting GE's 250,000 workers in 139 plants and speaking on public platforms. Reagan later described this as his 'apprenticeship for public life'. The 'New Dealer' came under the influence of the charismatic GE vice-president, Lemuel Boulware, who encouraged his move rightwards in what amounted to a 'postgraduate course in political science'. It was during his eight years on the road for GE that Reagan practised and perfected in front of live audiences 'The Speech' that would launch him onto the national stage during the 1964 presidential election.[31]

Success at the polls for governor of California followed in 1966, with re-election for a second term in 1970. He came within an ace of defeating President Gerald Ford for the Republican nomination in 1976 and delivered a short speech at the party convention in which he totally eclipsed the candidate. In 1980, any doubts that at sixty-nine Reagan was too old to be president were silenced by his vitality and obvious physical fitness. He won on a simple but highly effective message: 'Are you better off than you were four years ago?' Yet it was also a message of hope, one that he personified in his own cheerful and upbeat demeanour, that connected with the mood of change in the country. This impression crystallised in the presidential debates, when he reacted to shrill attacks by the incumbent Democratic president, Jimmy Carter, with a sad shake of the head and the line, 'There you go again.' People had had enough. On 4 November 1980 Reagan routed Carter by 50.8 per cent to 41 per cent of the vote, taking forty-four states, and was elected as the fortieth president of the United States.[32]

Listening to the results at three o'clock in the morning in London, the British prime minister, Margaret Thatcher, immediately dashed off a message of congratulations. 'Remembering our meeting in London in 1978,' she wrote, 'I look forward to working closely with you and with your colleagues in your new Administration. You will be assuming the presidency at a time when the close friendship between our two countries can, I believe, play a crucial role in strengthening cooperation within the alliance. I look forward to an early opportunity of discussing with you the urgent problems we all face.'[33] Ed Meese, Reagan's campaign chief of staff and an admirer of Thatcher, made sure her letter was at the top of the pile of correspondence on the president-elect's desk the next morning.

Thatcher would later write of her earlier meeting at Westminster with Ronald Reagan that 'When he left my study, I reflected on how different things might look if such a man were president of the United States. But in November 1978 such a prospect looked a long way off.'[34] Now it had come to pass. To many it had seemed unthinkable, but Reagan and Thatcher had both 'climbed to the top of the greasy pole'.[35]

3

Come In, It's Freezing!

White House. Thursday, 26 February 1981. Whatever anxieties Margaret Thatcher had felt on her way to Washington were gone by the time her motorcade arrived at the diplomatic entrance of the White House. There was a warm embrace for the waiting president. Friendly exchanges followed between Reagan's wife, Nancy, and Thatcher's husband, Denis, though the two had never previously met. Reagan introduced his vice-president, George H. W. Bush, and the secretary of state, Alexander Haig. Then came the spectacular 'ruffles and flourishes' on the South Lawn with the US Marine Band and a guard of honour presenting arms, playing the national anthems and firing a nineteen-gun salute. 'Your visit here renews the personal friendship we began in your country just before you took office,' Reagan declared from the podium after the two leaders had inspected the troops. 'When we talked in London just over two years ago – when neither of us was in office – I was impressed by the similar challenges our countries faced and by our determination to meet those challenges.'

Thatcher replied in an equally personal way. 'I count it a double joy that I am once again in the United States and as I'm being greeted here by you, Mr President, after a splendid victory but long since for me a trusted friend,' she observed. 'The message I have brought across the Atlantic is that we, in Britain, stand with you. America's successes will be our successes. Your problems will be our problems, and when you look for friends we will be there.'[1]

With the formalities concluded, Reagan put a hand on Thatcher's arm and steered her towards the South Portico balcony and into the Blue Room, before finally escorting her into the Oval Office for a private talk. Pointing at a large jar of jelly beans, Reagan explained that there were over thirty flavours in there, including peanut. 'We haven't yet had time to take them out,' he quipped, referring to President Carter's background as a peanut farmer. It was a cute ice-breaker for them both. Finally alone together for the first time as leaders, each realised that for all the talk of 'personal friendship', in reality they hardly knew each other at all.

The explicit policy of the White House national security team had been to play up in public and off the record the notion of a friendship between Thatcher and Reagan. 'The image which could most usefully emerge from these talks,' national security adviser Richard Allen had told the president, 'is of two like-minded leaders who have taken the measure of the difficulties their nations confront, who underestimate none of the situation's gravity, but who are neither daunted by such problems nor doubtful of ultimate success in dealing with them. Sleeves-rolled-up, sobriety-with-optimism is the main message you should be getting across with this visit; politically it can prove an effective chord both at home and abroad.' The hope was that a meeting between Reagan and Thatcher might dramatise something rare, at least on the political right, in recent exchanges between a US president and western European leaders – namely, a meeting of minds that encompassed not only philosophical affinities, similar economic outlooks, and a common allegiance to strong defence, but also a tough, pragmatic determination to do something about them.[2]

Yet while the administration was keen to 'love up' Thatcher, there seemed to be a concerted effort to 'buck' her up, too. Thatcher had arrived in Washington beset by economic problems at home. 'She is off to see President Reagan,' noted the Conservative MP Alan Clark in his diary, 'and I hope will be well received as she needs a bit of relaxation and a boost to her morale.' At home in Britain there was growing social and industrial unrest about the direction in which the country was heading. Thatcher had come to power in 1979 promising a fresh start. 'If we are to halt and then to reverse the long years of our country's economic decline,' she had promised, 'fundamental changes of policy and attitude are required at every level.' This would involve 'rolling back the frontiers of the state' and replacing the assumptions of the previous era of consensus. In short, said her first chancellor, Geoffrey Howe, there would be 'proper management of the money supply' and 'greater restraint and economy in public spending'. The principal aim of this policy was to bring under control inflation, which had been the scourge of the British economy throughout the 1970s. Thatcher was prepared to tolerate a higher level of unemployment than any of her predecessors. The end would justify the means if the principal objective – to bring down inflation – could be met. But as Howe conceded, there was a danger that unemployment could be 'unpalatable' and was likely to cause 'social strain'.[3]

By the time Reagan came to power in January 1981, many were already judging the painful UK economic adjustment a disaster. Britain was locked in recession. Unemployment was soaring, and twelve months later would hit three million – one in eight of the workforce. Bankruptcies were at record levels. Manufacturing industry was in crisis. Critics inside and outside Thatcher's own party were clamouring for a U-turn on economic policy. The head of the powerful Confederation of British Industry (CBI) was promising 'a bare knuckle fight' over policy. When Thatcher arrived in Washington, she generated strong media interest not just because of her perceived closeness to the new president, but also for other, less favourable reasons. 'Embattled but Unbowed' was the lead headline in *Time* magazine that greeted her. The article told of a country and a premiership in crisis. The *Economist* put it even better on its front page. Showing caricatures of Thatcher and Reagan in their bathing suits at the seaside, the prime minister beckons a dubious-looking president into the water with the words: 'Come in, it's freezing!'[4]

Critics of Thatcher included the most senior members of the Reagan economic team. David Stockman, Reagan's budget director and a zealot on supply-side economics, made no attempt to hide his belief that Thatcher had been insufficiently radical, particularly on tax cuts. Treasury Secretary Donald Regan pointedly chose Thatcher's visit to offer a similar analysis to a congressional committee. Thatcher noticed the barb, not least, she acidly observed, because Regan came immediately from Congress 'to join a lunch at which I was the main guest.'[5]

If the US administration would have liked to see more of the 'Iron Lady' in economic matters, then the sense of disappointment was two-way. Thatcher recognised that tax cuts and the economy were matters of difference between her and the president. Anyone who knew her understood that she welcomed combative debate on questions of policy. Indeed, getting the views of the president on Britain's economic problems was something she actively encouraged. Yet when Reagan raised the question of whether Britain intended to cut taxes harder and faster, her reply that it had to be done in stages – a classic 'art of the possible' answer – was accepted without much comment. Thatcher was astonished. Even if the president had not engaged personally, the least she had expected was a reiteration of the points made by Regan and Stockman. It was her first evidence that perhaps after all there would be no policy sparring or discussion of big ideas on this initial trip.

Thatcher had placed great emphasis on the possibility of such intellectual engagement in the weeks leading up to the visit. She had prepared in the usual way with officials, but had also convened a special 'seminar' at Chequers, with academics and specialists including Hugh Thomas, Sir Michael Howard, George Urban and Esmond Wright. The group had been assembled to help her think through broader strategic and philosophical questions, as well as some practical ones, in advance of talks in Washington. She had wanted to bring her 'A' game to the meetings with Reagan, anticipating a *tour d'horizon* on the great issues of the day. 'What was their reading of the president's mind?' she had wanted to know. These academic advisers had warned her that the president did not appear 'to suffer from an excess of reading or any marked thirst for the more complicated sorts of information.' This chimed with the advice of Nicholas Henderson, who had warned, 'The main worry is not just age but whether he possesses the mental vitality and political vision to cope.' Even members of cabinet had expressed doubts about whether Reagan was up to the job.

It was 'a fallacy', said minister Ian Gilmour, to think just because Carter had been bad that Reagan could not be worse. Thatcher had been more optimistic, believing that Reagan 'would give a strong lead.' Now, after her first meeting in the Oval Office, she was not so sure.[6]

Whatever doubts or disappointments Thatcher may have had, she was determined not to show them. Indeed, the prime minister's Chequers advisers had reminded her beforehand that even if the president were unable to 'keep up' with her, 'she must be careful not to embarrass him.' Indeed, such a scenario seemed to offer an opportunity. The president, Thatcher was told, 'sees himself as chairman of a board of governors and not a hands-on manager of the kind [prime ministers] tend to be and have to be.' There should be no misapprehension that Britain might, as Harold Macmillan had suggested decades earlier, play the role of Greeks to America's Romans. Nevertheless, an exceptional leader, Thatcher was advised, might find a way to insert herself into the policy-making debate surrounding the president.[7]

Thatcher had already seen to her cost how personal relationships could subtly alter diplomatic relations. The strong affinity between the president of France, Valéry Giscard d'Estaing, and the West German chancellor, Helmut Schmidt, had helped keep her isolated within the European Community. 'They have immense influence,' she judged. 'They shape European policy and are a powerful factor on the world scene.' It did not escape her notice that this 'influence' came about because 'they seem to hit it off; they are personal friends and speak the same sort of language.' In European affairs, where she was usually outside the loop of close personal relationships, the prime minister most often responded with the politics of confrontation. In 1979 and 1980, for example, Thatcher was involved in a series of bruising struggles over Britain's contributions to the EEC budget. Britain made the second highest net contribution after West Germany. Thatcher regarded that as insupportable. 'Its whole purpose is to demean Britain,' she told UK officials. 'We must fight this one – if necessary openly.' At the Dublin European summit meeting in November 1979, Thatcher bluntly demanded: 'I want my money back!' Continental European leaders were horrified, but it got the job done. Britain was granted a £350 million rebate in 1979 and a further £800 million the following year. A framework was put in place for future refunds in addition to a full review of the EEC budget process. But this came at a price. 'Margaret's firmness and intransigence were the key factors in getting us a proper solution,' noted the foreign secretary, Lord (Peter) Carrington, but 'the resultant atmosphere' created a foul odour around Britain's relations with its European partners that would last throughout the Thatcher years and beyond.[8]

Regarded as a difficult personality in Europe, Thatcher was determined to make the most of a relationship with a new American president with whom she had already established a personal rapport. This official first meeting with Reagan provided just such an opportunity. It also gave Thatcher an insight into how she might work within the gaps opened up by divisions inside the new administration.

In December 1979, President Carter had agreed to deploy 464 cruise missiles and 108 Pershing IIs in Europe. This decision was a NATO response to the SS-20 missiles that the Soviets were deploying in increasing numbers. The arrangement was highly controversial with western European public opinion. A wave of protests followed amid fears that a 'limited' nuclear war in Europe had moved a step closer. To counter popular anger, NATO had adopted a dual-track strategy: the decision to deploy was matched by an offer to the Soviet Union to negotiate on limiting this class of weapon. Thatcher supported this 'carrot and stick' approach, agreed in outline form by her predecessor, not least because it had been accompanied by a deal with Carter on the new Trident weapons system to replace Britain's aging nuclear deterrent. Dual-track also gave her a way to combat the growing popularity of the Campaign for Nuclear Disarmament (CND). Of Carter's new deployment, 160 cruise missiles would be sited at US bases in Britain. A quarter of a million people would take to the streets of London to protest. The nuclear dual-track approach helped Thatcher rebuff claims that she was a warmonger. But she had been left in a fix by the decision of the Reagan administration to reopen the debate on whether dual-track should be maintained. The Pentagon in particular, in the face of opposition from the

State Department, was arguing for immediate deployment without waiting for talks with the Soviets.[9]

Thatcher's way out came via the State Department, which had asked her to raise the dual-track issue at the meeting with the president on 26 February. Simultaneously, Paul Bremer, special assistant to Secretary of State Al Haig, had dispatched a note to James Rentschler in the White House, with speaking notes for the president's press conference after the Thatcher meeting. This included the statement that the president and prime minister had 'affirmed' the decision of December 1979 to modernise nuclear weapons 'and to pursue arms control efforts in parallel'. Rentschler passed this up to the national security adviser, Richard Allen, noting that it was an 'essential' point to be made at the press conference. Allen gave it to the president, who said it word for word to the press. The State Department and the National Security Council staff, with Thatcher's complicity, had outmanoeuvred the Pentagon, including a livid Caspar Weinberger, the secretary of defense.[10]

Even if Thatcher saw that Reagan might allow himself to get played on occasion by his advisers, she also seemed to recognise earlier than most that in important ways the president was entirely his own man. Obviously he rejected the foreign policy priorities of his immediate predecessor, although more unusually there was little effort to hide his disdain for the cold war policies of earlier Republican presidents, Nixon and Ford. What had not been anticipated was the way in which Reagan, who was often presented by the media as a good 'front man' who left the thinking to others, would in the end be his own most trusted adviser. He employed heavyweights in his administration such as Haig and Weinberger, but there was no one adviser who exercised the kind of influence that, for example, John Foster Dulles enjoyed with Eisenhower, Kissinger with Nixon, or Brzezinski with Carter. Shultz in the second term would come the closest. Reagan's self-sufficiency is demonstrated by the fact that he chewed up six national security advisers in eight years: Richard Allen, William Clark, Robert McFarlane, John Poindexter, Frank Carlucci and Colin Powell. Ultimately this president was the strategist-in-chief.[11]

Even beyond a set of pro-American, pro-libertarian instincts, Thatcher understood in this context that the best way to influence policy for her own national purposes was to convince the president directly on any given issue and to enlist allies in the administration on a case-by-case basis. Therefore it was imperative to her that the two hit it off. This she helped along with some panache at the black-tie dinner given in Reagan's honour at the British Embassy on 27 February. That night, Thatcher played every card in her hand to brilliant effect. 'She is very good at rising to an occasion,' noted an admiring Henderson afterwards, relieved that his 'trick' in getting the White House to accept the invitation had paid off in such style.[12]

The prime minister's speech delighted Reagan. Quoting Dickens's description of Americans as 'by nature frank, brave, cordial, hospitable, and affectionate', Thatcher turned to Reagan with a flourish: 'That seems to me, Mr President, to be a perfect description of the man who has been my host for the last 48 hours.' She departed from the official text to give a moving and robust description of political courage. 'There will, of course, Mr President, be times when yours perhaps is the loneliest job in the world, times when you need what one of my great friends in politics [Airey Neave] once called "two o'clock in the morning courage",' she explained. 'There will be times when you go through rough water. There will be times when the unexpected happens. There will be times when only you can make a certain decision.' Forcing home the message that she had complete faith in Reagan, Thatcher continued: 'I want to say this to you, Mr President, that when those moments come, we here in this room, on both sides of the Atlantic, have in you total faith that you will make the decision which is right for protecting the liberty of common humanity in the future. You will make that decision that we as partners in the English-speaking world know that, as Wordsworth wrote, "We must be be free or die who speak the tongue that Shakespeare spake".'[13]

It was a powerful piece of rhetoric, and one that left the president visibly affected. 'Prime Minister,' Reagan said in opening his reply, 'Bob Hope [who was present] will know what I mean when I speak in the language of my previous occupation and say you're a hard act to follow!' It was a sincere and unscripted moment, and one that drew delighted laughter and applause from the assembled guests. 'Dinner at the British Embassy,' Reagan recorded in his diary, 'truly a warm and beautiful occasion.' Afterwards, Mike Deaver, the deputy chief of staff and a close Reagan confidant, told Henderson 'without any prompting, that the President had been moved by Mrs T's embassy speech, especially the passage about two o'clock courage.'[14]

The personal good feeling that the embassy dinner engendered between the two leaders was reinforced the next day. Again in a departure from precedent, the president and first lady entertained the prime minister and Denis Thatcher for morning coffee in the Yellow Oval Room at the family residence in the White House. This was a private meeting, and essentially social in nature. The jovial but shrewd Denis played his part to a tee chatting amiably to the notoriously brittle Mrs Reagan. 'I believe a real friendship exists between the PM, her family and us,' Reagan wrote in his diary afterwards. 'Certainly we feel that way & I'm sure they do.'[15]

The prime minister could not have asked for more.

Thatcher left Washington on a high note. Such was the acclaim in the media that the Reagan administration had been forced into an about-turn halfway through the visit. On her arrival, the administration had distanced itself. The Treasury secretary and budget director had publicly highlighted differences between the two governments. Furthermore, in off-the-record briefings, the White House press secretary, James Brady, had emphasised that the administration, perhaps even the president, was bemused and disappointed by Thatcher's 'failed' economic policy. Brady even prepared a briefing paper for the press that outlined the differences between the economic policies of the two governments. If Thatcher was toxic, then the administration wanted to keep her at arm's length. However, by the end of her official visit the message could hardly have been more different. 'It took a crowbar to get them apart,' Brady joked to journalists on the last day. Whatever problems Thatcher may have had at home, she had star quality abroad. That was something the Reagan White House could respect and understand.[16]

'The visit resulted in great exposure for Mrs T, even more than planned, and in more favourable media coverage for her and the UK than the circumstances really warranted,' Henderson concluded. '[However], she returned to a very different type of reception in the UK where unemployment and bankruptcies accumulate, and there are widespread doubts about her within her cabinet and party about her policies. I think her acclaim in the USA may have helped to restore her.' In the House of Commons she gave a bracing performance on the trip to Washington, reporting that the Anglo-American relationship was in good health. That was thanks in no small part, she reminded MPs, 'to the excellent understanding that President Reagan and I had established even before either of us assumed our present responsibilities.'[17]

To Reagan, she wrote a warm letter thanking him for 'the friendliness of the welcome offered by you and Mrs Reagan', adding that 'our talks together were, for me, of particular and lasting significance.' Naturally she hoped 'that it will not be too long' before they met again. The letter was formally addressed to 'Dear Mr President' and signed 'Margaret Thatcher', but in her own hand, the prime minister added her own friendly encomium: 'We shall never have a happier visit.'[18] How close to the truth this was became clear a few short weeks later.

On 30 March 1981, John Hinckley fired six shots outside the Washington Hilton Hotel, wounding the president and three members of his party. Hinckley, who was later found to be insane, had no particular disagreement with Reagan: he had simply wanted to do something sensational to impress the actress Jodie Foster, with whom he had become obsessed. In a bizarre coincidence, Hinckley's family was friendly with that of Vice-President George H. W. Bush, who would have become president had Reagan died. That came closer to reality than most people realised at the time. An explosive Devastator bullet fired from Hinckley's gun lodged millimetres from the president's heart.

In the immediate aftermath of the attempt on his life, Reagan displayed one of the qualities of great leaders – grace under pressure – which reassured the country that all was well. 'I hope you're all Republicans,' he quipped to the surgeons about to operate on him. When a nurse enquired how he was doing, he echoed W. C. Fields, 'All in all, I'd rather be in Philadelphia.' This courage and humour at such a moment, observed the Pulitzer Prize-winning author Garry Wills, 'more than any other single event, added a mythical quality to his leadership, revealing his character in a way that made it almost impossible to dislike him.'[19]

Thatcher wrote immediately to Reagan. 'I was shocked to hear of the attempt on your life, and very distressed to learn that you have been injured,' she told him. 'I pray that the injuries are not serious.' She sent her thoughts to Nancy and also to 'your loyal staff' who had been wounded in the attack.[20]

The White House in the hours and days after the assassination attempt became a vipers' nest of competing egos and interests. The most notorious display of hubris came from Secretary of State Al Haig, who embarrassed himself and the administration with his breathless assertion that 'As of now, I am in control here in the White House.' In the Situation Room, the atmosphere between Haig, Secretary of Defense Caspar Weinberger, and national security adviser Richard Allen was extremely tense. Chief of staff James Baker apparently fretted about being 'left out'. When Lyn Nofziger, assistant to the president for political affairs, stepped in to brief the media in the absence of the press secretary, James Brady, who had been shot, he got a dressing-down from Baker. 'He was afraid I was going to get some publicity,' Nofziger concluded. 'Honest to God.'[21]

In such a febrile atmosphere, with confused lines of communication, it was even more important than usual to have friends in the right places. Fortunately for Thatcher, Richard Allen was an admirer, not least when it came to her strong views on the Soviet Union. He ensured that the prime minister's letter of concern went on the top of the first correspondence file Reagan read when he resumed light duties. To ram the point home, Allen gave a copy of the letter to Nancy Reagan. And he made sure the British knew what he had done.

Allen's was but one of several sympathetic ears in the White House in 1981, but Anglo-American relations might have been very different had Reagan died and been succeeded by George H. W. Bush. Certainly the relationship with Thatcher that actually emerged in 1989 when Bush became president was not a happy one. President Bush, like Thatcher's eventual successor, John Major, was essentially a managerialist, uneasy with 'the vision thing'. Thatcher and Bush shared no personal chemistry. In fact, the forty-first president seemed actively to dislike her. 'President Bush was sometimes exasperated by my habit of talking non-stop about issues which fascinated me and felt that he ought to have been leading the discussion,' she reasoned. Eventually she learnt to 'defer to him in conversation and not to stint the praise. If that was what was necessary to secure Britain's interests and influence I had no hesitation eating humble pie.' Yet this was a long way from the 'special position I had enjoyed in the Reagan administration's counsels and confidence.' That was the situation in 1989; it could have been the reality eight years earlier.[22]

Luckily for Thatcher, Reagan survived and was soon writing again to the PM in warm and familiar tones. 'Despite the rush of disturbing events two weeks ago, pleasant thoughts of your visit in February are still strong in our memories,' he told her on 27 April. 'It was not only a pleasure to renew our acquaintance, but even more special to get to know each other better.' Reagan reassured her that he was focused on 'the important policies and programs we have started' and signed off with 'I look forward to seeing you again in July in Ottawa.'[23]

In advance of that G-7 summit meeting, Reagan certainly gave every impression of renewed vigour and purpose following the attempt on his life. The day after writing to Thatcher he went to Congress to deliver a barnstorming performance in unveiling his plan for economic recovery, which was soon nicknamed 'Reaganomics'. 'The ovation he got was just phenomenal,' recalled White House staffer Max Friedersdorf. 'A month after being shot in the chest, and then that gave him the superman image as far as Congress was concerned . . . It was a hell of a way to do it, but that sort of worked out in his favor, that he was able to fully recover and also to capitalise on the fact of the assassination attempt on his life.' Reagan wanted to lower taxes across the board; he also wanted to increase the defence budget.

His speech to Congress came to be seen as the 'starter's orders' for the Reagan recovery that between 1981 and 1989 would see US inflation drop from 12 per cent to 4.5 per cent, the Standard

& Poor 500 Index rise from 130 points to 285, unemployment drop from 7.5 per cent to 5.7 per cent, the mortgage rate fall from 13.1 per cent to 9.3 per cent, and the top rate of tax drop from 70 per cent to 33 per cent. The cause of that recovery would remain in dispute for years afterwards, not least because Reaganomics entailed massive federal borrowing and spending totalling nearly $2 trillion. But the recovery enabled Reagan to keep his commitment to put pressure on the Soviet Union through a massive rearmament programme. Reagan had put the defence increases on the agenda within weeks of coming to office, outlining a five-year US defence budget that would increase by 10 per cent per year at a cost of $1.46 trillion.[24]

In foreign affairs, too, Reagan showed a new assertiveness in attempting to push the Soviet Union to breaking point while also seeking to abolish all nuclear weapons. These policies, which at times seemed to follow contradictory instincts, would become hallmarks of his presidency. The new approach caught even his own advisers off guard. On 18 April, sitting in the White House solarium, Reagan drafted a personal reply to an uncompromising letter from the Soviet leader, Leonid Brezhnev. 'Is it possible,' he asked, 'that we have let ideology, political and economical philosophy and governmental policies keep us from considering the very real, everyday problems of the people we represent?'[25] When officials at the State Department and the National Security Council saw the handwritten draft, they were appalled. 'I couldn't believe my eyes,' remembered the NSC Soviet specialist Richard Pipes, who later helped frame Reagan's 'evil empire' speech. 'It was written in a Christian turn-the-other-cheek spirit, sympathetic to the point of apology, fully of icky sentimentality.' When a more assertive draft was sent back to the president, containing hardly any of his own words, he signed it. But then he sat down to write a tighter version of his original letter, urging the Soviet leader to join him in 'the meaningful and constructive dialogue which will assist us in fulfilling our joint obligation of finding lasting peace.' He then ordered that both letters should be sent to Brezhnev. In doing so, he sent a strong message to his own foreign policy team that as president he would not be afraid to overrule them or take charge of the grand strategy of his own administration.[26]

Yet while the assassination attempt had brought a sharper focus and direction to Reagan's thinking on foreign affairs and the economy, it had also left him physically and mentally weakened. The public observed a president of renewed vigour; aides saw a septuagenarian recuperating from life-threatening wounds. 'What I saw was that for a period of months, he was sick,' recalled Martin Anderson, assistant to the president for policy development. 'I mean, he got a tremendous shock and he was in recovery.'[27]

That would become apparent at the G-7 summit.

Montebello, Ottawa. Sunday, 19 July 1981. As the presidential helicopter Marine One landed, Ronald Reagan admitted to feeling like 'the new boy at school'. This was his first meeting of world leaders, and from the moment they gathered for the initial meet-and-greet at the world's biggest log cabin, he found it difficult to get into his rhythm. It was one of the aspects about Reagan that often surprised observers. Watching him deliver a speech on TV or walking down a rope line, it was obvious that he was a natural. But at receptions or small gatherings where the president was expected to work the room, he often seemed ill at ease, particularly when Nancy was absent. Few understood that Reagan was actually a private and shy man. Here among the arrogance and hyper-egos of the global leaders, many of whom viewed him as a dangerous cold warrior, Reagan seemed oddly discomfited.

'My name is Ron'. His first tentative words at the conference table, reminiscent more of a group therapy participant than an American commander-in-chief, seemed to confirm everyone's fears that the new president might not be up to the job. Reagan's attempts to show a warm and approachable side only served to make him look weak and out of his depth. In the chair, Canadian prime minister Pierre Trudeau hardly bothered to hide his contempt. Even Margaret Thatcher, sitting next to Reagan, visibly tensed. Later, she would say the decision to use first names happened thanks to Reagan's effortless amiability. In reality, Thatcher detested informality of both manner and dress, believing that the public liked its leaders to look businesslike. But at Montebello, she valiantly struggled on in solidarity with the president, referring to him throughout as 'Ronald', a name that he never used. By the time they next met, she had learnt to call him Ron. He called her Margaret to her face; Maggie when talking to his staff.[28]

If Reagan had to battle with the language of international diplomacy, he also seemed to struggle with the pace. 'The schedule was heavy,' he complained in his diary. There were plenary meetings morning and afternoon – always preceded by sessions with his own advisers – and then one-on-one meetings, working lunches and formal dinners to attend. Reagan also found much of the left-of-centre company uncongenial. Trudeau, famed for his intellectual arrogance, sneered constantly at 'the cowboy'. The new French president, François Mitterrand, sided with Trudeau throughout and displayed a deep hostility to Reaganomics. Helmut Schmidt, the chancellor of West Germany, was even worse for the usually sunny-side-up Reagan. 'He was really down & in a pessimistic mood about the world,' the president gloomily noted. The sad shake of the head is almost perceptible.[29]

Reagan had come to Ottawa with high hopes of being able to 'sell' his foreign policy leadership to the allies as he had the US Congress on his economic policy. He was aware that reaction around the world to his election in 1980 had been 'laced with nervousness'. Now, in such a dispiriting and challenging environment for the president, Margaret Thatcher seemed like a godsend – and she knew it. At the conference table, where the United Kingdom was seated next to the United States, she fussed around him, buoying him up. During the opening pleasantries, she had demonstratively signalled her allegiances by planting a friendly kiss on Reagan's cheek. No one else was afforded this honour. Mitterrand would later famously describe Thatcher as 'having the eyes of Caligula and the lips of Marilyn Monroe'. But those lips, like Marilyn's for JFK, were reserved for the American president.[30]

Reagan came under constant attack on US economic policy from Trudeau and Mitterrand throughout the summit, setting the tone for future meetings. Thatcher agreed with them on a number of issues, particularly the high level of interest rates and concerns about the anti-European turn that American language had taken on defence matters. These reservations she retained for private bilateral talks with the president. In public, Thatcher was ferocious in her support. 'She and Reagan formed a very solid team,' Trudeau noted scornfully.[31]

At one stage in the sessions at Montebello, with Trudeau in full flight against Reagan, Thatcher cut across him to deliver a rebuke that perhaps only she could have got away with: 'Pierre, you're being obnoxious. Stop acting like a naughty schoolboy!' It was classic Thatcher and perfectly delivered to prick the pomposity of the haughty Canadian. No wonder that when the summit was over, a bruised Reagan recorded gratefully in his diary: 'Margaret Thatcher is a tower of strength and a solid friend of the US.' And, he might have added, of himself.[32]

A few days after returning from the G-7 summit, Reagan saw Nancy off for a visit to London to attend the wedding of Prince Charles and Lady Diana Spencer. Still suffering from his wounds, Reagan had been told not to risk the long transatlantic journey. He was pleased for Nancy, who had a fascination with the British royals, but he was concerned about the trip. 'I worry when she's out of sight 6 minutes,' he noted in his diary. In the Oval Office for the daily morning briefing, he found that 'my mind wasn't on it.' Television screens around the world had been dominated only weeks earlier by disturbing pictures from Britain of riots and cities in flames. Reagan had raised the matter with Thatcher in Canada and she had reassured him. In the end, the president was left to cross his fingers and take comfort in watching re-runs of *The Waltons*.[33]

For Thatcher, bolstering her relationship with Reagan at Montebello had been a rare success that summer. In contrast to her visit to Washington a few months earlier, this time it had been Thatcher who bucked up the president, walking him through his first summit. Her performance displayed another characteristic that even her enemies held in regard: fearlessness in debate. But while she was soothing ideological allies and dispatching awkward Canadians, Thatcher's leadership at home was under serious assault. For months, the government had been ripped apart by arguments between various economic monetarists and their opponents.

The term 'monetarism' was carelessly tossed back and forth in British political life in the early 1980s without anyone ever agreeing what it actually meant. Even 'monetarists' within cabinet were in constant dispute. At its most basic level, monetarism suggested an intimate correlation between inflation and the money supply. 'In essence, monetarism is simply a new name for an old maxim, formerly known as the quantity theory of money,' noted Nigel Lawson, financial secretary to the Treasury and a future chancellor. Its two basic propositions were that 'changes in the quantity of money determine, at the end of the day, changes in the general price level'; and that 'government is able to determine the quantity of money.' Translating even such clear explanations into hard policy was a harder trick to pull off. In March 1981, Thatcher and her chancellor, Geoffrey Howe, had identified the budget deficit as the principal enemy of economic growth. Having failed to cut back on public spending, Howe took the only option left to him to get the deficit under control: raising taxes. The result was a primal scream of national outrage.[34]

Opponents cited half a century of post-1930s economic thinking to deride a 'perversely contractionary' budget at a time when Britain faced recession and high unemployment. Serious observers pronounced Thatcher out of her depth. A letter was sent to the press by 364 leading economists from the nation's top universities denouncing her policies, which they said would 'deepen the depression, erode the industrial base of our economy and threaten its social and political stability.' They were wrong about the British economy, which began to recover after the 1981 budget. Predictions of social and political instability, however, seemed for a time to be more prescient. Beginning in Brixton, south London, and then spreading to the poorest areas of cities such as Liverpool and Birmingham, a series of violent riots erupted that summer the like of which had not been seen in Britain since the nineteenth century. Frightening images of violence, looting and burning dominated the news, including on televisions in the family residence of the White House. 'Those poor shopkeepers,' lamented Thatcher, the grocer's daughter. To her opponents, that comment showed how out of touch the prime minister had become. As unemployment headed towards 12 per cent of the active population, with a heavy concentration outside the prosperous south-east of England, it seemed that the social fabric of the nation might tear. It was just like the Crimean War, wailed one Tory backbencher, but with a crucial difference: 'Florence Nightingale is leading the Charge of the Light Brigade.'[35]

In truth, the riots that summer had more to do with racial tension and insensitive policing than economic policy. Many areas of high unemployment, such as the cities of Newcastle and Glasgow, did not riot. Yet the perception took hold that the issue was propelling Britain towards an abyss. On 23 July, two days after Montebello, Thatcher's own ministers panicked. At a meeting of cabinet that day, the monetarist chancellor Geoffrey Howe presented a paper outlining the slashing of public spending by £5 billion. His colleagues were outraged. 'No more!' shouted one. Minister after minister denounced the policy, observing that it would cause despair in the inner cities and spell electoral disaster for the Conservative Party. Inevitably someone ponderously quoted Churchill: 'However beautiful the strategy, you should occasionally look at the results.' Even Thatcher 'loyalists' in the cabinet, such as John Biffen, fell by the wayside.[36]

For the 'wets' in Thatcher's cabinet – those on the left of the Conservative Party who despised her – the summer of 1981 was their moment to strike. By 23 July the prime minister was facing a full-scale cabinet rebellion, with 'dry' support coming only from her mentor Keith Joseph, the chancellor Geoffrey Howe and the up-and-coming Leon Brittan. If ever there had been a moment when her opponents might have reined her in, perhaps even wielded the knife, this was it. But they were unwilling to threaten mass resignation if she did not back down, thus letting Thatcher off the hook. That failure warned of her own dangerous isolation in cabinet, but it also convinced her that these internal critics lacked her ruthlessness. Cabinet ministers such as Quintin Hailsham had been prepared to snipe to backbenchers that 'The Lady [is] like Herbert Hoover and would lead us to such a defeat that we would be out of office for thirty years'. But her opponents in cabinet were not prepared to act. While they hesitated, she moved against them. A few weeks after the pivotal cabinet meeting in July, Thatcher sacked three wets, including one of the most lauded, Ian Gilmour, and shuffled another, Jim Prior, to the governmental backwater of the Northern Ireland office. In their place she brought in keen 'Thatcherites' Cecil Parkinson, Nigel Lawson and Norman Tebbit.[37]

For Thatcher's supporters the battle over the 1981 budget and the rebellion of the 'wets' would soon take on a talismanic quality. It was, proclaimed Ferdinand Mount of the No. 10 policy unit, 'the turning point in post-war British economic management.' Thatcher at her core believed that progress came through confrontation, that there must be no U-turns, and above all that doing the right thing mattered more than consensus. A few years earlier, she had astonished the British diplomat, Sir Anthony Parsons, by the force of her contempt for those who believed in consensus politics. 'I regard them as Quislings, as traitors,' she spat.[38]

In retrospect, the summer of 1981 seems like the moment when Margaret Thatcher took control of the government. That was not how the White House saw it at the time. 'Thatcher has lost her grip,' national security adviser Richard Allen reported to the president, summarising reports from the embassy in London. 'With no British leader seeming to have a clear idea of where or how to go, some political turbulence is likely, with adverse effect on the country's reliability as a US ally.' Allen concluded that 'a visit by you to the UK early next year could significantly strengthen both British resolve and the Western Alliance itself.'[39]

Dismay within the White House about Thatcher's performance was intensified by frustration that, for all her protestations to the contrary, she was unwilling to follow Reagan's policy lead. For while Thatcher raised taxes and spurned consensus, Reagan was hitting the ball out of the park by doing the complete opposite. His signature tax cuts and defence increases were in their own way as controversial and divisive as Thatcher's policies. Yet where she ploughed through dissent, he patiently constructed a new consensus. By appealing to the wider public in general and southern conservative Democrats in particular, Reagan was able to get a bipartisan programme, notably the Economic Recovery Act, through the Democratic-controlled House of Representatives.

In part, Reagan's success came down to the ability to articulate a clear plan. By 1981, most Americans believed that the old order was broken. The economic data alone was terrifying. Inflation had hit 18 per cent the previous year. The prime rate notched 20 per cent. The threat of hyperinflation and currency collapse loomed. Bestseller charts, then as now, were filled with books predicting the demise of America as the world's number-one power. No wonder that *Time*, in the week that Reagan came to power, had judged the situation to be 'growing more frightening by the moment.' Just as in Britain, a sense began to develop that the Keynesian ideas underpinning the social democratic consensus of the previous fifty years were bankrupt. Supply-side economics – the belief that growth is spurred by tax cuts and deregulation – had begun to take hold from the mid-1970s. By 1980, the Democratic chair of the congressional Joint Economic Committee, the conservative Senator Lloyd Bentsen, had declared that America was 'in a new era of economic thinking'. His committee recommended a 'comprehensive set of policies designed to enhance the productive side – the supply side – of the economy.'[40]

Jimmy Carter had begun the process of realignment towards supply-side economics, but it was his successor who became the policy's most convincing advocate. Not the least of his success was in pushing a radical economic programme through Congress. Reagan worked the phones and met regularly with congressional members. In his first few weeks alone in office, he had taken 69 meetings with 467 members of the House. Most of those congressmen, even if they did not support Reagan, came away from the meetings at least liking him. That made it easier for the president to get business done.[41]

Reagan's approach was particularly successful in dealing with the speaker of the House, Thomas 'Tip' O'Neill. The brutal, hard-nosed speaker operated in bare-knuckle style reminiscent of Lyndon Johnson. He could not have been more different from the sunny-natured president, but he responded to Reagan's attempts to charm him and develop an amiable working relationship. One of the Reagans' first private dinners in the White House was as host to O'Neill and his wife. At the end of the evening, while Nancy gave Mrs O'Neill a tour of the residence, the president and speaker sat drinking whisky, swapping 'aul' Irish stories and enjoying the 'craic'. 'By the time O'Neill left that night,' noted Max Friedersdorf, assistant to the president for legislative affairs, 'I said, "This is going to be a little easier than I thought".

He [Reagan] could charm the socks off of you. He got on the elevator, went all the way down the elevator and walked out to the portico with the O'Neills and practically ushered them in the car. "Night, Tip". After that it was "Ron" . . . Then whenever Reagan would call him up on the phone . . . he'd say, "Tip, you know I've got this . . ."'[42]

The relationship that developed between Reagan and O'Neill demonstrates some of the complexities of politics and personalities in the 1980s. While both men had admired Roosevelt, only O'Neill remained an unreconstructed New Deal Democrat to the end. He was highly critical of Reaganomics, noting acerbically that 'When it comes to giving tax breaks to the wealthy of this country, the president has a heart of gold.' Yet O'Neill was enough of a realist to know that he had to work constructively with Reagan, if only because the support of conservative Democrats – the so-called 'boll weevils' – would make votes on tax cuts and defence rises tighter than they might otherwise have been. And beyond the amiable banter, the House speaker also recognised in Reagan a formidable and even admirable politician. He thought the president was 'the best public speaker I've ever seen', dwarfing his heroes Roosevelt and Kennedy. He liked the expert way in which Reagan dealt with business on the Hill. This engagement was in stark contrast to O'Neill's experience of President Carter, whom he had found arrogant and inept. Instead, Reagan impressed Congress with his civil manner and desire to consult. That approach signalled many things to O'Neill, but not the least of them was that the president, like the speaker himself, was a politician of more subtlety than most imagined.[43]

Reagan's way of keeping his enemies close was in stark contrast to Thatcher's method. Although she was often solicitous and considerate in private, when it came to politics her approach, particularly early on, was more often one of 'scorched earth'. That made her a deeply divisive figure among parliamentarians and the public alike. 'Often she was dismissive and aggressive if someone's reasoning was different from her own,' judged the defence secretary, John Nott. 'She would constantly interrupt and challenge, but if the victim did not hold his corner intellectually, she could be scathing. This did not endear her to her more timid, or should

I say more gentlemanly, colleagues.' In the end, Nott concluded, 'I always liked her very much, but I think that I might have been . . . in a minority.'[44]

What was true for the cabinet was also true for the country. Only 23 per cent of voters thought Thatcher was doing a good job. After little more than a year and a half in office, she had achieved the unenviable distinction of being the most unpopular prime minister since polling began.[45]

Thatcher's unpopularity caused real dismay in Washington, but whatever the disenchantment with her, there was no question but that the other options were worse for a Republican White House. As Allen warned the president, the Labour Party alternative – committed to unilateral nuclear disarmament – would 'prove harmful to our security interests'. Immediately after reading the note from Allen, Reagan wrote to Thatcher to buoy up her spirits. 'Dear Margaret', he began, addressing her in the familiar terms he would use for all future letters: 'I was delighted to be with you again at Montebello. You played such an important role in our discussions. We might still be drafting the communiqué if it were not for you.' Even though the visit of the first lady to London had been a 'state' not a political matter, he gave Thatcher credit for taking such personal effort to ensure 'Nancy thoroughly enjoyed the festivities of the Royal Wedding.' Then he ended with a great flourish: 'I look forward to the closest possible relations between our two countries. You know, of course, the esteem in which I hold our personal friendship.' The letter, signed 'Ron', was classic Reagan: uplifting, cheerful and appreciative.[46]

Thatcher's reply marked a new informal tone in their correspondence. She now wrote to him as 'Ron' and signed off as 'Margaret'. She agreed that Montebello had gone 'very well indeed', but saved her most glowing prose for the woman closest to the president's heart. 'It was wonderful to have Nancy with us for a week or so over the Royal Wedding,' Thatcher wrote warmly. 'She was a great hit everywhere she went – a real and true "Ambassador" for the President of the United States. We all loved her – and I hope she enjoyed our unique celebrations.' Thatcher had indeed kept a personal eye on making sure that Nancy Reagan was received with all possible bells-and-whistles during her visit.

The energy had not been wasted. 'Nancy still glows when she recounts her visit to England for the Royal Wedding,' the president told Thatcher again that autumn. It was pillow talk of great price for Thatcher and the British national interest.[47]

Reagan was able to offer warm words of friendship and encouragement to Thatcher, but in real terms over the next few months the president only added to her worries. On 1 October, he wrote to inform her of changes to the US nuclear weapons modernisation programme. Carter had previously agreed to sell Britain a new generation of submarine-launched ballistic missiles, the Lockheed Trident C-4, to replace the aging Polaris system. Britain would be buying the new system over ten years for £5 billion – the same figure that had caused such controversy when Howe cut public expenditure in July. This represented 3.5 per cent of the total defence budget. Now, in October 1981, Reagan wrote to say that the US had decided to substitute a new missile, the D-5 for the C-4, because it would have better range, accuracy and more warheads. In truth the more expensive D-5 was out of all proportion to Britain's defence requirements, but with the C-4 being phased out, the question was whether the UK still wanted its own nuclear deterrent.[48]

The position in which Thatcher found herself was just the latest in a long line of similarly awkward spots for a British prime minister. The delicate complexities of the modern Anglo-American nuclear relationship went back to the late 1950s. In 1957, President Eisenhower had indicated to the British that the McMahon Act of 1946 on atomic energy would be amended, thereby opening up the way for sharing nuclear technology. 'The great prize!' exclaimed a delighted Prime Minister Macmillan. That same year Macmillan agreed to the siting of sixty US intermediate-range nuclear missiles in Britain. In 1962 with Polaris and again in 1980–2 with Trident, America would provide the British with the latest nuclear technology. In 1979, James Callaghan verbally agreed to the siting of ninety-six American cruise missiles at US bases in Britain.

Both sides gained from these kinds of arrangements. America acquired nuclear bases that were vital to its logistics and forward defence, and benefited from Britain's not inconsiderable expertise in defence research. Britain accessed the technology needed to continue as a nuclear power without the expense of maintaining and developing its own deterrent. Yet the Anglo-American nuclear understanding left two awkward ambiguities. First, with Britain now a dependent partner rather an independent nuclear power, it pretty much had to take or leave whatever the United States offered – as was now clear over the D-5 missiles. Second, what veto exactly did the British government have over US nuclear weapons sited on British soil? For all the talk of consultation and cooperation, the answer to that question in Washington was 'none'. As former Secretary of State Henry Kissinger bluntly put it: 'we could not have accepted a judgment different from our own.' Ronald Reagan always tried to cover that awkward reality, noting that 'I don't think either one of us will do anything independent of the other . . . er . . . this constitutes a sort of veto doesn't it?' The more complicated truth lay not in the words, but in his pause and the question mark.[49]

Although the D-5 decision in 1981 had been made without much consideration for the British position, Thatcher was quick to talk up the outcome. 'These plans will greatly strengthen deterrence at the strategic level,' she told Reagan on 19 October, 'and the United Kingdom Government welcomes the improvement which this will bring in the deterrent posture of the NATO Alliance as a whole against the background of the increasing Soviet threat. I also welcome this renewed demonstration of your Administration's resolve to strengthen your defence capabilities as well as the incentive which the programme will offer to the Russians to engage seriously in arms control negotiations.'[50]

Whatever the complications, the offer to share the new D-5 system reinforced the 'special' nature of the defence relationship between Britain and the United States on nuclear technology, and by extension that between the president and the prime minister. Certainly this was not a repeat of the situation in 1962 when a similar change of technology – from Skybolt to Polaris – almost left Britain without a nuclear weapons system. Now there was no question of Britain not being offered the new weapons. Negotiations were swift, and in the medium term Reagan had also provided Thatcher with an unforeseen electoral bonus. Responding to the strength within its own ranks of the Campaign for Nuclear Disarmament, the Labour Party adopted a policy of unilateral nuclear disarmament that fatally undermined its claims as a government in waiting.

Reagan's programme of weapons modernisation was part of an overall strategy to put pressure on the Soviet Union. He believed the policy of détente, which had dominated American strategy since the 1960s, was defeatist and had outlived its usefulness. Even before entering the White House, Reagan had astonished Allen with a pithy summary of his approach. 'My idea of American policy towards the Soviet Union is simple, and some would say simplistic,' he said. 'It is this: We win and they lose. What do you think of that?'[51]

Margaret Thatcher later came to believe of the cold war that 'the west won. Above all, Ronald Reagan won it.' However, at the time she had grave misgivings about the president's strategy. These began to manifest themselves from the end of 1981 onwards. Throughout the autumn of that year, a row had been taking place within both NATO and the US administration about the direction of nuclear strategy. In late October, at a meeting in Scotland of the NATO nuclear planning group, West Germany proposed a 'zero option' for intermediate nuclear weapons in Europe. In essence, this amounted to an offer to the Soviet Union along the lines of 'if you withdraw yours, we will not deploy ours'. In 1979, Chancellor Schmidt had played a critical role in NATO's 'dual-track' decision, which was more about modernisation than arms control, by pushing for a 'coupling' of the US strategic deterrent to the defence of Europe in the face of Soviet deployment of SS-20 missiles. In other words, Germany wanted to make sure it was protected from the USSR by the most up-to-date nuclear weapons in the American arsenal. Under pressure from public opinion at home, however, Schmidt now seemed to be undermining the modernisation of nuclear forces that had been central to the dual-track decision.

This was an issue that transcended military considerations. It raised questions about political resolve and symbolism, intra-alliance solidarity, and the extent to which NATO policy could be directed by domestic political opinion. Many feared that US deployment of weapons might drag western Europe into an actual nuclear exchange with the Soviet Union; others worried about the potential 'decoupling' of European and American military strategy, which could leave western Europe at the mercy of Soviet SS-20s. It was a debate that cut to the heart of the Atlantic Alliance.[52]

Thatcher was horrified by the 'zero option'. This new American approach was not the same as Labour's unilateral disarmament policy, but it seemed to her to be cut from the same cloth by undermining the NATO commitment and the principle of nuclear deterrence. Thatcher supported arms control and even arms reduction, but she was deeply resistant to the idea of abolition. In Washington, she found support once again from the State Department and Al Haig, who believed that 'asking for the moon, for zero, could be turned against us and to our disadvantage.' Ranged against them, supporting the West German line, was Caspar Weinberger and the Defense Department. It seemed a complete inversion of Haig's and Weinberger's earlier positions, and was a good example of how policy in Washington could turn on a dime. Earlier in the year, Weinberger had opposed Haig's push for retaining Carter's 'dual-track' strategy. Now in an apparent contradiction Weinberger was supporting 'zero-zero'. In fact, his reasoning was about a combination of perception and throwing a spanner into Soviet policy. Like Haig, he believed the Soviets would reject a 'zero-zero' option. 'But whether they reject it or they accept it, they would be set back on their heels. We would be left in good shape and would be shown as the White Hats.'[53]

In the end, the decision was Reagan's to make. The division lines were clear enough. On one side he had Haig and Thatcher; on the other, Weinberger and the West German foreign minister, Hans Dietrich Genscher. At a National Security Council (NSC) meeting on 12 November, Reagan gave a green light to the 'zero option'. 'Al, we're not delivering an ultimatum,' he told Haig, who was visibly angry. 'We'll tell our Allies we're seeking "zero" and that we're negotiating for as long as it takes in good faith; and we'll ask for their support.' Weinberger drove the point home, surely with Thatcher in mind. 'Why would the Allies reject such a bold dramatic proposal?'

The following week, Reagan announced the new policy. 'The United States is prepared to cancel its deployment of Pershing II and ground-launched Cruise missiles if the Soviets will dismantle their SS-20, SS-4, and SS-5 missiles,' he said. 'This would be an historic step. With Soviet agreement, we could together substantially reduce the dread threat of nuclear war which hangs over the people of Europe.'[54]

This speech was the first indication of Reagan's interest not just in controlling the arms race, or even scaling it back by eliminating an entire class of weapons. 'Like the first footstep on the moon,' he promised, 'this would be a giant step for mankind'.[55]

Such was the importance of the speech to Reagan, he made it the first presidential address ever beamed live by satellite by the US government to western Europe. The timing was carefully chosen to maximise the impact on European television newscasts and to steal the thunder of the Soviet leader, Leonid Brezhnev, who was about to begin a visit to West Germany. An estimated 200 million people in forty countries, including Britain, were thought to have seen the televised speech. Reagan's speech did not please everyone. 'Over the years it has become a general axiom of diplomacy,' complained Hendrick Smith, the distinguished *New York Times* correspondent, 'that the most serious arms proposals are first put forward in private.'[56]

Thatcher's reaction to the speech seemed relatively blasé when she was asked about it in the House of Commons. 'I unreservedly welcome President Reagan's statement,' she blandly told the House. 'I hope that it finds a ready response in the Soviet Union. I see little point in going further than that.' Thatcher had private doubts about the wisdom of the zero option, but she was in no position to tell an American president what he could do with his own nuclear weapons; more importantly, the UK intended to maintain its own nuclear deterrent.[57]

To reassure the prime minister, Reagan dispatched Caspar Weinberger to brief her on recent developments. She was, the secretary of defense reported back apparently in earnest, as 'charming as usual' and delighted that the president wanted to make an official visit to London in June. That was a relief to the White House. 'Thatcher's domestic position,' Richard Allen noted, 'is getting more vulnerable and the possibility of a Tory defeat, with the present government replaced by a coalition government, cannot be discounted.' A presidential visit to the UK was 'the best possible way to shore up Mrs Thatcher'.[58]

The offer softened a diplomatic defeat for Thatcher. She was reassured that the zero option was an aberration in a policy that was otherwise characterised by a demonstrable military build-up. In his first press conference as president, Reagan had observed that détente had become a 'one way street that the Soviet Union had used to pursue its own ends.' He may now have been talking about the abolition of intermediate-range weapons, but simultaneously he was improving the power, accuracy and range of America's nuclear arsenal. Alongside the new D-5 Trident submarine-launched ballistic missile, Reagan was pressing ahead with the new B-1 bomber, which Carter had previously cancelled, and a new land-based missile, the MX.[59]

While Thatcher could bite her tongue over Reagan's zero option in Europe, other events on that continent at the end of 1981 provoked their first major public row.

On 13 December 1981, just days after Thatcher had seen Weinberger, the Communist government in Poland declared martial law. It cut telephone lines and imposed curfews. Security forces took to the streets. The Polish leader, General W. Jaruzelski, claimed that the country was 'on the edge of an abyss'. In an attempt to regain control he outlawed the new powerful 'Solidarity' federation of free trade unions, with more than ten million members, and interned its leaders. 'We must bind the hands of adventurers before they push the country into civil war,' Jaruzelski said.[60]

Reaction throughout the western world was one of outrage, not least inside the White House. After an NSC meeting on 21 December, Reagan recorded in his diary: 'I took a stand that this may be the last chance in our lifetime to see a change in the Soviet Empire's colonial policy re. Eastern Europe.' Unless martial law was ended, the US would quarantine the Soviet Union and Poland. On 29 December, he followed up these words with action, announcing sanctions against Poland and the USSR to make clear 'our displeasure over the crushing of human rights in Poland.' These included suspending negotiations on selling grain; banning flights to the US by the Soviet airline, Aeroflot; suspending a number of science, technology and energy agreements; and an embargo on the shipment to the USSR of high-tech US products, including most provocatively the critical pipe-laying equipment needed to build the Siberian gas pipeline.[61]

At the pivotal NSC meetings on 21–2 December, Reagan had made clear that the United States must tell its NATO allies 'to join us in such sanctions or risk an estrangement.' Weinberger confidently assured him that if 'you take the lead . . . [the Europeans will] be dragged along with our actions.'[62]

That was to underestimate Thatcher, who never liked being dragged anywhere. When sanctions were announced, she was incandescent. A message had been received from Reagan ten days earlier, but the decision had been taken without any further consultation. In particular, her anger, and that of her European allies, focused on sanctions that affected the Siberian pipeline. British companies already had existing contracts to provide pipeline equipment, much of which involved components sourced in the United States. Vital jobs and more than £200 million of business were now at risk. It was a naive and heavy-handed piece of gesture politics that took little or no account of the realities of a globalised economy. 'This was no longer a time for concessions but for some straight talking to our American friends,' Thatcher recalled. She decided to approach the president.[63]

Reagan was sufficiently troubled to instruct Al Haig to stop off in London, en route from the Middle East, for talks with Thatcher in the New Year. The secretary of state received a blistering reception – ironic given that he himself had reservations about the policy. 'I have just spent an hour and a half with Mrs Thatcher and several of her colleagues,' he told the president afterwards. 'She raised [her] concerns with unusual vehemence.'[64]

'Whatever the perception in America,' the furious PM had told him, 'the cost of the sanctions are [sic] greater to Europe than the United States. There will be dire consequences for the Western Alliance if you proceed.'

'The perception in the US,' Haig shot back, 'is that the allies have not done nearly enough.'

When tempers had calmed, Thatcher suggested an urgent meeting of Britain, the United States, West Germany, France and Italy to devise 'a tough and credible' set of measures against the USSR that would be 'fairly shared among the allies.' Haig had promised to pass the message on to Reagan, but he left with a warning: 'For [the president] to step back, however slightly from the action [he has] taken will require a much stronger set of decisions on the part of our allies and even then would be politically dangerous.'[65]

As soon as Haig had left, Thatcher composed a long letter to Reagan, setting out in more measured terms the European objections to sanctions and requesting a secret meeting of the allies to discuss a way forward. She proposed that if this meeting agreed on tough new sanctions, the US would then lift the current ones on exports by subsidiaries in western Europe and take no further unilateral steps. In fact, soon afterwards, Reagan would anger Thatcher by extending sanctions through a ban on the supply of oil and gas technology to the Soviet Union that would apply not only to US companies but also to their foreign subsidiaries and companies manufacturing American-designed components under licence.[66]

'We must support American leadership,' Thatcher wrote, but that did not mean the United States could pursue its interests 'regardless of the opinion of their European allies.'[67]

The disagreement between Reagan and Thatcher over the sanctions and the Siberian pipeline has often been presented as an aberration in their partnership, a 'lovers' tiff' in an otherwise happy political marriage. In fact, it established a *modus vivendi* for their relationship. 'Her allegedly heart-to-heart relationship with President Reagan, which I know to be less close than supposed because I saw them together,' noted George Walden, principal private secretary to the foreign secretary Lord Carrington, 'was widely accepted because it suited Mrs Thatcher and the British press, not to speak of the president himself, to encourage the illusion.' Certainly Reagan was always pleased to have Thatcher on the team if her position fitted into his overall strategy for the cold war. At other times, when they disagreed, he simply brushed her aside. In the end she always remained a junior partner, a fact that she – more than most – rarely forgot.[68]

Much of Thatcher's diplomatic effort was spent trying to influence US national security policy and the wider NATO strategy. Devising a grand strategy for the cold war, however, was the preserve of American presidents. By late 1981, Reagan had found his game plan. Pipeline diplomacy would be part of a new strategy developed from that winter onwards with the explicit aim of winning the cold war. Reagan's policy would become the subject of fierce debate in the years after the collapse of Communism, as the president's supporters and critics argued about the extent to which he had brought about the demise of the Soviet Union, or had simply got lucky.[69] It seemed clear to commentators of all persuasions during the 1980s that when the president began his 'pipeline politics' in 1981, he had a clear strategy in mind. 'By denying the Soviet Union access to Western technology, credit, and markets for its natural gas, Reagan had hopes of undermining what he saw as a teetering economy,' one cold-war historian summed up: 'The Soviets would then be forced to abate their military build-up and to liberalize their regime. The United States, with the support of its allies, would win the Cold War.' Pipeline politics formed part of a broader strategy to reverse the course of the cold war. In addition to limiting access to western technology, this would entail a massive defence build-up, a series of covert intelligence actions and an overhaul of strategy through a series of secret national security directives. The explicit aim of this activity was to challenge and undermine the Soviet Union. The question afterwards became what underpinned that strategy? Critics argued that the administration was moved by ideology, not hard analysis. Recent releases of national security documents suggest that was not the case.[70]

A few months earlier, amid the awkwardness of the Ottawa G-7 summit, the French president, François Mitterrand, had drawn Reagan aside to give him incredible news. The French had recruited a high-level agent, code-named 'Farewell', in the KGB's technology directorate. Mitterrand offered to share the material with the United States. Reagan gratefully accepted. (It was a sign of Mitterrand's complicated relationship with the US that he subsequently came to believe that 'Farewell' was a CIA plant all along, which led him to sack the chief of the French secret service, Yves Bonnet.) In August 1981, however, the French in good faith passed, via Vice-President George Bush, more than 4,000 pages of documents to the CIA. 'Reading the material caused my worst nightmares to come true,' said Gus Weiss, one of a handful of White House officials who saw the 'Farewell' dossier. 'Since 1970, [the KGB] had obtained thousands of documents and sample products in such quantity that it appeared the Soviet military and civilian sectors were in large measure running their research on that of the West, particularly the United States. Our science was supporting their national defense.'[71]

Right at the very top of the Soviets' shopping list was oil and gas technology for the Siberian pipeline. This massive project, extending 3,600 miles from Siberia to western Europe, was not just a pipeline for the Soviet Union, it was also a lifeline. The implications of the 'Farewell' dossier were clear enough: the billions of dollars that the pipeline would generate by supplying gas to western Europe represented the way in which the Soviet Union planned to rescue its ailing economy.

This assessment gave a new focus to national security policy in the White House. It reinforced Reagan's belief that it was time to apply pressure on the Soviet economy. 'We actually got word that [Reagan] was going to try to "prevail" over the USSR,' remembered Weiss. The first step in that process was to impede the pipeline project. 'He knew what the Soviet Union needed very much was hard currency,' said Caspar Weinberger. 'And he knew that the construction of the pipeline would give them that. He felt very strongly that you didn't want to assist them in any way in getting hard currency.'[72]

The declassified minutes of the National Security Council make clear that by October 1981 the administration had in principle 'decided to impede' construction of the Siberian pipeline. The declaration of martial law in Poland two months later provided an ideal pretext to implement the decision. In that same meeting, Secretary of State Haig made clear to the president that the United States would be 'pressuring our Allies,' but that if he was looking for allied support of unilateral sanctions, 'We won't get it!' Reagan went ahead anyway. By 9 February 1982, a National Security Decision Directive (NSDD 24) had formalised the policy of disrupting the pipeline, including strenuous efforts to limit western Europe's role in construction.[73]

'Gentlemen,' the president had told his foreign policy staff in December 1981, 'our concentration has been on domestic matters this year, and I want to roll the sleeves up now and get to foreign policy, defense and intelligence.' NSDD 24 was one of a series of 120 secret decision directives that would be formulated in 1982. They would provide the backbone of the administration's national security policy. Mostly written under the direction of a new national security adviser, William P. Clark ('The Judge'), these directives were, Clark said, Reagan's 'strategy to accelerate the demise of the Soviet Union.'[74]

Reagan was personally involved in all the NSDDs. 'This wasn't a workshop situation where elves sat around pounding out shoes for the king,' said Clark. 'He was very much part of it. Not just signing, but also progression, briefing, discussion, and guidance.' Richard Pipes put this even more robustly. 'As someone involved in the formulation of Soviet policy,' he said, 'I can attest that the direction of this policy was set by the president and not by his staff, and that it was vigorously implemented over the objections of several more dovish secretaries.' Many had expected the administration to moderate its views and tone down its rhetoric on coming to power in January 1981. Yet while the administration would continue to rely on moderate figures such as Alexander Haig and then George Shultz to implement policy, the president stuck doggedly to his own agenda, ensuring that the voice of hawkish radicals such as Richard Perle and Fred Ikle did not get lost in policy discussions.[75]

Among the more important directives developed in early 1982 was NSDD 32, which became known as 'The Plan to Prevail'. It stated the US objective 'to contain and reverse the expansion of Soviet control and military presence throughout the world [and . . .] to contain and reverse the expansion of Soviet influence worldwide.' As Clark pointed out, 'We must force our principal adversary, the Soviet Union, to bear the brunt of its economic shortcomings. 'This was followed up by NSDD 66, which stated that it would be US policy to disrupt the Soviet economy by attacking a 'strategic triad' of critical resources – financial credits, high technology, and natural gas. The directive was tantamount to a 'secret declaration of economic war on the Soviet Union.' NSDD 75 stated that the United States would no longer co-exist with the Soviet system but would seek to change it fundamentally. Reagan intended to roll back Soviet influence at every available opportunity.[76]

Taken together, these National Security Decision Directives represented a new strategy to defeat the Soviet Union. Certainly, as Reagan's critics pointed out, it was driven by ideology, including the president's personal conviction that the United States was on the right side of history. But it was also supported by hard analysis, not least the forensic assessment of the 'Farewell' dossier, which showed that the bloated military expenditure of the Soviet Union was unsustainable.

'The Plan to Prevail' was a bold step, and one that would need global partners. But it was also one that Reagan was determined to pursue even in the face of allied opposition. In 1981–2, Reagan would try various strategies to bring western allies on board, including the invocation of American prestige as the alliance leader and an economic package to help compensate for losses associated with the Siberian pipeline. Yet, as a State Department paper made clear, the president was sending 'an important message to our allies . . . about our seriousness of purpose' and the future direction of policy. Not only would the president 'brave Soviet wrath', one official told the conservative magazine *Human Events*, 'but the howls of our allies'.[77]

Those howls were of anguish in western Europe, where the prospect of cheaper gas and billions of dollars in technology contracts were now under threat. Helmut Schmidt simply announced that 'the pipeline will be built.' Even the French, who had provided much of the vital intelligence that underpinned the strategy, talked about 'a progressive divorce' because 'we no longer speak the same language.' Ordinarily, this might have presented a dilemma for Thatcher, for whom it was almost an article of faith never to criticise the US president in public. On this occasion, however, such was the level of her anger that she unambiguously condemned 'one very powerful nation' riding roughshod over the economic interests and legal contracts of British business. She even joined in a united European Community formal protest against 'unacceptable interference' in the sovereign affairs of nations.

A compromise would be reached down the road, but for Thatcher the experience and implications of pipeline politics were deeply unsettling. Like the president, and in contrast to her European allies, Thatcher believed that strong defence was more important than détente. Yet she also believed that strong defence came through the unity of NATO and the western alliance. Reagan's new strategy taught her that the president was prepared to ignore allied concerns, including her own, when they conflicted with US policy. The result was not only a more fragile British defence, but a weakened western alliance.[78]

On this occasion Thatcher had narrowly avoided being left exposed, because both her policy and instincts coincided with those of her European partners. It was not long, however, before Reagan's shifting global priorities would threaten to leave her isolated on the world stage, facing the gravest political and international crisis of her premiership.

4

Little Ice-Cold Bunch of Land

House of Commons, Westminster. 2 April 1982. The Conservative backbencher Alan Clark had called in to Westminster that day only to collect his post. He had been due to take the train down to his Plymouth constituency for the weekend. Now he found fellow MPs shocked and stunned by breaking news: the Falkland Islands in the South Atlantic had been invaded. For many outside Westminster, the first reaction to that news would be 'the *which* islands?' followed by a quick consultation of an atlas. But Clark not only knew where the islands were, he understood what the invasion might mean. 'We've lost the Falklands,' he told his wife that evening. 'It's all over. We're a Third World country, no good for anything.'

Clark, an Old Etonian millionaire, was an easy man not to take seriously. Raffish, lecherous, and often gratuitously offensive, he exasperated even his friends and effortlessly collected enemies, of whom there were many. Yet Clark was acknowledged as a leading defence specialist in the House and, as the author of *The Donkeys* – an iconoclastic history of British generals in the early campaigns of the First World War – he had a knack for setting contemporary politics in their historical perspective.

Now, in 1982, it seemed to Clark that the Falklands crisis was a defining moment in the British national story. 'Can it have felt like this in the Thirties, from time to time,' he asked in his diary, 'on those fine weekends when the dictators, Hitler and Musso[lini], decided to help themselves to something – Durazzo,

Memel, Prague – and all we could do was wring our hands and talk about "bad faith". I have a terrible feeling that this is a step change, down, for England. Humiliation for sure and, not impossible, military defeat. An apparition that must have been stalking us, since we were so dreadfully weakened at Passchendaele I suppose, for the last sixty-five years.'[1]

For Clark it was history that came to mind; for others it was farce. On that same day, 2 April, another Old Etonian, the Foreign Office junior minister Douglas Hurd, found himself at his alma mater Trinity College, Cambridge, entertaining a party of German MPs. 'The waiter dropped on the floor a huge dish of creme brulee, the pudding for which my college is famous, creating an awesome mess,' he recalled. 'The omen proved accurate.'[2]

This sense of dismay was felt by many, not least in Westminster, where for an instant it looked as if the prime minister might fall. The House of Commons was recalled for an emergency sitting on 3 April, the first Saturday debate since the Suez crisis in 1956.

The modern House of Commons had witnessed many moments of intense drama since its opening in 1852, and the debates during the Falklands crisis would rank high among them. The squalor and humiliation of the situation in which the government found itself seemed intensified by the glory of the surroundings. The magnificent Palace of Westminster by Charles Barry and Augustus Pugin, faithfully restored after bombing during the Second World War, proclaimed the power, confidence, prosperity and majesty of mid-Victorian Britain. It was perhaps the nation's most iconic building, symbolised by 'Big Ben' and its tower, which were instantly recognisable around the world. From the dispatch box in the Commons chamber, Gladstone and Disraeli had ruled an empire and brought the 'common' man within the 'pale of the constitution', Asquith had nonchalantly played 'wait and see', and Churchill had proclaimed Britain's 'finest hour'.

This palace of Gothic enchantment, with its gilded celebration of the past, was not somewhere that encouraged failure. Indeed, the Commons chamber seemed almost designed to destroy the weak. The green benches of the government and the opposition were ranged adversarially against each other. There were not enough places for every MP to be seated, so those without a spot would cram into the gangways and behind the Speaker's Chair, creating a claustrophobic bear pit of an atmosphere. Convention demanded shouting, jeering and the waving of papers. From the dispatch box, the prime minister of the day stood 'two swords lengths' away from the leader of the opposition. Each remained behind a line that could be 'toed' but not crossed; but in all other senses, this was a political duel to the death. No quarter was asked or given. And the fatal blow could often come from behind. At any time, a prime minister might be enjoined by one of his own backbenchers, as Leo Amery demanded of Neville Chamberlain in May 1940, 'In the name of God, go!'[3]

Chamberlain resigned after the 1940 Narvik debate to make way for Churchill. The Suez crisis too had eventually caused the downfall of a prime minister. Indeed, the parallel with Anthony Eden and Suez was one that most MPs were already making as they prepared for the emergency debate on the Falklands. Members from all sides of the House rose to condemn the invasion and to chastise the government that had allowed it to happen. 'For a government that was so avowedly patriotic,' wrote the official historian of the war, Sir Lawrence Freedman, 'it was galling to be castigated by an Opposition that was so clearly to its left for losing British sovereign territory to a military dictatorship in such a surprising and convincing manner.'[4]

Reaction was fiercer than it might otherwise have been because this was so clearly a self-inflicted blow. Thatcher, like Reagan, believed in 'strong defence', but unlike the president she could not afford to invest heavily in both conventional and nuclear weapons. In 1981 she had put the monetarist John Nott into the Ministry of Defence to slash spending. Nott's defence review had laid out cuts to Britain's surface naval fleet. The future of the Royal Navy was to be in submarines armed with the expensive Trident nuclear weapons system. The aging aircraft carrier *Hermes* would be scrapped, and the mini-carrier *Invincible* sold to Australia. This would leave Britain with just one mini-carrier, *Illustrious,* in its fleet. The number of frigates and destroyers would be cut by a third. Dockyard capacity was to be significantly reduced. Such was the ferocity of these cuts that the navy minister, Keith Speed, resigned in protest.[5]

One of the side effects of these naval cuts was that the British ice patrol vessel HMS *Endurance* – known affectionately as the 'Red Plum' for its bright paintwork – would be withdrawn from the region. The Foreign Office had warned in vain that such a move was likely to signal to Argentina that Britain had little interest in protecting its possessions in the South Atlantic. These comprised the East and West Falkland Islands, a hundred smaller islands, and the dependencies of South Georgia and the South Sandwich Islands. They had been in British hands since 1833, with a claim that went back to 1690. When Thatcher came to power in 1979, she had privately told ministers that she was 'very worried about the whole subject.' In November 1980 a Foreign Office minister, Nicholas Ridley, went to the Falkland Islands to propose a solution. This included an arrangement by which sovereignty over the islands would be ceded to Argentina, but with Britain leasing back the islands. When islanders, and later the House of Commons, angrily rejected any such change of status, the plans were quietly dropped. Nevertheless, the impression abroad remained that the British government was far from committed to maintaining its absolute claim to sovereignty of the islands. Indeed, to many it seemed as if Britain couldn't wait to get rid of the Falklands.[6]

Argentina also made a centuries-old claim to the islands it called *Las Malvinas*. Buenos Aires argued that it gained sovereignty over the islands with independence in 1816 from Spain, which had never relinquished its own claim to them. Moreover, as the islands were on Argentina's continental shelf, the government also claimed the islands under the 1958 UN Convention on the Continental Shelf. It was not so much the strategic value of the Malvinas that mattered to Argentina. The geopolitical importance of the Falklands had diminished since the mid-twentieth century, when the islands had commanded the naval route around Cape Horn. Economic interest was negligible, although the potential certainly existed for oil exploration.

The population was less than 2,000, with more sheep than there were people. The terrain of the islands was predominantly bare and windswept. Their land area of 4,700 square miles was less than that of Northern Ireland. But as one London newspaper put it: 'For the Falklands as for Northern Ireland, politics and raw emotion outweigh most dispassionate economic calculations.' British rule was a national humiliation for Argentina.[7]

Although the authoritarian Argentine junta had been successful in suppressing domestic dissent since it came to power in 1976, the Malvinas question was just one of a number of embarrassing foreign policy failures. These included a losing struggle with Brazil to become the dominant regional power in South America, and another territorial dispute, this time with Chile over the Beagle Channel Islands. In response to these failures, the junta in 1978 began a vigorous programme of rearmament, including a commitment to acquiring a nuclear capability. By 1982, Argentina was testing its first ballistic missile. Operational capability was expected by 1984. One anticipated result of this process was that Argentine nuclear weapons capacity, when combined with British defence cuts in the region, would lead inevitably to a negotiated transfer of sovereignty over the Malvinas.[8]

What changed that long-term calculation was the emergence, following President Roberto Viola's heart attack, of General Leopoldo Galtieri at the head of the junta in December 1981. He purged the army of its top five generals and ordered that immediate plans be drawn up to seize the Malvinas. The Argentine economy was close to breaking point, with a debt of more than $35 billion. The junta was deeply unpopular in the country. Galtieri needed some good news to reinforce the regime. He set a date by which capture of the islands must be complete: 25 May – Argentina's national day.[9]

On 19 March 1982 the Argentine flag was seen on South Georgia. Britain reacted cautiously by dispatching HMS *Endurance* to monitor the situation. Shortly afterwards an Argentine invasion fleet set sail unhindered for the Falkland Islands. On 2 April, the Argentine flag was reported as flying over Government House in the Falkland Islands capital, Port Stanley. The governor and representative of the crown, Sir Rex Hunt, had surrendered.

It had only taken about 1,000 Argentine soldiers to complete the task.[10] Three days earlier, a baying mob had stood in the main square in Buenos Aires calling for the downfall of the junta. Now Galtieri appeared on the balcony of Casa Rosada to acknowledge the adulation of a frenzied crowd chanting his name.

In Britain the mood in the House of Commons during an emergency debate the following day was a mixture of fury and disbelief. Thatcher was visibly nervous as she addressed the House – 'clearly shaken,' noted the former foreign secretary, David Owen. Her pitch of voice betrayed anxiety and she gabbled much of what she said. For one moment she hit her stride, speaking in Churchillian terms of the people of the Falkland Islands, who 'like the people of the United Kingdom, are an island race'. She continued: 'They are few in number, but they have the right to live in peace, to choose their own way of life and to determine their own allegiance. Their way of life is British: their allegiance is to the Crown. It is the wish of the British people and the duty of Her Majesty's Government to do everything that we can to uphold that right. That will be our hope and our endeavour and, I believe, the resolve of every member of the House.'[11]

It was a fine piece of rhetoric, but words were not enough. What saved Thatcher was that she could announce a task force ready to sail for the South Atlantic.[12] Serious questions about her leadership remained. Enoch Powell, whom she admired greatly, summed up the feeling in the House. 'The Prime Minister, shortly after she came into office, received a sobriquet as the "Iron Lady",' he said. 'It arose in the context of remarks which she made about defence against the Soviet Union and its allies; but there was no reason to suppose that the Right Hon. Lady did not welcome and, indeed, take pride in that description. In the next week or two this House, the nation and the Right Hon. Lady herself will learn of what metal she is made.'

Thatcher was helped in re-establishing her political authority by the acumen and sense of honour displayed by her foreign secretary, Lord Carrington. He understood that public and politicians alike required a scapegoat for the loss of the Falklands.

'The nation feels that there has been a disgrace,' he wrote afterwards. 'Someone must have been to blame. The disgrace must be purged. The person to purge it should be the minister in charge. That was me.' Thatcher, who liked and respected Carrington, tried to talk him out of going, but his mind was made up. 'My departure would put a stop to the search for scapegoats,' he told her. 'It would serve the cause of unity and help turn the eyes of all from the past to the immediate future.' For the sake of that party unity, Thatcher was forced to appoint Francis Pym in his place, thus replacing, she reflected ruefully, an 'amusing' Whig with a 'gloomy' one. Pym would be a thorn in her side throughout the Falklands campaign.[13]

One feature that Pym brought to proceedings was actual experience of war. In fact, of the members of the war cabinet, Thatcher was the only one not to have served under the Queen's colours. Pym had won the military cross in Italy during the Second World War. William Whitelaw, Thatcher's deputy, had had the military cross pinned on his chest by Field Marshal Montgomery himself for gallantry in Normandy in 1944. John Nott, the defence secretary, had seen active service in Malaya. Conservative Party chairman Cecil Parkinson had done national service in the Royal Air Force.

Thatcher was unafraid to draw on the advice of those with greater experience if she needed to. Now she consulted one of her predecessors as prime minister, Harold Macmillan, to use his knowledge of battle and wartime leadership. Macmillan had served in the trenches during the First World War, had been close to Churchill during the Second World War, and was chancellor of the exchequer during the disastrous Suez crisis in 1956. It was Macmillan, said Thatcher afterwards, who advised her to form the small war cabinet that would meet daily. He also advised her not to include the chancellor in that group, perhaps the most telling indication he ever gave that his own advice given from the Treasury during the Suez crisis had been less than helpful to the prime minister at the time, Anthony Eden.

Thatcher had no military background, but she seemed to have an instinctive understanding that her role was to give political direction to the overall strategy of the war. Tactics were not her concern: she left the military to get on with them. Robert Wade-Gery, deputy secretary to the cabinet, observed of her relationship with the chiefs of staff that 'Right at the beginning she said, "Look, you run this war because you know how to. I don't, but when you need a political decision of any kind, come to me, if necessary at 3 o'clock in the morning, and I will give it to you". And she was as good as her word.' Thatcher, he concludes, 'was a frightfully good war leader in that respect, which I didn't think she'd be.'[14]

If the military, particularly the navy, responded to the clarity that Thatcher offered, so she in turn respected their decisiveness. It was something she had seen right at the outset of the crisis. Days earlier, on 31 March, having received intelligence that an invasion was imminent, Thatcher had met with advisers and ministers in her rooms at the House of Commons. The mood was one of gloom and defeatism. John Nott stated that Britain would not have the capability to retake the islands. Richard Luce from the Foreign Office urged restraint so as not to make a bad situation worse. Thatcher was stunned. 'I think we [had] all got into a frame of mind which didn't actually believe there could be war again involving our country,' John Coles, the prime minister's private secretary, recalled. 'We got into a frame of mind that negotiation was the answer to everything.'[15]

Only with the arrival at Westminster of Sir Henry Leach, the chief of the naval staff, had this 'dark moment' passed and Thatcher's mood changed. Yes, he told the PM, he could put together a task force of destroyers, frigates, landing craft and supporting vessels, which would be led by the aircraft carriers *Hermes* and *Invincible*. It could be ready to leave in forty-eight hours. 'Before this, I had been outraged and determined,' she wrote afterwards. 'Now my outrage and determination were matched by a sense of relief and confidence.' This encounter, when the quiet authority of military commanders superseded political timidity and caution, established a framework for Thatcher's war.[16]

At that same meeting, as the Argentine fleet had been sailing towards the Falkland Islands, Thatcher understood that the best chance of avoiding conflict was to turn those ships around. 'Our only hope now lay with the Americans,' she wrote. 'Friends and allies, and people to whom Galtieri, if he was still behaving rationally, should listen.' Thatcher sent an urgent personal message to the president asking him to intervene.

Reagan replied immediately. 'We share your concern over the disturbing military steps which the Argentines are taking and regret that negotiations have not succeeded in defusing the problem,' noted the president. 'Accordingly, we are contacting the Argentine government at the highest levels to urge them not to take military measures which would make a just solution more difficult to achieve. As you requested, we are also asking for assurances from them that they will show restraint and not initiate hostilities.' Reagan ended with a personal flourish for Thatcher: 'I want you to know how we have valued your cooperation on the challenges we both face in many different parts of the world. We will do what we can to assist you here.'[17]

Thatcher was delighted, but her relief was short-lived. Within hours, the president had sent another telegram. 'I have just talked at length with General Galtieri about the situation in the Falklands,' he told her. 'I conveyed to him my personal concern about the possibility of an Argentinian invasion . . . The General heard my message, but gave me no commitment that he would comply with it. Indeed, he spoke in terms of ultimatums and left me with a clear impression that he has embarked on a course of armed conflict.' Only the president's personal reassurances offered a boost. 'While we have a policy of neutrality on the sovereignty issue,' he promised her, 'we will not be neutral on the issue involving Argentine use of force.'[18]

These were resolute words, but in truth the mood inside the White House was one of bemusement more than anger. No one could quite understand why Britain and Argentina were getting so worked up about a few scattered islands in the South Atlantic.

British Embassy staff were at the forefront of efforts to get the Americans to take the issue more seriously. The danger, noted Peter Hall, the head of British Information Services in New York, was that the dispute 'would be regarded as a faintly ludicrous Gilbert and Sullivan cocked-hat thing.' In fact, it was worse than that. Jim Rentschler, the White House official responsible for handling the Falklands, summed it up in his diary as 'Gilbert and Sullivan as told to Anthony Trollope by Alistair Cooke.'[19]

In the days leading up to the outbreak of war, the British Embassy in Washington had been astonished by the lukewarm support the Americans had expressed. On occasion this spilled over into outrage, such as when Jeane Kirkpatrick, the US ambassador to the UN, dined at the Argentine Embassy on the night of the invasion of the Falklands. It was, protested the British ambassador, Nicholas Henderson, as if he had joined the Iranians for tea on the day that fifty-two Americans were taken hostage in Tehran. Henderson found officials at the State Department 'immensely detached', adding sadly, 'I suppose that's the impression British diplomats gave a century ago when we were a great power and some lesser country sought our support.'[20]

It had not helped that the British public relations effort had been so slow to get off the ground. 'Initially the Argentines were getting rather good [coverage], and this was beginning to affect the Administration,' recalled John Coles. 'We therefore had to step up our campaign, and the ambassador in Washington, Nicholas Henderson, and Tony Parsons, the ambassador in New York [at the UN], became familiar figures on the American screen, and that was very important, because, with those and other efforts, the attitude of the American media changed.'[21]

Comical though a Gilbert and Sullivan dispute might have seemed, the conflict between Britain and Argentina cut right to the heart of the foreign policy dilemma that confronted the United States as a superpower with both global and regional interests. America had its Atlantic relationship with Britain, which was rooted in shared defence and intelligence, and was reinforced by language, culture and the experience of fighting two world wars and the cold war together. Yet the United States also had to take a 'hemispheric' view, which meant looking after its own back yard. The question for policy makers was whether the United States should oppose one of the largest and most important countries – Argentina – in its own hemisphere, particularly when that country was such a vital player in US cold war strategy in the region.

Argentina had a history of difficult relations with the United States. During the 1930s, it had repeatedly challenged American political and cultural hegemony. When the United States entered the Second World War in 1941, Argentina infuriated Roosevelt by remaining neutral. Fears about Argentinian fascism were heightened by a military coup in 1943 led by Juan Perón among others. Only a last-minute declaration of war against the Axis powers in March 1945 secured Argentina an invitation to the inaugural United Nations Conference in San Francisco a few weeks later. Resentment in Washington would be long-lasting; Argentina and the United States never enjoyed the sense of shared wartime experience that helped sustain Anglo-American relations.[22]

Nevertheless by 1982 strategic considerations had ensured that Argentina was seen as a key ally in an important cold war battleground. Latin America, said Jeane Kirkpatrick, had become 'the most important place in the world for us'. The Reagan administration would expend enormous amounts of energy and resources in trying to roll back Communism and Socialism in this traditional sphere of influence. In some cases, such as Nicaragua, this would involve using military force to attempt the overthrow of left-wing regimes. In other cases, such as El Salvador, it meant propping up authoritarian regimes against leftist threats. Trade was also a vital part of the calculation, as the US looked to remove strong competition in an established market from Japan and western Europe, including Britain.[23]

The Reagan administration had vigorously pursued a US-Argentine alliance from the outset. President Viola arrived in Washington on a full state visit in March 1981, just weeks after Thatcher. The administration announced that it would end Argentina's trade isolation. The Humphrey-Kennedy amendment, which prevented arms sales, would be undone. In addition, the administration indicated that it would cease to criticise Argentina's human rights record. In return, the United States looked to Buenos Aires for help on a number of international projects, particularly El Salvador and the Sinai Peace Force, as well as support for the Contras in Nicaragua. When Viola proved less amenable than hoped, the administration turned to General Galtieri, whom it had already identified as the likely successor to the ailing Argentine president. Galtieri made two visits to the United States in 1981, meeting Vice-President George H.W. Bush and then being taken to Disneyland by Reagan's roving ambassador, General Vernon Walters. When Walters subsequently held talks with the junta in Buenos Aires in the autumn that year, he was asked specifically about what would happen in the event of Argentina seizing the Falkland Islands. The British would 'huff, puff and protest, and do nothing,' Walters told them. America would deal with Britain's wounded pride. It was a promise that Galtieri took to heart.[24]

Competing American views on the Falklands crisis – Atlantacist vs. Hemispheric – came to a head on 7 April in a fiery meeting of the National Security Planning Group (NSPG), chaired by the president. Jeane Kirkpatrick, US ambassador to the United Nations and an expert on Argentina, outlined a strong case for preserving the inner-American system and the viability of 'hemispheric defense' as outlined in the Rio Pact. This inter-American treaty of reciprocal assistance, signed in 1947, stated that an attack against one power in the hemisphere should be considered an attack against them all. Atlanticists were astonished by this approach. 'I couldn't disagree more with Jeane's statement,' boomed Admiral Bobby Inman from the CIA. 'It's the most wrongheaded thing I've ever heard!' He went on to evoke the ties of language, alliance, tradition and strategic interest that the US shared with Britain. He also added a chilling warning about Argentina's ballistic missile programme: 'If we let the Argentines get away with aggression now using conventional stuff, who is to say that ten or fifteen years down the road they won't be tempted to try again with nuclear?'[25]

Thatcher might have expected Reagan's view to have been firmly behind his self-styled 'closest ally'. In fact, he was non-committal. He was certainly impatient for a decision at the NSPG meeting, as Marine One was on standby to transport him to the Caribbean for an Easter vacation. Yet he was reluctant to tilt policy in one direction or another, still hoping the issue might blow over. To help this along, the president backed a suggestion by Al Haig that the secretary himself might visit each of the rival capitals to negotiate a settlement. While Reagan left for the beach, Haig headed to the airport to begin an exhausting two-week, 3,000-mile diplomatic shuttle mission.

Thatcher, kept up to date with developments in Washington, could not hide her concern. 'Unfortunately the attitudes of Mrs Kirkpatrick and some other members of the US administration [are] at this point of considerable importance,' she noted. Yet the prime minister was utterly convinced that at the end of the day the president would come through for her. It was only when Al Haig arrived in London on 8 April that real doubts began to set in. 'I certainly [couldn't] imply that American support was immediate and full – it wasn't,' recalled John Coles. The 'awkwardness was the American determination to try to negotiate a settlement.'[26]

Haig came to 10 Downing Street with a three-step process to avoid war in the Falklands. This involved, first, the withdrawal of Argentine troops from the islands; second, the return of British administration under an interim international authority; and third, a swift return to negotiations on the question of sovereignty.

Thatcher had agreed with Ambassador Henderson's advice that Haig should be received not as a negotiator, but as a close friend and ally. Talks took place over dinner to try and lend a more collegial atmosphere, although the Americans were slightly bemused to find their British counterparts dressed in black tie for the event. Perhaps this was a Gilbert and Sullivan operetta after all. Thatcher fussed around with the drinks, but then, in a pointed reminder of what was at stake, showed her guests two oil portraits that been put on display especially for the occasion. One was of Lord Nelson and the other of the Duke of Wellington.

If the heroes of Trafalgar and Waterloo had in some way failed to emphasise to Haig that Britain was resolved to stand and fight, then Thatcher's own rhetoric left him in no doubt whatsoever. 'Wooliness!' she spat contemptuously after hearing him out. Flushed in the face, her voice rising in indignation, Thatcher let fly. 'I did not dispatch a fleet to install some nebulous arrangement which would have no authority,' she continued. 'Interim authority! To do *what*? I beg you to remember that in 1938 Neville Chamberlain sat *at this same table* discussing an arrangement which sounds very much like the one you are asking me to accept; and were I to do so, I would be censured in the House of Commons – and properly so! Britain simply will not reward aggression – that is the lesson of 1938.'[27]

'Tough lady,' concluded Jim Rentschler. All the while, as Thatcher hammered away, Al Haig sat nervously tapping his foot and chain-smoking Merits. For a man still recovering from a heart bypass operation, the cigarettes were probably less harmful than the stress of Thatcher in full flight. As he left, Thatcher pulled the secretary of state to one side. 'I do hope you realise how much we appreciate and are thankful for your presence here, and how the kind of candour we have displayed could only be possible among the closest of friends,' she told him – 'With everyone else we're merely *nice*!'[28]

Back on the plane, Haig penned a long memo for the president in which he did not try to hide his dismay at Thatcher's attitude. 'The prime minister has the bit in her teeth,' he reported. 'She is clearly prepared to use force, though she admits a preference for a diplomatic solution. She is rigid in her insistence on a return to the *status quo ante*, and indeed seemingly determined that any solution involve some retribution.' The only positive that Haig could find was in the attitude of the foreign secretary, Francis Pym, who had shown a certain flexibility, albeit 'not appreciated by Mrs Thatcher'. Ruefully, Haig noted that he had taken a pre-arranged downbeat line with the press to avoid any suggestion that there was cause for encouragement, which was lucky as 'There is, in fact, little basis for encouragement in any event.'[29]

Reagan replied immediately to restate his desire for an accommodation on the crisis. 'The report of your discussion in London makes clear how difficult it will be to foster a compromise that gives Maggie enough to carry on and at the same time meets the test of "equity" with our Latin neighbors,' he noted. 'As you expected there isn't much room for maneuver in the British position . . . It's my guess from the [British] stance that any compromise on Thatcher's part will take time.'[30]

Haig's next stop was Buenos Aires, where he promised General Galtieri that the United States was pressing Britain to compromise. 'Thatcher's demands were clear: You must withdraw before they will consider negotiations,' the secretary reported. 'I told her I was sure you could not accept this – and frankly I don't believe you should. The British position is tantamount to an ultimatum.'[31]

This explicit criticism of the British position was a calculated attempt to show the United States as an honest broker. 'After twelve hours of back and forth – and ups and downs – we came up with a package which the Argentines *may* be able to accept,' the exhausted Haig told Thatcher when he returned to London on 12 April. 'I say "may" because as I left they reintroduced unacceptable demands involving Argentine interim rule and assured sovereignty.'

Haig assured the British that this was mere posturing on the part of Buenos Aires before delivering his conclusions to the prime minister: 'The package I have brought here is not a US proposal, but I must tell you in candor, I would have to say it's reasonable.' These terms included the idea of UK forces withdrawing 4,000 miles to Ascension Island. Then came the *coup de grâce*: 'If the choice is between this package and war, the view of the United States is clear.' This was a point he had agreed with Reagan, who was being held in reserve to apply pressure at a later stage. 'The time for a possible personal intervention by you with Mrs Thatcher has not yet arrived,' Haig had cabled the president. 'We must first see how she reacts to the proposed interim solution . . . as well as my appeal for British military restraint.'[32]

Although Thatcher believed the US plan was 'full of holes', she was momentarily put on the defensive by Haig's declaration that the package was better than war. John Nott recalled that 'Haig talked and talked, speaking up for his proposals with some vigour and skill.' In the end it was Argentine diplomatic incompetence and duplicity that let Thatcher off the hook. As the discussions were going on, Haig was called to the phone. The private thoughts which the Argentine foreign minister Nicanor Costa Mendes had given the secretary as he had been boarding the plane in Buenos Aires had now appeared in the *New York Times*. The deal that Haig had brought to London was worthless. When Haig came back into the room, disappointment and lack of sleep left him looking like a 'zombie' – and a fool.[33]

Haig's initial efforts to find a negotiated settlement had been a genuine attempt to plot a course between America's 'hemispheric' and 'Atlantic' allies. However, as the talks floundered, and the crisis began to gain momentum towards war, so desperation for a solution began to set in. In an attempt to achieve it, he began pushing harder for concessions from Britain, in particular a pre-condition that negotiations could not lead to a return to the earlier status quo, and that the task force should be stopped.[34]

'Unthinkable!' Thatcher told Haig. There was no question of the fleet standing down. 'That is our only leverage. I cannot possibly give it up at this point, one simply doesn't trust burglars who have tried to steal [our] property. No, Al, absolutely not: the fleet must steam on!'[35]

So the weary Haig set out for the airport on 13 April with his tail firmly between his legs. 'The countenance staring into the cameras from beneath that Irish tweed cap looks not merely grim but downright mortuary,' reflected Rentschler as they left Downing Street together. Thatcher concurred. 'He was obviously very depressed,' she observed, not entirely sympathetically. Reagan shared the prime minister's sense of disappointment in the secretary, albeit for different reasons. For with Haig on the way home, the chances of avoiding war now seemed 'very dim'.[36]

House of Commons. 14 April 1982. Margaret Thatcher resumed her seat on the green leather benches of the chamber to cheers from both sides of the House. MPs had listened in respectful silence, but her closing rallying cry was enough to prompt these loud expressions of solidarity and approval. It had been a resolute performance, setting out a position on the Falkland Islands that was firm while keeping to the moral high ground. 'The eyes of the world are now focused on the Falkland Islands,' she had concluded: 'Others are watching anxiously to see whether brute force or the rule of law will triumph. Wherever naked aggression occurs it must be overcome. The cost now, however high, must be set against the cost we would one day have to pay if this principle went by default. That is why, through diplomatic, economic and, if necessary, through military means, we shall persevere until freedom and democracy are restored to the people of the Falkland Islands.' It was more political showmanship than high policy, but she had perfectly captured the mood of the House.[37]

Thatcher's aim had been to show the outside world that she had the support of a united House of Commons. As she sat listening to the debate, the prime minister could reflect on a job well done. Where a week and a half earlier there had been fury and humiliation, now there seemed only to be resolve and unity. Those few MPs, mostly Labour left-wingers, who spoke out against the government's policy were met with howls of derision from both sides of the House. 'It is bound to happen,' recorded the former Labour cabinet minister, Tony Benn, in his diary the next day. 'You couldn't expect otherwise at this early stage of jingoistic fervour.'[38]

As the debate continued, Francis Pym passed along a note to the prime minister. What Thatcher read astonished her. Haig was on the telephone. He wanted to announce, following complaints from Argentina about 'fair play', that Britain's use of US facilities on Ascension Island – where the task force was now gathering – would cease. Thatcher immediately understood what this move signalled. It was more than a diplomatic manoeuvre. This was a direct threat to her entire military strategy to recover the Falklands.

The prime minister hurriedly left her seat to speak to Haig. Playing for time, she explained that the debate was going on and that she would telephone back within the hour. Just before ending the call, she acidly pointed out that many in the Commons that afternoon had expressed deep anger and disappointment at the US position of 'neutrality'. With that she rang off. When Thatcher returned half an hour later, it became immediately clear to Haig that she had wound herself up to a high pitch of indignation. 'The US [is] already doing less for us than we deserve,' she insisted. The British government simply could not and would not accept being put 'on an equal footing with the Junta.' The time had come for the US to choose exactly which side it was on.

'It's getting hairy, fellas,' Haig told his staff afterwards. 'It's getting hairier and hairier.'[39]

From his aeroplane to Buenos Aires the following day, Haig signalled to Reagan that the time was approaching when as president he would need to intervene personally. 'We should begin to prepare for the worst,' he warned. 'In this regard, I may need very soon to seek your decisions on . . . whether and how far to push Mrs Thatcher to come forth with a significant concession . . . Whether you should, or could, push Mrs Thatcher to this bitter conclusion – that they cannot in any event resist the course of history and that they are now paying the price for previous UK vacillation on the sovereignty question – with all that it would mean for her, for our relationship, and our own principles, will require very careful thought'.[40]

Five days later, now returned from Argentina, Haig briefed the president in the Oval Office. In the intervening period, the *New York Times* had reported on general British unhappiness with the American position as reflected in a poll showing 28 per cent of Britons had a lower opinion of the president as a result. Reagan still greeted the secretary warmly: 'Home is the sailor, home from the sea!' Haig confirmed to the president that 'now comes the delicate part of the problem. Military pressures are rising. Britain may debark on South Georgia tomorrow [and] the British will step up pressure on us to back them openly.' The question of how to proceed was not easy. The United States should 'keep to a neutral press line'. The British foreign secretary, Francis Pym, was flying to Washington, and Haig would be exerting extreme pressure 'to identify the British bottom line.' But there was no simple solution, the secretary concluded. 'This game is excruciatingly difficult and may well be impossible to win,' he advised. 'But every time I recalculate the cost to us of war in the South Atlantic, I cannot avoid concluding that we would be a major loser, on both continents.'[41] The Falklands crisis, Reagan noted in his diary that week, was coming to its 'moment of truth'.

When Pym arrived in Washington, the foreign secretary came under intense pressure to reach a compromise. Haig had identified Pym as the only representative of the 'peace party' in Thatcher's war cabinet. If anyone was going to be susceptible to a diplomatic solution, it was him. Haig pulled no punches. He had been angered the previous day when Ambassador Henderson had informed him that the operation to retake South Georgia was about to begin. Now the secretary of state warned Pym that if Britain continued on the path to war, the UK 'might be on [its] own.' Many in Washington wanted the US to keep itself in reserve for a later peace effort. Haig even doubted that Britain could achieve any kind of quick or satisfactory military victory in the South Atlantic. International opinion would turn against Britain as soon as shots were fired. Even if Britain did win, victory would come at the price of having to keep a permanent military presence in the region. None of this, Haig urged, would be as satisfactory for Britain as the deal that was currently on the table.[42]

Years afterwards, in his book *The Politics of Consent*, Francis Pym included a pithy sketch of how many people perceived the difference between himself and the prime minister. 'Margaret Thatcher is courageous and resolute,' he wrote. 'She speaks for the people of Britain and is the first prime minister for decades to have the guts to do what is necessary to put the country back on its feet . . . She has put pride and purpose back into the nation. Francis Pym is ineffective and negative. He epitomises the willingness to compromise that has led Britain downhill.'[43]

This characterisation was a stereotype, to be sure, but it captured in a nutshell Thatcher's mood at the cabinet meeting on the evening of 24 April when Pym returned to London. He had with him Haig's new draft proposals, which the foreign secretary was recommending should be accepted. Thatcher was shaken to her core. Haig had bullied Pym into accepting a 'conditional surrender'. If these terms were accepted, Thatcher told William Whitelaw, the deputy prime minister and her closest colleague throughout the conflict, she would resign.[44]

The meeting of the war cabinet that evening was a close-run thing. Pym, supported by Foreign Office diplomats, presented his paper arguing that the terms laid out by Haig should be accepted. It was an assured performance, given added authority by the fact that he could present this as an American plan. Thatcher countered by displaying one of her defining characteristics as prime minister: mastery of detail. Five hours had gone by since she had initially spoken to Pym and she had marked up her brief in intricate detail. Now she took Pym through the plan clause by clause, bombarding him with questions about what each point actually meant. By the end of the meeting, John Nott recalled, there was 'something of an impasse'. In the end it was Nott himself who came up with the solution. He suggested that Britain should make no comment on the draft, but ask Haig to put it to the Argentines first. If they accepted, then the matter could be put to Parliament on that basis. This 'brainwave', said Nicholas Henderson afterwards, was 'a finesse of which Talleyrand would have been proud.'[45]

Any poker player can appreciate the value of checking the bet, but in many ways it was a risky manoeuvre, as Nott himself acknowledged. Because the deal did not concede sovereignty, the full cabinet and the Commons might well have accepted it. That would have forced Thatcher to consider resignation. Fortunately for her, as throughout the conflict, the Argentines could always be relied upon to look an American gift horse in the mouth. On 29 April they informed Haig that his plan was unacceptable. The secretary of state had one last fruitless meeting with the Argentine foreign minister, Nicanor Costa Mendes, to urge acceptance, noting that if Buenos Aires adopted the deal, he would force Britain to take it as well. But the game was up. Haig's three-week peace mission was over, at least for the time being.[46]

That same day, Reagan chaired a meeting of the National Security Council to discuss what to do next. The US Senate had already heaped pressure on him by passing a resolution stating that the US 'cannot stand neutral' and must help Britain achieve 'full withdrawal' of Argentine forces. ('Don't mind all that crap about self-determination,' Democratic senator Joe Biden of Delaware told Henderson. 'We're with you because you're British.') At the NSC meeting Jeane Kirkpatrick made a last attempt to counter moves that would damage America's hemispheric interests. 'The Argentines will do anything to avoid war,' she pleaded. 'They don't want it, they'll slip out of it. I would even anticipate a UN démarche which will settle the issue this weekend.' The president responded scathingly: 'Wouldn't it be nice if, after all these years, the UN actually did something to promote peace?' His comment confirmed what Kirkpatrick already knew: that she was fighting a losing battle. 'There wasn't any question about where President Reagan stood on this issue, from start to finish,' she recalled, not without a certain bitterness. The NSC meeting concluded that US policy would now take 'an explicit pro-UK tilt', including the supply of matériel, and would include a series of 'concrete steps underscoring US determination not to condone the use of unlawful force to resolve disputes.' These included limited economic sanctions and the suspension of all military exports to Argentina.[47]

Reagan wrote to Thatcher to inform her of the change to a pro-UK policy. 'I am sure you agree that it is essential now to make clear to the world that every effort was made to achieve a fair and peaceful solution, and that the Argentine government was offered a choice between such a solution and further hostilities,' he wrote. He agreed not to publish the full draft of the Haig proposal 'because of the difficulty that might cause you', and noted – was it peevishly? – that 'I recognize that while you see fundamental difficulties in the proposal, you have not rejected it.' In the end, however, Reagan gave Thatcher at least some reassurance, noting that 'We will leave no doubt that Her Majesty's government worked with us in good faith and was left with no choice but to proceed with military action based on the right of self-defense.' Or, as he put it in his private diary: 'I don't think Margaret Thatcher should be asked to concede any more.'[48]

This was hardly the forceful Rooseveltian response that Thatcher had been looking for now that her 'house' was on fire. Reagan had not even tried to hide his belief that 'a strictly military outcome cannot endure over time. In the end, there will have to be a negotiated outcome acceptable to the interested parties. Otherwise, we will all face unending hostility and insecurity in the South Atlantic.'

Thatcher described Reagan's intervention as 'a substantial moral boost to our position'. In fact, that was far from the case. The president's warning could hardly have been clearer: eventually London and Buenos Aires would have to return to the negotiating table. Of course he was opposed to the use of force as a means to decide international disputes. But was it really worth going to war, he asked reporters, over that 'little ice-cold bunch of land down there'? It was the question Thatcher did not want to hear. Just as in the pipeline dispute, Reagan had little sympathy with the interests and designs of his British ally.[49]

Whatever her disappointment in Reagan, Thatcher's political position by the end of April 1982 was considerably stronger than it had been at the beginning of the month. For a brief moment it had seemed as if she might be forced from office by her own party. Now the domestic situation was more secure. She had united the country behind her decision to send the task force. The 'peace party' at home and abroad had been shown the door. The first military action of the campaign had been successfully undertaken and the morale-boosting signal received: 'Be pleased to inform Her Majesty that the White Ensign flies alongside the Union Jack in South Georgia. God save the Queen.' Outside No. 10, Thatcher admonished waiting journalists to 'Just rejoice at that news!'

A 200-mile 'total exclusion zone' was now in place around the Falkland Islands, with a warning to Argentine forces that they would be fired upon without warning if they breached that zone. It was clear to everyone, not least Margaret Thatcher, that the diplomatic phase of the Falklands crisis was over and that full scale military conflict was imminent. 'I felt proud and exhilarated,' she wrote after an ovation at a Conservative Party rally on 30 April, 'but I felt too an almost crushing burden of responsibility. I knew the task force would enter the waters around the Falkland Islands the following day.'[50]

With the task force in position, Thatcher must have hoped that she could finally count on the Americans. It had been a disconcerting few weeks for such an instinctive Atlanticist. Divisions within the Reagan administration about the direction of strategy had often blindsided Thatcher. Jeane Kirkpatrick, with her hemispheric inclinations and doctrine of supporting anti-Communist authoritarian regimes in the area, had been easy to read. '[She] was very mixed up with Latin American policy,' Britain's UN ambassador, Sir Anthony Parsons dryly commented. But the attitude of Al Haig had been an unwelcome surprise. As a former NATO commander, he had seemed the ideal person to support Britain's position in the face of Argentine aggression. His attitude that the US was 'friends with both' had come as a shock. On occasion the British had been unable to contain their fury. When Henderson had informed Haig that the operation to retake South Georgia was about to begin, the secretary had primly told him that the US was duty-bound to inform Argentina. The tirade from Henderson that followed was doubly effective in stopping this development because it came from such a usually urbane source.[51]

Britain was often left confused by the competing interests at the heart of the US administration. When Pym had arrived in Washington for his talks with Haig, which resulted in the 'unacceptable' plan over which Thatcher threatened to resign, he had beforehand met the national security adviser, 'Judge' Bill Clark. Breakfasting on the beautiful terrace at the British Embassy, amid the cherry and apple blossom, Clark threw out the idea that the Falklands might become a US trusteeship. Would Pym like to meet the president to discuss it? Clark asked. No British foreign secretary was going to turn down a meeting in the Oval Office, so Pym indicated a willingness to discuss the idea. Soon afterwards, an apoplectic Al Haig arrived to see Pym. Ever the prima donna, the secretary was indignant that Clark should have raised the question of a trusteeship. 'Am I not in charge of the negotiations?' he bellowed. Pym never heard from Clark again during the visit, and he did not get his meeting in the White House. Instead, he returned home to London with Haig's new peace proposal to face the wrath of Thatcher.[52]

Fortunately for Thatcher, the man who had become the face of the administration during the Falklands conflict – Al Haig – was not the most important one in ensuring that Britain successfully recaptured the Falklands. The secretary of defense,

Caspar Weinberger, had proven more helpful to Thatcher's war plans. He had conducted a very quiet Falklands war, almost entirely out of the public eye. Much later, after the war, Henderson would write to him from retirement to express regret that he was forbidden from revealing the details of Weinberger's role during the conflict. For while the camera-hungry Haig jetted between continents in a search for peace, Weinberger simply got on with the business of making sure that Britain won the war.

Caspar Weinberger was Jeane Kirkpatrick's photo negative during the Falklands crisis. He was clear from the outset that Atlantic interests trumped hemispheric ones. 'I believed at the beginning – and did not change my views later on – that this was an attempt by a corrupt military dictatorship to interfere with the rights that had been exercised by one of our oldest and closest allies,' he recalled, 'and among other things, a fellow member of NATO to whom we had treaty obligations under the NATO agreement.' Weinberger was immediately hostile to Haig's mediation efforts, not just because he disliked Haig personally, but because 'I was very skeptical about the results, and also very worried that in the course of mediation we might forget some of our basic obligations to Great Britain and to the fact that she was a NATO ally.' Margaret Thatcher could not have expressed it better herself.[53]

Weinberger's pro-British view ensured that London got vital support in the area it needed most: intelligence and military matériel. Weinberger understood that Britain in 1982 was ill equipped to fight a war in the South Atlantic. It lacked air surveillance. Satellite communications were inadequate. The Harriers had no effective air-to-air missile system. There was no base in the South Atlantic. Weinberger recognised these deficiencies and moved to overcome them, even as Haig was pushing his peace plan. First, Weinberger offered use of the American Wideawake Air Base on Ascension Island, which the US held on long-term lease from Britain. Supplies immediately cascaded in for the task force, including aviation fuel, Stinger anti-aircraft systems, and weapons and ammunition of all kinds. Most important of all were the new Sidewinder air-to-air missiles

– the decisive weapon of the conflict. Matériel was supplemented by intelligence and communications support. Weinberger even offered to make a US carrier available to Britain in the South Atlantic. 'It is impossible to exaggerate,' judged Henderson, 'the contribution Weinberger made to our cause.'[54]

Weinberger's support for the British had begun as soon as the task force set sail at the beginning of April. Yet it was clear that the president had only the haziest notion of what was going on. 'They [*The Washington Post*] have charged that we are lending aid to Britain's navy in the Falklands dispute,' Reagan noted on 14 April. 'This of course has set the Argentinians on fire. The charge is false. We are providing Eng. with a communications channel via satellite but that is part of a regular routine that existed before the dispute. To have cancelled it would have been taken as supporting the Argentine. [But] we're still in the game as to trying for a peaceful settlement . . .'[55]

Reagan's assertion that 'The charge is false' was contradicted by the military and intelligence support Weinberger was in fact giving Britain. Either the president was lying (even to his diary), or else he was unaware of the major thrust of defence policy within his own administration. Two years afterwards, an embittered Al Haig, now out of office, would point to this as a wider characteristic of policy making under Reagan. 'The White House was as mysterious as a ghost ship,' he wrote in exasperation. 'You heard the creak of the rigging and the groan of the timbers, and sometimes even glimpsed the crew on deck. But which of the crew had the helm?' In the end, Haig concluded, 'It was impossible to know.'[56]

Certainly not Haig, as it turned out. The Falklands peace shuttle would be his last hurrah, or rather, damp squib: Haig resigned at the end of June 1982. Events in the South Atlantic would be part of a broader shift in the administration's foreign policy that saw Judge Clark and the NSC take the leading role in making US cold-war strategy more robust.

This change of direction did not offer much in the way of comfort to Thatcher and the British during the conflict. In fact, as confusion mounted, so too did the prime minister's frustration and anger.

If Reagan in his memoirs recorded incorrectly that his administration had done little or nothing to help Britain before hostilities broke out, he also noted that 'once fighting started, after the Argentineans had repeatedly rejected reasonable offers of a settlement, we declared our full support of Britain, and provided her with whatever aid we could.'[57]

The reality was considerably less satisfactory for Britain. Thatcher was about to face her lowest and most controversial moments in the conflict. And when she needed Reagan, he wasn't there.

5

Even More of a Wimp than Jimmy Carter

Total Exclusion Zone, South Atlantic. 4 May 1982. 'A dull forenoon with little happening,' wrote Admiral Sandy Woodward, the Falklands battle group commander, in his diary that night, 'until 1415 when an Exocet from an Étendard blew my old ship *Sheffield* away. As I write ten hours later she's still burning out there . . .'

The Super Étendard aircraft of the Argentine navy had been practising with its own ships to perfect avoidance of radar detection. Only two days earlier, in the first and most controversial action of the war, a British nuclear submarine using Mark 8 torpedoes had sunk the Argentine carrier *Belgrano*, a controversial act that cost 368 lives. The attack on the *Sheffield* was a direct response. On 4 May, two planes slipped away from their base at Rio Grande and then successfully refuelled in mid-air. When they got to within twelve miles of the British destroyer, each plane fired an Exocet and made their escape. The missiles took a minute to reach the *Sheffield*. One missed; the other hit the destroyer amidships, where it failed to explode. However, the fire from the blast of impact was enough to kill twenty people and badly wound twenty-six more. Soon the order was given to abandon ship, leaving the *Sheffield* to go down. She was the first British naval vessel to have been sunk by enemy action since the Second World War.[1]

The sinking of the *Sheffield*, noted defence secretary John Nott, brought home to everyone 'that we were really at war'. Admiral Woodward's wife heard the news back in London. 'As from that moment,' she remembered, 'I rather stopped regarding the Argentinian navy as something out of Gilbert and Sullivan.' That the Falklands conflict was not a scene from *HMS Pinafore* now seemed a matter on which everyone could agree.[2]

This attitude penetrated the White House as well, where reaction to the sinking of the *Belgrano* and the *Sheffield* was one of astonishment and horror. 'The stance of these two disputants increasingly resembles that of a couple of staggering streetfighters, spastically-swinging at each other while blinded into fury by the flow of their own blood,' national security staffer James Rentschler recorded in his diary. An NSC paper, *The Falkland Islands: What Now? What Next?* was not as colourful, but its incomprehension at what was happening was no less clear. 'The sinkings of the *Belgrano* and the *Sheffield* bring the South Atlantic conflict to an alarmingly new and perhaps desperate stage, one which throws into sharper relief the negative strategic factors which the US will increasingly confront as the hostilities persist,' the paper bluntly stated. 'We are in a situation where only an act of sanity may now save not only the belligerents themselves from further loss, but larger US interests as well.'

Assessment of the British position and its impact on US strategy was particularly harsh. 'Continuation of the British blockade with sporadic military action,' the NSC paper noted, 'will result in a grave setback to all our policies in this hemisphere as Latin American positions harden, while tying down the Royal Navy 8000 miles from its NATO responsibilities.' But the United States did have one ace to play: 'Now that we have come down on the British side, our leverage with Mrs Thatcher is greatly increased,' the NSC paper concluded. 'We are a *de facto* partner in the enterprise and can use that position to push our own interests in ways denied to us in our previous "honest broker" role.'[3]

The paper served to focus minds in the White House. Although Secretary of State Al Haig was still trying to resurrect his peace plan, this time with assistance from Peru, national security adviser William Clark decided it was time for the president to use his personal authority with the British prime minister to push for compromise. Later that same day, 4 May, Reagan sent a letter to Thatcher making a personal appeal. Lives had already been lost, he reminded her. It was time to call a halt.[4]

Thatcher's reaction when she read the letter was one of shock mixed with rage. Only hours earlier she had received news of the attack on the *Sheffield*. It had been a dark moment and her spirits were low. Now here was her closest ally urging a policy of 'appeasement'. Such 'constant pressure to weaken our stance' was quite simply unacceptable. Immediately, she sat down to write a personal response to Reagan that pulled no punches about how disappointed and angry she was. That letter, she said afterwards, 'revealed perhaps too much of my frustration.' Having got it out of her system, and urged by officials not to undermine her relationship with the president, she then toned down the note before it was sent. But even this more nuanced response remained a clear rebuke. She complained about US attempts to bulldoze Britain into compromise, and appealed to the president as 'the only person who will understand the significance of what I am trying to say.' Naturally she wanted a peaceful settlement and would work with Haig to try to achieve it. But the United States and Britain, as friends and allies, stood for the same principles of freedom and democracy. Surely the president understood that there could be no long-term solution to the Falklands crisis that did not 'provide unambiguously for a right to self-determination'? It was a matter of principle for Britain and for her. Time and again the Falkland Islanders had made clear their wish to remain under British rule. She would not desert them.[5]

Reagan sat on the letter for almost a week before countering. During that time negotiations for a peaceful resolution had moved to the United Nations, where the secretary-general, Pérez de Cuéllar, was complaining about Britain's lack of flexibility. Britain had been bombarding the Falkland Islands by sea and air, and had sunk the Argentine ship *De Los Estados* and a trawler, *Narwal*. The campaign was escalating. This time Reagan tried to bring more personal pressure to bear on the prime minister by telephoning instead of writing. 'I talked to Margaret,' he noted afterwards, 'but don't think I persuaded her against further action.'[6]

It was a bland account of an acrimonious call. Finally the mask of friendliness had slipped. Reagan told Thatcher that if rumours of Britain preparing to attack the Argentine mainland were true, this would put the United States in an extremely difficult position. She assured him that was not the case, because the international political damage would be too great. Reagan was relieved, but reminded her that military action and perceived intransigence were already damaging Britain's reputation. Surely it was time to hold off further military action, he urged, to give the UN a chance to work. This was too much for Thatcher. 'Argentina attacked our ships only yesterday,' she told him. 'We cannot delay military options simply because of negotiations.'[7]

Reagan explained his concerns that world opinion might see the war as a 'David v. Goliath' battle, with Britain in the role of Goliath. 'This could hardly be true at a distance of 8,000 miles,' Thatcher retorted. She then launched a tirade against the president, asking if he would like any Americans to live under a brutal dictatorship such as the Argentine junta, pointing out how long many of the families in the Falklands had lived there, and playing up the strategic importance of the islands. 'What if the Panama canal were ever closed?' she asked. Then America would understand the value of this 'bunch of land' in the South Atlantic.[8]

Afterwards, Thatcher expressed herself 'dismayed' by the president's attitude and 'horrified' by his suggestion that Britain should halt military operations. 'I can't see Reagan getting on to her on the phone again in a hurry,' Nicholas Henderson predicted.[9]

What made the situation all the more inexplicable to Thatcher was that Reagan's attitude contrasted so poorly with that of François Mitterrand, the Socialist president of France. Mitterrand had pledged unambiguous support from the outset. Jacques Attali, his former aide, wrote that the French president called Thatcher on the day after the invasion and told her: 'I am with you.' According to Attali, who acted as interpreter, 'she was stunned and did not expect it'.[10]

'I remember being in Downing Street the Saturday afternoon after the Argentinian invasion,' recalled John Coles, the prime minister's private secretary, 'and he was actually the first foreign statesman to ring up and say . . . "You have my support. This is important". That was significant.'[11]

'In so many ways Mitterrand and the French were our greatest allies,' wrote the defence secretary, John Nott, after the war. France had earlier supplied Argentina with the Mirage and Super Étendard aircraft. The Argentine navy was equipped with French-built Exocet missiles. Mitterrand now instructed the French Defence Ministry to give Britain access to Super Étendard and Mirage aircraft for training purposes. The French also supplied detailed technical information on how to tamper with the Exocet. A 'remarkable worldwide operation then ensued,' said Nott, to prevent Argentina from acquiring further Exocets. This involved the intelligence services of Britain and France working together to find Exocet missiles and render them inoperable.[12]

This did not mean there were not moments of Anglo-French tension. According to Mitterrand's psychoanalyst, Ali Magoudi, Mitterrand spoke in their sessions that May of his exasperation with the British prime minister. 'What an impossible woman, that Thatcher!' the president exclaimed. 'With her four nuclear submarines on mission in the southern Atlantic, she threatens to launch the atomic weapon against Argentina – unless I supply her with the secret codes that render deaf and blind the missiles we have sold to the Argentinians. Margaret has given me very precise instructions on the telephone . . . I have been forced to yield. She has them now, the codes. If our customers find out that the French wreck the weapons they sell, it's not going to reflect well on our exports.' How do you react to such an intransigent woman? asked Magoudi. 'What do you expect?' replied the exasperated president: 'You can't win a struggle against the insular syndrome of an unbridled Englishwoman.'[13]

Admiral Henry Leach, chief of the naval staff during the conflict, later denied the nuclear claim, saying that 'we did not contemplate a nuclear attack and did not make any even potentially preparatory moves for such action.' In which case Thatcher had excelled in the art of bluffing. Nevertheless, whatever sharp exchanges there may have been, Thatcher was clear in her own mind that the French were 'absolutely staunch' in their support. 'I was to have many disputes with President Mitterrand in later years,' she wrote, 'but I never forgot the debt we owed him for his personal support throughout the Falklands crisis.'[14]

It was left to her defence secretary to draw the obvious comparison. 'For all Margaret Thatcher's friendship with Ronald Reagan, he remained a West Coast American looking south to Latin America and west to the Pacific,' observed Nott. 'Sometimes I wondered if he even knew or cared where Europe was. There was incredible pressure from the White House and the State Department to negotiate. It was hugely damaging. They couldn't understand that to us any negotiated settlement would have seemed like a defeat.'[15]

In its own way the Falklands crisis – an imperial farce to many Americans – had turned out to be deeply revealing of US feelings of humiliation from its own failed imperial venture in Vietnam. Reagan had come to power in 1980 promising to banish the gloom of the Vietnam syndrome. Yet in many ways his defence policy exemplified it. Over the course of eight years in power, the administration would put more than $2 trillion into defence spending. Between 1980 and 1990, defence spending as a percentage of GDP rose from 4.9 per cent to 5.2 per cent, and accounted for around a quarter of federal expenditure for most of that decade. The aim of this defence build-up, which had already begun under President Carter, was to intimidate America's enemies to such an extent that war with the United States would become unthinkable. Behind that calculation lay a post-Vietnam understanding shared across the political divide: the strongest desire to avoid sending troops into battle – and home in body bags.

This policy would be made explicit the following year by Secretary of Defense Weinberger, who argued that the United States should only fight when it could win without significant loss of life. 'We have learned that there are limits to how much of our spirit and blood and treasure we can afford to forfeit in meeting our responsibility to keep peace and freedom,' he explained in a speech on 'The Uses of Military Power'. It became known as the Weinberger Doctrine, and would later became the foundation for the Powell Doctrine that underwrote American military strategy until 9/11. With Reagan's own personal hatred of war and violence thrown into this mix, it was not difficult to see why his attitude towards Thatcher during the Falklands crisis was one of anger and bafflement. To see her convictions intensified by the loss of a destroyer such as the *Sheffield* astounded him. The thought of what bloodshed might yet come was incomprehensible. It was the duty of a friend and ally to pull Thatcher back from the brink.[16]

Tensions escalated as the Falklands conflict moved from an aerial and naval battle to a ground war. On 21 May, British troops landed near the port of San Carlos and rapidly established a bridgehead. A week later, those forces took the defended positions of Darwin and Goose Green. The British lost 17 men; Argentinian forces lost ten times that number and had well over 1,000 soldiers taken prisoner. By 29 May, British forces had surrounded the capital, Port Stanley.

As the war intensified and more reports of deaths came in, anxiety within the Reagan administration spilled over. 'There is now an immediate and urgent need for a dramatic new effort on the part of the United States,' drummed a hyperbolic NSC paper entitled *UK–Argentine War*, 'in order to prevent huge losses on both sides with grave consequences for the entire free world (weakening of NATO, disruption of international financial systems, etc).' Many of the Latin American countries, led by Venezuela, were publicly and privately taking every opportunity to stoke American fears of a continent on their doorstep seething with resentment and anger. 'I scarcely need to say,' observed the US ambassador in Buenos Aires, 'that a bloody battle on the Islands leading to Argentine defeat would produce grave consequences for US interests here and elsewhere in Latin America.'[17]

Staggeringly, it now seemed as if the 'little ice-cold bunch of land down there' was in danger of wrecking Reagan's entire strategy in Latin America – identified by the administration as 'the most important place in the world for us'.[18]

Anxiety inside the White House manifested itself publicly in *Washington Post* reports that Reagan might be forced to cancel his official visit to Britain in June. This initiative had been arranged the previous year as a way to bolster Thatcher at a time of intense political and social instability. Now there was a fear that the glamour of state banquets and rides on horseback in the grounds of Windsor Castle with the Queen would contrast badly with the horror of war. They might also provoke further Latin American hostility. The

White House officially denied the story in the *Post*, but even talk of cancellation was a further shot across Britain's bow.

By the end of May, the Reagan administration had concluded that the best means to stop the fighting was to bring the president himself into play. 'The only remaining level at which the United States could mount a peace effort,' noted another NSC paper on Falklands strategy, 'will be the President's personal intervention.'[19]

The arrangements were left to Haig. 'It's getting like Duck Soup down there,' the secretary told Henderson, in a reference to the famous Marx brothers war film. Haig explained that Reagan would be telephoning the prime minister to inform her that the United States would be calling for a ceasefire in order to avoid a bloody battle and the total defeat of the Argentine garrison. Henderson agreed that it would be good for the two leaders to talk. 'I said that normally I thought these heads of government telephone talks were apt to lead to trouble and acrimony as had occurred over a previous call from Reagan, but . . . I did not think a call could do any harm now,' he recorded. 'How wrong I was.'[20]

Reagan telephoned Thatcher on 31 May. He began with charm and a play on her vanity: 'I want to congratulate you on what you and your young men are doing down there. You've taken major risks and you've demonstrated to the whole world that unprovoked aggression does not pay.' He then moved to outline 'some of our ideas on how we might capitalize on the success you've had, with a diplomatic initiative.' Of course, Argentina might turn it down, but 'I think an effort to show we're all still willing to seek a settlement . . . would undercut the effort of . . . the leftists in South America who are actively seeking to exploit the crisis. Now, I'm thinking about this plan . . .'

Before Reagan could say what that plan might entail, Thatcher sharply cut him off.

> 'This is democracy and our island,' she warned him, 'and the very worst thing for democracy would be if we failed now.'
>
> 'Yes . . .' began Reagan.

Thatcher cut across him again.

'Ron, I'm not handing over . . . I'm not handing over the island now. I can't lose the lives and blood of our soldiers to hand the islands over to a contact [group]. It's not possible.'

'Margaret, but I thought that part of this proposal . . .'

'You are surely not asking me, Ron, after we've lost some of our finest young men, you are surely not saying, that after the Argentine withdrawal, that our forces, and our administration, become immediately idle? I had to go to immense distances and mobilise half my country. I just had to go.'

'Margaret, I . . .'

'I wonder if anyone over there realises, I'd like to ask them. Just supposing Alaska was invaded? Now you've put all your people up there to retake it and someone suggested that a contact could come in . . . you wouldn't do it!'

'No, no, although, Margaret, I have to say I don't quite think Alaska is a similar situation.'

'More or less so,' she snapped back.

'Yeah, well, uh . . . uh . . . Well, Margaret, I know I'm intruding on you . . .'

Reagan, stumbling and unable to get a word in edgeways, could hardly get off the phone fast enough.[21]

When Thatcher finished the call, she was in a blind and reckless fury. She told her private secretary to get the British ambassador in Washington on the telephone. She did not even bother with a secure line. Henderson was given an immediate ear-bashing for not warning her about what the president might say. But the real focus of the prime minister's rage was Reagan himself. She was 'dismayed', she kept repeating, 'dismayed by his attitude.' How could he propose another peace initiative at such a time? She was 'most upset'. The proposals had 'horrified' her. There was 'no possibility' of compromise. Britain had been prepared to engage with Haig's earlier initiatives. But no longer. 'We have lost a lot of blood and it is the best blood,' Thatcher lamented. 'Do they not realise that it is an issue of principle. We cannot surrender principles for expediency.' Thatcher would put up with it no longer: the president must be told to stop calling.

As Henderson listened, his private secretary brought in a note saying that Al Haig wanted to speak to him urgently. He knew immediately that the secretary of state must have received the transcript of the president's conversation with the prime minister. Henderson also knew – as did Thatcher – that the secretary of state would soon be reading the transcript of this unsecured call. The luckless ambassador must have winced as Thatcher spat out her contempt for the new initiative as 'pure Haigism'.

No sooner had Henderson finished the call than Haig came on the line. The secretary did not even attempt to hide his own displeasure or that of the president at what had just happened.

> 'Opinion is moving against you,' he warned.
>
> 'Do you mean in Congress and the media?' Henderson inquired.
>
> 'No,' Haig replied bluntly, 'I mean with me – and the President.'

He then offered Britain both a carrot and a stick. 'We are with you, make no mistake of that, we are on your side,' Haig said, 'but we can't accept intransigence.' If Thatcher continued to take such a dogmatic approach, the United States would be forced to reassess its position. 'Can we rely on you in the UN Security Council?' Henderson asked. 'Perhaps not,' Haig replied. 'You must help the Argentinians to find a way out, short of total humiliation.'[22]

Although there was anger within the administration about the way in which Thatcher had spoken to Reagan, there was also embarrassment at how clueless the president had appeared. 'As usual', complained one NSC staffer, nobody in the West Wing had asked them to give Reagan a substantive briefing before making the call. As a result, 'The president came off sounding like even more of a wimp than Jimmy Carter.'[23]

Where in the past Reagan's tactic had been to leave Thatcher time to cool off before making another attempt to apply pressure, that was not an option on this occasion. The two leaders would be meeting at the G-7 summit at Versailles a few days later. To help clear the air, a private meeting between them was set up for

4 June at which no one else would be present. Haig thought this was 'a terrible mistake', but was overruled by the president. By this stage, it had become clear to Haig that he had been superseded by 'Judge' Clark as the president's closest foreign policy adviser. That led to a terrible atmosphere within the American delegation at Versailles. 'An uptight Haig is in as foul a mood as I've ever seen him,' noted one member of the team, as he watched the secretary 'chewing out' subordinates. Meanwhile, Clark was running around undermining Haig, telling aides, 'I don't know what's gotten into Al, I love him . . . but lately . . .' The secretary in response was constantly threatening to resign. 'Goddamn it, I've had it,' he shouted at one aide. 'I'm leaving. This is it.' The personal gulf between the national security and the foreign policy principals increasingly appeared unbridgeable.[24]

After the telephone debacle, Clark and the national security team took the lead in preparing Reagan for his meeting with Thatcher. 'The trick now,' they advised him, 'is to make the Iron Maiden realise that we will *not* be signing in for a permanent state of war in the South Atlantic.'[25]

In the British camp, Thatcher's resentment continued to fester. Taking a briefing from Henderson, 'glaring at me, she said that she would be very reasonable in her conversation with the president *provided I get my way*'. Flexibility, Henderson reflected afterwards, 'is almost as odious a word to the prime minister as is magnanimity.'[26]

Thatcher arrived on foot for her showdown with the president at the US Residence, strolling down the rue du Faubourg St-Honoré in warm sunshine. 'She looks great coming into the courtyard,' noted Rentschler admiringly. The prime minister was greeted by the president before being ushered by him into a private room alone.

Reagan emphasised how much the United States admired her 'courage' and the 'impressive' military campaign. 'We have supported you in this effort because you are right,' Reagan said. But he then delivered his unwelcome message. 'The conflict, however, is not over and will not be over in our view even with stunning British military success. It is time now to focus on the next phase of this problem.' In particular, America demanded flexibility. 'To be candid,' the president said, 'I am worried about a situation which could lead to a permanent state of war between Argentina and your country . . . The inescapable fact is that the US has risked a great deal in the Hemisphere and is likely to risk a great deal more. For this reason, we do not believe that an indefinitely prolonged military occupation of the Falklands is in either of our interests.' Reagan concluded with a plea: 'I do not believe we are asking too much in requesting you to take our own concerns carefully into account.' He knew that they would continue to 'consult fully and frankly on this issue'.[27]

Thatcher responded with an expression of thanks for American support, but also noted that Argentina had made no effort to find a negotiated outcome. She had even accepted, on 17 May, the proposal to install a United Nations administrator in the Falklands, only to see the idea rebuffed by Buenos Aires. Britain had now moved beyond gestures. The only deal that interested Thatcher was 'a ceasefire, irrevocably linked to Argentine withdrawal within 14 days.' Repossession of the islands, she argued, was not inconsistent with improving the position of the West in Latin America, because it sent the right message about self-determination and the rule of law. As to the islands themselves, Britain would be prepared to discuss the long-term future, including a greater degree of self-government, but only once things were back to normal.[28]

Without note-takers present, there is no formal record of how the conversation developed. What seems clear, however, is that Reagan recognised there would be no movement from the British until after Port Stanley had been recaptured. Immediately after the meeting he affirmed his support for the British, which was widely interpreted as a 'green light' for the battle for Port Stanley.

That was an oversimplification. As the G-7 host President Mitterrand of France observed: 'We wanted to affirm our solidarity with Great Britain, who, as it happens, had been the victim of aggression against both its national interests and its national pride . . . Great Britain must regain its right, it being understood that we shall do everything once its right has been regained so that peace triumphs over war.' Mitterrand had been a supportive ally of Britain throughout the conflict, but his view reflected that of other G-7 leaders, including Reagan: when the war was over, Britain would be expected to show flexibility in addressing Argentina's claims to the islands. 'Magnanimity before victory became their watchword,' John Nott bitterly observed of Britain's G-7 allies. 'Bravely, Margaret Thatcher held firm – and it needed a massive exercise of will to resist these pressures, but she did so.'[29]

The private meeting between Reagan and Thatcher on 4 June had been an attempt to help the two leaders get past their personal *froideur* before the president's upcoming official visit to London. Any benefits it brought in lowering Thatcher's irritation with US policy barely lasted the day.

In New York at the United Nations, Spain and Panama had put forward a new resolution calling for 'an immediate ceasefire in the Islands'. When it came to a vote of the Security Council, both Britain and the United States vetoed the motion. But moments after the vote had taken place, the American UN ambassador, Jeane Kirkpatrick, emerged to make a flustered statement to the press. She had voted the wrong way. Al Haig in Paris had done a last-minute *volte-face*. He had wanted the United States to abstain, not veto the motion, presumably on the grounds that such a move would curry favour with Latin American countries. However, Kirkpatrick did not receive the instruction until after she had cast her vote. 'My government has asked me to put [that] on the record,' she announced to general incredulity. Not only had the United States sought to double-cross Britain, it had done so incompetently.

On one level American ineptitude was a plus for Britain. 'Any odium which might have attached to us for using our veto was diverted by the astonishing statement by Mrs Kirkpatrick,' noted the British ambassador, Anthony Parsons. 'This revelation left the Council and the media stunned and I was able to escape from the chamber almost unnoticed by the press, the microphones and the television cameras as they engulfed Mrs Kirkpatrick.'

Britain reacted furiously to the substance of what had happened in the Security Council. Henderson tore a strip off Haig's deputy, Walter Stoessel, pointing out that the secretary of state had not long before told the foreign secretary, Francis Pym, that the United

States would be vetoing the resolution. The deception even looked pre-meditated given Haig's threat to Henderson a few days earlier that Britain should not take American support at the United Nations as a given. In the early hours of 5 June, the hapless secretary of state had first called Pym to tell him America had abstained, only to phone back ten minutes later to say that they had vetoed.[30]

Certainly Thatcher did not hesitate privately to express her 'consternation' at this further example of American prevarication. Later that day came what she called 'a still more embarrassing' public sequel. As the G-7 leaders took their seats for lunch in the Palace of Versailles, a US journalist took advantage of Reagan and Thatcher being side by side to ask an awkward question about the veto. The president, amid sharp intakes of breath, replied that he did not know anything about it. He had not been told. The reporter immediately turned for a reaction to the prime minister, who tartly informed him that she did not give interviews over lunch.[31]

Thatcher's answer was the perfect riposte to an incendiary question. Reagan had been let off the hook, although he appeared not to notice. The president was becoming complaisant that, whatever differences they might have, Thatcher's harsh words would be reserved for private conversations and not aired in public. After all the high tension of recent weeks, the focus of his attention now moved elsewhere.

Windsor Castle. 8 June 1982. Here was the image that the White House had been planning for so long: President Reagan and the Queen side by side, both on horseback, riding through the grounds of Windsor Castle. 'Carter couldn't have done a thing like that!' snorted the deputy chief of staff, Mike Deaver. There had been weeks of endless conversations about these few minutes of equestrianism: what kind of horse would the president ride, which saddle did he use, should he wear a hat? There were some concerns in London that a movie-star cowboy might not be the same thing as a real one: would the president end up making a fool of himself next to the Queen, who was a fine horsewoman? After all, there was some history here with the Reagans. During Nancy's visit for the Royal Wedding the previous year, there had been much comment about her behaviour at a polo match featuring Prince Charles. The first lady had arrived, sirens blaring, in a long motorcade of limousines with blackened windows. Out she had stepped onto the soggy field in six-inch heels, wearing a $1,200 bright red Adolfo suit. 'I hope we don't lose her!' quipped the BBC commentator as those heels sunk into the muddy turf, 'or that she doesn't fall and break her hair!' The Queen's reported comment was less jolly. 'That damned woman!' a royal clerk claims she snapped during the visit.[32]

On this occasion, everything was perfectly judged. The president looked the part, with a nod to traditional British dress with his tweed jacket and to the carefree cowboy spirit in his open-neck shirt. The Queen wore her trademark headscarf. Neither donned a hard hat, much to the irritation of safety campaigners. Reagan was, in fact, an experienced horseman and had owned ranches in California since the 1950s. Just to be on the safe side the crown equerry who ran the royal stables had given him a horse that 'looked and was powerful, but behaved like a lamb.' Reagan shared with the Queen one of his favourite and oft-repeated sayings of Winston Churchill, that 'there is something about the outside of a horse that is good for the inside of a man.' The horse benefited from another well-known Reagan trick when out riding: a handful of jelly beans.[33]

More than six hundred members of the media turned out to watch the ride. Pictures went around the world. 'Reagan is just a movie star acting the part of a king, and the Queen is like a movie star in a film about Britain,' complained the labour MP Tony Benn in his diary. 'I find it embarrassing to live in Britain at the moment.' The Americans on the other hand were delighted. 'Buckingham Palace really went out of their way for the Reagans,' noted James Kuhn, personal assistant to the president.[34]

Reagan had a Hollywood star's understanding of how the royal family fascinated the American imagination. Many Americans, including Nancy Reagan, had been enthralled by the wedding of the Prince of Wales to Lady Diana Spencer. Now the public was swept along by the imminent arrival of a first child (Prince William). There was much excitement on the subject, Reagan told the Queen. To British eyes such interest seemed strange coming from a republic whose founding document had described the British monarch as 'a tyrant'. Yet attraction to the royal family remained a feature of American life. The year before Reagan's 1982 visit, seventeen million American TV viewers had watched the Royal Wedding. Thirty years later the wedding of Prince William to Kate Middleton would attract twenty-three million American viewers. In a society that so admires celebrity, the British royal family, with its wealth, glamour and scandals played out over centuries, provided an enthralling, long-running soap opera that made all other fame look like 'fifteen minutes'.[35]

Theodore Roosevelt, the twenty-sixth president, once described the role of the commander-in-chief as that of an 'elected king'. Certainly Reagan was not afraid to maximise the quasi-regal status and trappings of the job. Speaker of the House 'Tip' O'Neill believed that much of Reagan's popularity came from an understanding that Americans wanted 'a magisterial air in the White House'. Limousines made a return, as did 'Hail to the Chief'. Entertainment at the Reagan White House was spectacular, beginning with Frank Sinatra at the inaugural gala. After the grey parsimony of Carter, the inelegance of Ford, the seediness of Nixon, and the 'I'm on the can' vulgarity of Johnson, the American public seemed anxious for a return to the easy glamour of JFK and 'Camelot'. In fact, what they got was closer to the court of the first president, George Washington – another 'lucky' and often ridiculed figure who nevertheless succeeded in embodying the dignity of the state and commanding affection among the people.[36]

Thatcher would adopt something of this more presidential style herself as her premiership went on. Her outfits became more glamorous, and the prime ministerial Rover P5 ('the poor man's Rolls-Royce') was replaced with an altogether more elegant Jaguar. Yet life for a British prime minister lacked the institutionalised comforts of the presidency. When Thatcher arrived for meetings in foreign capitals she did so without a vast entourage, and was usually accompanied only by a few civil servants.

She lived modestly – far more so than she had been accustomed to as the wife of a paint business millionaire – 'above the shop' in 10 Downing Street. It was a poky little flat, 'up in the rafters in fact', that reminded her of 'my girlhood in Grantham' as the grocer's daughter. It was the kind of accommodation, remarked a private secretary, 'that I doubt many councils would offer to an asylum seeker.' Not much had changed since the days of Disraeli, who had complained that his wife 'can do nothing with Downing street, it is so dingy and decaying.' There was no housekeeper, so Mrs Thatcher made sure to organise her diary in a way that allowed her to cook breakfast for Denis each morning. ('If you want me to poach your egg, *come now*,' she could occasionally be heard to call out.) Phone calls were answered by whoever happened to be around at the time. When Reagan phoned the Thatchers after their son Mark had got himself lost in the Sahara Desert, his call was taken by an assistant helping the prime minister pick out a dress. This was a distinct contrast to the hushed tones and smooth service provided by the seventy or so servants and household staff who tended to the president in the White House.[37]

The poise that Reagan had displayed in his outing with the Queen also emphasised another important difference from Thatcher. While he was both head of state and head of government, she was only the latter: the trappings of being the 'first citizen' in the land were never hers to enjoy. On any state occasion, the prime minister always came well down the order of precedence, not just falling after various royals but also two archbishops and the lord chancellor. Moreover, as the unwritten British constitution intended, prime ministers were constantly put in their place by the machinery of state: a party leader can win a huge majority at the polls, but still has to wait for an invitation from the Queen to 'kiss hands' and form a government; prime ministers must report to her every week; the troops they send into battle swear an oath of allegiance to her. And the Queen gets to wear the crown.

At times elevated above politics in a way that Thatcher was not, Reagan was able to enjoy and exploit the deference afforded to a head of state. Ruffles and flourishes greeted him wherever he went. People stood up whenever he entered the room. The military saluted him. Reporters even applauded his speeches and refrained from asking tricky questions when he was abroad. On the one occasion in the year when he was held accountable by the legislature, lawmakers welcomed him to the 'State of the Union' with a standing ovation. For this reason Reagan never really understood the Darwinian arena of the House of Commons. There was no equivalent for Reagan of Prime Minister's Questions (PMQs), that twice-weekly ritual at which MPs could ask questions on any subject. Tony Blair would later describe PMQs as the most 'discombobulating, nail-biting, bowel-moving, terror-inspiring, courage-draining experience in my prime ministerial life, without question.' Thatcher believed it was the real test of her political authority. 'No head of government anywhere in the world has to face this kind of regular pressure,' she would pointedly remind Reagan.[38]

On the occasion when Reagan did face British parliamentarians, he saw them on their best behaviour. Following his horse ride at Windsor, he went to the Royal Gallery at the Palace of Westminster to address a joint session of Parliament. There he delivered a blistering and unexpected attack on the Soviet Union. 'I believe we live now at a turning point,' he declared. 'In an ironic sense Karl Marx was right. We are witnessing today a great revolutionary crisis, a crisis where the demands of the economic order are conflicting directly with those of the political order. But the crisis is happening not in the free, non-Marxist West, but in the home of Marxist-Leninism, the Soviet Union. It is the Soviet Union that runs against the tide of history by denying human freedom. It also is in deep economic difficulty.'

Reagan went on to lay out the battle ahead, in which the most powerful weapons would be ideas. 'What I am describing now is a plan and a hope for the long term – the march of freedom and democracy which will leave Marxism-Leninism on the ash heap of history as it has left other tyrannies which stifle the freedom and muzzle the self-expression of the people,' he declared. '. . . The ultimate determinant in the struggle now going on for the world will not be bombs and rockets, but a test of wills and ideas – a trial of spiritual resolve: the values we hold, the beliefs we cherish, the ideals to which we are dedicated.'[39]

Reagan's 'ash heap of history' speech – the phrase was cleverly borrowed from Trotsky – would turn out to be perhaps the most prescient of his entire presidency. The timing was not chance.

Only a few weeks before, Reagan had signed the secret NSDD 32, 'The Plan to Prevail' – the culmination of that shift in national security policy towards the defeat of the Soviet Union ordered by the president at the turn of the year during the Siberian pipeline crisis. The Westminster speech represented an important public outing for that policy.

In the month leading up to the speech, 'Reaganauts' and 'pragmatists' within the administration battled over the president's text. The initial draft was written by Tony Dolan, a Pulitzer Prize-winning reporter and protégé of the conservative writer William F. Buckley. Dolan was already despised by many senior staff and State Department officials as the creator of Reagan's most right-wing rhetoric. With this particular speech, Reagan startled 'Judge' Clark by demanding to see a very early draft, before it could be watered down. The president heavily edited the text himself, and added several new passages in his own hand. These personal additions included a line about 'the march of freedom and democracy which will leave Marxism-Leninism on the ash heap of history.' Two days later, Dolan sent a memo to the president registering 'a vigorous dissent' to efforts by pragmatists to soften the tone of the speech. Reagan backed him. 'I [was] amazed that our national leaders had not philosophically and intellectually taken on the principles of Marxism-Leninism,' Reagan later explained. 'We were always too worried we would offend the Soviets if we struck at anything so basic. Well, so what? Marxism-Leninism thought is an empty cupboard. Everyone knew it by the 1980s, but no one was saying it. I decided to articulate a few of these things.'[40]

Historians would later see the speech in the Royal Gallery as perhaps the most complete statement of Reagan's foreign policy world-view that he ever gave. Few commentators thought so at the time. Most of the western media dismissed the speech as 'wishful thinking, bordering on the delusional.' British reaction ranged from lukewarm to personally hostile. For the left-of-centre *Guardian* newspaper, Reagan had shown that he was just an amiable senior citizen who 'when crisis breaks' is left to doze. 'Very little can be built on the president's words,' it concluded, because they reflected only his 'benign, blank helplessness'. American media reaction was muted. The *New York Times* summed up by noting that, 'characteristically', Reagan had 'failed to point the way from here to there, or to give the Russians a plausible range of policy options.' Even those who liked the speech, such as the veteran White House correspondent Helen Thomas, complained that there were 'few specifics'. NBC News anchor Tom Brokaw simply thought it 'naive'. As for the politicians in attendance, one grandee was heard to observe that 'everyone had been less interested in the substance than in the audio-visual prompters used by Reagan to enable him to give the impression of speaking without a text.'[41]

The directness of Reagan's rhetoric, not to mention his teleprompters, had helped mask another striking feature of the president's speech: what was missing. For in a speech of almost 5,000 words, there were only five sentences on Britain's ongoing war in the Falklands, which was reaching its climax. And where there might have been an opportunity for a personal tribute to Thatcher to praise her principled stand or courageous leadership, there was none. In fact the speech, aside from a quick joke at the outset, was notable for its lack of comment on Thatcher and their shared conservative revolution. Protocol may have demanded that partisan politics should be avoided in a speech to Parliament, but the lack of any sense of a shared journey was an obvious symptom of the coolness that had entered their relationship. During the president's visit, Thatcher hosted a formal lunch at Downing Street, which she had to leave early to attend Prime Minister's Questions in the House of Commons, and she also held a short breakfast meeting with him. Otherwise, she saw little of the president. In her memoirs, the visit is accorded two sentences. Instead, it was the final campaign of the Falklands War, and in particular the sinking that day of the landing ship *Sir Galahad*, that was etched on her mind.[42]

There could be no doubt, concluded Nicholas Henderson, that the recent American attitude over the Falklands 'has had a bad effect here'. Even as she was waiting to greet the president, Thatcher again 'spoke to me about it with consternation'. It was a long way from the happier days of her visit to Washington in 1981, when 'your problems will be our problems'.[43]

Irritation with Reagan was temporarily put to one side in the euphoria of victory in the Falklands. The assault on Port Stanley had begun before dawn on Friday, 11 June. Fighting was particularly heavy on Mount Longdon, Mount Tumbledown and Wireless Ridge, where Argentine forces put up fierce resistance from prepared positions. When British forces breached the line at Tumbledown, it gave them a stranglehold on the Argentine garrison in Port Stanley. At 2359 hours on 14 June, the Argentine commander, General Mario Menéndez, surrendered to Major-General Jeremy Moore of the Royal Marines. In total, 255 members of the British forces and 649 members of the Argentine forces had died in the campaign, along with three civilian Falkland Islanders.[44]

On 15 June, Thatcher went to the House of Commons to announce the Argentine surrender. 'So ends the Falklands Affair – which began in such despair and humiliation,' the Tory MP Alan Clark noted in his diary. As he was leaving the chamber, he came face to face with Thatcher behind the Speaker's Chair. 'Prime Minister, only you could have done this,' he told her. 'You did it alone, and your place in history is assured.' Thatcher looked a 'little startled . . . and bemused by the triumph.' But she could hardly have doubted that he spoke for the majority in the Conservative Party and the country.[45]

Two days later, during Prime Minister's Questions on 17 June, Enoch Powell returned to a point that he had made at the beginning of the crisis. Then he had observed that soon they would all know 'of what metal she is made.' Now with the rhetorical finesse for which he was admired on both sides of the House, Powell asked if the prime minister was 'aware that the report has now been received from the public analyst on a certain substance recently subjected to analysis and that I have obtained a copy of the report? It shows that the substance under test consisted of ferrous matter of the highest quality, that it is of exceptional tensile strength, is highly resistant to wear and tear and to stress, and may be used with advantage for all national purposes?'[46]

This brought the House down. MPs bellowed and waved their order papers.

'I agree with every word that he said!' replied Thatcher, flushed with victory.

The fog of the cold war meant there were not many conflicts

left that yielded clear outcomes; few leaders of western countries got to take the salute at victory parades: now Thatcher had achieved both.

Washington, DC. Saturday, 19 June 1982. Nicholas Henderson had only a few weeks remaining before he left his post as British ambassador to the United States and retired from the diplomatic service. He had already been persuaded out of retirement once to take the post in Washington. Victory in the Falklands provided a suitably upbeat ending to a distinguished career. His public profile had been high during the conflict and he was generally considered to have had a 'good' war. There had been widespread scepticism in Washington about the whole endeavour in the South Atlantic. Now in victory, he reported, there was 'admiration and applause', with people approaching him in restaurants and on the street to say how delighted they were with the British victory. This was not, however, a sentiment that appeared to be shared inside the White House.

Henderson had got some inkling of discontent at a meeting with Al Haig to discuss the post-conflict situation in the Falklands. Haig was already showing 'signs of restlessness' in wanting Britain to start the process of involving Argentina in the future of the islands as soon as possible. In particular, he had recoiled from the prime minister's statement in the House of Commons when announcing the recapture of Port Stanley, which he thought was 'too high in decibel content'. As the president had written to Thatcher on 18 June, a just peace 'in my judgment must include enhancement of the long-term security of the South Atlantic, mitigation of Argentine hostility and improvement in the relations of both our countries with Latin America.'[47]

To get the ball rolling, Haig suggested an early meeting between the president and the prime minister. Thatcher was due to fly in to New York the following week to give a talk at the United Nations on disarmament. Why not have her come down to Washington to see the president as well? Haig suggested. Henderson sent a telegram to London. Thatcher agreed to the meeting. Everything was set. Until Henderson received a telephone call from the national security adviser, 'Judge' Clark.

The president, Clark told Henderson bluntly, was increasingly out of sync with Britain in general and the prime minister in particular. Therefore he was cancelling the meeting between Reagan and Thatcher. Henderson was astonished. 'The invitation has already been extended,' he told Clark, 'with Haig's authority, based he had told me on a talk with the president.' Clark paused. 'That's very awkward,' he said slowly. 'Yes,' replied Henderson, not letting him off the hook. 'What do you recommend?' Clark asked, clearly irritated. The prime minister had been invited, Henderson told him. The idea had not been hers. If the Americans were going to withdraw the invitation, there would have to be 'a plausible reason for cancelling'. Twenty-four hours passed without Henderson hearing anything further. To complicate matters, Downing Street had confirmed the prime minister's diary. Eventually Henderson phoned Mike Deaver, who controlled the president's schedule, to get an answer one way or another. 'Deaver said, not altogether graciously, that as things had gone so far and Mrs T had actually been invited, there was no alternative but to go through with the visit.'[48]

Henderson put the attempt to cancel the meeting with Thatcher down to the dysfunctional relationship between the State Department and the White House. That in part led to the resignation a week later of Al Haig, who had lost his battle to be 'vicar' of foreign policy. But it was also indicative of a general cooling of relations between Reagan and Thatcher. The White House was beginning to tire of constant scolding.

Reagan's reluctance to see the prime minister had something to do with personal pique at the tone Thatcher was taking in their conversations. There was even a hint of jealousy. Thatcher, after all, was now enjoying the laurels of victory in the American media for her determination not to allow Britain to be pushed around. It was a long time since an American president had attended a victory parade. 'The prime minister was the most courted person on the international scene,' John Coles remarked. 'Every country wanted her to visit, and British foreign policy became alive and successful again.' It was the prime minister after all, not the president, whose recent actions had 'said a great deal about Western resolve and determination.'[49]

Differences between the two leaders went beyond a disagreement over the Falkland Islands, which remained, despite any wider hemispheric importance, Reagan's 'little ice-cold bunch of land'. This particular Anglo-American disagreement cut to the heart of Reagan's cold-war strategy. At a meeting on 18 June, a few days before Thatcher arrived, the president had come under intense pressure from senior figures in the administration to abandon his policy of sanctions against the Soviet pipeline. At the end of a bad-tempered debate, with the president clearly in the minority, Reagan had summed up and given his decision. 'Well, they can have their damned pipeline,' he said. Everyone in the room exhaled. Then after a pause the president spoke again. 'But not with American equipment and not with American technology!' With that, he stood up, and before others were even able to get to their feet, the president had left the room.[50] 'Cabinet very divided,' Reagan wrote in his diary afterwards. 'I ruled we would not remove sanctions. There hadn't been the slightest move on the Soviets part to change their evil ways.'[51]

The decision to keep sanctions in place had shown the president standing firm. It had also been a victory for Clark and the NSC over Haig. This helps to explain why immediately after losing the debate, Haig wanted to get Thatcher into the Oval Office – and why Clark tried to keep her out. For within the western alliance there was no more robust opponent of these sanctions than Thatcher. Much of this centred on the engineering firm, John Brown Ltd, which had $279 million in pipeline contracts with the Soviets and was dependent on rotors supplied by General Electric of America. The prime minister had personally urged the president on at least two occasions to ease the sanctions. More generally, noted the State Department brief for the Thatcher meeting, 'the British have been among the most vociferous critics of US efforts to apply our laws and regulations in foreign jurisdictions. The British have been blocking legislation on the books to prevent UK companies from complying with US laws if we try to enforce them in Britain, and can be expected to use it if necessary.'[52]

Thatcher, still bullish from her Falklands victory, arrived at the White House on 23 June ready for a fight. The White House seemed to be expecting one. In reaction to the awkward recent bilateral meeting between the pair at Versailles a few weeks earlier, the president this time protected himself with a larger group, which included Clark, Haig and Vice-President Bush, along with several NSC officials.[53]

When Reagan raised the issue of the Falkland Islands, Thatcher interrupted before the president had even finished speaking. 'I want to give you an account of the present position,' she told him. Her sketch did not refrain from gruesome detail. Morale was so poor that the Argentine officers had insisted on being allowed to keep their pistols to protect themselves against their own men. She described the poor state of the Argentineans who had been captured: malnutrition, trench-foot, diarrhoea. 'We were spared nothing,' Henderson recorded. The president 'made another effort to get into the act, perhaps to deliver a warning about intransigence and the need for magnanimity, a word the Americans keep trying to put into Mrs Thatcher's vocabulary, quite unsuccessfully.' The prime minister gave them no opening, but simply went off again, talking about the battle and the sacrifices.

Reagan tried to regain the initiative by turning to pipeline sanctions. This too was a matter of principle, he told the prime minister. In the immediate aftermath of events in Poland the previous December, he had warned the Soviets that unless certain steps were taken, such as the release of Lech Walesa, sanctions would be extended. He was now 'proceeding to carry out this threat.' As to the specific British grievance, it was regrettable, but there was no way that US pipeline equipment could be provided to John Brown, even though it was part of a pre-December 1981 contract. Reagan then delivered a hard punch: the administration had been in touch with John Brown Ltd and they were 'quite happy' with this decision.

If the large group Reagan had assembled was a misguided attempt to intimidate or subdue Thatcher, it failed. 'Mrs T's eyes blazed and she launched into a fierce attack on the president's decision,' recorded Henderson (who was present). 'Look!' she said. 'We stick to our deals, we said we would deliver, we shall deliver, we want to deliver. Now will you please not understand this, especially as after all you in the United States are going to deliver wheat to the Soviet Union?' At this point 'The Judge' rose from his chair, walked to the president's desk and took out a sheet of White House writing paper. 'I hope the prime minister will recognize that the president's decision was based on strong principle,' he wrote. He then ostentatiously passed it to Henderson. It was an unmistakable rebuke: Thatcher had crossed a line.[54]

By the time an hour had passed and he had to leave for his next engagement, Reagan had barely got a word in edgeways. For the second time in a matter of weeks, Thatcher had battered the president into silence if not submission. Days afterwards, when a reporter asked Reagan about pipeline sanctions, pointing out that even Thatcher disagreed with him, the president offered an uncompromising defence. 'I understand that it's a hardship [for Britain],' he said, but 'the Soviet Union, now hard pressed for cash because of its own actions, can receive anywhere from ten to twelve billion dollars a year in hard cash payments in return for the energy when the pipeline is completed – which I could assume, if they continued the present policies, would be used to arm further against the rest of us and against our allies and thus force more cost for armaments for the rest of the world.' A few weeks later Reagan put it even more forcefully. 'They're up against a wall,' he said of the Soviets. The pipeline would give them 'cold, hard cash' aided and abetted by 'cash customers' such as Britain. The sanctions would stand.[55]

What Thatcher found difficult to stomach was that Britain was being called upon to make a principled sacrifice at a time when the United States itself was prepared to be more flexible about exports. By raising the issue of US wheat sales to the Soviet Union in her talks with Reagan, Thatcher had highlighted an awkward inconsistency in the administration's strategy. Reagan had long talked about putting the Soviet Union into 'quarantine', but his administration had overturned the grain embargo introduced in January 1980 by President Carter. A number of explanations were put forward to justify this reversal, including that the embargo hit American farmers as hard as it did the Soviet economy. By the early 1980s, American agriculture was enduring the worst decline since the Depression of the 1930s. Exports to the Soviet Union amounted to 6.2 per cent of total grain production. It was a market that could not be sacrificed without significant cost. But the political cost was just as important. The embargo had contributed to Carter's defeat in the 1980 presidential election, as voters in the Midwest took their revenge. In April 1981 Reagan fulfilled a campaign pledge to lift the ban. The secretary of state, Al Haig, had opposed the decision, not understanding that for Reagan this was a political imperative that trumped cold-war strategy. In 1983 – a year before fighting another presidential election – Reagan would sign a new agreement with the Soviets that included a pledge never to repeat the grain embargo.[56]

Thatcher was a political realist, but she saw the American policy as hypocrisy. Shortly after her meeting in the White House, she brought her anger out into the open. She delivered a stinging rebuke to Reagan, drawing attention in uncharacteristic public terms to the disappointment she felt. Interviewed by the BBC, she made clear her objections to US pipeline sanctions. 'I spoke to President Reagan about it when I saw him because you know how deeply concerned I was,' she said. It was an observation worded in the politesse of diplomacy. But when asked if the president was out of line, Thatcher escalated the dispute to a new level:

> Well, I have not made any secret of that. We make a contract, we make a deal, we keep it unless there's some overriding reason. Had he said right at that beginning, before the contracts were made, 'look, no American technology or licences will be permitted', we wouldn't have put in for the contracts. But it wasn't said at the beginning and I don't believe that now is the right time to do it and naturally we feel . . . [pause] . . . particularly . . . [pause] . . . *deeply* wounded by a friend. I would like to say one thing. We've been a staunch friend of the United States and we must continue to be that, the alliance must hold because that is in our interests, but from that basis we must be pretty frank with our American friends.[57]

This was uncharacteristic behaviour from Thatcher. The pauses said everything. She was reluctant to criticise the president in such direct and personal terms, but at a time when she was often accused of being Reagan's poodle, this was an occasion when she seemed determined to show both bark and bite. Her comments were backed up by action: John Brown Ltd shipped gas turbines to the Soviet Union at the end of August in defiance of US sanctions. This meant daring the White House to retaliate by issuing 'denial orders' to the American firms involved, stopping them from any more pipeline-related dealings with the UK firm, and thereby sending John Brown Ltd into bankruptcy. 'This dispute cannot but spill over into other aspects of our relationship,' the US ambassador in London, John Louis, warned Washington.[58]

A few days after the BBC interview, Secretary of Defense Caspar Weinberger was dispatched across the Atlantic for urgent talks with the prime minister. He had built up a debt of gratitude in London for his pro-British policy during the Falklands War. If anyone had credit to spend on the president's behalf, it was 'Cap'. 'You were absolutely marvellous,' Thatcher assured him at that meeting on 8 September, and 'could not thank us enough for our generous and prompt assistance.' The secretary in turn was 'full of praise' for the 'discipline and leadership' that Thatcher had demonstrated.

Yet, as the American minutes of the meeting reveal, this love-in was not the reason for the talks. 'Finally turning to the pipeline . . .', they noted with a kind of weariness what actually followed. 'The only fly in the ointment is the John Brown thing,' Thatcher told Weinberger. Her fervent hope was that whatever the United States did 'would be so minimal that she could ignore it. She desperately needed some face-saving solution.' If John Brown Ltd and four or five other similar firms went under, she warned, there would be huge popular anger directed against her 'closest friend' the United States.

Weinberger countered, making it clear that this was about more than one company. Sanctions were the keystone of a new strategy to apply pressure on the Soviet Union. There had been 'little progress toward a relaxation of oppressive measures' in Poland. There was also 'concern about the large amount of hard currency that would flow to the Soviets from the completion of the pipeline.' Obviously, the United States wanted to find 'some formula through which our differences could be minimized.' But it was also vital 'that we not help the Soviet military, which always seemed to have first claim on Soviet financial resources.'

The meeting ended without a resolution. Thatcher rejected outright Weinberger's practical solution that the US would make sure companies like John Brown 'get some substitute orders' by way of compensation. 'The President genuinely wants to help achieve a satisfactory solution,' the secretary told her, 'and he doesn't want to hurt UK business.' Thatcher blandly replied that she 'hoped there would be a way out'. Almost as an afterthought, she added the standard courtesies that whatever their differences, she retained 'great admiration' for the president, whom she considered 'a humane, honest, and straightforward person.'[59]

The pipeline dispute would simmer on throughout 1982 and into the following year before an awkward compromise was agreed between America and its European allies. The US would allow a one-strand pipeline (but not the two-strand originally planned) to proceed in exchange for tighter western European restrictions on technology exports and low-interest loans to the Soviet Union. The NSC estimated this would deprive the Soviets of at least $10 billion in annual revenue, out of a total hard-currency income of $32 billion. This was a massive hit for the Soviets and one which ensured that Reagan's policy, as expressed in NSDD 66 – to 'cause such stress' on the Soviet economy that 'it will implode' – remained intact, even in the face of strong reservations by European allies.[60]

If disagreement over the pipeline seemed to suggest a cooling between Reagan and Thatcher, then ongoing differences over the Falkland Islands confirmed it. At the end of October, the new Argentine military government led by General Reynaldo Benito Bignone put forward a UN draft resolution. This reaffirmed the principles of the UN Charter concerning the non-use of force, took account of the de facto cessation of hostilities and the intention of the two sides not to renew them, and stated that the interests of the islanders must be taken into account. References in earlier resolutions to colonialism had been skilfully withdrawn. Argentina, having lost the war, was now keen to sit at the negotiating table as a seemingly reasonable partner. The strategy worked in Washington. On 30 October 1982, Paul Bremer at the State Department recommended that the president should tell Thatcher of 'our desire to see the dispute between Argentina and the UK resolved peacefully and stating that we consider the Argentine draft to be moderate enough not to prejudice the position of either party to the dispute.'[61]

Soon afterwards Reagan sent Thatcher a long letter explaining why his administration would be supporting the Argentine resolution at the UN. 'I fully understand that negotiations are not acceptable to you, having paid so much in blood and treasure to repulse the Argentine invasion,' he began reassuringly. 'We have no intention to press you – or to see you pressed – into negotiations before you are ready. Equally we have no intention to take a position on the substance of the matter that is in any way prejudicial to your position on the questions of sovereignty and self determination.'

'Margaret, my country has always supported you, and always will in defeating any effort to solve the Falklands dispute by force,' Reagan told her, glossing over recent disagreements. But his current position was clear: 'You know that we have always been neutral on the question of sovereignty. And we have always favored peaceful solution of the issue by negotiation. I am well aware that it was the Argentines that interrupted negotiations by attacking the islands. But I do not think that in itself is reason not to support a solution by negotiations sometime in the future. It is hard for the United States to have any other position.' For this reason he had 'informed Argentina . . . that we would support [the resolution].'

Reagan ended with a plea. 'I am truly sorry that we disagree on this matter and for my part will do everything in my power to make sure this resolution is not abused,' he wrote. 'You may be confident that the United States will continue to abide by the jointly shared principles which guided both our countries through the Falklands crisis to its successful conclusion.'[62]

The tone of Reagan's letter attempted to pre-empt Thatcher's predictable outrage. Her reaction came not face to face, but was delivered by proxy at a meeting between the new secretary of state, George Shultz, and the new British ambassador to the United States, Sir Oliver Wright. It was the very first occasion that the two men had met. 'Her ambassador, on instructions, read me off like a sergeant would a recruit in the Marine Corps boot camp,' recorded Shultz (a former Marine). 'I felt Mrs Thatcher was wrong to oppose us for taking a reasonable position on a critical issue in our neighborhood,' he concluded. 'And Wright was wrong to lay it on so thick.'[63]

Shultz had entered the State Department in July 1982 as a voice of calm after the emotional volatility of the Haig era. He had been close to Reagan in California and during the presidential campaign. Many people had been surprised when he was not appointed secretary of state in 1981. He had an unflappable style that also hinted in a somewhat menacing fashion at the toughness underneath. He was a United States Marine, a Princeton footballer and an MIT economics professor. As Treasury secretary under Nixon, he had seen and survived intact the worst political crisis of modern American history. In short, George Shultz was not a man easily intimidated.

A few weeks after his encounter with Ambassador Wright, Shultz went to Downing Street to have the matter out with Thatcher in person. She launched a furious attack, arguing that on principle and for strategic reasons the US had to give Britain firmer support on the Falklands. 'What if the Panama Canal were to be closed', she demanded again, 'requiring ships to go "around the Horn" as in the days of clipper-ships? The location of the Falklands in the shipping lanes of the South Atlantic would then be vital.' This was 'far-fetched', thought Shultz. While he had agreed with the decision to support Britain during the conflict, the president's priority now was to repair the damage done with American interests in Latin America. 'She listened,' Shultz recalled, 'but not sympathetically.'

'Every American secretary of state in recent history, at an early point, has had to think through the matter of the "special relationship" between Britain and the United States,' Shultz would later record. The meeting in Downing Street had been his first experience as secretary of state with Thatcher, and while he could admire her intellectual and moral clarity, he came away foreseeing problems. 'I worried that President Reagan would be alarmed at Margaret Thatcher's reaction,' Shultz reflected, 'but I found that he, too, was getting a little fed up with her imperious attitude.'[64]

The new secretary of state had taken it as a given that Reagan and Thatcher were 'soulmates'. Now their relationship was just one more problem on his overcrowded desk.

6

Another Island, Another War

Rancho del Cielo, California. 1 March 1983. Her Majesty Queen Elizabeth II, it was fair to say, was not amused. Her visit to the Golden State at the invitation of the president had been beset by difficulties and misunderstandings. There had been a furore over protocol in San Diego. Then on a US aircraft carrier HMQ had been served lobster, despite her well-known aversion to shellfish. And worst of all, California's sunny climes had been replaced by terrible Pacific storms, with rain, gales, and even a tornado. At Reagan's mountaintop Rancho del Cielo near Santa Barbara, everything was now shrouded in thick fog so that the magnificent views were nowhere to be seen. The first couple, said the president's personal assistant, Jim Kuhn, had so wanted to 'make that trip go as well as it could possibly go.' Now, after a Tex-Mex lunch that consisted of enchiladas, stuffed chillies and refried beans, the Queen re-emerged, one British reporter noted, looking 'like she had backed a loser at the Newmarket races.' When she got spritzed by the rain, Reagan seemed mortified. 'I knew before we came that we have exported many of our traditions to the United States,' the Queen laconically observed, 'but I had not realised that weather was one of them.'[1]

If the royals were unimpressed at being dragged out into the wind and the rain by the Reagans, they also saw, as in London the previous year, another display of the president's star quality. For a thirty-first wedding anniversary celebration, Ron and Nancy were invited to spend the night on board the royal yacht *Britannia*. After a small private dinner hosted by the Queen, more than eighty guests joined them for a reception. Kuhn recalled being struck that while the Queen and Prince Philip entertained in one room 'with just a small number of people there,' the adjoining room with the Reagans 'was crammed with people, people hanging all over the president, Mrs. Reagan, everything . . . pulling his neck off trying to get to him.' No doubt those guests would be glad to say they had met the Queen, but everyone understood which of these heads of state was *primus inter pares*.[2]

Seeing such power in the raw may have added to royal bafflement at Reagan's easygoing style of government. The following morning, Mike Deaver, the deputy chief of staff, caught Reagan after breakfast to give him a copy of the speech the president was due to deliver later in the day. It was Reagan's first sight of the text, so Deaver told him to look out for one particularly tricky foreign name and a slight modification of policy towards Nicaragua. 'Fine – thanks, Mike,' the president responded pleasantly.

Royal aides were astonished. One retold the story to the Queen, observing that they would never dare give her a speech to deliver unseen. 'And they call me a constitutional monarch!' the Queen noted acidly. It was a common misperception across the Atlantic that Reagan was merely a 'figurehead' president; the next few days would show just how wrong that analysis was.[3]

A week later, on 8 March 1983, Reagan delivered one of the most important and controversial speeches of the cold war. The original text had been written by Tony Dolan, the White House staffer who the previous year had drafted Reagan's Westminster 'ash heap of history' speech. Reagan took Dolan's text of this new speech and worked extensively on it himself, in particular adding his own conviction of an imminent Soviet collapse. 'Now and forever, the Soviet empire is an evil empire . . .' read the first draft. Reagan deleted 'Now and forever'. The revision would become perhaps his most famous line.[4]

Reagan's 'evil empire' speech, delivered at the annual convention of the National Association of Evangelicals, took almost everyone by surprise, including his own national security team.

'If it had been a major foreign policy-related speech,' recalled his director of speechwriting, Aram Bakshian, 'the NSC and State would be more highly focused on it, and chances are it would have been spotted.' Just as in his very first press conference as president, when he had said that the Soviets would 'lie, cheat and steal to get whatever they want', Reagan had stepped outside traditional diplomatic language to make clear his utter revulsion for the Soviet system.[5]

Two weeks later, Reagan followed up with a call to action. In a televised address on 23 March, the president mapped out a 'vision of the future which offers hope'. He outlined a new programme 'to counter the awesome Soviet missile threat with measures that are defensive'. This was the Strategic Defense Initiative (SDI), 'an effort which holds the promise of changing the course of human history'. The scope of his ambition was clear. 'I call upon the scientific community which gave us nuclear weapons,' Reagan declared, 'to turn their talents to the cause of mankind and world peace; to give us the means of rendering these weapons impotent and obsolete.' It was a line that he had added in his own hand.[6]

'Said it might take 20 yrs. or more, but we had to do it,' Reagan wrote in his diary afterwards. 'I felt good.'[7]

How exactly weapons in the Strategic Defense Initiative might work would become a highly contentious question, prompting 'the science wars' among experts. An official outline was given in 1984 when the Strategic Defense Initiative Organization (SDIO) explained to Congress a multi-tiered weapons system with the capability to destroy an incoming ballistic missile at any stage of its trajectory. This system would include space-based radars and sensors alongside with state-of-the-art command and control. Interceptors would include kinetic-energy and directed-energy weapons beamed up from Earth and directed onto their target from space. 'There is very little question that we can build a very highly effective defense against ballistic missiles someday,' noted General James Abrahamson, director of SDIO. 'The question is how soon and how affordable and what degree of effectiveness can initial steps allow us.'[8]

Reagan's SDI announcement in March 1983, and in particular

the commitment to making nuclear weapons obsolete, had come as a shock even to senior figures in his own administration. 'He didn't share that with anybody before that,' recalls Kenneth Adelman, director of the US Arms Control and Disarmament Agency. 'I know that Shultz was kind of blindsided by it, Weinberger, they may have had two days notice or something like that. But it was stunning, stunning.' In particular, the speech confirmed to Adelman just how anti-nuclear Ronald Reagan was. 'The fact was he couldn't stand nuclear weapons; he wanted to get rid of nuclear weapons,' Adelman remembered. 'I'd never met an antinuclear hawk before in my life. It was just part of Reagan's makeup.'[9]

Shultz was furious at not being consulted on SDI, not least because it fell to him to justify the initiative to allies. Within months, western European countries would be expected to accept the siting of US cruise and Pershing missiles on their soil, as agreed by NATO in November 1979. 'Shultz felt that the White House staff ignored these diplomatic realities,' wrote Jack Matlock, who would be appointed as special assistant to the president for European and Soviet affairs that year. 'The president's national security advisers appeared more interested in blocking steps to improve relations with Moscow than in promoting a dialogue.'[10]

Reagan's speech marked the beginning of a series of bitter disputes within the administration about the Strategic Defense Initiative. To be sure, both Shultz and Weinberger soon became committed advocates of SDI, but each did so for incompatible reasons. Shultz quickly came to recognise that the Soviets were mesmerised by the prospect of extending the arms race into space. Indeed, the Soviet leadership seemed to view SDI with something approaching terror. 'Every Soviet official one met was running around like a chicken without a head . . . ,' noted James Buchan of the *Financial Times*, 'talking in the most ghastly and dire terms of real hot war – of fighting war, of nuclear war.' That Soviet panic was caused by the recognition that SDI was a technological escalation in the cold war that was simply beyond them. Shultz believed that such a calculation provided the United States with an opportunity, because it would encourage the Soviets to negotiate deep cuts in their offensive arsenal in return for compromise on space weaponry.[11]

Weinberger also viewed SDI as a means to an end, but his pay-off was the opposite of that envisaged by Shultz. While the secretary of state wanted a negotiated reduction in offensive nuclear weapons, his counterpart at the Department of Defense saw the initiative as a way to enhance American offensive nuclear forces. In particular, this idea was taken up by Assistant Secretary of Defense Richard Perle, an initial sceptic of SDI, who soon came to see it as the ultimate spanner in the works of arms control. Perle believed that the United States could only benefit from an arms race with the Soviets. He hoped that by moving SDI from the research to the development phase as quickly as possible it might wreck Shultz's plans for arms control talks and even derail the 1972 ABM Treaty, which limited strategic defensive systems.[12]

For opposing reasons Shultz and Weinberger would combine to ensure that the president's Strategic Defense Initiative got through Congress. Their most high-profile adversary on the Hill was Senator Edward Kennedy, who did his best to turn the very concept of weapons in space into a sick joke. 'This really is a very strange idea,' Kennedy declared after Reagan's SDI speech. 'We cannot found national policy on fond memories of radio serials, dreams of the Old West, and the thrilling days of yesteryear. We must reject the preposterous notion of a Lone Ranger in the sky, firing silver laser bullets and shooting missiles out of the hands of Soviet outlaws.' Instead, Kennedy reiterated his earlier demands for 'an immediate, mutual and verifiable freeze between the United States and the Soviet Union on the testing, production, and deployment of nuclear weapons.'[13]

Many in Europe shared Kennedy's view that SDI was something straight out of a Hollywood B-movie rather than a credible defense strategy. SDI 'was greatly derided on [the European] side of the Atlantic,' recalled the British ambassador, Sir Oliver Wright, 'but I managed to persuade Mrs Thatcher to take it seriously.' Although Thatcher's initial reaction was sceptical, what captured her imagination was the science involved in such an ambitious project – not least how it might work. 'Laid-back generalists from the Foreign Office – let alone the ministerial muddlers in charge of them – could not be relied upon,' she wrote later (forgetting

Sir Oliver). 'By contrast, I was in my element.' Soon this Oxford-trained scientist was firing off requests for research papers on the technical possibilities. 'Science is unstoppable,' she instructed doubters. 'It will not stop for being ignored!'[14]

But Thatcher's intellectual enthusiasm could not hide her opposition to the thrust of Reagan's new strategy. While she was in favour of the US going ahead with SDI, Thatcher did not share the president's hope that it might lead to the abolition of nuclear weapons. 'This seemed to me an unattainable dream,' she surmised. Reagan had rejected mutually assured destruction as literally MAD, but for Thatcher it was the bedrock of Britain's strategy to protect itself from the Soviets. She differed sharply from the president's view that SDI should be a major step towards a nuclear weapons-free world. And the idea that the Americans, when they had SDI, would share the technology with the Soviet Union was even worse. She was 'horrified' to think that the United States might throw away a vital technological advantage in the cold war.[15]

The prime minister's hostility about the new direction in American nuclear strategy was mitigated by her assessment that it did not present any immediate threat. SDI was a research project, not a system ready for deployment. Reagan himself had said it could take twenty years or more to bring to completion. Later, Thatcher's concerns would become more sharply focused, but in this initial phase she was content to support the president. In fact, she recognised the tactical advantage of doing so. She insisted on keeping 'a tight personal control' over discussions in Britain about SDI, only too aware that irreparable harm could be done to Britain's relationship with the United States if the wrong line or even tone was adopted. This policy was close to the president's heart. His scheme had been derided around the world as, at best, the delusional ramblings of a Hollywood ham and, at worst, the weaponisation of space – 'Star Wars'. Thatcher was determined not to add her voice to the chorus of boos.

After a period of irritation and disagreement between Reagan and Thatcher throughout 1982, the issue of nuclear weapons helped restore a certain equilibrium in their relationship. In addition to SDI, which had stolen the headlines that spring, there was also a more immediate nuclear weapons issue on the table for which the president needed British reinforcement.

Since the 1970s, the Soviets had enjoyed an advantage in intermediate-range nuclear forces (INF) in Europe after they deployed the SS-20 Pioneer missile. The SS-20 had a range of more than 3,000 miles and could easily hit London or Paris. And there were more than 200 of these missiles pointed in that direction. In response, NATO had decided in 1979 to deploy 108 single-warhead Pershing IIs and 464 ground-launched cruise missiles in Europe, with a strike capacity on the Soviet Union. The Pershing II was a fearsome weapon. It could fly at nearly Mach 8, faster than 6,000 miles per hour, and carried a high-precision guidance system. The ground-launched cruise missiles could fly under radar. If this was the ballistic 'stick', the US had matched it with a disarmament 'carrot'. The 'zero-zero option' offered by Reagan in 1981 had proposed eliminating an entire class of medium-range missiles in Europe. Divisions among the western allies over this 'zero-zero' option had in part been mitigated through its rejection by the Soviets. Deployment of the US weapons was scheduled to begin in western Europe at the end of 1983.[16]

In preparation for this action, Reagan had sent Vice-President George Bush to western Europe in early 1983 for talks with the allies. Afterwards, the president wrote to western leaders, including Thatcher, to express his desire to 'continue in a way which will be most helpful to you in sustaining the INF deployment schedule . . . It seems to me that our current position – one of commitment to zero-zero as the optimal and most moral outcome – buttressed by clear openness to consider any reasonable alternative, is as far as we should go at this time.'[17]

Thatcher was sceptical about zero-zero, fearing it could leave western Europe defenseless against the superior conventional forces of the Soviet Union. She attempted to modify the policy, suggesting to Vice-President Bush that the West might make a new initiative to agree some finite level of INF weapons above zero – arms control rather than abolition. Reagan wrote to her later that month to say that he had 'considered it at some length', but believed that such a policy 'might be exploited' by left-wing opponents, particularly in Germany, where the more sympathetic centre-right coalition was facing an imminent election. 'I am disinclined to even mention it now,' Reagan wrote, adding smoothly that 'nevertheless I value your counsel on this very deeply and would welcome your thoughts on both the substance and timing aspects.'[18]

Thatcher may have been wary of the zero-zero option, but in the end she could accept it as a bargaining position. Her calculation was that Soviet intransigence would always make a deal unlikely. It was more important to her that the deployment of Pershing II take place. That issue came to a head at a stormy G-7 summit held at Williamsburg, Virginia, in May 1983.

Reagan by now was a far more assured character on the world stage than 'the new boy in school' who had struggled at Ottawa two years earlier. As the host at Williamsburg, he junked the usual procedure whereby the final communiqué was drafted in advance and then the leaders argued over fine-tuning the wording for a few days. Instead, he put forward an agenda for substantive discussion, with a final communiqué to be based on the conversation that had taken place. If Reagan wanted to take his fellow leaders out of the comfort zone, it worked. For Thatcher, this was a welcome move: she always loved a good row.

At dinner on the first night, the talks began promisingly. Reagan was in good form, having spent the previous night watching the movie of *The Sound of Music*. The leaders discussed nuclear strategy and disarmament in general terms, and also talked more specifically about the deployment of Pershing II missiles in western Europe. All seemed well in a calm and reasoned debate. Afterwards, Reagan gave the secretary of state, George Shultz, detailed notes to help officials prepare a draft declaration. The leaders would resume mid-morning the next day. Reagan expected to have everything wrapped up by lunchtime.

Only when the text appeared on Sunday morning did trouble begin. The draft declaration approved both INF deployment and the desire for negotiations with the Soviets in order to stabilise and eventually eliminate such intermediate-range weapons – in other words, an interim version of zero-zero. 'Out of the blue both Mitterrand & Trudeau said they couldn't support such a statement,' Reagan recorded in his diary. Discussion on the deployment of American cruise and Pershing II missiles in Europe grew very agitated. Mitterrand argued that the US administration was favouring 'modernisation' (deployment) over 'negotiation' in the 'dual-track' approach to arms control. France, supported by Canada, demanded a recalibration of that balance. George Shultz recalled that Reagan became extremely 'upset . . . at one point he threw down his pencil in exasperation.' Thatcher weighed in emphatically behind the president, accusing Mitterrand and Trudeau of making trouble for its own sake. 'I thought at one point Margaret was going to order Pierre to go stand in a corner,' the American president said afterwards.[19]

Reagan would later note that the matter was 'resolved', with 'no winners or losers'. This sentiment was simply magnanimity in victory. There had been a clear loser at Williamsburg: the French president, François Mitterrand. Throughout the summit, Shultz remembered, Mitterrand had been 'sour and imperial'. Now with the clock counting down on securing a formal declaration, it was Mitterrand who had been put in the corner, and not by Thatcher. The US national security adviser, William Clark, took aside the French president's chief of staff, Jacques Attali, and unmistakably threatened him. Since the 1970s, France had benefited from informal American advice to help with its nuclear deterrent. The policy, known as 'negative guidance', had seen US nuclear experts tip the wink to their French counterparts on technology to let them know if they were heading up the right path. It was a clever way of helping an ally without actually breaching national security. Unless you get on board with the statement, Clark now told Attali bluntly, the president has authorised me to say that negative guidance will come to an end. At the G-7 summit, Mitterrand had attempted to recalibrate the balance between deployment and negotiation in arms control; but faced with Clark's choice, he quickly capitulated. Reagan got his unified declaration. 'Our nations express the strong wish that a balanced INF agreement be reached shortly,' it read. 'Should this not occur, the negotiations will determine the level of deployment. It is well-known that should this not occur, the countries concerned will proceed with the planned deployment of the US systems in Europe beginning at the end of 1983.'[20]

If international summits were a zero-sum game, then with Mitterrand down, Thatcher was clearly up. She could still be annoying, not least in stealing the president's punchlines. At dinner on the first evening, held in what had been the colonial governor's mansion, Reagan had theatrically turned to Thatcher with a big smile, saying, 'Margaret, if one of your predecessors had been a little more clever . . .' Thatcher cut him off mid-sentence. 'I know, I would have been hosting this gathering.' But Reagan let her lack of comic timing go, not least because at meetings such as these he found her other virtues helpful. While the new wording on missile deployment was being worked out, Thatcher was a useful battering ram to use on the other leaders. 'Some European ministers were coming up with a really weasel-worded statement,' Reagan's director of communications, David Gergen recalled. 'They took it to her. She was on the other side of the room and I remember when she took one look at this thing, stalked across the room, threw down the piece of paper and said to one of the German ministers and the Italian: "This is impossible. I will not sign this," and forced them to change it.' Gergen was 'terribly impressed. A lot of the Americans just held her in awe.'[21]

That sense of awe could intimidate the team around Reagan, and perhaps even revealed their own reservations about the president's abilities. 'Margaret Thatcher . . . felt that President Reagan had been poorly prepared at the [1982] Versailles summit, and she was sharply critical of his staff,' noted George Shultz, who was not involved in those preparations. He had been determined to avoid repeating the performance at Williamsburg. Shultz got the president's attention 'by putting on a little show'. Various White House staffers were chosen to play the parts of the G-7 leaders and the president role-played with them. 'The young fellow who played PM of England – Margaret Thatcher was a stranger to me,' Reagan recorded in his diary. 'When I called on him I told him his gown was lovely.' No doubt the president practised his 'if one of your predecessors' line. If the stand-in was any good, 'she' would have butted in.

Shultz thought the president loved the 'drama and the fun' of this acted-out summit meeting. 'We caught the president's interest, and he became increasingly involved,' he recalled. 'Once you get him into an operational frame of mind, then he starts paying attention in a more aggressive way.' It must have given Shultz satisfaction to hear Thatcher, on leaving the summit, privately praising Reagan's 'superb chairmanship'. Reagan himself was pleased too, noting that 'apparently PM Thatcher' planned to run the London G-7 summit along the lines 'we used in Williamsburg'.[22]

Having been so critical of Reagan after Versailles, Thatcher was quick to write after Williamsburg to express her admiration. She praised Reagan 'for conducting the formal talks towards such a successful outcome', and was fulsome, almost gushing, in expressing her hope that the talks would 'bring to the United States and to you personally encouragement and support in your leadership of the Western Alliance. We in Britain remain deeply indebted to America and its President.' Thatcher even recognised in Reagan the tactical use of charm that she herself often lacked. He really was 'a master politician.'[23]

By the time the president replied almost a fortnight later, there was other news to discuss: Thatcher had won a general election.

Margaret Thatcher had spent most of her first term with critics believing that she was certain to lose the next election. Soaring unemployment, riots in the streets, a divided cabinet: these and other issues had contributed to giving Thatcher record low approval numbers. Back in the summer of 1981, the American ambassador to London had delivered a brutal summary of the 'troubling political, social and economic drift' in Britain. 'Thatcher has lost her grip on the political rudder,' the national security adviser at the time, Richard Allen, informed the president. Now, less than two years later, Thatcher had delivered a landslide victory and given the Conservatives their largest majority in the House of Commons in the twentieth century.

Commentators would argue about the extent to which the 'Falklands factor' helped Thatcher. Certainly there were other ingredients: the self-confessed 'suicide' of the opposition Labour Party; the clashing egos within the new Social Democratic Party (SDP); and an apparent public acceptance that high unemployment was the unpleasant medicine that had to be taken in order to restore the economy to health. Yet it was indisputable that Thatcher's role during the Falklands conflict had come to represent some broader truth about her leadership: that she was a 'warrior queen', a leader of vision and courage, who would walk where others feared to tread and deliver victory in the most unpromising of circumstances. There was much talk of Britain's pride being restored. Admirers on the political right and left agreed that some kind of emotional and psychological hurdle had been jumped: Britain for the first time in more than a generation did not seem to be lurching towards inevitable decline.[24]

Across the Atlantic, there was no question that Reagan wanted Thatcher to win. 'I wish you every success in the election and in gaining another mandate to carry out the courageous and principled policies which you have begun,' he wrote to her at the beginning of the campaign, not bothering with the usual niceties of avoiding even the appearance of interfering in the democratic affairs of an ally. To his advisers he was even more explicit. 'Hell, the main thing is for her to get re-elected,' he exclaimed when they asked him about the role Thatcher might play at the Williamsburg summit, which had taken place during the British election campaign. 'I shared his analysis,' Thatcher noted dryly when the remark was reported back to her.[25]

Whatever personal irritations and disappointments Reagan may have endured with Thatcher over the previous two years, notably during the Falklands crisis, there was little doubt that he viewed the alternative as far worse. Michael Foot, the leader of the Labour Party, was exactly the kind of old-fashioned Socialist Reagan despised. Of particular concern was Foot's policy on defence, which included a commitment to unilateral disarmament. This was a direct and immediate threat to the president's own cold-war strategy, not least because Foot had promised to stop the deployment of cruise missiles in Britain later that year.

Although Reagan made no mention whatsoever of Thatcher's re-election in his personal diary, he certainly seemed keen to use the moment to reinforce and revivify his own relationship with her. The phone calls and correspondence in the days and weeks after her victory brimmed with satisfaction. 'As I said on the telephone, I am overjoyed,' he told her effusively a week after the election. 'Your landslide win certainly gives a positive shot in the arm to the Western Alliance.' The next day, he wrote once more to offer 'congratulations again on your well-deserved landslide victory.' And four days after that he began a third letter by noting that 'I could not let the occasion of Secretary Weinberger's [London] visit pass without asking him to convey to you again my personal congratulations on your splendid election victory.'[26]

Everyone likes to be associated with success. For Reagan, pondering a run for a second term the following year, it was only natural for him to applaud long and hard Thatcher's achievement in Britain. This was after all a vindication of the transatlantic 'conservative revolution'. When the prime minister suggested getting together in Washington, Reagan readily agreed. Everyone understood that the meeting was as much about symbolism as substance. 'Prime minister Thatcher's visit to Washington will mark the effective start of her second term in office,' noted John Louis, the US ambassador in London. 'The timing is intentional. The US link is central to her foreign policy, and the trip is designed in part to make that point as her second term begins.' William Clark repeated this view directly to the president. 'Mrs Thatcher remains among your strongest supporters,' he noted. 'The US is central to Britain's foreign policy, and her visit is designed to "kick-off" her second term. In a sense, the visit itself is the message.'[27]

Margaret Thatcher had spent much of her first term in office on the back foot. Having secured a huge majority at the polls, she was now determined to move onto the offensive. She had ambitious plans at home centred on privatisation and trade union reform. And abroad Thatcher was determined to capitalise on the new spirit of self-confidence that the Falklands conflict had given Britain – and her.

In particular, Thatcher turned her thoughts to the question of the cold war and the role that Britain might play in engaging the Soviet Union. On 8 September, a few weeks before leaving for Washington, she convened a two-day seminar at Chequers on the subject. A hand-picked group of ministers, officials and Soviet specialists analysed the worsening state of cold-war relations. This deterioration had been horribly demonstrated seven days earlier by the Soviet shooting down of a South Korean commercial airline, killing 269 passengers. The Soviet general secretary Yuri Andropov accused Reagan of an 'insidious provocation involving a South Korean plane engineered by US special services.' In fact, his own tapes showed that pilot error had inadvertently taken the plane over Soviet territory. Korean Airways flight KE007 was shot down when only seconds from neutral airspace. 'This incident has vividly illustrated the true nature of the Soviet regime,' Thatcher wrote to Reagan. 'Its rigidity and ruthlessness, its neuroses about spying and security, its mendacity, and its apparent inability to understand, let alone apply, the normal rules of civilised conduct between nations, have been an object lesson to those who believe that goodwill and reason alone will be sufficient to ensure our security and world peace.'[28]

The shooting down of KE007 gave a heightened sense of urgency to Thatcher's Chequers seminar. 'One notable success,' an official noted afterwards, was 'to convince the PM that there was very little scope for destabilizing the Soviet Union'. Thatcher argued that Britain must seek out, cultivate and sustain the rising generation of Soviet leaders to encourage reform and better relations. Professor Archie Brown, a Soviet expert attending the seminar, identified the youngest member of the Politburo, Mikhail Gorbachev, as 'the most hopeful choice from the point of view both of Soviet citizens and the outside world.' Sir Geoffrey Howe, the new foreign secretary, later remarked that 'our September seminar at Chequers was, therefore, more important than we knew,' for it catalysed 'her greatest achievement in foreign affairs' – the relationship with Mikhail Gorbachev.[29]

Coming three months after the election victory in June 1983, the Chequers seminar visibly thrilled Thatcher. The forthcoming trip to Washington, during which she would receive the Winston Churchill Foundation Award, provided an ideal setting for a major speech on her new thinking about cold-war strategy. Despite the Foreign Office having participated in the seminar, Thatcher brought in more outside experts to help prevent the text from getting watered down – after the Falklands War, she never lost her sense of the diplomatic service as vacillating and weak. At a private meeting at Chequers, it was clear that 'she was now in full flood' on the subject of the cold war. There was much discussion about the current state of the Soviet Union, and in particular – it would become the main thrust of the speech – of the cold war as a battle of ideas that could be won. But what surprised those gathered at the prime minister's country retreat was Thatcher's hostility to American policy in general, and Reagan in particular.

Thatcher had only belatedly come to recognise that Reagan's Westminster speech had marked the beginning of a new thrust in US cold-war policy. At the time, with the battle for the Falklands reaching its climax, her attention had been elsewhere. 'I don't think it crossed my mind that the president was making a fighting, ideological speech that would change western policy,' she explained at Chequers. 'Reagan was making jokes, and he was reading his words in such a mellifluous way, with such a natural sweet expression on his face, that I did not quite catch the tremendous significance of what he was saying.'

Now Thatcher got it, and was not happy. In particular, she feared this shift in US policy took no account of allied priorities and concerns. That suspicion had been reinforced by Reagan's more recent speeches on the 'evil empire' and SDI. 'It is outrageous to imply that the Americans are alone in this game,' she told her astonished group of advisers. 'We're all in it: we're all part of it, and it's quite wrong for the Americans to throw their weight around and to imply that we are just satellites.'

'The Americans must have conducted themselves with very little finesse if they've managed to alienate Margaret Thatcher, a more pro-American politician than whom we haven't got in the whole of Europe,' reflected one of her Soviet experts. 'There is a lot of tension between the two governments, and the cause of that tension appears to be, in the British view at any rate, the Americans' overbearing style in dealing with their partners.'[30]

When Thatcher arrived in Washington for her meeting on 29 September with the president, she was greeted with the usual military pomp and personal warmth. Yet Reagan's own speaking notes made it clear that the Americans were not prepared for a wide-ranging discussion on cold-war strategy. However, Thatcher quickly brought the conversation round. Reporting on the seminars at Chequers, she explained that the key was to establish a realistic relationship with the Soviets. After all, she declared – previewing a line from her Churchill Foundation speech the next day – 'We all had to live on the same planet.'[31]

Thatcher's line illustrated a divide that was opening up with the White House on the question of how to approach the Soviet Union. For all her transatlantic credentials and occasional anti-European rhetoric, Thatcher's conception of the relationship between defence and détente was often closer to that of her continental partners than to Reagan. His view of an 'evil empire' hell-bent on totalitarian expansion could often seem crudely one-dimensional when seen from across the Atlantic. Reagan had explicitly rejected détente as failed policy, but western European capitals, including London, still viewed it as an essential 'ying' to the 'yang' of strong defence. This was the rationale for the deployment of Pershing and cruise missiles on the continent while at the same time rejecting sanctions against the Siberian pipeline. Americans saw this as contradictory. But as one official from Britain's Washington embassy put it, while Europeans – not least Mrs Thatcher – did not dismiss the Soviet threat, they felt an urgent need to constrain 'the American habit of overreacting.'

The president's reply to Thatcher made clear their differences on the Soviet Union and the cold war. The West, Reagan argued, had to remember that the Soviets would never be influenced by 'sweet reason'. If they saw that the US had the will and the money to keep building up its defences, the Soviet attitude would inevitably change because they knew they could not keep up. The Russians, he believed, were now close to their economic limit. Eventually they would have to 'cry uncle'. It's a bit like that old cartoon about Brezhnev, the president told Thatcher: 'I liked the arms race better when we were the only ones in it!'[32]

But what did this all mean, Thatcher wanted to know, irritated by Reagan's lack of detail. She kept coming back at him on 'the need to consider precisely how we should deal with the Soviets when they faced up to reality and returned to the negotiating table in a more reasonable frame of mind.' 'We [are] very different people,' Thatcher wearily reflected when the meeting was over. 'He had an accurate grasp of the strategic picture but left the tactical detail to others. I was conscious that we must arrange our relations with the communists on a day to day basis in such a way that events never got out of control.'[33]

If she had known what Reagan was really mulling over, she would have been angry, not weary. 'If things get hotter and hotter and arms control remains an issue,' the president told George Shultz a few days afterwards, 'maybe I should go see Andropov and propose eliminating all nuclear weapons.'[34]

In the end, however, it was not arms control but military action on another small island, this time in the Caribbean, that would ratchet up Anglo-American discontent to new levels.

Eisenhower Cabin, Augusta National Golf Club. Saturday, 22 October 1983. Shortly before 4 am. Ronald Reagan always cheerfully admitted that he was not a good golfer, and this trip to Augusta was not going to win him any green jackets. 'I was better than at Andrews [Air Force Base] but still not good,' he noted ruefully in his diary. 'I guess you have to play more than 4 times in almost three years.' But Reagan did love sunshine and fresh air, so when this trip to the famous home of the Master's was planned by George Shultz, it had seemed like a welcome escape from Washington. But even before Reagan had gone to bed on Friday night, he knew this was unlikely to turn out to be the relaxed trip everyone had expected. The president was woken just before 4 am. It came as no surprise: there was a decision to be made.

The man tasked with briefing the president in the early hours was Bud McFarlane, who just a week earlier had taken over from William Clark the job of national security adviser. A former Marine who had served two tours of duty in Vietnam, McFarlane had previously held junior positions in the National Security Council during the Nixon and Ford administrations, and had been a key foreign policy adviser to Reagan since the 1980 presidential election. A few days into his new job, McFarlane had been a late addition to the golfing party – the calculation being that it would cause less comment in the media if McFarlane was brought along rather than have the trip cancelled at the last minute, as the president would have preferred. Now in the early hours of Saturday morning, Reagan (still in his pyjamas), Shultz and McFarlane gathered in the living room of the secure Eisenhower Cabin, built for 'Ike' when he became president in 1953. 'We were on the phone with Wash[ington] about the Grenada situation,' Reagan wrote in his diary afterwards. 'I've OK'd an outright invasion.'[35]

A few days beforehand, an ultra-hard-line Marxist group within the government of Grenada – an island in the eastern Caribbean with a population of around 100,000 – had launched a violent internal coup and shot and killed the prime minister, Maurice Bishop (himself a Marxist). This sounded immediate warning bells in the United States. Intelligence showed that the USSR and Cuba had been building military installations on the island, including a 10,000-foot aircraft landing strip, and were stockpiling matériel. Reagan had already warned about the strategic danger of the island in his televised speech of 23 March 1983, although this aspect had been overshadowed by the announcement of the Strategic Defense Initiative in the same address.

Within weeks of Reagan coming to power in 1981, neo-conservatives in the administration, led by UN Ambassador Jeane Kirkpatrick, had tilted US policy towards a more offensive cold-war strategy in the hemisphere. Reagan himself saw the region as a crucial battleground to stem Communist expansion, and spoke often of 'the actual involvement of the Soviet Union, of Cuba, of the PLO, of even Gaddafi in Libya, and others in the Communist Block [sic] nations' to ferment revolution and terror in the region. Even before the October coup Reagan had been worried about Grenada as another 'Cuba' on America's doorstep. In the summer, he had ordered Vice-President Bush to draw up contingency plans. Now that the worst had happened, Reagan was ready to go. 'Do it', he ordered when Grenada's neighbours in the Organisation of East Caribbean States (OECS) called for a military response from the United States. 'He was very unequivocal. He couldn't wait,' recalled McFarlane of that decision to invade Grenada taken in the early hours of 22 October at Augusta. When one White House staffer in Washington tried to caution the president that there would inevitably be 'a harsh political reaction' to a US invasion, he was brushed off. 'I know that,' the president told him. 'I can accept that.'[36]

If the coup in Grenada had been met with urgency in Washington, the reaction in Britain was altogether more leisurely. Grenada was a former British colony and a member of the Commonwealth. Queen Elizabeth II was the island's head of state. Her Majesty's representative, Governor-General Sir Paul Scoon, remained in residence there. Yet in dealing with former colonies such as Grenada there was always great reluctance, particularly on the part of the Foreign Office, to be seen as interfering with the internal affairs of a sovereign nation, above all a black one. The charge of neo-imperialism and, worse, racism was always lurking in the background. And if truth be told, this small island hardly seemed to matter a great deal when seen from thousands of miles away in London. Grenada, in contrast to the Falkland Islands, lacked any intrinsic strategic value. Britain did not share US fears about the island as a threat to the stability of the Caribbean. Neither had Grenada been invaded by a foreign power. Geoffrey Howe, the British foreign secretary, barely even knew where it was, this 'place called Grenada, a Caribbean island-state of which before that time I had been no more than vaguely informed.' It would soon become etched in his memory. The chapter in his autobiography on the crisis would be unambiguously titled: 'HUMILIATION IN GRENADA'.[37]

For Howe, that humiliation stemmed primarily from being left to twist in the wind by his American counterpart, George Shultz. On Monday, 24 October, two days after Reagan had given the go-ahead for the invasion of Grenada, Howe answered a question in the House of Commons from the opposition spokesman, Denis Healey, by asserting that the new regime in Grenada posed no imminent danger to British citizens on the island, or to the governor-general. 'Grenada is an independent country,' the foreign secretary reassured the House. 'Our concern and what we are prepared to do about it must be determined by recognition of that fact.' When questioned about a possible US invasion, Howe reassured the House that he was 'in the closest possible touch with the US and Caribbean governments' and he had 'no reason to think that American intervention is likely.' Any US naval forces in the area, he explained, 'are in that position solely because of the requirement that may arise to rescue their own very sizable community in Grenada.'[38]

Less than four hours after Howe's assertion, an urgent tele-letter arrived in London from President Reagan. It was Thatcher's first warning that military action was imminent. 'Dear Margaret,' the president began, 'I have followed closely the political turmoil in Grenada in recent days':

> I know that you share my concern for the impact which the killing of the leadership there has had on our friends in the Western hemisphere, particular on the democratic government of the English-speaking Caribbean states. The prospect that the blood-stained group who appear to be the only authority on the island could perpetuate their power also raises questions about the welfare of the people of Grenada themselves, as well as our own nationals resident there . . . The nations of the OECS have unanimously decided to pursue a collective security effort to restore peace and order in Grenada and have formally requested United States support and participation. I understand a similar request was to have been presented to Her Majesty's Government. I am writing to inform you that I am giving serious consideration to the OECS request.

Reagan concluded by asking Thatcher for 'your thoughts on these matters,' and promising 'to inform you in advance should our forces take part in the proposed collective security force . . .' At such a time of crisis, Reagan observed, 'It is of some assurance to know that I can count on your advice and support on these important issues.'[39]

Thatcher was alarmed by this change in tone. Over the previous forty-eight hours informal contact with Washington had suggested that military invasion was not under consideration. Now it seemed imminent. As luck would have it, Thatcher was due to attend a farewell dinner that night for the outgoing American ambassador, John Louis. She instructed her officials to draft a reply to the president expressing her firm opposition to intervention. She then left for the dinner, where she cornered Louis to ask for an explanation. 'Something is going on,' she told him fiercely. He professed to know nothing about it, which turned out to be the truth rather than a diplomatic sleight of hand. Later, during the dinner itself, Thatcher was slipped a note, which urged her return to Downing Street immediately. There had been another message from the president.[40]

When Thatcher saw the letter, she could hardly believe what she was reading. 'Dear Margaret,' it began. 'In a message to you earlier today, I expressed my desire to keep you informed of the United States' response to a formal request by the [OECS] to support and participate in a collective security effort to restore peace, order, and democracy in Grenada. I have decided to respond positively to this request . . . We will inform you of further developments as they occur.'[41]

Geoffrey Howe and the defence secretary, Michael Heseltine, were summoned to No. 10 where, in a small upstairs drawing room, Thatcher showed them the letter. 'I was indignant,' recalled Heseltine. Howe was 'dumbfounded' and immediately saw the wider implications. 'What on earth were we to make of a relationship, special or otherwise, in which a message requesting the benefit of advice was so quickly succeeded by another which made it brutally clear that that advice was being treated as of no consequence whatsoever?'[42]

Just after midnight on Tuesday, 25 October, within an hour of receiving the letter from Reagan, a strongly worded reply was sent to Washington. 'The action will be seen as intervention by a western country in the internal affairs of a small independent nation, however unattractive its regime,' Thatcher wrote. 'I cannot conceal that I am deeply disturbed by your latest communication. You asked for my advice. I have set it out and hope that even at this late stage you will take it into account before events are irrevocable.'[43]

Such was Thatcher's fury that she decided a written communication was not enough. She needed to talk directly to Reagan. Twenty minutes after sending the letter, she got on the 'hot line' – the secure telephone connection to the White House – and asked for the president.

Upstairs in the family residence at the White House, Reagan was meeting congressional leaders in the Yellow Oval Room to brief them on the imminent military action in Grenada. George Shultz and Caspar Weinberger, along with the chairman of the Joint Chiefs of Staff, General John Vessey, had barely started their briefing when they were interrupted. 'Just as they were getting started,' recalled Howard Baker, the Senate minority leader, 'one of the White House butlers came in and said to the president in a rather firm, loud voice, because he [Reagan] didn't hear very well, and we could all hear. He said, "Mr President, the prime minister is on the phone."'

Reagan excused himself and went next door to take the call. 'But as is typical of many people who don't hear very well,' continued Baker, 'he also spoke in a loud voice. I could hear him plain as day. He said, "Margaret," long pause. "But Margaret," and he went through that about three times, and he came back sort of sheepish and said, "Mrs Thatcher has strong reservations about this."' Caspar Weinberger and General Vessey, who were both engaged in a vicious turf war with Shultz and the State Department, had also opposed the plan to invade Grenada, and they must have been buoyed to hear the prime minister battering the president into silence on the matter. But her contribution had no impact on policy. Reagan went ahead anyway.

'I believe Maggie Thatcher was the only person who could intimidate Ronald Reagan,' Baker reflected afterwards. 'He'd make friends with about anybody.' On this occasion the president, if not intimidated, was at least abashed. 'In the middle of the meeting, Margaret Thatcher called,' Reagan wrote in his diary that night. 'She was upset & doesn't think we should do it. I couldn't tell her it had started.'[44]

A few hours after their telephone conversation, Reagan replied to Thatcher's letter, setting out his reasons for the invasion. His reply had a formulaic feel to it and was obviously culled in part from a general letter to America's allies. Three considerations had proved persuasive in the decision to intervene: concern for 'the welfare of our citizens' on Grenada; the OECS request for support, which was 'so clear an expression of the will of the nations of the region [that] I would find it difficult to explain either to them or to others who depend upon us why we had not acted'; and finally, wider 'US national security interests . . . Grenada's recent drift into the Soviet bloc,' which meant that 'the alternative to decisive action on our part may well be to allow the imposition by the Cubans of the regime whose actions would be even more inimical to our interests.'

Only at the end did Reagan's letter address Thatcher directly, although his suggestion that she get on the team offered little comfort. 'I appreciate your comments,' he began. 'I share many of your concerns, but believe that they are outweighed by the factors outlined above. I would hope that as we proceed, in cooperation with the OECS countries, we would have the active cooperation of Her Majesty's Government and, in particular, that the Governor General will exercise his constitutional powers to form an interim government which would restore democracy to Grenada and facilitate the rapid departure of all foreign forces.' This was the nub of the assistance America had wanted from Britain: help to garrison the island after the invasion as part of an international force and a broad willingness to use existing constitutional levers advantageously.[45]

By the time Thatcher received the letter, she already knew the game was up. 'I felt dismayed and let down by what had happened,' she wrote afterwards. 'At best, the British Government had been made to look impotent; at worst we looked deceitful.' Only a day earlier, Geoffrey Howe had stood in the House of Commons complaisantly dismissing all rumours of an American invasion. Now he faced the embarrassment of having to explain how it had happened that a member of the Commonwealth had been invaded by Britain's closest ally without so much as a by-your-leave. This was 'an unpardonable humiliation of an ally,' summed up Labour's Denis Healey when he faced Howe across the dispatch box in the Commons later that day. 'The British people,' he suggested, 'will not relish the spectacle of their prime minister allowing President Reagan to walk all over her'.[46]

Thatcher would hardly have disagreed, but it was not simply the humiliation that bothered her. Reagan's actions had exposed an ideological divide between them. She was convinced that a country had the right to defend itself against aggression, as Britain had against Argentina during the Falklands conflict, and that it should expect the support of allies in such an endeavour. But she also believed that to invade a country to effect 'regime change' was nothing short of folly. 'We in the Western democracies use our force to defend our way of life,' Thatcher explained during a BBC World Service phone-in on 30 October. 'We do not use it to walk into independent sovereign territories . . . If you're going to pronounce a new law that wherever communism reigns against the will of the people, even though it's happened internally, there the USA shall enter, then we are going to have really terrible wars in the world.'[47]

Thatcher also understood that the invasion raised important new questions about the 'special relationship'. In the context of the times, these had implications for Britain's entire cold-war strategy. Thatcher in her advice to Reagan in the early hours of 25 October had pointed out that any invasion of Grenada was bound to have an adverse effect in the House of Commons, which was about to debate the question of the siting of cruise missiles in Britain. The failure by the United States to consult over Grenada raised obvious concerns about whether it would do so on the use of cruise missiles. Sure enough, at her first PMQs following the invasion, Enoch Powell, whose contributions she always feared, rose to ask the question on everyone's mind. 'Will the prime minister learn the lesson,' he demanded to know, 'that no undertakings that may be offered by the United States – either as to the use that it might make of missiles stationed in this country or as to the consultation that would precede such use – ought to be relied upon?' Thatcher replied that there was 'no parallel at all'. But a public opinion poll a few days afterwards suggested otherwise: three-quarters of those questioned did not trust the United States to consult before pressing the nuclear button on cruise missiles sited in Britain.[48]

In contrast, across the Atlantic, the US administration was exultant about the success of the operation in Grenada. American forces completely secured the island within days of the invasion. The strategic value of the country may have been limited, but the symbolism of its capture was a shot in the arm for Reagan's more offensive cold-war strategy. 'Grenada showed that it could be done,' commented one Reaganaut. '[It] proved that boldness and determination could defeat Communists.' National Security Decision Directive 75, signed by the president on 17 January 1983, had stated that the 'primary focus' of American foreign policy would be 'to contain and over time reverse Soviet expansionism'. The president had feared that a legacy of defeatism from the Vietnam War might prejudice public opinion against a counter-revolutionary strategy. Much as the Falklands War had done for Margaret Thatcher, success in Grenada gave Reagan an important morale-boasting victory to offer as a symbol of a new general direction in American strategy: the push back against Communism.[49]

Only belatedly did the administration absorb the extent to which this success had humiliated Margaret Thatcher and damaged Anglo-American relations. 'Mrs. Thatcher and Geoffrey Howe have been hurt domestically by what appears to many in the UK to have been our failure to consult adequately with Her Majesty's government,' Shultz's office told McFarlane. Everyone had to understand that life had been made 'more difficult for our staunchest supporters.'[50]

In an attempt to cheer Thatcher up, Reagan phoned her on 26 October. His timing could hardly have been worse. She took the call in her room in the House of Commons, having been summoned out of a brutal emergency debate on the Grenada invasion. 'I was not in the sunniest of moods,' she recalled afterwards.[51]

'Hello, Margaret Thatcher here,' she began frostily.

Reagan tried to turn on the charm. 'If I were there, Margaret,' he chuckled, 'I'd throw my hat in the door before I came in.'

'There's no need to do that,' Thatcher replied, still without any warmth.

Reagan was well used to Thatcher interrupting him. The cold-shoulder treatment was something new. And momentarily he seemed to panic. Audibly falling back on his 'talking points', the president launched into a long-winded, blow-by-blow account of the events leading up to the invasion of Grenada. 'We regret very much the embarrassment caused you, and I would like to tell you what the story is from our end,' he began. 'I was awakened at 3:00 in the morning, supposedly on a golfing vacation down in Georgia . . .'

Reagan burbled on stiltedly for two or three minutes without interruption, often stumbling over his prepared lines. He explained that the administration had 'a loose source, a leak here' and was 'greatly concerned, because of [the] problem here – and not at your end at all – but here.' His fear was that someone on the US side would leak the planned invasion to the press. That was why he had to restrict the operation to a need-to-know basis. Unfortunately that meant he had been unable to consult. 'But I want you to know it was no feeling on our part of lack of confidence at your end,' he reassured Thatcher. 'It's at our end.'

Eventually, when Reagan's monologue petered out, Thatcher spoke. Reagan must have expected the famous 'hairdryer' treatment. Instead, she barely engaged with him. 'I'm very much aware of the sensitivities,' she said quietly. 'The action is underway now and we just hope it will be successful.'

Reagan tried again, this time setting off on another long, prepared update on what was happening in Grenada. 'It's going beautifully,' he began. 'The two landings immediately took the two airfields. Then we managed to secure that medical school, St George's Medical School, where we have about 800 students. We've moved on, but there is still some combat. All those several hundred Cuban construction workers down there must have been military personnel or reserves, because, as I told you, we got word that a little group had arrived before we could get anything underway. They looked like they were pretty prominent Cubans because they were being treated with great deference. They turned out to be a military command and the opposition that still remains, as the last word we have here – in about three spots on the Island – is led by these Cubans. They are the leading combat forces, not the Grenadian forces. We have captured 250 of them already.'

Again Reagan ground to a halt.

'Well, let's hope it's soon over, Ron, and that you manage to get democracy restored,' replied Thatcher. And then silence.

Undeterred, Reagan tried to nudge the conversation back to allied solidarity. 'We're very hopeful that it is going to be short

(ALL PHOTOS COURTESY RONALD REAGAN LIBRARY UNLESS OTHERWISE NOTED)

Mrs. Thatcher goes to Washington.

The prime minister with the new president on the White House South Lawn, 26 February 1981.

With Nancy Reagan and Denis Thatcher walking along the cross hall at a state dinner in the White House, 26 February 1981.

G-7 leaders at the Grand Trianon Palace in Versailles.

Left to right: Gaston Thorn, Zenko Suzuki, Thatcher and Reagan, François Mitterrand, Helmut Schmidt, Pierre Trudeau, Giovanni Spadolini and Wilfried Martens, 4 June 1982.

At 10 Downing Street during the Falklands War, 9 June 1982.

'Marxism-Leninism on the ash heap of history.'

Reagan addresses the British Parliament at Westminster, flanked by Yeomen of the Guard, 8 June 1982.

'In the middle of the meeting, Margaret Thatcher called. She was upset.'

Interrupted while briefing congressional leaders in the White House cabinet room on the invasion of Grenada, 25 October 1983.

'She really turned him [Reagan] round.'

Thatcher at Camp David immediately after talks with Gorbachev in London, 22 December 1984.

In Churchill's shadow.

Reagan holds a National Security Council meeting in the White House Situation Room, 16 June 1985.

Long faces at Reykjavik.

Reagan says goodbye to Gorbachev after their summit in Iceland, 12 October 1986.

And some explaining to do.

Camp David, 15 November 1986.

The last visit.

Reviewing troops on the South Lawn, 16 November 1988.

A perfectly choreographed photo opportunity in the White House Rose Garden.

And an awkward one at 10 Downing Street.

Thatcher with the new president, George H. W. Bush, on 1 June 1989.
(Courtesy of the George Bush Presidential Library and Museum)

and then your role is going to be very critical, as we all try to return Grenada to democracy under that constitution that you left them,' he explained. 'The leader that was murdered [Bishop], and of course those that murdered him, have abandoned that constitution.'

This was too much for Thatcher. Almost despite herself, she could not allow it to pass. 'Well, the constitution, I'm afraid, was suspended in 1979,' she informed Reagan, almost as if talking to an eager but misinformed child.

'Yes, that was when Bishop made his coup and took over,' Reagan continued, missing Thatcher's ironic tone.

And so the conversation went on. As the president raised various points and made observations about the personalities involved, Thatcher replied each time with a few brief words. Even when Reagan tried to invoke the shared heritage of the English-speaking peoples – 'kith and kin' – the prime minister refused to be drawn in.

Finally, Reagan made one last attempt to apologise to Thatcher for landing her in such political hot water. 'I'm sorry for any embarrassment that we have caused you,' he said, 'but please understand that it was just our fear of our own weakness over here with regard to secrecy.'

'It was very kind of you to have rung, Ron,' Thatcher replied, pointedly not accepting the apology. In the end, she simply excused herself. 'I must return to this debate in the House,' she told the president. 'It is a bit tricky.'

'All right,' Reagan replied, with a joviality that seemed inappropriate to the situation. 'Go get 'em! Eat 'em alive!'

'Good-bye,' said Thatcher. And she was gone.[52]

Reaction in Washington to the exchange between Reagan and Thatcher, and more broadly to Britain's general refusal to support the enterprise, was one of bemusement and anger, not least because it seemed so ungrateful.

'I was annoyed,' explained the secretary of state, George Shultz. 'We had turned ourselves into pretzels for Mrs Thatcher over the Falklands crisis.' Whatever reasons she may have had for opposing intervention in Grenada in the first place, 'she did not exhibit any particular concern for "the special relationship" between Britain and America.'[53]

The same frustration was felt inside the Oval Office. Reagan 'clearly was unhappy,' recalled the deputy chief of staff, Mike Deaver. Bud McFarlane knew that 'the president was very disappointed'. And this was personal frustration with Thatcher. President Reagan, summed up Shultz, 'felt that she was plain wrong. He had supported her in the Falklands. He felt he was absolutely right about Grenada. She didn't share his judgment at all. He was deeply disappointed.' When Sir Anthony Kershaw, chairman of the House of Commons Foreign Affairs Select Committee, had the opportunity to ask the president in Washington why he had not given the prime minister notice ahead of time, the answer was blunt: 'Because I didn't want her to say no.'[54]

7

This is How Large Powers Behave

The American invasion of Grenada in October 1983 had stunned Margaret Thatcher. And in turn her reaction to it came as an even more profound shock to the intellectuals who surrounded her. Certainly George Urban, the director of Radio Free Europe in Munich and an adviser to Thatcher on Soviet affairs, did not fully appreciate the impact of Grenada on the prime minister's mindset until he received an alarming letter from Hugh Thomas, the director of the Centre for Policy Studies (CPS).

A few weeks earlier, Thomas had approached Urban to ask if he would speak on the Soviet Union at the CPS annual meeting, which would be presided over by the PM herself. 'Because of her presence,' Urban had noted enthusiastically in his diary, 'we always drew the cream of the intellectual-spiritual element in the Conservative party, tangling with whom was stimulating and frequently pleasurable.' On 15 December, however, Thomas wrote again to Urban, this time to signal a problem. 'I think, for good or evil, the prime minister is toying with the idea of some kind of an approach to the USSR,' he explained, 'so she does not want to be undercut, as it were, by us saying such things more fully. Also she has not yet come out of the fury with the US over Grenada and that needs to be considered.'

Urban grasped the meaning immediately. 'I might say things at the annual general meeting that would undoubtedly reach Soviet ears,' he noted, 'and prejudice the PM's freedom of manoeuvre if, indeed, there was to be a "new approach" to the Kremlin in the wake of Grenada.' Soon afterwards, when Urban saw Thomas in London, the full significance of Grenada in Margaret Thatcher's thinking revealed itself. The prime minister was looking for 'a launching pad for an Anglo-Gaullism of sorts' – a more independent foreign policy, less dependent on the relationship with the United States.[1]

Thatcher's right-wing intellectuals at the CPS were concerned about the new tilt in policy; others elsewhere were more positive. Inside the Foreign Office, a planning paper written for Sir Geoffrey Howe articulated a fear that, when it came to the use of force, the US was now a greater threat than the Soviet Union. The Reagan administration, the paper noted, 'believes that it [force] worked in Grenada – and it did. The risk is the thought that it can also be applied successfully in other Third World situations.' Howe himself was sympathetic to this Foreign Office view. Certainly he recognised that something important had been changed by Grenada. He put aside and kept a press cutting of a column by the *Financial Times*'s chief political commentator, Malcolm Rutherford, who had warned that 'British governments have been living in a fool's paradise in looking to Washington first, and Europe second. In future, it should be the other way round.' The foreign secretary agreed, and recognised this as a game-changing moment. 'I had no doubt,' he observed, 'that we should base our future strategic planning increasingly upon the premise that Grenada, rather than the Falklands, offered the best evidence of American instincts.'[2]

Thatcher agreed with Howe. 'The Americans are worse than the Soviets,' she told an astonished Irish prime minister, Garret FitzGerald, at an Anglo-Irish summit at Chequers shortly afterwards: 'Persuading the Governor [of Grenada] to issue a retrospective invitation to invade after they had taken him aboard an American warship.' It was no better than the 'fraternal' Soviet invasions of Hungary and Czechoslovakia. To an intelligence adviser, Brian Crozier, Thatcher was even more forthright. 'That man!' she exclaimed of Reagan. 'After all I have done for him, he didn't even consult me.'[3]

Relations between Reagan and Thatcher were made worse by

events in Lebanon. On Sunday, 23 October, the day after the president had given the go-ahead for an invasion of Grenada, Reagan had once again been awoken in the middle of the night, this time with devastating news of a terrorist attack. Suicide bombers in an 18-ton Mercedes truck loaded with explosives equivalent to more than 12,000 pounds of TNT had driven into the lobby of the US Marine Barracks in Beirut. This was the nerve centre of the multi-national force (MNF) that had been stationed in Lebanon since the summer of 1982 in the wake of an invasion by Israel. The MNF comprised American, French, Italian and British soldiers. On this day, 242 Americans and 38 Frenchmen lost their lives. The death toll represented the largest American loss of life to enemy action on a single day between the end of the Second World War and 9/11. It was, wrote Reagan in his diary, 'tragic news'.[4]

The president's reaction to the bombing in Beirut would become another source of tension between Reagan and Thatcher, but it was also a contributory factor in Thatcher's fury with Reagan over Grenada. On receiving news of the terrorist attack on 23 October, Reagan wrote immediately to Thatcher. 'There is no doubt that the perpetrators of the latest bombings in Beirut have attempted once more to undermine our collective will and sense of purpose,' he told her, 'as we work to support the legitimate government of Lebanon in its efforts to secure a more stable and peaceful future.' Yet crucially, despite writing to her about Lebanon, the president continued to conceal from Thatcher the impending invasion of Grenada, which he had sanctioned the night before. When she discovered this omission, it only added to her anger and sense of exclusion.[5]

Fearing a unilateral move by the United States, Thatcher warned Reagan to 'think carefully' before taking retaliatory action for the bomb attack in Lebanon. It was vital, she urged, that 'no hasty action be undertaken,' and that MNF ministers should have the chance to discuss a coordinated response at the forthcoming NATO meeting in December. The Americans must not escalate the crisis by attacking Iran and Syria even though both were implicated in terrorism in the region.

Thatcher's letter provoked more outrage in Washington. On 4

November, Secretary of State Shultz made it clear to national security adviser Bud McFarlane that the White House must respond to Thatcher in a way that 'sets the record straight on US intentions to engage in measures of self-defense against the perpetrators of the bomb attack'. The United States expected 'allies to stand firm at this delicate juncture.' That message was delivered in two letters from the president. In the first, he told Thatcher that 'any action would be a matter of self-defense, not revenge.' In the second, he informed her that he was now 'inclined' to take limited but decisive military action. Undeterred, Thatcher responded to these letters quickly – and negatively. 'My message was as clear as it could be,' she recorded. 'I did not believe that retaliatory action was advisable.'[6]

Once more, as with Grenada, Thatcher's advice counted for little. On 4 December, a week before NATO foreign ministers were due to discuss the crisis, US Navy aircraft from the Sixth Fleet launched an air strike on Syrian air defence positions in Lebanon. In this action they were supported by France, which launched an air strike against Iranian Revolutionary Guard positions in the Bekaa Valley of Lebanon. Even though French citizens had been killed in the October terrorist attack, the participation of France in the military operation, said Richard Allen, Reagan's first national security adviser, demonstrated 'an alliance with Mitterrand that exceeded everyone's expectations.' The French president later told Thatcher, somewhat sheepishly, that air strikes had been carried out 'at American urging'. The combined strikes began an escalation of a conflict that would see the Lebanese government collapse two months later, leaving the country in chaos, and the subsequent 'redeployment' of the multi-national force to ships offshore before a final withdrawal in March 1984.[7]

Thatcher concluded that American intervention in Lebanon was a naive failure. Many Americans agreed. The United States, said Colonel Colin Powell, a top military adviser to Weinberger, had stuck 'its hand into a thousand-year-old hornets nest with the expectation that our mere presence might pacify the hornets.' It only added to the growing sense of well-intentioned amateurishness and disarray that surrounded US policy in the Middle East. Such clumsiness would eventually come to hurt Reagan during 'Iran-Contra' – the most damaging scandal of his presidency.[8]

Even the practicalities of getting MNF forces out of Beirut were a source of tension and misunderstanding between Reagan and Thatcher. Plans had been drawn up for an orderly withdrawal. Thatcher left the decision on British forces to the commander on the ground, but then a message came from the White House on 7 February to say the president would be making a television broadcast that night about the withdrawal. Thatcher immediately notified the British commander that any element of surprise was about to disappear. No sooner had that message gone out than another tele-letter arrived in Downing Street from the president: he had decided to cancel the broadcast. Thatcher again was livid and, despite US pressure, refused to delay the British withdrawal. That turned out to be the right call. 'In spite of my earlier message to you,' an apologetic Reagan wrote to her the next day, 'I had to go public with our own plans last night, in part to preempt a news leak on the plan which all the networks would have carried in the evening news.' There would, NSC staff warned the president, be an 'inevitable rumpus' with Britain about the way in which the announcement had been handled.[9]

The discord over Lebanon had come to a head at the exact moment that Thatcher was putting her new Soviet strategy into practice. US indifference to her views seemed to confirm the prime minister's belief that Britain needed an independent approach to international affairs. A month earlier, she had taken a bold initial step. Thatcher undertook her first visit to the Eastern bloc with a three-day trip to Hungary – considered one of the most flexible regimes within the Warsaw Pact. Immediately afterwards she signalled to Reagan that she was changing tack. 'I am becoming convinced that we are more likely to make progress on the detailed arms control negotiation if we can first establish a broader basis of understanding between East and West,' she told him. 'It will be a slow and gradual process, during which we must never lower our guard. However, I believe that the effort has to be made.' Thatcher's statement, however cautiously expressed, signalled a new diplomatic strategy with an emphasis on détente.[10]

Grenada had played an important part in Thatcher's thinking, but so too had the astonishing new information received by British intelligence (SIS): the world, so it seemed, had only narrowly avoided a nuclear attack months earlier. In November 1983, NATO had conducted one of its annual war games – *Able Archer-83*. Only when the exercise concluded did British intelligence learn, through the double-agent Oleg Gordievsky, that Moscow had genuinely believed this activity might be the cover for a first strike on the Soviet Union. What really alarmed the British was the report that Soviet aircraft 'capable' of carrying nuclear weapons had been put on runway-alert in East Germany during *Able Archer*. For Thatcher, it only confirmed her view that the West needed to communicate more effectively with the Soviet Union. 'The time had come to move beyond the rhetoric of the evil empire,' said Charles Powell, her private secretary for foreign affairs.[11]

Thatcher's first move was to attend the funeral of the Soviet leader, Yuri Andropov, who had died on 9 February. To reinforce the necessity of her trip, the prime minister also chose the date of the funeral to give Washington material from Gordievsky. It was a fine example of the utility of Britain's 'intelligence power' in the Anglo-American relationship. When Robert Gates, the deputy director of intelligence at the CIA, saw the report, he gasped that it was 'terrifying'.[12]

Thatcher's objective in going to Moscow was not to make progress with Andropov's feeble replacement. She was unimpressed after meeting Konstantin Chernenko on 14 February, mordantly reflecting that the new fur-lined boots bought for the occasion would probably be needed again sooner rather than later. But at her Chequers seminar the previous autumn, Thatcher had decided to seek out potential 'change agents' within the Soviet system such as Grigory Romanov and Mikhail Gorbachev. When she approached Gorbachev at the funeral, he was immediately responsive to her overtures. He had noted that while other western leaders had chatted among themselves as the cortège passed, the Iron Lady had stood, like the Soviet leadership, in respectful silence. Sensing his goodwill, Thatcher grasped the initiative by inviting him to London. He indicated a willingness to come.[13]

Thus the seeds were sown of a new 'special relationship' for

Thatcher. And it was a partnership that in time would put even greater strain on the older one with her 'friend' in the White House.

In the months following Grenada and Lebanon, neither Reagan nor Thatcher showed any particular inclination to kiss and make up. In fact media commentators began remarking on the distinctly chilly note that had entered the relationship. 'Eisenhower and Eden, Kennedy and Macmillan, Johnson and Wilson, Nixon and Heath, Reagan and Thatcher: the Anglo-American marriage always starts well, falters and collapses in scowling and scolding,' judged the *Economist* in a two-part special report ('Say Something, If Only Goodbye') on the state of Anglo-American relations. The past two years had seen the relationship go through its 'most drastic tests since Suez'. In the end, the magazine concluded, Washington had shown that 'superpowers do not need allies, only cheerleaders.'[14]

On the index of alliance politics, as Thatcher's stock in Washington fell, so that of the French president, François Mitterrand, began to rise. At the end of March, Mitterrand conducted a grand tour of the United States, which included 'two sets of private talks and much jollification with Mr Reagan'. They made an 'odd couple', but the president seemed to have a new best friend. As US officials were keen to make clear: 'America can count on France'. The tacit rebuke of Britain was clear enough.[15]

Charles Wick, the director of the US Information Agency in DC and an old friend of the president, was sufficiently concerned by stories of a rift that he wrote to Bud McFarlane. A 'new coolness' had developed in Britain about relations with the United States, he warned. Recent misunderstandings had taken a serious toll. 'The drop in favorable opinion of the United States is essentially the result of a number of events that occurred during the last half of 1983,' he explained, 'which revived British commentary about our failure to consult and the unreliability and bellicosity of this Administration.' George Shultz warned Reagan that 'the "special relationship" has come under severe strain' since the president and the prime minister had last met in September. McFarlane agreed with Shultz that the new dip in relations needed 'watching'.[16]

In the end, it was hard political realities as much as sentiment that pushed Reagan and Thatcher back together. A G-7 summit meeting in London was scheduled for June 1984. As that event approached, both leaders recognised that they were each vital to the other's interests. Thatcher as host wanted a success to emphasise her global stature. She could expect, and even welcome, theatrical battles with left-wing leaders such as Pierre Trudeau and François Mitterrand. Yet even a hint of coolness, or worse a slap-down, from Reagan would immediately be pounced upon by the media and her political enemies as a sign of dwindling influence in the wake of Grenada. The summit might well represent her first opportunity to upbraid the president in person about the operation in the Caribbean, but for her own sake it was important to resist that urge and let bygones be bygones.

Reagan, too, needed to move on. With a presidential election only months away, it was crucial for him to do well at the G-7 meeting to burnish his credentials as the leader of the free world. There was no question of Reagan coasting to victory at the polls; many were asking whether, at the age of seventy-three, he was simply too old to be commander-in-chief. Even more significantly, he could not have the summit turning into an attack on US economic policy. Reagan was vulnerable on high interest rates and an out-of-control budget deficit. Thatcher herself had spoken in forceful terms to Reagan at previous summits about the dangers of the deficit. Now the US expected Thatcher to swallow those concerns. She would have to defend the president from the chair against assaults from the left and to deliver a final communiqué that avoided any hint of criticising American economic policy. 'The prime minister is conscious of the US political scene,' reassured the NSC officials in the brief for Reagan, 'and will not try to embarrass the president.'[17]

Thatcher's price for that support was greater access. The two leaders held a bilateral meeting in Downing Street on 5 June, which, McFarlane advised the president, 'reflects Mrs Thatcher's publicly stated desire for more frequent, high-level, exchanges of view with the USG [US government] in as informal a setting as possible.' The informality of these talks was followed immediately by a shared act of commemoration the following day, when both leaders travelled to Normandy to attend services marking the fortieth anniversary of D-Day. These deeply affected Reagan, who found the day 'an emotional experience' and 'had difficulty getting through my speech'. As a young man Reagan had volunteered for the US Army, but had been turned down due to deafness in one ear and poor eyesight. He always felt ashamed that 'all I did in the war was fly a desk' in the US Army/Air Force Motion Picture Unit. He would show great personal humility around veterans of the war. The ceremony with 'the boys who helped end a war' at Pointe de Hoc, the site of a key battle in the Normandy landings, was a particularly moving occasion for him. It was a telling reminder of American fortitude and a shared history of Allied solidarity and sacrifice in the battle to free Europe.[18]

The G-7 summit began in London the next day. Despite their 'love-in' in Washington only weeks earlier, Reagan found himself put on the economic defensive for much of the time by Mitterrand, supported by Trudeau. Thatcher took up the sword on Reagan's behalf. 'Margaret handled the meetings brilliantly,' Reagan recorded in his diary. 'More protests by Pierre and Francois,' he added later. 'There was blood on the floor – but not ours.'[19]

At one point, with tensions running high, Trudeau launched a bitter attack on Thatcher for her 'heavy handed and undemocratic' behaviour in the chair. Reagan was horrified by the Canadian's tone, but admired how Thatcher kept her cool. Later, as they were leaving the room together, the president expressed his outrage. 'Oh, women know when men are being childish,' snorted Thatcher.[20]

That night at Buckingham Palace, a relieved president recited by heart for the Queen Mother 'The Shooting of Dan McGrew' to gales of laughter from the royal family and the assembled world leaders. As Thatcher looked on, she could reflect with some satisfaction that all vestiges of recent coolness in the Anglo-American relationship appeared to have been swept away. Nevertheless, she had learnt a lesson: her trust in transatlantic consultation would never be as strong again.

When Reagan returned to Washington, he wrote to Thatcher in warm terms to thank her for the way in which she had chaired the summit. 'I want to express by letter what I told you in London,' he began. 'I admire the masterful job you did in organizing and presiding over this year's summit. Thanks to your leadership, the summit was an outstanding success.'[21]

'An outstanding success' for a president seeking re-election meant avoiding any public loss of face. A working draft of the final communiqué had targeted the need for the G-7 nations to exercise monetary restraint and curb budget deficits. The text had singled out the United States for specific criticism in failing to make promised 'downpayments' on the deficit. Thatcher eventually calculated that it was in her political interest to get that censure removed. She bludgeoned other G-7 leaders into a vapid statement promising 'to continue with and where necessary strengthen policies to reduce inflation and interest rates, to control monetary growth and where necessary reduce budgetary deficits.' Even Reagan could accept that commitment, because it did not criticise him or give specific policy directives. In particular, the president avoided any awkward demands to raise taxes (as Thatcher had done in 1981).[22]

For Reagan to have dodged so many potential brickbats in London was only possible with help from Thatcher as a human shield. Something more personal also changed between the two leaders at the G-7 summit. The small, habitual gestures of friendship and solidarity that once characterised their relationship, but that had been absent in recent months, now began to return. A few weeks after the summit, Reagan wrote to Thatcher apropos of nothing to let her know that he was thinking of her during the political troubles of a national mineworkers' strike. 'In recent weeks I have thought often of you with considerable empathy as I follow the activities of the miners' and dockworkers' unions,' he wrote. 'I know they present a difficult set of issues for your government. I just wanted you to know that my thoughts are with you as you address these important issues; I'm confident as ever that you and your government will come out of this well.' This was the entire text of the letter. There was no business to be transacted, only good wishes to be passed along.[23]

A few weeks later, Thatcher reciprocated. When Sandra Day O'Connor visited her in Downing Street – the first woman to be a US Supreme Court justice calling on the first woman to be Britain's prime minister – Thatcher gave her a message to pass along to the president as he geared up for the election: 'I've got my fingers crossed, my toes crossed, my everything crossed!' she told him. No one could have doubted it.[24]

As it turned out, it was Thatcher who needed the luck more than Reagan. In the early hours of 12 October 1984, in her suite at the Grand Hotel in Brighton, the prime minister had just finished working on the final text of her speech to the Conservative Party Conference. As she was about to retire for bed, there came a knock at the door. An apologetic Robin Butler, her principal private secretary, entered with one last paper for approval. While Thatcher was reading it, a massive explosion shook the room. 'A car bomb', she exclaimed, before rushing next door to the bedroom to see if Denis was all right. 'It touched me,' Butler said afterwards, 'because it was one of those moments where there could be no play-acting.'

When the security services swept in and moved the Thatchers out of the building, it became apparent that the explosion was more than a car bomb. 'I think this was an assassination attempt, don't you?' she asked Ronnie Millar, her speechwriter. In fact, it had been an attempt by the Provisional IRA to murder the entire British cabinet. A 100-pound bomb had been planted weeks beforehand. In total, five people died and thirty-four were injured.

While Thatcher was praised for her coolness under fire, live TV pictures of the aftermath of the attack made it clear how close the prime minister had come to death. If she had not been momentarily delayed by Butler and had instead been in the bathroom, which collapsed, Thatcher would in all likelihood have been badly injured or died. Her personal good fortune held that day, but no British prime minister would ever be quite so carefree again. 'Today we were unlucky,' read the chilling statement issued by the IRA, 'but remember we only have to be lucky once; you will have to be lucky always.'[25]

Reagan was campaigning when he heard the news that a bomb had 'almost got her'. He telephoned Thatcher immediately to say 'personally how much we deplore this horrible attack.' It was, thought Bud McFarlane, 'a nice gesture'.[26]

A follow-up letter from the president also made clear his sense of relief and outrage. Fortunately, he told Thatcher, no sooner had 'word of the Brighton attack reached me' than it was overriden 'immediately by the most welcome news that you were unharmed.' Now he had 'been told of deaths and injuries, and particularly of the grievious [sic] wounds to your colleagues, Norman Tebbit and John Wakeham.' Reagan sent his condolences, telling Thatcher that 'the thoughts and sympathies of all Americans are with you and with the families of those struck down by this barbarous act.' He also offered practical assistance. 'In the context of our special relationship,' he reassured the prime minister, 'I have directed that my experts be available to work with yours to assist in bringing the perpetrators to justice.'[27]

Thatcher was grateful, but not just for the warm words. The bomb, she told Reagan, had been detonated by a 'long delay timing device'. These were difficult to detect and any help that the US could offer would be welcome. As good as his word, Reagan replied before the month was out that 'we have identified four individuals who are experts in the area of long delay timing devices for terrorist explosives. I have directed that these personnel be made available to confer with your experts in this area.' It was – the president told Thatcher – 'by working together [that] we can more quickly deny this brutal tactic to those who would use terrorism to attack the foundations of democracy.'[28]

On 6 November 1984, a few weeks after the terrorist attack in Brighton, democracy in action saw Ronald Reagan re-elected president in a landslide victory over Walter Mondale. He carried forty-nine out of the fifty states. Thatcher was thrilled. Whatever her difficulties with Reagan, she had no desire to see Jimmy Carter's vice-president in the White House. Reagan at least was on the right (wing) side of the angels. 'What a victory!' she telegraphed him when she heard the news. 'I cannot tell you how delighted I am. It will be a great tonic and reassurance for all America's friends who can continue to have the fullest confidence in your nation's leadership.'

Just as she had done after Reagan's election in 1980, and after her own re-election in 1983, Thatcher immediately began agitating for an early visit to Washington. 'We are now both in a second term and confront many formidable challenges,' she told the president. 'My fondest hope is that we can continue to work as closely together as we have over the past four years, and consult privately and with complete frankness on all major international problems.'

To this end, she wanted to arrange not one but two meetings in the next few months. George Shultz, she reminded Reagan, had 'made an interesting suggestion for a small seminar between us, with particular attention to arms control issues, early in your new administration'. It was an idea she would 'certainly be ready to go along with'. However, 'more immediately', if Reagan was going to be in California for Christmas, 'I could stop over for an hour or two' on the way back from a trip to China. 'It would be good to have a talk,' she trilled.[29]

At face value, the solicitous tone of Thatcher's message did not seem that much different from earlier requests. In fact, it masked her hardened and coldly calculating view of the relationship with the president. 'I feel very strongly that the Atlantic Alliance is most important,' she told advisers, 'even though I also feel that the Americans have done us a disservice by invading Grenada. But – I have learnt to think that this is how large powers behave. Morality does not come into the picture. The more the pity.' For such a conviction politician, it was a telling admission of the frustrations of a junior partner.[30]

Reagan took up Thatcher's request with the suggestion that they find 'a mutually convenient date early in 1985'. There could be no trip to California, as he would not be there until after Christmas. An undeterred Thatcher – never one to take a hint – immediately offered to come to Washington instead and ended up with an invitation to Camp David for her perseverance.

'I dare to say that I almost feel as if I am in your electoral league,' Reagan replied self-deprecatingly, adding that he looked forward 'to continuing closest consultations. Indeed, I pledge to do so.' Warm words were backed up by actions, including one outrageous piece of favouritism towards Thatcher. It was an intervention that made clear Reagan's personal determination to draw a line under any remaining bad feeling about Grenada. The result stunned many in his administration.[31]

For well over a year, Thatcher had been urging the president to intervene to stop a proposed anti-trust investigation by the US Department of Justice into whether price-fixing by British Airways (BA) and other European airlines had unfairly forced Laker Airways out of business in 1982. In addition, the trustees of the bankrupt Laker Airways had brought a private anti-trust action seeking massive damages from airlines, including BA. Thatcher had first written to the president about the matter in the lead-up to the 1983 general election, when she worried that it might scupper her manifesto promises to privatise BA. 'I want to take up with you personally and urgently my deep concern at the proposed antitrust investigation,' she had told him. 'The matter is urgent which is why I am contacting you immediately. I am most disturbed about it and do hope you will feel able to take it up personally and very quickly.' In an electoral context, the use of the word 'personally' – as in favour – was explicit: Thatcher wanted Reagan to stop the investigation.[32]

Wide-scale privatisation would become an ideological centrepiece of Thatcher's second term. This free-market policy had the twin advantages of reducing government expenditure by ending subsidies while increasing government revenues through selling national assets. It also promised to weaken trades unions, which were strong in nationalised industries, and encourage a more flexible marketplace. Political and economic realities made privatisation too complicated during Thatcher's first term. A Conservative electoral landslide in 1983 changed that equation. The first big sell-off was British Telecom in 1984. BT was followed by British Gas, British Airways, the British Airports Authority and the electricity companies. A total of forty sell-offs not only raised vast sums for the exchequer, they also remodelled the political landscape in Britain. 'The transfer of ownership and control of industries and services to a wide public,' observed Enoch Powell, an early advocate of monetarism, 'gave the Conservative government precisely the sense of irreversibility that is daunting to political opponents.'[33]

In 1983, Reagan had been in no position to help Thatcher

with her Laker problem. National security adviser William Clark had warned on the anti-trust investigation that 'it would be wrong to suspend it.' Reagan had conveyed the news to Thatcher apologetically. 'You know how highly I value our personal relationship and the unique co-operation between our countries on important matters,' he explained. 'However in this case I feel that I do not have the latitude to respond to your concerns.'

The investigation continued to loom over Thatcher's privatisation plans throughout 1983–4. She never lost an opportunity to raise it with the president whenever the two met. Her argument was that the investigation was an illegal and improper unilateral attempt by the US to regulate international aviation. Reagan's briefing book for the London G-7 summit made it clear that this was one of the major irritants in the relationship between the two countries.[34]

The issue was also a source of division within the Reagan administration itself. The Justice Department believed that it could 'investigate and prosecute effectively'. The State Department thought 'these arrangements are shaky' and worried that they would make relations between Britain and America 'increasingly contentious'. The matter came to a head in the Oval Office ten days after the presidential election. Carol Dinkins, deputy attorney-general since 1984, argued that Justice should pursue the case and bring criminal charges of anti-trust violations. George Shultz maintained this would be a disaster for the Atlantic Alliance. 'PM Thatcher has really dug in her heels,' Reagan noted in his diary. 'George thinks our relations with the UK are more important than the case. Hearing both sides I came down on the side of foreign relations – case closed.' It was a stunning decision, one that emphasised the growing influence of Shultz on the president as well as Thatcher's return to favour.

The *Financial Times* would later report that the Justice Department had been unable to prove any conspiracy to operate predatory pricing on transatlantic routes for the purpose of ruining Freddie Laker. Most experts believed that Laker Airways would have gone bankrupt even without the price war with BA. But the reaction at the Justice Department at the time was one of fury. They refused to cooperate with the British Embassy in announcing the decision and leaked to the press that this had been a direct political intervention by the president. Within months, Carol Dinkins had resigned as deputy attorney-general and left the administration.[35]

With a new electoral mandate in his pocket – and almost exactly a year after they had fallen out so badly over Grenada – Ronald Reagan with one very public and controversial gesture had signalled to Margaret Thatcher his continuing belief in their special relationship. It seemed the perfect prelude to their meeting at the president's mountainside retreat of Camp David in December.

If the president expected gratitude, he should have known better. 'They thanked us when you quashed the indictments,' Ambassador Charles Price complained to the president shortly afterwards, 'but so far we have nothing in hand but a bag of air.' The ambassador's frustration went deeper. 'During my first year in London, I have met with the PM perhaps 15 times,' he wrote. 'In every meeting she does most of the talking . . . It's time she did some listening.'[36]

It had become a familiar refrain.

Despite Reagan's gesture in the autumn of 1984, it was clear as winter set in that uneasiness still pervaded the relationship. For Thatcher, her acceptance of 'how large powers behave' was combined with an acute sense of personal disappointment in the president himself. He was the most powerful man in the world, yet – say it quietly and never in public – she did not consider Reagan to be her intellectual equal.[37] Nothing illustrated that gulf, not to mention the limited power of a British prime minister, better than the new relationship she struck up a few days before seeing Reagan at Camp David.

On the morning of 16 December, Thatcher welcomed Mikhail Gorbachev of the Soviet Politburo to Chequers. This visit, she noted later, was 'the next step in my strategy of gaining closer relations – on the right terms – with the Soviet Union'. Beforehand, she had held another seminar with Soviet experts in preparation for what they warned her would be a dynamic exchange of views. Gorbachev was part of a new generation

– one of the 'children of the 20th Party Congress' – that many hoped would fulfil Khrushchev's aim of 'socialism with a human face'. He was known to read widely, including western studies of the Soviet Union, and by virtue of having been a protégé of Andropov, was thought to be a tough political realist. By 1984 he had risen to the suitably Orwellian post of secretary in charge of ideology – in effect the party number two and favourite to be the next Soviet leader.[38]

Gorbachev arrived in Britain with a tantalising reputation as a reformer. He did not disappoint. 'The second he came into the great hall at Chequers you knew that here was an entirely different sort of Russian leader,' recalled private secretary Charles Powell. 'Here was a man bursting with energy, a broad grin on his face, a readiness to engage in argument.' When the talks began, Thatcher found her exchanges revelatory. 'His personality could not have been more different from the wooden ventriloquism of the average Soviet apparatchik,' she recalled. 'He smiled, laughed, used his hands for emphasis, modulated his voice, followed an argument through and was a sharp debater . . . He did not seem in the least uneasy about entering into controversial areas of high politics.' At one point, Gorbachev produced a sheet of paper from his pocket. 'I showed her a kind of diagram with 1,000 little squares,' he recalled, 'and every little square represented 1,000th of the nuclear weapons accumulated in the world by that time. Each square by itself contained enough weapons to destroy life on earth. So life on earth could be destroyed 1,000 times over, and the arms race continued.' A robust debate followed. 'We had a very open dialogue,' Gorbachev wryly observed. For Thatcher, the contrast with Reagan was striking. The Russian wasn't glued to his prepared note cards. He relished the strategic *tour d'horizon* as much as the prime minister herself did. 'I found myself liking him,' Thatcher reflected. These were not words she used often.[39]

Geoffrey Howe looked on in wonderment at the transformation in Thatcher during the talks. Her hectoring tone – so often used in frustration when she felt she was dealing with someone weak or dim – was gone. Instead, her eyes burned with enthusiasm as she thrilled to an intellectual and political debate of the highest order. 'Margaret was at her best,' Howe remembered.

'Fluent but measured, thoughtful but shiningly and convincingly sincere.' She also had a useful 'cheat sheet': the double-agent Oleg Gordievsky had provided her with Gorbachev's brief for the meeting. The moment when the British realised Gorbachev was something different came when he quoted the nineteenth-century prime minister, Lord Palmerston, who said, 'Nations have no permanent friends or allies, they only have permanent interests.' Thatcher and her foreign secretary found this 'remarkable', not because Gorbachev knew the quote, but 'for the precisely effective way in which it was deployed.' No wonder that when she emerged from the meeting and spoke to the BBC, Thatcher famously declared of Gorbachev that 'We can do business together.' The prime minister had at last met her match, and she loved it.[40]

The most difficult moment for Thatcher at Chequers had come when Gorbachev pressed her on the Strategic Defense Initiative. The Soviet politician knew that Thatcher was close to Reagan. Indeed, Charles Powell noted the Soviets seemed to have calculated that Thatcher was 'somebody who could both persuade President Reagan to deal with them and in a sense help explain them to President Reagan.' Gorbachev, who knew that the prime minister had her own reservations about SDI, hoped she might convince Reagan to scrap this new programme. It was a theme he would take up in public the next day at a lunch hosted by Geoffrey Howe. 'The Soviet Union is prepared . . . to advance towards the complete prohibition and eventual elimination of nuclear weapons,' he declared. But 'I would like to stress that in present circumstances it is especially important to avert the transfer of the arms race to outer space. If it is not done it would be unreal to hope to stop the nuclear arms race.' When Gorbachev tried out that line on Thatcher at Chequers, he got short shrift. 'Do not waste any time,' she warned him, 'on trying to persuade me to say to Ron Reagan: "Do not go ahead with SDI". That will get nowhere.' Yet despite the forceful rejection of any notion that she would deliver a message to Reagan from Gorbachev on SDI, this was in fact exactly what she intended to do.[41]

In Washington, the Soviet overture to Margaret Thatcher through Gorbachev was followed up immediately by a personal letter from Chernenko to Reagan on 20 December. The message was as clear as it had been in London. 'Recently you have spoken on more than one occasion . . . in favour of moving along the road leading eventually to the liquidation of nuclear weapons, completely and everywhere,' the Soviet leader wrote. 'We, of course welcome that.' But there was a catch. 'To be quite frank: emergence and deployment of strike space systems would make it impossible to conduct serious negotiations on the limitation and reduction of strategic arms.'

It was an ultimatum Reagan had been expecting. Just three days earlier, at a meeting of the National Security Planning Group, the president had interrupted a long briefing by McFarlane to point out that 'SDI is the main target of the Soviet Union' in talks about disarmament. 'They are coming to the table to get at SDI,' he predicted. 'We need to stay with our SDI research program no matter what.' Later, in private, he noted that he would stand firm no matter what they offered.[42]

In fact, the first test of his resolve would come from Margaret Thatcher.

Camp David. 22 December 1984. 'Sat. dawned clear and bright,' Reagan wrote cheerfully that day, 'which was fine because PM Margaret Thatcher was coming in for a visit.' In fact the weather almost stopped her coming altogether.

To get to Washington had required a Herculean effort from the British prime minister. Following her Sunday meeting with Gorbachev at Chequers, she left the next day for Beijing, where she signed an agreement with the Chinese government on the future of Hong Kong. After a visit to Hong Kong itself to reassure its people that the agreement was not a British sell-out, she then carried on across the Pacific and continental America to Washington. This extraordinary journey, prompted by her determination to see the newly re-elected President Reagan, took approximately fifty-five hours. Not that the prime minister, who famously only slept four to five hours a night, seemed to demonstrate any noticeable flagging of energy. At a stop-off to refuel the plane at Hickham Air Force Base in Hawaii, she insisted on getting off to see Pearl Harbor. As flustered officials chased about trying to organise a car, she waved them away, pulled out a torch from her own handbag and marched off into the darkness to find it herself. Just over half a mile later, at the water's edge, she looked out towards the memorial to the stricken USS *Arizona*, reflecting on the 'date which will live in infamy' and perhaps on her sixteen-year-old self.[43]

After spending the equivalent of more than two days in the air, severe fog in the Washington, DC, area saw her plane diverted from Andrews Air Force Base to Dulles international airport. This time it was embassy staff who were left scrambling around, as they dashed from Andrews to Dulles to greet her. When they got there, Thatcher was already waiting. 'Don't worry,' she told them. 'I've worked out the rearrangements.' It was typical Thatcher – intimidatingly considerate.[44]

With Washington still socked in by fog, Thatcher had to wait hours after her breakfast with Vice-President George Bush before getting word that Marine Two had been cleared to transport them down to Maryland. By the time they arrived, the presidential retreat was bathed in bright sunshine.

Thatcher had strained every sinew to get to Camp David for a few hours of face time with the president. For the senior partner, however, things were rather more relaxed. He buzzed across the lawn – coatless, windswept and cheerful – in his golf buggy as the helicopter landed. When Thatcher came down the steps, he moved forward to embrace her warmly and kiss her cheek. 'I sometimes thought I was directing *Gone with the Wind*,' her press secretary, Bernard Ingham, mordantly reflected. Then the president gestured towards his golf cart, saw Thatcher into the passenger seat, and hopped in beside her. Waving happily to the assembled media, Reagan executed a half-turn and sped off, as Thatcher looked at him with a mixture of affection and bemusement. 'Be careful,' shouted a member of the White House press corps. 'You bet!' shot back the president.[45]

The attitude of the administration towards the Thatcher visit had been fairly relaxed beforehand. McFarlane had briefed the president that the meeting had come about because the prime minister was 'obviously eager' to re-establish her position at the start of the second term. Despite a number of 'irritants', he counselled, the relationship remained essentially 'close, sound and special'. If anything, Thatcher seemed a bit too eager. 'We have been going back and forth with the British on the possibility of Mrs Thatcher meeting with you again in February,' McFarlane complained. 'We originally thought the Camp David meeting would fill the bill, but she will be in the US on a speaking tour in February and has pushed to meet with you again.'[46]

George Shultz also briefed the president that Thatcher was coming 'in order to stress the close links she hopes to continue to have with you in your new administration'. But he reminded the president that Thatcher being Thatcher, she 'will want a frank exchange of views'. Not the least of these would be on arms control. 'Thatcher is generally supportive,' Shultz warned, 'but is critical of SDI.'[47]

McFarlane had correctly predicted that Thatcher would want to make Gorbachev and SDI the 'centerpiece' of her talks with the president. Reagan in his golf buggy had driven Thatcher straight to the presidential Aspen Lodge, where Nancy was waiting. This was more than a simple courtesy. 'Past experience', Peter Sommer at the NSC noted, taught that Thatcher always wanted 'a small one-on-one meeting with the President' before any formal talks began, and this trip to Camp David was no different. In fact, so determined was Thatcher to get that one-on-one time that (in the absence of Denis) she brought along her principal private secretary, Robin Butler, to this initial session. His explicit instructions were to entertain Mrs Reagan and to make sure she did not interrupt this important first opportunity to chat with the president. In the event, Nancy was too accomplished a political wife not to know when to make herself scarce. Butler confined himself to taking a note of the meeting.[48]

Thatcher began by congratulating Reagan on his 'fantastic victory' at the polls. 'The victory,' she told him, 'was even more impressive given that he had so significantly changed US politics. Such a wide victory was an endorsement of [your] policies and a clear call for a continuation of these policies.' While Thatcher laid on her compliments with a trowel, the president received them with characteristic 'aw-shucks' humour. Certainly it was 'an honour to win by such a margin,' he told her, but he knew what he wanted from Santa for Christmas: 'Minnesota!' It was the only state he had lost.[49]

Thatcher was never a great one for small talk and it wasn't long before she steered the conversation back to policy. And she played the highest card in her hand straight away. She had met the coming man in the Politburo a week earlier. Now she wanted to tell the president all about him. Gorbachev was 'an unusual Russian', she explained, 'in that he was much less constrained, more charming, open to discussion and debate.' Carelessly, given Reagan's dependence on them, she added that the Russian 'did not stick to prepared notes.' On matters of substance, Thatcher had the sense that Gorbachev was 'an advocate of economic reform.' Certainly he was 'worried' about the Soviet Union's poor economic performance.

The Iron Lady was keen to emphasise to the president that there was no corrosion in cold-war views. Indeed, she reminded him, 'the more charming the adversary, the more dangerous.' As such, she had warned Gorbachev in the bluntest terms that 'there is no point in trying to divide Britain from the United States. This ploy will never succeed.' The PM had reminded Gorbachev that she and Reagan 'have known each other since long before' they assumed their current positions. Dividing them was simply 'not on'. She had also emphasised that 'the president is an honorable man who sincerely wants to improve relations with the Soviet Union.'

If Thatcher was trying to charm Reagan, it did not work. He made no comment whatsoever in reaction to her character analysis of Gorbachev. Instead, he turned almost immediately to the crux of the disagreement he had with Thatcher herself – the Strategic Defense Initiative – giving her due warning to back off. The Soviets had fared 'so poorly' in the propaganda battles of recent months. Now they were returning to the negotiating table at the Geneva disarmament talks to try to regain some initiative. But Reagan's fear was that they simply wanted to use these talks as a 'propaganda forum' to attack SDI, saying that it was weaponising space. That was never his intention. The new technology would be put 'into international hands.' And there was a higher purpose, an impassioned Reagan told Thatcher. 'The new Strategic Defense

Initiative also has a moral context,' he explained. 'We must search for ways to build a more stable peace. Our goal is to reduce, and eventually eliminate nuclear weapons.'

Thatcher was horrified. Once again the gap between US and UK conceptions of defence and détente had been exposed. Days earlier at Chequers, the prime minister had admitted to Gorbachev that she 'did not share' Reagan's dream of ridding the world of nuclear weapons. Now it rattled her to hear the president speaking in such frank terms. And in an uncharacteristic moment of panic, she blurted out the ultimatum from Gorbarchev: 'tell your friend President Reagan not to go ahead with space weapons'. If the programme went ahead, Gorbachev had promised, 'the Russians would either develop their own, or more probably, develop new offensive systems superior to SDI.'[50]

A few beats of stunned silence followed. Reagan, so often the one to break an awkward moment, said nothing. Then Thatcher started blathering about being 'interested in learning more about SDI'. But each knew what had happened. 'Thatcher delivered the message,' spat Martin Anderson, a member of the president's foreign intelligence advisory board.[51]

With uncharacteristic brusqueness, Reagan simply cut Thatcher off and said it was 'time to join the others at Laurel Lodge'. The private meeting was over. But Thatcher was only just getting going. 'In the three hours she was there,' Anderson noted of the Camp David meeting, 'it seemed that her main mission was to get Reagan to kill SDI.'

If Thatcher showed little tact during the meeting, she also showed no fear. The president was accompanied by the vice-president, the secretary of state, the national security adviser and a phalanx of officials. The prime minister came alone, save for three officials, who did not speak throughout the session. Once the opening pleasantries were out of the way, Thatcher launched straight in again. Of course 'the US SDI research program must go ahead,' she explained, but not in a way that compromised security. 'Nuclear weapons,' she reminded the president, 'have served not only to prevent a nuclear war, but they have also given us forty years of unprecedented peace in Europe. It would be unwise to abandon a deterrence system that had prevented both nuclear and conventional war.' Her final warning was blunt: Britain had 'real worries'.

After this long opening from Thatcher, with its apparently contradictory impulses, the president finally was able to speak. He emphasised again that 'research is promising and SDI may be feasible.' And he reiterated his overall aim in simple terms: 'My ultimate goal is to eliminate nuclear weapons.' SDI was the best way to achieve that objective. Not only would it provide an international defensive system in the long term; more immediately, it would put pressure on the Soviets, who 'must be concerned about our economic strength. It will be especially difficult for them to keep spending such vast sums on defense.' So his strategy was straightforward: 'We must deal with the Soviets from a position of strength. But we also know that in a nuclear war there would be no winners.'

Reagan had been deeply affected by the apparent near-miss of *Able Archer-83*. The American report into that NATO war game had grimly predicted that it marked the beginning of a 'more perilous strategic and political struggle over the rest of the decade.' According to Bud McFarlane, the president had been 'very moved' by reading the summaries of Gordievsky's reports. It had reinforced his belief that something needed to be done not simply to reduce tension with the Soviet Union, but more ambitiously to end the cold war and the threat of nuclear annihilation.[52]

Thatcher had provided those intelligence reports, but her conclusions were different. With all this talk of abolishing nuclear weapons, the prime minister could hold her tongue no longer. Surely, she interjected, deterrence was the best way to achieve this, and 'Strength is our best deterrence.' Reagan agreed, but continued that it was also important to 'convince the Soviets that we mean them no harm.'

Yes, shot back Thatcher, but that was why 'it is correct to emphasize military balance, not superiority.' History taught a simple lesson: 'Balance gives us security.' The unspoken assumption was left hanging in the air: SDI risked destroying that balance and was therefore a threat to security. Research was one thing; deployment quite another. Once again Thatcher was arguing for the need to emphasise détente over defence.

As Reagan became increasingly exasperated, he asked McFarlane to expand on the SDI programme. The national security adviser spoke bluntly of 'our inability to match the Soviet offensive build up', which was why the president was exploring 'other alternatives'. 'It is prudent and responsible for the President to undertake the SDI research,' said McFarlane.

'SDI as I understand it seems to suggest inherent US superiority,' Thatcher shot back.

'Deterrence as we know it today may no longer meet our future needs,' McFarlane replied.[53]

It was the confirmation of Thatcher's worst fears. Playing for time, she demanded that 'someone could come to London to give [me] a top-level US technical briefing on the US and Soviet strategic defense programmes.' Relieved to have found a way out, Reagan 'nodded agreement and said it was time to break for lunch.'

Not for Thatcher, it wasn't. With the president rising from his seat, the PM told him that she 'would appreciate' further discussions before lunch, and proceeded to speak at great length. After an already bruising session, Reagan had simply had enough. When Thatcher stopped talking, he brushed her off for the second time that day. Certainly he was 'eager to make further progress'. But not now. 'Time for lunch,' he said. Even then Thatcher would not relax. The weariness of the minute of the meeting captures the atmosphere. 'During the cocktail session before lunch,' it records, 'the president, Mrs. Thatcher and Ambassador Price' continued discussions 'at some length.'

When the formal sessions resumed, Reagan and Thatcher began a more general survey of international and economic affairs. Only towards the end of the session did they return to the question of SDI. Discussions between officials had been going on at the margins of the talks, much of it choreographed by George Shultz. Now at the main session the secretary explained that the goal of the initiative was to maintain and strengthen deterrence. 'SDI is not a departure from deterrence,' he said clearly. It seemed an obvious contradiction of what McFarlane had said earlier.

Thatcher then produced from her handbag a brief statement that she intended making to the press on her departure. 'It has been worked out by respective staffs,' she told the president. There were four specific points and she read them out: They were '(1) the U.S. and Western aim is to maintain balance, i.e., not achieve superiority, while taking account of Soviet developments; (2) SDI-related testing and deployment, in view of treaty obligations, would be a matter for negotiations; (3) the overall aim is to maintain, not undercut, deterrence; and (4) East–West negotiations should aim to achieve security at reduced levels of offensive systems.'

'We agree with these points,' Reagan replied nonchalantly, adding that he hoped they would 'quell reports of disagreements between us.' His only substantive changes were that deterrence should be 'enhanced' rather than 'maintained', and to delete the words 'testing and' from the phrase 'SDI-related testing and deployment'.

Thatcher, who had been so keen to discuss the issue of SDI, now immediately switched subjects, presumably in case the president changed his mind. After a few cursory exchanges, the talks came to an end, with Reagan amicably telling Thatcher he 'highly valued' the discussion and 'looked forward to seeing [you] again in February.' Thatcher in turn thanked the president for a 'warm pre-Christmas reception', and looked forward 'to an early reunion.' The only hint of tension came in a final exchange with the national security adviser. 'Looking at Mr. McFarlane,' records the minute of the meeting, 'she reiterated her desire for a technical briefing in London.' McFarlane, surely with a touch of sarcasm, replied that 'he was interested in personally giving her the briefing.'

It had been a difficult meeting, but afterwards Reagan seemed contented enough. 'Main topic was our Strategic Defense Research ("Star Wars"),' he noted. 'I believe [we] eased some concerns she had.' Thatcher believed that the president had done more than just ease her concerns. She left Camp David thinking that Britain had secured major concessions for western Europe from Reagan on his pet project. 'It was intensely political,' remembered Charles Powell. 'She really turned him round.' Thatcher had agreed to give public support to SDI. In turn, Reagan had conceded that he would neither abandon the broad principle of deterrence nor unilaterally deploy SDI. Moreover, the president had agreed that Thatcher should announce this publicly at her press conference.[54]

In one regard the British had been lucky that their reservations about the important distinction between SDI as a research initiative and as a deployed system coincided with those of George Shultz. As during the Falklands War, Thatcher was able to take advantage of bitter disputes within the administration, although on this occasion she found herself on the opposite side of the argument from Caspar Weinberger at the Defense Department. As the Geneva disarmament talks with the Soviets approached, Weinberger was adamant that the Strategic Defense Initiative should not form any part of the negotiations. Shultz in contrast was determined that SDI should at least be on the table. Thatcher's visit had offered the secretary of state an opportunity to ensure that his view prevailed. State Department officials had worked directly with the British to produce the document that emerged from Camp David. 'It was an excellent statement,' the secretary judged; 'it differentiated between research and deployment of space-based defense and gave me some running room in Geneva. Since the president had signed on, my instructions would reflect what had been agreed upon.'

This was a classic example of how members of the administration could use Thatcher to gain leverage during internal policy disputes. Thatcher understood this, and often turned it to her advantage. She had come genuinely to admire Shultz, who was both tough and adept at playing the diplomatic game. He had already outmanoeuvred one longtime Reagan supporter in 'Judge' Clark, who had resigned in frustration as national security adviser in 1983. Now 'Cap' Weinberger, another old Reagan friend, found himself on the back foot. Despite the fact that the British had signalled SDI as the main topic of conversation at Camp David, Shultz (who as secretary of state coordinated the visit) contrived to keep Weinberger out of the meeting by not informing him that SDI was the substantive item on the agenda. When the secretary of defense learnt of the deceit, he was furious, and demanded that the president issue clarification that the Soviets were not being given a veto over SDI at the Geneva arms talks.

Weinberger got his statement, but he need not have worried.

As Thatcher and Shultz would soon find out, the president remained as committed as ever to his dream of SDI and the abolition of all nuclear weapons. Soon Reagan would be facing a Soviet leader who, just as he predicted, was ready to 'cry uncle'.

8

Not a Great Listener

Inauguration Day. Monday, 21 January 1985. 'The big but very cold day,' Ronald Reagan noted in his diary. Outside, wind chill temperatures were -20°F. Frostbite took ten minutes. 'There is no way we should inflict this risk on all the people who would have to be out in the cold for hours,' the president wrote. So the parade had been cancelled. The ceremony itself was postponed and moved inside to the Capitol building, where Washington's elite would gather under the magnificent rotunda – 96 feet in diameter and soaring to 180 feet in height. The previous day, in a small ceremony at the White House, Reagan had taken the oath of office on the date – 20 January – laid down in the Twentieth Amendment. Today an elaborate motorcade of more than fifty vehicles, including two identical presidential Lincoln limousines, one of which contained the commander-in-chief and the first lady, swept up Pennsylvania Avenue to the Capitol, for Reagan to give his second inaugural address.[1]

The speech had been outlined by the president himself. And on foreign policy it bore the rhetorical simplicity that had been a hallmark of his first term. His straightforwardness, together with the significance of the occasion, made the second inaugural address among the most important of Reagan's speeches. 'We seek the total elimination one day of nuclear weapons from the face of the Earth,' he declared. 'Is there either logic or morality,' he asked, 'in believing that if one side threatens to kill tens of millions of our people our only recourse is to threaten killing tens of millions of theirs?' Moving beyond that calculation was the objective to which he committed his second term. 'We will meet the Soviets,' he promised, 'hoping that we can agree on a way to rid the world of the threat of nuclear destruction.' And the United States would intensify its commitment to the Strategic Defense Initiative, 'a research program to find, if we can, a security shield that will destroy nuclear missiles before they reach their target.' The objective of this twin-track approach was to 'render nuclear weapons obsolete'.[2]

Reagan, as so often in major foreign policy speeches, had laid out in simple and direct terms the objectives of his strategy. He would engage the Soviet Union in a process of radical disarmament that sought to reduce and eliminate nuclear weapons. He would fund a research programme that might in the longer term offer a protective shield against nuclear attack. The aim of this twin-track approach was clear: to end the game of nuclear deterrence and move from mutually assured destruction to mutually assured survival.[3]

The aspirations of the second inaugural were greeted in 10 Downing Street with barely concealed contempt. Margaret Thatcher had never taken much trouble to hide her disagreement with the president's hopes for a nuclear-free world. Only a few weeks earlier, she had even conceded to Mikhail Gorbachev that she 'did not share' Reagan's vision of a world without nuclear weapons. After the sharp exchanges with Reagan on this subject at Camp David before Christmas, national security adviser Bud McFarlane had flown to London to give her an up-to-date briefing on both SDI and George Shultz's preliminary talks with the Soviet foreign minister, Andrei Gromyko. 'I am indebted to Mr McFarlane for his comprehensive briefing,' Thatcher wrote to Reagan afterwards. 'We now have a clear idea of how you expect the subsequent negotiations may develop. I look forward very much to further discussions with you on these all-important issues . . . when I come to Washington next month.'[4]

In the weeks leading up to Thatcher's February 1985 visit, the Reagan administration did everything possible to coax along the prime minister They made sure to organise any number of public displays of the uniqueness of the relationship. The most visible of these, as in 1981, was the acceptance by the president and first lady of an invitation to dinner at the British Embassy. 'Their attendance,' explained McFarlane, 'would . . . send a highly positive signal about US-British relations.'[5]

Also in advance of the visit, Secretary of Defense Weinberger travelled to London to give Thatcher a further technical presentation on SDI, saying how much he wanted 'especially to thank you' for such a valuable opportunity. As a trained scientist, Thatcher was particularly interested in ongoing research to determine the feasibility of 'an effective ballistic missile defense'. And yet that same training also made her an instinctive sceptic. To begin with, there had been no precise definition of what exactly 'effective' meant in the context of ballistic missile defence. Officials in the Strategic Defense Initiative Organization spoke of 'a multi-layered defense designed to stop missiles in their boost phase and warheads in their mid-course trajectories.' These might in time become effective in stopping around 80 per cent of the Soviet missile fleet. Thatcher, like experts in the United States and around the world, wanted to know how it was going to work. Would missile defence comprise directed-energy weapons, such as lasers and particle beams, or kinetic-energy weapons, which used force of impact? What kinds of sensors and computers would be needed? What was the role of individual decision making? By 1985, Weinberger was talking of genuine advances. 'The barriers we saw to progress are crumbling,' he asserted. SDIO officials reported on 'technical marvels', including experiments with low-powered laser beams bouncing off the space shuttle.[6]

Positive briefings on SDI by Weinberger and McFarlane only confirmed Thatcher's fear that testing might move out of the laboratory sooner than anticipated. Her apprehension also grew when Reagan followed the second inaugural with a State of the Union address that declared, 'All of us have no greater dream than to see the day when nuclear weapons are banned from this Earth forever'. The fact that such a statement coincided with the imminent resumption of East–West disarmament talks in Geneva only compounded her anxiety.[7]

Part of Thatcher's problem now was that it was becoming increasingly difficult to find the right place to insert herself into policy divisions within the administration. In December 1984, at Camp David, she had been able to manipulate the infighting between Weinberger and Shultz over SDI to Britain's advantage. But to a certain extent she had been played, too. The agreement she made with Reagan at Camp David was essential to Shultz's strategy heading into discussions with the Soviet foreign minister, Andrei Gromyko. These in turn would lead to further disarmament talks and a summit meeting. Such developments left the prime minister in a bind. In the president's twin-track strategy, Weinberger had SDI and Shultz had nuclear disarmament. Thatcher disliked both, believing each to be equally unwelcome for European nuclear deterrence. But it also meant she had no dog in the Washington fight.

Short on diplomatic options, Thatcher decided her only recourse was to attack the strategy in public. Her choice of venue was Reagan's own back yard. Thatcher asked Sir Oliver Wright, the British ambassador in Washington, to petition Speaker 'Tip' O'Neill for an invitation to address a joint session of Congress during her forthcoming trip. Not only would the occasion be 'symbolic of the special ties of tradition and friendship between our two countries and parliaments,' Wright told O'Neill, it would also give the prime minister an 'opportunity to speak about some of the challenges facing our democracies in the final years of this century.' The White House, unwittingly as part of its strategy to keep Thatcher sweet, was only too happy to help. Reagan wrote a fulsome personal letter of support to O'Neill. 'Britain is among our closest and most important Allies,' he said. 'The prime minister's visit presents a wonderful opportunity for American political leaders and our public to hear her views first-hand on the major issues of the day, including the state of the trans-Atlantic alliance and East–West relations.'[8]

Thatcher took personal control of writing her address to Congress. 'She had one draft from the foreign office which she didn't much like,' noted her informal adviser on Soviet affairs, George Urban, who was invited to send notes for the speech. Hugh Thomas from the Centre for Policy Studies, former UK ambassador to the Soviet Union Frank Roberts, and the former disarmament minister, Lord Chalfont, also contributed, and attended a seminar with the prime minister at Chequers to discuss ideas. Thatcher also gave much thought to the delivery as well as the substance of the speech. She resolved to practise speaking the text until every intonation and emphasis was right. This homework was done in her customarily thorough and sleep-deprived fashion.[9]

Arriving in Washington late on 19 February, Thatcher went straight to the British Embassy, where the ambassador had set up an American autocue for her to rehearse with. The prime minister had already had a master class from the Great Communicator himself. George Shultz recalled 'a fascinating time at a little luncheon' when the president taught Thatcher how to use the most up-to-the-minute teleprompter. 'He explained to her why our way was better and she should shift,' Shultz noted. 'Then he said, "Now you want to be sure that the numbers of the pages are on the teleprompter and you turn the page, no one even notices you're turning the page, but you always want your text in front of you because you never know when something will go wrong with the teleprompter and then you want to be able to pick it right up".' There were also tricks to help Thatcher appear more natural. 'Be sure to have a few good quotations in your speech,' Reagan suggested, 'and when you come to one of those, pick up the piece of paper so people see it and you read it and then you put it down. That makes the rest of it look less read.'[10]

Thatcher had always been a diligent pupil. Once she was in front of the president's personal autocue, sent over to the embassy by the White House on his instruction, there was work to be done. 'Ignoring any jet lag,' she remembered, 'I practised until 4 am. I did not go to bed, beginning the new day with my usual black coffee and vitamin pills, then gave television interviews from 6.45 am, had my hair done and was ready at 10.30 to leave for the Capitol.'[11]

An address to the US Congress by an overseas leader can often end up as a 'dud', with scant attendance by members of both houses and little in the way of media interest. Margaret Thatcher, on the other hand, was a big draw in Washington, where politicians and press alike had come to enjoy her forthright style. Her speech did not disappoint. For on the question of a world without nuclear weapons, the Iron Lady could not and would not hold her tongue.

Thatcher's address was an impassioned defence of 'the shield' of nuclear deterrence, which had kept Europe safe in a way that 'seemed unattainable amid the mud and slaughter of the First World War and the suffering and sacrifice of the Second'. She continued:

> Mr Speaker, wars are not caused by the build-up of weapons. They are caused when an aggressor believes he can achieve his objectives at an acceptable price (*applause*) . . . Our task is to see that potential aggressors, from whatever quarter, understand plainly that the capacity and the resolve of the West would deny them victory in war and that the price they would pay would be intolerable (*applause*). That is the basis of deterrence and it is the same whatever the nature of the weapons, for let us never forget the horrors of conventional war and the hideous sacrifice of those who have suffered in them. Our task is not only to prevent nuclear war, but to prevent conventional war as well (*applause*). No-one understood the importance of deterrence more clearly than Winston Churchill, when in his last speech to you he said: 'Be careful above all things not to let go of the atomic weapon until you are sure and more than sure that other means of preserving peace are in your hands!'[12]

Thatcher's speech was rapturously received by Congress, with many Republican defence hawks chanting 'Maggie! Maggie!' during her standing ovation. However, Edward Kennedy, the liberal conscience of the Democratic Party and a leader of the Nuclear Weapons Freeze Campaign, remained ostentatiously seated. 'Bad manners,' complained the UK defence secretary, Michael Heseltine. Kennedy was appalled by Thatcher's enthusiasm for nuclear weapons, but he was not the only American politician whose nose was put out of joint. The speech, it soon became clear, had also outraged the White House.[13]

After a short reception with members of Congress, Thatcher

sped down Pennsylvania Avenue for her meeting with Reagan. Unlike the intimacy of Camp David before Christmas, this gathering was more formal, including cabinet members from both sides. ('Turn to George and Cap if asked for details,' advised Reagan's speaking notes.) After a few brief moments for the two leaders alone in the Oval Office, the full meeting began with a working lunch and was followed by a formal session on 'strategic stability'.[14]

White House anger was clear right from the outset. Michael Heseltine recalled a member of the president's staff immediately taking him aside to warn that nuclear weapons and SDI were 'not a subject upon which the president wished to dwell.' The formal discussions were curiously flat and *chétif*, with the president showing none of the easy charm that usually helped along even the most difficult meetings. Thatcher thought the presence of her own cabinet ministers, Geoffrey Howe and Heseltine, might have cramped conversation. She resolved not to bring them again. Her ministers were no happier. Heseltine recorded that his role in the discussions was at best 'perfunctory'.[15]

Thatcher put the bad atmosphere down to having too many people in the room. In reality it had more to do with the substance of her remarks and the force with which she expressed them. 'As regards the Strategic Defense Initiative,' she told Reagan, raising the subject anyway, 'I hope that I [am] able to explain to you clearly my preoccupation with the need not to weaken our efforts to consolidate support in Britain for the deployment of cruise and for the modernization of Trident by giving the impression that a future without nuclear weapons is near at hand. We must continue to make the case for deterrence based on nuclear weapons for several years to come.'[16]

'Bud, you know, she's really missing the point,' Reagan exclaimed to McFarlane afterwards. 'And she's doing us a lot of damage with all this sniping about it.' Reagan, as his diary records, still believed in 'the friendship between our two countries & with the PM.' But it was clear from the exchanges with Thatcher that his patience was stretched thin. 'Continued Alliance solidarity,' he warned her, 'is vital to induce the Soviets to negotiate seriously.'[17]

In the end it was the foreign secretary, not the prime minister, who proved to be the British straw that broke the American camel's back. Geoffrey Howe had expressed himself 'dismayed' by the hawkish tone of Thatcher's congressional speech, the writing of which the prime minister had kept within her own tight circle. A few weeks later, on 15 March, Howe presented his own strategic vision in a speech at the Royal United Services Institute in London. Howe was not a charismatic speaker. Debating with this 'tedious and tendentious' character, said his opposite number, Denis Healey, was 'like being savaged by a dead sheep'. However, on this occasion, as in his later resignation speech in 1990, the very understatement of his delivery made the thrust of an attack all the more effective.[18]

Howe began with the 'Camp David accords', agreed between Reagan and Thatcher in December 1984, which established that research into defensive systems was permitted by the ABM Treaty. But like all research systems, Howe continued, these raised as many questions as they answered. What would happen if and when 'decisions are required on moving from the research to the development stage?' Would the technology 'actually work'? Would it (as the veteran US arms control expert Paul Nitze had asked) 'provide defences that not only worked but were sensible and cost-effective? And would NATO security 'be enhanced as a result of defensive deployment?'

In pressing home his point, Howe then delivered a line that was a gift to opponents everywhere. 'There would be no advantage,' the foreign secretary warned, 'in creating a new Maginot Line of the twenty-first century in space.' It was a devastating historical analogy: the president's new defensive 'shield' might be as useless as the vast wall that had failed to stop the Nazis' advance through France in 1940.

Howe's critique provoked, in his own words, 'a transatlantic explosion'. *The Washington Post* reported 'considerable concern' within the Reagan administration about the speech, which was 'the most comprehensive list of questions and concerns about the initiative voiced publicly by any allied official.' Even so, no one could have predicted the verbal ferocity of the US response.[19]

A week later, the administration eviscerated Howe. The beating was handed out by one of the fiercest political pugilists – Richard Perle, assistant secretary of defense. Perle was admired and loathed in equal measure in Washington. A brilliant defence analyst and political strategist, he was dubbed 'the prince of darkness' by those who despised his Machiavellian ways and feared he lacked any sense of potential nuclear apocalypse. Throughout the 1970s, as a staffer to the conservative Democratic senator Henry 'Scoop' Jackson, he had marked himself out as the bête noire of Henry Kissinger and the policy of détente. Now installed in the Department of Defense, working for a Secretary in Weinberger who lacked expertise in the area, Perle had arms control to himself. His policy objective was clear, noted a colleague: 'He thinks that we should run an arms race with the Russians and win.'[20]

For maximum effect, Perle launched his assault on Howe not in Washington, but during a visit to London, where he was addressing a conference on 'Communism and Liberal Democracy'. He began with a personal insult, observing that Howe's policy speech 'proved again an axiom of geometry, that length is no substitute for depth.' His analysis of the substance of Howe's argument was no less brutal. 'In a mere 27 pages,' Perle continued, the foreign secretary had 'succeeded in rewriting the recent history of the Soviet-American relationship, rendering it unrecognizable to anyone who has charted its course.' He accused Howe of 'mistaking the unfulfilled promise' of the 1972 US-Soviet treaty limiting anti-missile defences 'with the reality that followed,' and of a 'tendentious and obliquely declaratory manner' in questioning the president's Strategic Defense Initiative. Perle continued: 'In what may earn its place as the understatement of 1985 on the unrelenting buildup of Soviet nuclear forces, Sir Geoffrey observes that Russia's "historical experience has inclined them towards overinsurance." Even in this city of Lloyd's [the world's leading insurance market], I find the concept of insurance a less than persuasive description of the Soviet strategic nuclear buildup.'[21]

Perle's onslaught was remarkable coming from Britain's closest ally. Foreign Office mandarins admitted that they could not recall any similar instance in which a US official of Perle's rank had publicly rebuked a British foreign secretary in such a way. 'It's certainly not the kind of thing that happens every day,' observed one member of the diplomatic service. In Washington, Perle was frequently at odds with the State Department, not least his opposite number, Richard Burt, who often would not even speak to him. On this occasion, however, both Defense and State spoke with one voice. The day after Perle's speech, Ambassador Charles Price reinforced its message by calling on Howe at the Foreign Office, where he 'cocked an eyebrow' at the foreign secretary. There should be no mistaking, the ambassador warned, the anger and bewilderment felt in Washington about why, with new arms talks beginning in Geneva, Britain had chosen this time to embarrass the president by undermining SDI so publicly. The foreign secretary had brought this rebuke upon himself.[22]

Margaret Thatcher's motives and behaviour during this incident were, at best, mixed. Howe had followed the principle of collective responsibility to the letter by sending his speech in advance to the private offices of the prime minister and the defence secretary for comment. Heseltine's office had approved it. A day before the speech was due to be given – 'to our slight surprise,' said Howe – word came from Charles Powell at No. 10 that the prime minister 'had seen and approved' the text. All of which makes it difficult to explain why afterwards she was reported to be furious with her foreign secretary, and even phoned the White House to apologise to the president. Thatcher told Reagan that she had not been given sight of the speech before it was delivered – a statement of fact contradicted by Powell's letter to Howe.

Gossip flashed around Whitehall about what might have happened. Some said that the prime minister, while on a long international flight, had fallen asleep with the 'red box' of official papers on her lap, meaning the speech had gone unread. Others suggested this was not the stuff of which the Iron Lady was made. It had in fact been Charles Powell who had nodded off. 'We all have our bad moments,' the private secretary reflected, 'and that was one of mine.' Either way someone had fallen asleep on the job.[23]

As an explanation, it did not seem to stand up. In reality, Howe had been offered up as a patsy. Despite Thatcher's subsequent 'fury', the foreign secretary had expressed in public many of the concerns that she shared in private. She may have been taken aback by the strength of the US reaction, and embarrassed by the rebuke from Perle, but this did not stop her from continuing to harass the Americans on the very questions raised by her hapless foreign secretary. 'Now, Bud,' she badgered McFarlane only weeks afterwards at a summit in Bonn, 'are you keeping SDI under appropriate restraint, adhering to the ABM treaty and so forth?' If Perle's rebuke had been meant as a warning to the British to quieten down, then much to the exasperation of the White House, it had failed.[24]

Thatcher returned to Washington in July 1985 for an arms control seminar. There she delivered a critique of American nuclear strategy that was as damning in its own way as Howe's speech had been. Only this time it was delivered with greater verve, in Thatcher's trademark style. The president, the secretaries of state and defense, the chief of staff, the national security adviser and assorted top-level officials had to sit in silence as the prime minister lectured them. Reagan had begun with a warm welcome, and invited Thatcher to say a few words to open. Once started, she did not stop, expanding on the theme of her February speech to Congress that nuclear deterrence was the only effective way to keep the peace.

As the torrent of argument flowed, Kenneth Adelman, the director of the Arms Control and Disarmament Agency, passed a note to the chief of staff, Don Regan. 'Thatcher loves the bomb,' it said bluntly. Later Adelman recalled, 'She said it many, many different ways. Her point was that all this talk surrounding SDI was delegitimizing nuclear weapons and basically taking away any kind of justification for the presence of nuclear weapons in Europe, or anywhere around the world to protect Western Europe.' Adelman himself was a hard-liner on the nuclear deterrent, but even he grew weary as 'she went on and on in that vein.' Frustrated members of the administration attempted to interrupt the prime minister. She was having none of it. 'Several of us tried to get into the act,' reflected Adelman wearily, but 'she said "Let me make one more point" when we held up our fingers or did whatever one does in a situation like that.'[25]

When the seminar was over, the American team trooped away, not knowing whether to be amused or annoyed. 'I walked out with Reagan afterwards,' recalled Adelman, 'and Reagan said to me, "Boy, she's a great talker, she's not a great listener".' The president explained his tactics for dealing with Thatcher to his personal aide, James Kuhn. 'She's a woman and she had a lot she wanted to say,' Reagan told him, 'and I just thought I would let her do that.'[26]

For most of the meeting Reagan had kept his habitual good humour without engaging Thatcher directly. But in the end he was the one who delivered the put-down that brought Thatcher to a juddering halt. The prime minister kept up her line that even with SDI, it would be foolhardy to abandon nuclear deterrence. 'If you follow that logic to its implied conclusion,' she scolded the president, 'and do get rid of nuclear weapons, you expose a dramatic conventional imbalance, do you not? And would we not have to restore that balance at considerable expense?'

Reagan looked her straight in the eye and replied, 'Yes, that's exactly what I imagined.'

For the first time it seemed in hours, Thatcher stopped talking. Even with her thick skin, impervious as she was to criticism or embarrassment, the prime minister understood that she had gone too far. Around the table, nobody moved as Reagan maintained eye contact. 'It was a rather awkward silence there while both sides absorbed the weight of just what had been exchanged,' recalled McFarlane. 'I think the staffs of both sides agreed that this had better never get out.'

Once Thatcher had returned to the British Embassy, McFarlane went to see her there to make it clear that Britain had reached a crossroads. Reagan was planning a superpower summit in the autumn with the new Soviet leader, Mikhail Gorbachev. As Thatcher had seen for herself that day in Congress, this move was attracting criticism from hard-liners in the Republican Party. Even some within the administration feared that the president might be going 'soft' on Communism. If Thatcher spoke in public the way she had just addressed Reagan in private, it would do huge damage. 'He had problems with his own White House staff,' recalled Max Kampelman, the chief US arms negotiator in Geneva, 'he had problems with his friends and he had problems with the right wing of the Republican Party'. The fact that Thatcher had been the first to identify Gorbachev as a man the West could 'do business with' had provided Reagan with good cover: if the Iron Lady approved, then the new Soviet leader must be worth talking to. But, McFarlane warned, if Thatcher now chose to say that the president's nuclear strategy was a sell-out, the results would be disastrous for the president, and in turn for the Anglo-American relationship.

'It was very good of you to come up to the embassy . . . for a talk,' Thatcher wrote to McFarlane afterwards, 'and I found it extremely useful. I shall of course treat what you said with the greatest possible discretion.' McFarlane replied that he had given 'the president a full report on our discussions and he, like I, found your comments very thoughtful.'[27]

The correspondence was unusually oblique. On Thatcher's side, it established the fact that the talk had been 'useful' and that 'the greatest possible discretion' was required. That sense of circumspection was reinforced by the complaint to McFarlane by one of his senior staffers, Peter Sommer, that 'I am not aware of the details of your meeting'.[28] McFarlane in his own note to Thatcher made sure to make it clear that he had reported their conversation back to the president. Even the word 'thoughtful' seems unusual.

In truth, McFarlane had bought Thatcher's silence. After her meeting at the embassy, and another with him in London, Thatcher kept quiet about her reservations on SDI and nuclear disarmament. She was careful not to criticise the president before his meeting with Gorbachev at the Geneva summit in November. The reason why became clear two weeks later. On 6 December 1985, Britain became the first ally to sign an agreement to participate in SDI research. The UK Ministry of Defence predicted (wrongly as it turned out) that the contract would be worth a billion pounds. These were the hard-nosed realities even of a special relationship, a fact that the prime minister understood only too well. It was an aspect of her success as a politician that many often overlooked. At heart, Thatcher was a realist. 'Whilst she was principled and idealistic,' observed her friend and adviser Tim Bell, 'she was also intensely pragmatic.'[29]

That pragmatism was an unspoken assumption in relations with

Reagan. Thatcher understood that Britain as the junior partner could only push disagreement so far, and that she should eventually take what money there was on the table. Better to stick with the president than twist and bust.

Villa Fleur d'Eau, Geneva. Tuesday, 19 November 1985. The president's security team had been advised that the Soviet general secretary, Mikhail Gorbachev, was on his way. Standing around uneasily in the entrance of this beautiful château on the banks of Lake Geneva, officials exchanged nervous glances. This president seemed not to be the same character who would cheerfully wait for Thatcher in his golf buggy. He looked old, even shaky, huddled in a big overcoat. 'What we all feared about Geneva was that here was the man who was seventy-five years old and Gorbachev was a generation younger,' recalled Ken Adelman, the US arms control negotiator. 'It's one thing dealing with Thatcher, and Kohl and Mitterrand: it's a different thing being at a superpower summit. There hadn't been a summit for seven years. There is now going to be a summit with Gorbachev, and it was an order of magnitude difference. We were very afraid that Reagan wouldn't pull it off.'[30]

The president was usually the master of tense situations, always knowing how to break the atmosphere with a joke or an anecdote. Today he was strangely quiet, more concerned to follow the instructions left for him in a personal note by the young son of the Aga Khan, who had lent this house for the summit. 'Please feed the goldfish,' the boy had asked. Which was exactly what the president was now doing.[31]

Only when the key moment finally arrived did old Hollywood instincts kick in. Hatless and now coatless despite the bitter cold, Reagan bounded out onto the terrace, hand outstretched and smiling broadly. When Gorbachev emerged from his black limousine, wrapped up against the cold in an overcoat, thick scarf and hat, the Russian knew instantly that he had lost the first propaganda battle. Reagan, sleek, handsome and relaxed, seemed the younger man, despite being twenty years older. The Soviet leader reacted to the situation by whipping off his fedora, which only served to emphasise that the president also had a better head of hair. Gorbachev's humiliation was completed when a gust of wind caught his own remaining tufts of hair and stood them on end, forcing the general secretary awkwardly to pat them down. Round one to Reagan.[32]

Gorbachev's aides were furious at the PR disaster. The Americans were exultant. This was the first meeting between a US president and a Soviet leader since Jimmy Carter and Leonid Brezhnev in June 1979. That year the Soviets had organised the entire schedule to keep the media from seeing the extreme frailty of Brezhnev. This time they had hoped to capitalise on having the younger man. Instead, recalled Adelman, 'Reagan comes down the stairs like he's a Labrador retriever. They talk for a minute . . . Obviously they don't speak each other's language but it's kind of like, "You have no coat on, I have a coat on," which absolutely emphasized, as everybody could physically see, "You're chicken shit".'[33]

For all the one-upmanship and nerves on each side, this meeting was an historic moment. Geneva was the summit that would come to symbolise the beginning of the end of the cold war.

Reagan recognised something fresh in Gorbachev. 'As we shook hands for the first time,' he said afterwards, 'I had to admit – as Margaret Thatcher . . . predicted I would – that there was something likable about Gorbachev. There was a warmth in his face and his style, not the coldness bordering on hatred I'd seen in most senior Soviet officials I'd met until then.'[34]

That did not mean that the discussions were not tough, especially when they got onto the Strategic Defense Initiative. Gorbachev denounced this 'primitive approach' to East–West relations. Inevitably, it would lead to 'an arms race in space'. If Reagan went ahead, the Soviet leader warned, 'we will build up in order to smash your shield.' Gorbachev's assault was delivered with verbal passion and physical energy. Not to be outdone, Reagan responded with equal intensity. 'SDI is my idea,' he declared. 'If a defensive system is found, we would prefer to sit down and get rid of nuclear weapons and, with them, the threat of war.'[35]

It looked, said Gorbachev on reviewing the transcripts many years later, like the 'No.1 Communist' and the 'No.1 Imperialist' trying 'to out-argue each other'. The turning point between the two men came when they took a stroll in the grounds together out to the pool house. As Reagan spoke passionately about SDI and his dream of a nuclear-free world, Gorbachev came to recognise, he later said, that the president was sincere 'on a human level'. That facilitated an agreement to accelerate arms control talks on intermediate-range nuclear forces (INF). It also made a further summit possible. Officials had expected to spend months negotiating another meeting, but when the two leaders breezed in from their talk, Reagan announced that they had already agreed to rendezvous together again in 1986. 'You could almost get to like the guy,' Reagan told his staff afterwards.[36]

The Geneva summit produced a number of significant results. Airline services between the two countries were resumed, with new cooperative measures implemented in the North Pacific to avoid another disaster like the shooting down of Korean Airlines flight KE007. Cultural and education projects, suspended by the Carter administration in the wake of the 1979 Soviet invasion of Afghanistan, were now restored and expanded. On nuclear weapons, there was some closing of the gap between American and Soviet positions. Gorbachev agreed to a 50 per cent reduction of strategic nuclear weapons. In turn, Reagan modified his position on INF, moving away from an earlier insistence on total elimination. Furthermore, each leader acknowledged 'that a nuclear war cannot be won and must never be fought'. Both sides claimed this last point as a diplomatic victory – the Soviets because it addressed fears that had convulsed them since the 1983 *Able Archer* war scare; the US because, said NSC staffer Jack Matlock, 'Soviet negotiators accepted for the first time a flat, non-ideological statement'. But perhaps the most important outcome at Geneva was the public declaration that momentum would be maintained. Both leaders committed to meeting 'on a regular basis' and to 'intensify dialogue' on all levels.[37]

From Geneva, Reagan flew straight to Brussels to brief allied leaders at NATO on the summit. To a degree this gesture towards partnership was a reaction to Thatcher's constant refrain, made most forcefully at Camp David the previous year, that the allies must be consulted about negotiations with the Soviets.[38]

The president's session at NATO was conducted amid great elation, with compliments and jokes flowing from all sides. Reagan praised member governments as having been instrumental in helping the United States and him personally to prepare for the Geneva meeting. 'NATO can rightfully claim part of the credit for the talks' success,' Reagan told them. They had all taken 'an important step forward' in constructing a basis for stable and constructive East–West relations. 'All in all,' he concluded, 'the Geneva talks produced more results than many had anticipated. The atmosphere was cordial. [I] believe that Mr Gorbachev knows as I do that progress in US-Soviet relations would be a benefit to all the world.'

In the open session NATO leaders queued up to congratulate the president and hail the beginning of a new era. Chancellor Helmut Kohl of West Germany said that people 'could only imagine' how good he felt today 'because of the positive results which President Reagan had brought back from Geneva.' Progress at the summit 'was important for everyone'. Canadian prime minister Brian Mulroney said that the president had 'reestablished many simple but powerful truths'. The president could return to the United States 'with the respect and admiration of the Alliance, to which he had given true leadership.' The Danes, the Italians and the Dutch echoed those sentiments. And so it went on with encomium after encomium, each responded to by the president with confidence, grace and humour.

Only Margaret Thatcher failed to share in the mood. The prime minister had agreed with McFarlane that she would not criticise the president. Instead, she damned him with faint praise. When it came to her turn to address Reagan at NATO, her comments were flat and sour.

She began with tepid congratulations for making progress 'on far more things than had been generally expected.' But then her tone became increasingly sharp. The West, she said, should follow Reagan's public lead in describing the meeting positively, but should not be 'euphoric' about it. 'We should not build exaggerated public expectations which prove difficult to fulfil when the real nitty-gritty of agreements is being worked out,' she warned. 'The presentation and style of the Soviet leadership have changed but the substance appears the same.' Based on Gorbachev's comments about SDI, she predicted that the Soviets would 'continue a major propaganda effort against SDI in the coming year by promising radical weapons reductions in return for giving up SDI'. The West 'must resist such a campaign, counter Soviet propaganda, and support the President in his efforts.' As a final jab, Thatcher could not resist a pointed reminder about deploying SDI. She was 'very pleased to hear that the United States would continue to abide by the ABM Treaty and planned to respect the SALT II Agreement'. After all, it was vital 'in an uncertain world' that 'the two great powers observed existing arms control treaties.'

Thatcher's remarks were surprisingly ungracious. Reagan's reaction gave away his disappointment. Where his previous responses had been upbeat, warm and personal, now with Thatcher he was bland and generic. He simply thanked the prime minister for her words and said the United States needed all the help and support possible from its allies. Then he invited the next question.[39] The British prime minister may well have played matchmaker to Ronald Reagan and Mikhail Gorbachev. Only now did she realise that this meant the president might have a new 'best friend'.

9

The Day the Earth Shook

By the mid-1980s, Britain had discovered a new TV celebrity pundit. The BBC's John Cole, owlish behind his thick spectacles and with a strong Belfast accent, made an unlikely Voice of the Establishment. Yet the public seemed to enjoy his wry tone and deep love of politics, which he communicated with the enthusiasm of a commentator at the FA Cup Final. Among his most lasting contributions was to popularise what soon became among the most ubiquitous quotation in British politics. Peering into the camera from a windswept College Green, framed in his trademark herringbone coat by the Houses of Parliament, Cole would remind everyone that Harold Macmillan had got it right all those years ago. What did Macmillan fear most? 'Events, dear boy, *events*.'

Running true to form, it was unexpected events in 1986 that had brought Margaret Thatcher to the worst crisis of her second term. The issue at hand seemed anodyne enough, but it had enveloped the government in accusations of conspiracy and deceit. At the end of 1985, Britain's only helicopter firm, Westland Aerospace, had been on the verge of collapse. United Technologies, the American firm that ran Sikorsky helicopters, put a rescue bid on the table. The British defence secretary, Michael Heseltine, was not hostile to Anglo-American defence collaboration – indeed he had been pushing to intensify it through SDI. But he was also an advocate of the need for European cooperation in defence projects to counterbalance American technological dominance. Heseltine cobbled together a last-minute European bid for the company. But the Westland board opted to accept Sikorsky. Once they had made their decision, Thatcher supported them. The rest of the cabinet got into step, leaving Heseltine to resign on 9 January 1986 while muttering about dark goings-on behind the scenes. Two weeks later, the home secretary, Leon Brittan, resigned after admitting that he had leaked official government papers to undermine Heseltine's position. The question then became whether Brittan had authorised the leak at the behest of the prime minister.

The atmosphere in the lobby of the House of Commons on 27 January was tense and grave ahead of an emergency debate on Westland. But in the MPs' dining room, parliamentarians could barely conceal their excitement at the drama of the whole occasion. Alan Clark, a Thatcher acolyte, joined a table for lunch with fellow Conservative MPs Julian Amery and Robert Jackson. 'I say "with",' he recorded afterwards, 'but there was much jocularity at our end of the room, and shouting across from one table to another.' As they gossiped noisily, quaffing good Burgundy, they were joined 'unexpectedly' by the chief whip, John Biffen. He had a copy of the statement that the prime minister intended to make later that afternoon, which explained away the affair as 'a genuine difference in understanding between officials'.

'I read a few paragraphs,' wrote Clark, 'started a *faux-rire*. I couldn't help it. "I'm sorry, John. I simply can't keep a straight face" . . . How *can* she say these things without faltering? But she did. Kept her nerve beautifully.'[1]

Thatcher may have kept her nerve, but she was badly wounded by the Westland affair. It had shown her contempt of and impatience with colleagues, a willingness to use the dark arts to undermine those who disagreed with her and, in the departure of Brittan, a ruthlessness in cutting loose someone who had loyally served her. Moreover, she had shaken the faith of those MPs who had entered the House of Commons on her coattails at the 1983 election. 'Many of them are inexperienced and afraid of gunfire and run for cover when they hear it,' complained one of their number, Nicholas Soames, who was Churchill's grandson. But as his interlocutor, the journalist Woodrow Wyatt, noted slyly, 'He didn't sound very robustly behind her either.' It was a long way off, but the seeds of Thatcher's eventual destruction had been sown. Michael Heseltine's leadership challenge in 1990 would see her forced tearfully from office, brought down by a fatal combination of conspiracy and 'events'.[2]

Thatcher was extremely low as Westland unfolded. When her favourite speechwriter, Ronnie Millar, visited her on the day of the emergency debate, she told him frankly that she might not be prime minister by six o'clock that evening. In the middle of all this crisis came a phone call from Ronald Reagan, which must have inspired in Thatcher feelings of gratitude tinged with embarrassment. Afterwards the president wrote, 'She's being rousted around by the parliament & her integrity challenged – the first time ever that has happened. I told her I just thought she needed to hear a friendly voice.'[3]

The phone call was a thoughtful touch, not least because Reagan was aware that the Westland affair had brought his own relationship with Thatcher into sharp relief. For at the heart of this crisis for most commentators was a 'Europe v. America' tug of love. 'The Westland helicopter row is intrinsically unimportant,' judged *The Times*. 'And yet, for better or worse, it has become a symbolic test case involving not just the standing and careers of Messrs Leon Brittan and Michael Heseltine but [one] of the most important and emotive issues of contemporary British politics – Europeanism versus the Atlantic "special relationship".'[4]

Certainly it is true that Heseltine had come to see the future of Westland in such a way. He was an instinctive European and as defence secretary had enthusiastically backed a number of high-profile European initiatives, including the European policy group within NATO, the revival of the Western European Union, and the European Fighter Aircraft (EFA). Any reservations he had about transatlantic cooperation were not helped by his poor personal relationship with the US secretary of defense, Caspar Weinberger, although these concerns were put to one side to sign what seemed a lucrative agreement on SDI technology.

While ideology had played a part in Heseltine's thinking, Thatcher's own response was more practical. The Sikorsky Sea

King helicopter, which had been hugely successful during the Falklands War, was made under licence by Westland. Much of the original system design for the Sea King had been developed by Westland in Britain, which made it an important weapon for the UK military. Sikorsky were interested in a rescue deal for Westland precisely because there was already synergy between the two companies and the Americans valued the British technological expertise. The European consortium, on the other hand, seemed only to be interested in Westland making 'bits' of helicopters, meaning that the technology would be lost to Britain. Moreover, there were concerns that Aérospatiale, the French company leading the European consortium, was planning to sack thousands of its own workers, thus making it an unstable partner for Westland.[5]

Aside from the short-term factors in favour of Sikorsky – Thatcher believed it was the better deal for Westland and for Britain – there were also longer-term implications for the future of the British defence industry that went way beyond a prestigious but small-scale helicopter firm. American defence contracts, as Thatcher had demonstrated over SDI, were highly prized. For all the talk of European cooperation, the competition for US contracts among allies was ferocious. Even if the prime minister had a direct line to the president, it was by no means a given that Britain would get what it wanted. Thatcher had felt this keenly in the months leading up to the Westland controversy when a highly lucrative contract for a battlefield communication system was awarded to France, not Britain.

Thatcher had spoken to Reagan personally about the matter on several occasions in 1985 and, Peter Sommer reported, had 'leaned hard on the president for the US to buy the British MSE [mobile subscription equipment].' Thatcher had told him the British system was 'a good system, and unlike the competing French system, is compatible with NATO standards.' She had also added that 'the sale is important because [we] need to find the money for Trident.' Reagan had assured her that 'the decision would be based entirely on the technical superiority of the system chosen.' In that case, Thatcher told him, 'We will get it.'[6]

Whatever Reagan's assurances and Thatcher's confidence, the

contract was in fact awarded to the cheaper French bid. McFarlane had even told the president that 'the UK system does indeed exhibit superior performance' while 'the French competitor has poor performance'. When a 'saddened' Reagan wrote to Thatcher on 4 November to inform her of the decision, he explicitly made a promise, despite this most recent failure, of future closer co-operation. 'We will renew our efforts to integrate UK firms and capabilities into our SDI program, and indeed into our defense requirements more generally,' he told her. 'We will look for ways to share our technological assets with you within the constraints of special bilateral agreements on sensitive technologies that we both hope will allow the UK to assume more rapidly a position of technological leadership in its various European cooperative development programs. We will be in contact with you in regard to both approaches in the near future.'[7]

This letter of 4 November 1985 coincided with the moment that the row over Westland came into the public domain. It was just one more reason, and a multi-million-dollar one at that, why Thatcher was determined to go with Sikorsky.[8]

Westland had brought renewed accusations that Margaret Thatcher was too willing to fall into line behind President Reagan. Ironically, this coincided with a period of intense irritation in Washington over another issue on which Thatcher was seen to be displaying anything but solidarity. In time, however, the question of how to deal with Colonel Muammar Gaddafi of Libya would bring fresh criticism that Thatcher was, as *Private Eye* put it, nothing more than 'President Reagan's answering machine'.

On 27 December 1985, in simultaneous twin terrorist attacks at Rome and Vienna airports, gunmen had opened fire on passengers queuing at departure desks for Israel's national airline, El Al. Eighteen people, including five Americans, were killed and one hundred and twenty injured. Evidence soon emerged that the attacks had been masterminded by Abu Nidal, the leader of the Palestinian Fatah Revolutionary Council – the world's most feared terrorist organisation until the rise of al-Qaeda. Evidence was also produced to show that Nidal had been supported by the Libyan government.[9]

There had been frequent skirmishes between the United States and Libya since Reagan had taken office, beginning in August 1981, when two American F-14s shot down two Soviet-built SU-22s of the Libyan air force over the Gulf of Sidra. The incident was broadly welcomed in the US, only attracting controversy when it emerged that Ed Meese, counsellor to the president, had not bothered to wake Reagan to tell him about the encounter. By the time of the bombings during Christmas 1985, following earlier such attacks at Frankfurt's international airport and the nearby American air base, Reagan was more than awake to the growing threat of Libyan state-sponsored terrorism. 'We all feel we must do something,' he wrote in his diary, 'yet there are problems including thousands of Americans living and working in the mad clown's country.' On 7 January 1986, Reagan imposed economic sanctions, including bans on imports and exports (except food, clothing and medical supplies), on travel to or from Libya, and on loans and credits to Libya. Libyan assets in the United States were frozen. US citizens in Libya were ordered to leave. It was the clearest warning possible to Gaddafi. 'Now that the American oil workers were out of Libya,' recalled Reagan, 'I knew we had to do something about that crackpot in Tripoli.[10]

Having made the decision to impose sanctions, the administration immediately began to enlist the support of allies, including the British. On 8 January, Ambassador Price called on Geoffrey Howe at the Foreign Office to inform him about the US sanctions against Libya. Howe signalled that he could foresee no problem, and immediately after the meeting issued a broadly supportive statement, which drew attention to the restrictions Britain itself had put in place in 1984 following the killing of WPC Yvonne Fletcher outside the Libyan Embassy in London.[11]

Thatcher on the other hand was more concerned. This situation looked like Grenada all over again. Determined to speak up, she gave a press conference for American correspondents in London on 10 January at which her message was unmistakable. Time and again, the prime minister repeated the line that 'sanctions do not work.' Naturally, she wished 'in many ways that we could all get together against nations which have terrorist camps and practise terrorism and supply armaments to terrorists.'

But unilateral sanctions were not the way to achieve this. 'They only work if you go through the United Nations and get a Resolution and, even then, if everyone actually agrees to operate them.'

This was direct opposition to American policy on Libya, but Thatcher also took her opposition to the next level with a frank warning against any kind of military action. 'When it comes to retaliatory strikes,' she declared unambiguously, 'I must warn you that I do not believe in retaliatory strikes which are against international law . . . Once you start to go across borders, then I do not see an end to it and I uphold international law very firmly.'[12]

Thatcher followed up her strong words to the press with a direct letter to Reagan that was more reflective in tone but with a message that was understood in the White House. 'Mrs Thatcher has sent the president a letter condemning Libyan terrorism and noting Britain's long standing opposition to economic sanctions,' Peter Sommer wrote to John Poindexter, who was next after McFarlane through the revolving door that was the office of the national security adviser to President Reagan. 'She also makes nice noises about cooperating in the struggle against terrorism,' continued Sommer. However, he went on, 'The letter is perhaps more important for what it does not say. She makes no mention of her public remarks to the effect that international law prohibits punitive strikes against states that harbor terrorists. She does, however, subtly ask that "we remain in close touch as our thinking develops".' Thatcher expected no repeat of the lead-up to the invasion of Grenada.[13]

'It sounds to me,' summed up Bob Pearson, an NSC staffer, to Poindexter, 'as though the Brits have stiffed us completely.'[14]

The question was how to respond. Poindexter and Secretary Shultz agreed on a threefold approach to convey the administration's displeasure, involving a reply from the president, a high-level trip to London and a speech by the secretary of state. First came a letter from Reagan. His staff had thought it best 'in the light of the president's personal relationship with Mrs Thatcher [and] his style . . . the president's reply does not challenge her on this question.' Instead, he wrote more in disappointment than in anger. He thanked Thatcher for her 'assurance that Britain will not do anything to undercut our measures.' He then outlined his view that 'Gaddafi's repugnant acts are a moral issue that merit an exceptional approach.' Finally, he advised her that his deputy secretary of state, John Whitehead, had gone to London 'at my request' in order to explore 'ways we can work more effectively together to curb terrorism.' He would not hide that 'I am disappointed that Britain apparently is not prepared to take additional steps', but he promised that he would be 'staying in close touch' as she had requested.[15]

Whether it was a British oversight or a snub, Whitehead did not meet with Thatcher, but he was nevertheless able to report back that he had conveyed 'US "disappointed" that HMG not able to take additional steps.' This was accompanied by a broadside from the secretary of state on the claim that international law prohibited punitive or pre-emptive strikes. 'As you know,' Poindexter advised the president, 'George, without mentioning her by name, has publicly challenged this'.[16]

Shultz's speech at the National Defense University in Washington, DC, on 15 January 1986 may not have named Thatcher, but no one in the British government doubted that the secretary had the prime minister in his sights. 'There should be no confusion about the status of nations that sponsor terrorism against Americans and American property,' he announced. 'There is substantial legal authority for the view that a state which supports terrorist or subversive attacks against another state, or which supports or encourages terrorist planning and other activities within its own territory, is responsible for such attacks. Such conduct can amount to an ongoing armed aggression against the other state under international law.'

'Later,' Shultz wrote, 'Margaret Thatcher issued a blast at what I had said.'[17] Another transatlantic row seemed inevitable.

On Saturday, 5 April 1986, a terrorist bomb exploded in an American nightclub in Berlin, killing three people and injuring more than 200. Two of the dead were US Army personnel and sixty of the injured were American citizens. 'Our intelligence is pretty final that this bombing was the work of Gaddafi,' wrote

Ronald Reagan in his diary. He was presented with 'targets for retaliation' in order to deal with 'the villain'. On 8 April, Reagan sent personal messages to Margaret Thatcher and to President Mitterrand asking for permission for American F-111s to leave from a British base with overflights across France in a strike against Libya. Although A-6 and A-7 strike aircraft were available on carriers in the Gulf of Sidra, the F-111s were much more capable aircraft, with a bigger payload and greater accuracy.[18]

Thatcher was hosting a dinner at 10 Downing Street for President Chun Doo-hwan of South Korea when an official slipped her the letter from Reagan. It was general in tone, asking for permission to use the UK-based F-111s, but with no specifics about targets or timing. As luck would have it, both the foreign secretary, Geoffrey Howe, and the new defence secretary, George Younger, were attending the dinner. As soon as the South Korean president could decently be dispatched, the three sat down to hammer out an early response to Reagan's letter. For Howe and Thatcher it must have been uncomfortably reminiscent of the disastrous falling-out with America over Grenada. Yet in many ways their first response was almost identical to that of 1983: play for time. By 1 a.m., they had prepared an interim reply for the president asking him not to act precipitately. Thatcher wanted more information on the targets in Libya. She thought that US action might begin a cycle of revenge. She was worried that Gaddafi's standing would be strengthened. There were concerns about the implications for British hostages in Lebanon. Thatcher fully shared the American anguish over terrorist activities, but any response had to be in accordance with international law. This included the right to self-defence, which in her view did not include acts of retaliation.[19]

Many years afterwards, Thatcher would write that 'Looking back, I think that this initial response was probably too negative. Certainly the Americans thought so.' That was an understatement. Confronted once again, as over Grenada in 1983, by British hesitation, the White House dispatched the American UN ambassador, Vernon ('Dick') Walters, to London to read Thatcher the riot act. It was a shrewd choice. The son of a British immigrant to the United States, he had been educated by the Jesuits at Stonyhurst College in Lancashire, which had given him both an English sensibility and a ferocious intellectual capacity. Combined with his US military training, it made Walters a tough and clever adversary.

By the time General Walters arrived on 12 April, his job was already half done. Thatcher reluctantly saw that Reagan had backed her into a corner. He had sent a detailed response to the points she had raised. 'I have no illusion,' it read, 'that these actions will eliminate entirely the terrorist threat. But it will show that officially sponsored terrorist actions by a government – such as Libya has repeatedly perpetrated – will not be without cost.' The arguments themselves did not convince Thatcher. On 10 April, at a meeting of ministers and officials, Geoffrey Howe had put his finger on the nub of the problem that confronted them. 'We *all* started out from the premise that Margaret herself had publicly identified only three months before,' he wrote, 'that it would be very difficult to justify action of the kind proposed. But, now that the request had been made, the political difficulties in refusing it became equally apparent.' American frustration at having consulted and still getting a 'no' was palpable. A subsequent phone call with Reagan made it absolutely clear to Thatcher that the president was determined to strike with or without her.[20]

That Saturday, recalled Howe with characteristic understatement, Vernon Walters 'argued his case vigorously, as always.' It was a difficult meeting. Thatcher told Walters how 'appalled' she was that 'the gist of my exchanges with President Reagan was by now openly reported in the US press.' She expressed her reservations about the action and pressed Walters for the list of targets. 'I suspect that the General knew precisely which targets the US would hit by the time he came to see me.' It was not, however, information that Walters was prepared to share. Thatcher was at least reassured that the targets would be military, not civilian. 'By the end of the weekend,' Howe wrote of the Walters mission, 'the prime minister and her key secretaries of state (Foreign and Defence) were of one mind. The White House was told that we would allow US aircraft to fly from British bases for action consistent with the right of self-defence "against specific targets demonstrably involved in the conduct and support of terrorist activities".' But it was not done with enthusiasm. As Walters was leaving, he remarked to Thatcher, 'You know, prime minister, my normal job is US representative to the United Nations, and when I go back there, I'm going into the eye of the storm.' It was too much for Thatcher. 'General,' she shot back acidly, 'when I go back to the British electorate *I'm* going back into the eye of the storm.'[21]

On Monday, 14 April 1986, eighteen US Air Force F-111 bombers took off from RAF Lakenheath in Suffolk to attack three targets near Tripoli. Those targets were the military side of the Tripoli airport; a port section called Sidi Bilal, where Libyan commandos were trained; and the military barracks el-Azziziya. Overflight permission had been denied by the French government, with Mitterrand swayed by concerns about how participating in an attack on Gaddafi would affect the situation in Chad, where France and Libya were both enmeshed in the civil war. In a separate attack, fifteen A-6 and A-7 aircraft from the USS *Coral Sea* and USS *America*, the two US Navy aircraft carriers in the central Mediterranean, attacked two Libyan bases near Benghazi. A number of non-military buildings, including the French Embassy, were accidentally hit, resulting in around a dozen civilian deaths and further casualties. 'Thatcher is a murderer,' Gaddafi said. 'Thatcher is a prostitute. She sold herself to Reagan and now she has sold her country too.'[22]

Reagan had personally phoned Thatcher on Monday evening to tell her that the raid was about to begin. A few hours earlier, Thatcher had launched a book at the offices of the *Economist* on the great constitutionalist Walter Bagehot, edited by the former leader of the House of Commons, Norman St John Stevas (who had christened her 'The Blessed Margaret'). As she went in, someone remarked to her 'with some concern' how pale she looked. 'Since my complexion is never ruddy,' she recalled, 'I must have appeared like Banquo's ghost.'[23]

When news of the attack and the resulting civilian casualties came through, she looked more like Lady Macbeth. 'Television reports', she wrote, 'concentrated all but exclusively not on the strategic importance of the targets but on weeping mothers and children.' The backlash began immediately. 'The initial impact on public opinion in Britain, as elsewhere, was even worse that I had feared,' she remembered. 'I was depicted as cringing towards the US but callous towards their victims.'[24]

That judgement was shared by some members of her own government. The decision to allow use of British bases had been made by a small group of ministers. The full cabinet had not been consulted. The first that most ministers heard of the attack was when it was reported on the news. At the cabinet meeting on the morning after the raid, wounded pride and concern at the public reaction resulted in a stormy meeting. Of those ministers who had not been privy to the decision, only Viscount Hailsham, the Lord Chancellor, spoke in favour during a rambling disquisition on the special relationship and his American mother. Leading the charge against was Norman Tebbit, himself no bleeding-heart liberal, with heavyweight support from John Biffen, Nigel Lawson and Kenneth Baker. Thatcher was resilient, countering criticism by saying, 'We would have been in a much worse position if we had withheld our support.' Towards the end of the discussion, the chancellor of the exchequer, Nigel Lawson, ruefully said, 'The Americans owe you a lot for this.' Kenneth Baker had a different take. 'The Americans had jeopardized their own Latin American policy by helping us during the Falklands War,' he reflected. 'The fact was that Ronald Reagan had done Margaret a favour and she was now repaying him.'[25]

Thatcher admitted to her friend the columnist Woodrow Wyatt that she felt 'very lonely' during this period. She also believed her colleagues were a useless lot. 'As I go on in this job,' she told Wyatt, 'I sometimes think I can't go because who on earth is there to succeed me?'[26]

It was this latter sense of conviction that got Thatcher through the next difficult days. In Washington, Reagan basked in the glow of public approval. A *New York Times*–CBS News poll recorded that 77 per cent of the American people approved the strike on Libya. The same poll showed that support for Reagan's handling of foreign policy in general was up from 51 per cent the previous week to 76 per cent following the attack. In stark contrast, public opinion polls in the UK showed that two-thirds of the British population opposed Thatcher's actions over Libya. Many of her usual allies in the right-wing press were hostile. Even her own backbench MPs were deeply unhappy. 'People are worried,' commented one backbencher after Geoffrey Howe addressed a meeting of backbench MPs.[27]

Thatcher did not give an inch. 'The United States is our greatest ally,' she proclaimed from the dispatch box on 16 April. 'Terrorism exploits the natural reluctance of a free society to defend itself, in the last resort, with arms. Terrorism thrives on appeasement. Of course we shall continue to make every effort to defeat it by political means. But in this case that was not enough. The time had come for action. The United States took it. Its decision was justified, and, as friends and allies, we support it.'[28]

Before the debate, there had been speculation that Heathite enemies within Thatcher's own ranks – 'men grey in years and opinions' – hoped to use the parliamentary occasion to bring her down. 'As so often before, however,' reported *The Times* afterwards, 'she proved to be a lioness in a den of Daniels. Every criticism from the Opposition benches was turned away with remorseless logic; every hint of nervousness on the Tory benches was soothed away with painstaking explanation.'[29]

Certainly there were some embarrassing and high-profile swipes made at Thatcher during the debate. David Steel, the Liberal Party leader, told the PM that she had turned 'the British bulldog into a Reagan poodle.' Thatcher's hapless predecessor as Conservative leader, Edward Heath, reminded the House that when he had faced a similar request from President Nixon during the Yom Kippur War in 1973, he had refused permission. 'I cannot come to the conclusion that this action by the United States will destroy terrorism,' he said, 'nor do I believe that bombing cities is the right way to attempt to destroy terrorism.'[30]

Others came to a different judgement. 'Her refusal would have done immense damage to our relations with the Reagan Administration,' concluded David Owen, the Social Democratic Party leader and a former foreign secretary. 'She showed courage and loyalty, but she also demonstrated one of the distinguishing features of great leadership – the ability to turn a blind eye to instruction or to legal niceties and just to follow one's instincts.'[31]

Whatever the cost to Thatcher in the UK, Britain's support for the raid renewed her favoured status in the United States, where the *New York Times* now reported 'Anglophilia rules'. Certainly that was the case in the White House. 'PM Thatcher as always was right solidly behind us,' wrote Reagan in his diary, banishing all memories of recent conflicts over SDI and Grenada. That sense of solidarity was aided significantly by the fact that 'France was violently against us'.[32]

The contrast served Britain well. 'For the raid on Libya,' recalled Secretary of Defense Weinberger, 'we wanted to fly many of the bombers from England [via France] to Libya to participate in the raid. The English gave us permission immediately, and the French did not. As a result, we had to fly eight hundred miles out of the way, at night, in radio silence, and refuel three extra times, which I thought were very hazardous additions to the trip . . . The French were not cooperative.' To make matters worse, President Mitterrand had told Weinberger, while refusing permission, that the US should make the strike 'a real attack', not a 'pinprick'. The secretary was incensed. 'Very difficult,' he remembered. 'No, they were not helpful.'[33]

In reality, 'very difficult' might just as easily have initially applied to Thatcher, with her list of questions for the president and the set-to with Dick Walters. Yet in the end that was forgotten, because she had chosen to put aside her doubts in order to be helpful. Many were struck at the press conference on the night of the raid by the 'sickle-shaped' line Weinberger drew with his finger, which traced the flight path of the US planes that struck Libya. The head of the sickle was at Lakenheath air base in England. The base of its handle was in Tripoli. And the arc extended out into the Atlantic, bypassing France, Spain and Portugal, and heading down through Gibraltar to the Mediterranean. 'The Weinberger line divides the Atlantic alliance in two,' wrote Charles Krauthammer in *The Washington Post*. 'Margaret Thatcher chose our side of the line.' In the words of George Shultz, Thatcher 'had come through'.[34]

Having done so, Thatcher was immediately rewarded. A week

after the Libyan raid, the White House made clear that it was determined to enact a revised extradition treaty – which had been stuck in the Senate Foreign Relations Committee since the previous year – with Britain. The original treaty had been negotiated by John Jay, the first Chief Justice of the United States, in 1794. The difficulty with the current version, dating from 1972, was that it barred extradition of those who had committed political crimes. That meant, for example, that the IRA members who had attempted to assassinate Thatcher in Brighton in 1984 would not have met the grounds for extradition. The revised treaty aimed to prevent terrorists from seeking a safe haven in the United States by claiming their crimes were politically motivated. This was a change being opposed by some Democrats on the committee, and one maverick Republican, Jesse Helms of North Carolina.[35]

Reagan now took the unexpected step of making a direct personal plea to the US Senate to pass this revised treaty. Britain had recently shown that 'she is our staunchest ally in our battle against international terrorism,' the president reminded the senators. 'We need to stand tall with our British allies at this important moment.' Later, in his weekly radio broadcast, Reagan spelled out the same message. 'Rejection would be an affront to British prime minister Margaret Thatcher,' he said, 'one European leader who, at great political risk, stood shoulder to shoulder with us during our operations against Gaddafi's terrorists.' It was a point the British were happy to make for themselves. The Americans 'owe us one,' briefed an embassy staffer off the record. 'Although the comment raised a few eyebrows for its bluntness,' reported the Washington correspondent for *The Times*, 'it reflected a sentiment not unshared here.'[36]

On 12 June 1986 the treaty, along with structural funds to support the Northern Ireland peace process, was voted out of the committee by 12 votes to 2. On 17 July, the treaty was ratified by the full Senate by 87 votes to 10. 'I called Margaret Thatcher, tracked her down at a dinner party,' Reagan noted in his diary. 'She's delighted.'[37]

Britain's support for the bombing of Libya had brought great kudos in the United States, and even a political reward in the revised extradition treaty. But it had also been a warning about the limitations of British influence in the White House. In January 1986 Thatcher had told Reagan of her reservations about a military response to terrorist activity. In April those warnings had been ignored. Thatcher then chose to execute a U-turn by giving precedence to the 'special relationship' over and above her belief that the best way to deal with terrorism was through international institutions. She had already fallen out with Reagan over Grenada and SDI. In the end, the prime minister had calculated that the potential damage to Anglo-American relations of withholding support for the attack on Libya was too great to risk. But it was no coincidence that immediately after the raid she used the Tokyo G-7 summit in May to win acceptance of a 'firm' British draft on terrorism and state-sponsored terrorism that brought the issue back into the fold of international cooperation rather than unilateral action.[38]

Libya had been a wake-up call for Thatcher. Within months she would have her faith – not just in Reagan, but in the very nature of the Atlantic Alliance – shaken again.

On Saturday, 11 October 1986, Ronald Reagan and Mikhail Gorbachev picked up where they had left off the previous year in Geneva. This time they were meeting at Reykjavik in Iceland. Gorbachev had proposed London or Reykjavik as a venue, and the Americans had plumped for the latter, perhaps on this occasion thinking that London would have had Mrs Thatcher too close for comfort. Nevertheless, the British made their presence felt in other ways. The meeting took place in Hofdi House, a bleak, isolated spot looking out towards the Icelandic fishing grounds. It had belonged to the British government until 1952, when the ambassador had persuaded the Foreign Office to sell on the grounds that it was haunted by a mysterious 'white lady' who regularly caused the pictures to fall off the walls. If the Iron Lady had been in the house in October 1986, the damage would have been considerably worse.

Reykjavik was meant to be an interim summit, but it very quickly turned into a full-blown one, with almost all the action taking place in one-on-one meetings between the two leaders, who were sometimes accompanied by their two foreign ministers.[39] Gorbachev began with a bold initiative, offering 50 per cent cuts in nuclear arsenals and an INF treaty. 'This is the best Soviet proposal we have received in 25 years,' the veteran arms negotiator Paul Nitze told the president during the first break. Strategic nuclear disarmament, zero INF in Europe, a comprehensive test ban treaty, on-site verification: 'He was laying gifts at our feet,' recalled Shultz.[40]

Alexander Bessmertnykh, one of only five members of the Soviet Defence Council, later confirmed that by 1986, Gorbachev 'understood that we did not have a chance of catching up with the United States.' The 'economic side of the arms race,' he thought, 'was very much on Gorbachev's mind' at Reykjavik. Gorbachev's foreign minister, Eduard Shevardnadze, put it even more bluntly. 'The point was to stop the arms race,' he recalled. 'Our country could not remain a militarized state.' According to Soviet estimates, 63 per cent of the money spent on machine building in 1986 was for military purposes. An extra $20 billion per annum had been committed to military spending. Marshal Sergey Akhromeyer, the chief of staff of the Soviet armed forces, recalled, 'The USSR was not able to continue the military confrontation with the USA and NATO. The economic possibilities for such a policy were exhausted.'[41]

The Soviet proposals at Reykjavik were just a beginning. As the talks continued, Reagan stunned everyone by setting an objective that was rooted in his own sense of the immorality of nuclear weapons. 'I think it would be very good,' he told Gorbachev, 'that by the end of [ten years], all nuclear explosive devices would be eliminated, including bombs, battlefield systems, cruise missiles, submarine weapons, intermediate-range, and so on.'

'We could say that,' responded Gorbachev simply.

In ten years' time, Reagan joked, they would meet again in Iceland. He would be very old by then and Gorbachev would not recognise him. 'The president would say, "Hello, Mikhail." And Gorbachev would say, "Ron, is it you?" And then they would destroy the last missiles.' It sounded like a movie script. But in a matter of seconds the two leaders had agreed in principle to eliminate their entire nuclear arsenals – and Britain's.

The sticking point to this extraordinary proposal was SDI. Gorbachev demanded a commitment that research would be confined to the laboratory; Reagan refused. 'It is a question of one word,' he implored the Soviet leader. 'This should not be turned down over a word.'

'If we say research and testing in laboratories, I could sign it,' Gorbachev responded. 'But if I went back and said that research, testing and development could go on outside the laboratory and the system could go ahead in ten years, I would be called a dummy and not a leader.'

'I'm asking you to change your mind as a favor to me,' Reagan appealed, 'so that hopefully we can go on and bring peace to the world.'

'I cannot do it,' Gorbachev told him. 'If we could agree to ban research in space, I would sign in two minutes.'[42]

Reagan passed a note to Shultz. 'Am I wrong?' it read. Shultz whispered back, 'No you're not'.[43] And with that, Reagan gathered up his papers and left. The summit was over.

Outside, the two men shook hands as limousines with engines running waited to depart.

'Well, Ron, I don't know what else we could have done,' Gorbachev said.

'You could have said yes,' Reagan replied. And he turned his back.[44]

Ronald Reagan only rarely displayed emotion over politics. His easygoing style and steady temperament meant that even the most tense political circumstances would not rattle him. The immediate aftermath of Reykjavik was different. James Kuhn, executive assistant to the president, recalled that 'I'd just never seen Ronald Reagan that way before, had never seen him with such a look. I mean he looked distraught to me.' Reagan's staff left him alone on the flight back to the United States, asking themselves, 'Is he going to be alright.' Reagan spent several hours by himself reflecting on what had happened. About halfway through the six-hour flight, he reappeared. 'I'm okay now,' he told his staff. 'I gave it a lot of thought. I know I made the right decision back there. We couldn't give up SDI, not for America's future. I made the right decision. I wasn't sure, but I know now I did.'[45]

Reagan would be criticised from the left for 'blowing' the best chance in a generation to end the cold-war hostility between Russia and the United States. Barney Frank, a Democratic congressman from Massachusetts, employed a mixed metaphor to make the point. The president, he said, was rejecting 'a bird in the hand for pie in the sky.' Others took a more nuanced view. 'The Reagan-Gorbachev meeting in Iceland should be judged by the immensity of the task,' wrote James Reston in the *New York Times*. 'Seldom have two leaders of divided nations tried to do so much in so short a time. Maybe this effort to negotiate the dangerous intricacies of the nuclear balance of power was a blunder. But it was not, as so many are now saying, a disaster. Everything was attempted without success, but nothing was irretrievably lost.'[46]

That was a view shared by many inside the administration. The United States and the Soviet Union had each seen where the other stood. 'As we all know, once you put your positions on the table, you can say, "I've withdrawn them," but they're not withdrawn,' noted George Shultz. 'They're there. We've seen your bottom line, and so we know where it is . . .' Moreover, as officials began poring over the notes from the meetings, they came to realise that the debate on SDI had masked another important factor. 'Gorbachev never accepted the idea of eliminating ballistic missiles, even as part of a package that included all strategic offensive weapons,' noted Jack Matlock, who had been in the room for some of the talks at Reykjavik. For all the talk of abolishing nuclear weapons, 'Gorbachev's refusal to ban ballistic missiles made the whole question moot.' It was no coincidence that only a few weeks after the summit, Reagan directed the administration to work on how best to press the Soviets on making the 'transition to a world without offensive ballistic missiles.'[47]

Others in the administration were less sanguine. Richard Perle, the hawkish assistant secretary of defense, thought Reykjavik showed in a 'very stark' way that the president 'was vulnerable to the view that the world would be better off without nuclear weapons'. Nuclear deterrence had been the foundation of US national security policy since the 1950s. In coming so close to abandoning that strategy, Reagan had convinced senior military figures that he had put the United States in peril. 'The chiefs thought they had dodged a bullet when Gorbachev insisted the price had to be SDI,' remembered Colin Powell, soon to be national security adviser. One of his staff, Nelson Ledsky, was more blunt. 'Reykjavik scared everyone,' he recalled. 'It was seen as scary proof that Ronald Reagan might do something terribly reckless.'[48]

Reagan believed in complete nuclear disarmament as a principled objective, but he also reckoned that the Soviet Union could no longer compete in the arms race. In refusing to give up SDI at Reykjavik, the president had effectively called Gorbachev's bluff. 'Ninety-nine per cent of the Russian people,' judged Genrikh Trofimenko, a high-ranking official from the Brezhnev era, 'believe that [America] won the cold war because of your president's insistence on SDI.' Before the summit, Gorbachev had often spoken of the president as a 'fool and a clown', who was unfit to lead a superpower. On his return, he angrily told the Politburo that Reagan was 'extremely primitive, has the looks of a troglodyte and exhibits mental incapacity.' But he soon stopped such trash talk. Asked many years later by George Shultz what he considered the turning point in the cold war, Gorbachev 'didn't hesitate one second' before replying, 'Reykjavik'.

Even a week after the summit, the Soviets understood that they had overplayed their hand on SDI. Shevardnadze dispatched a leading scientist to New York in November to give a lecture on how manned space stations were considered orbital laboratories. '"Modest" SDI testing called compatible with ABM pact,' stated the next day's *Washington Post*. The Soviets soon caved in altogether by taking SDI off the table. On 1 March 1987, Gorbachev announced that he was decoupling SDI from the INF negotiations. The following month he said he would do the same for short-range nuclear forces. In 1984, Gorbachev had used Thatcher as the messenger to tell Reagan to scrap SDI in return for progress on arms control. The two men had been engaged in high-stakes poker over the issue ever since. Now

Gorbachev had blinked. The summit at Reykjavik, concluded the senior US arms negotiator Ken Adelman, had turned out to be 'Reagan's finest moment'.[49]

This upbeat assessment was not one shared across the Atlantic. 'My own reaction,' recalled Margaret Thatcher, 'when I heard how far the Americans had been prepared to go was as if there had been an earthquake beneath my feet.' One cabinet minister, Michael Jopling, who was with the prime minister as she was briefed, 'never saw her more incandescent.' The implications of what had happened seemed devastatingly clear: the whole system of nuclear deterrence, 'which had kept the peace for forty years', was set to be abandoned. For Britain in particular, this would have meant killing off the Trident missile and buying a different system in order to maintain an independent nuclear deterrent. The president, said Geoffrey Howe, had come within an inch of 'falling into a Russian trap', in which 'we should have moved, via Reagan's dream of a nuclear-free world, into a nightmare world where notions of deterrence – the key to western defence policy for decades – had been suddenly discarded.'[50]

Howe recognised that 'one supreme irony' of the situation was that only Reagan's attachment to SDI – which the European allies distrusted – had saved the very basis of western strategic deterrence. Irony was never part of Margaret Thatcher's make-up and she was certainly not prepared to entrust British defence policy to it. She still had a 'gnawing anxiety' that something similar could happen again. So in the course of a telephone call to the president the day after he returned from Reykjavik, she invited herself to Washington for talks. Helmut Kohl, the furious German chancellor, would do the same. For Thatcher it would mean a fourteen-hour round trip for a three-hour meeting with the president – such was the lot of a junior partner – but it was an inconvenience she was willing to endure. 'Somehow,' she said, 'I had to get the Americans back onto the firm ground of a credible policy of nuclear deterrence.'[51]

'She believed in being a candid friend,' reflected her press secretary Bernard Ingham, 'and when Mrs Thatcher is candid, she can be *really* candid.'[52]

★

After many years of dealing with Margaret Thatcher, the White House understood that she would need to be handled with some care after Reykjavik. This was not least because they recognised that her concerns were not just strategic: there was a large measure of politics involved. John Poindexter made this clear to the president in his briefing for Camp David. 'Mrs Thatcher is clearly coming to seek reassurances about Reykjavik,' he explained, 'in particular, that strategic reductions . . . will not undercut deterrence and will not overlook the conventional imbalance; and reassurances that our negotiating proposals will not put in question the UK Trident program and undermine her reelection chances.'[53]

It was these final sensitivities to a likely British general election in 1987, more than Thatcher's strategic concerns, that made the administration determined to give her something positive to take home from the visit. 'How we do it, however,' noted Poindexter, 'is a delicate matter.' After all, the last time Thatcher had come to Washington, she had lectured the president beyond endurance. Then there were the common statements likely to be produced mid-meeting from her handbag. '[We] have found that in most cases,' warned Poindexter, 'even with friends like Mrs Thatcher – that joint statements, which are frequently a compromise, do not serve our policy interests.'[54]

To help smooth the way, George Shultz visited Thatcher at the British Embassy in Washington before she helicoptered down to Camp David. Unlike many in the administration, including Caspar Weinberger and John Poindexter, Shultz was a firm supporter of the president's strategy at Reykjavik. He was also a wily political operator. 'What does Mrs. Thatcher want?' he had raised with the president. 'Generally to strengthen her pre-election position by bringing US and UK positions on arms control into harmony.' In order to do that, Shultz told Reagan, it would be necessary 'to indicate our strong support for Mrs. Thatcher and HMG [Her Majesty's Government] policies on defense, specifically nuclear modernization and increased expenditure on defense.' If this could be done, they would be able 'to ensure that she returns to London . . . reassured about the direction of our policies.'[55]

Once Shultz and Thatcher had discussed a common line to take, British and US officials began work on a statement to give to the press at Camp David. Afterwards, the British would claim that the language started with them, although in fact a draft of 'common press points' was already in Reagan's brief before the meeting. The trick, explained Rozanne Ridgway, the State Department official in the talks, was 'to produce a statement consistent with both US policy and positions at Reykjavik and affirmations of the validity of current nuclear policy of importance to her [the PM].' In fact, Ridgway advised, 'Mrs Thatcher's overriding focus will be British public perception of her performance at Camp David. Our interest is in assuring that the results of the meeting support a staunch friend and ally of the US.'[56]

When Thatcher arrived at Camp David at 10.45 am on 15 November, her arrival had all the *bonhomie* of her earlier visit in 1984. Reagan was there waiting to give her a peck on the cheek and to whisk her off again in his golf buggy to Aspen Lodge. In reality, the atmosphere was tense. In 1984, the president had still been on a high from his re-election; now he was reeling from the disappointment of Reykjavik and political troubles at home – the Republicans had lost control of the Senate in recent elections, leaving the Democrats in control of Congress, and a scandal involving arms sales to Iran was beginning to spiral. On top of this, here was Margaret Thatcher to give him a dressing-down. No wonder that even the usually amiable Reagan seemed in poor humour.

Unusually for such meetings, no note-takers accompanied the two principals as they met alone on this occasion. Whatever sentiments were exchanged, they were heard by no one and remained private. Afterwards, the two walked unaccompanied, still deep in conversation, from the Aspen to the Laurel Lodge. With Thatcher in high heels and camel-hair coat, and Reagan in a bomber jacket and boots, they seemed an incongruous pair. The body language looked awkward and incompatible. Yet it was clear to observers that something important had passed between them.

While the odd couple talked, staff from both sides were left anxiously hanging around. With the Americans preoccupied by their own political difficulties, the atmosphere was strained, not least because Reagan's team did not particularly like the prime minister. 'She was okay to deal with, but nothing from a staff point of view,' recalled James Kuhn, the president's personal aide. 'You could say hello and she would say hello back, but not that personable.' On this occasion, however, things warmed up when Thatcher and Reagan arrived at the Laurel Lodge for drinks before lunch. The PM cheerfully informed everyone that she had enjoyed a wonderful chat with the president. As usual, she produced a document from her handbag and announced that it contained what they had chosen she should say at her press conference afterwards. To the relief of American officials, it was the document that had been agreed in advance. Then, with great enthusiasm, Thatcher told everyone how she had just watched the president record his weekly five-minute radio address. Reagan chuckled appreciatively as she explained how it had been done in one take. Even in the aftermath of a difficult conversation with Thatcher, Reagan was nothing if not a professional.[57]

As if to demonstrate that all was well between them, Reagan also threw Thatcher a bone during the hour-long meeting that followed. It had been agreed that the two leaders would discuss the question of arms to Argentina. Reagan's talking points had suggested that he would say that although he knew 'this is a delicate subject', he was 'deeply concerned about democracy in Argentina'. The situation required 'the development of [a] security relationship' with the Alfonsin government. That would mean a 'return *sooner* rather than later' to the question of military aircraft for Argentina. Officials kept expecting the president to raise the subject, but as the minutes ticked by, it never came up. At the very end of the meeting, Thatcher looked down her list of topics, ticking them all off one by one. Then she stopped. 'Oh, arms to Argentina,' she said coquettishly. 'You won't, will you?' 'No,' replied Reagan, 'we won't.'[58]

Thatcher returned to the British Embassy in Washington for a press conference on the talks at Camp David in ebullient form, telling journalists that she had prepared 'a small statement' for them. 'Shall I read it,' she asked with a smile, 'and then you can cross-examine me on it.'

The prime minister then read out the statement that had been agreed in advance of Camp David. It noted that 'priority should be given to an INF agreement'; confirmed 'the need to press ahead with the SDI research programme'; observed that 'nuclear weapons cannot be dealt with in isolation, given the need for stable overall balance at all times'; and offered reassurance that all 'these matters should continue to be the subject of close consultation within the alliance'. For her audience at home, Thatcher gleefully reported that the president had 'reaffirmed the United States' intention to proceed with its strategic modernisation programme, including Trident,' as well as confirming 'his full support for the arrangements made to modernise Britain's independent nuclear deterrent with Trident.'

In case anyone thought she was flying solo, Thatcher ended with a comment accompanied by one of her famous concluding stern looks. 'May I make it quite clear,' she said, 'that the statement on arms control which I read out is an agreed statement between the President and myself.'[59] 'Thatcher Wins Reagan Pledge to Sell Trident,' read the headline the next day in the *Sunday Times*. 'I had reason to be well pleased,' the prime minister noted afterwards. Pleased, but not convinced: she would never forget that nuclear weapons remained the 'issue on which I knew I could not take the Reagan Administration's soundness for granted'.[60]

The White House was similarly delighted with the visit to Camp David, not least because Thatcher had signed up to the US statement drawn up in advance. But the Americans also had other reasons to be relieved.

After Thatcher finished making her statement at the British Embassy, she took questions from the press. The first American network to be called immediately moved away from arms control to the subject that was convulsing Washington. 'Can you give us your view of US policy on Iran, specifically . . . the delivery of arms to Iran,' asked the CBS reporter. 'Does that strike you as a wise policy?' The next US reporter to be called asked the same question with a more personal twist. 'Do you believe the president's actions,' asked the reporter from ABC, 'have in any way weakened the United States' ability to pursue a policy of not dealing with terrorists?'[61]

As Thatcher answered, she knew that the entire American political establishment was watching to see whether the president retained the trust of his self-styled closest ally.

On 13 November, before Thatcher had arrived in Washington, President Reagan had been forced to go on television to tell the nation that arms had been sold to Iran, although he denied that the weapons had bought the release of American hostages in Lebanon. The story had begun in a small Lebanese newspaper, *Al Shiraa*, which claimed that Bud McFarlane had offered Iran an arms deal involving Israel as an intermediary. An investigation by US Attorney-General Ed Meese soon found that the story was true, and discovered a new twist: the Israelis had also been used to divert money to anti-Communist forces in Latin America – the 'Contras' – to circumvent congressional rulings about such funding. At a meeting of the National Security Planning Group on 25 November, Meese would announce not only that White House staff had acted in a way that was contemptuous of the president – he had not been informed – but that the law had been broken.

When the press were told Reagan wrote in his diary, 'they were like a circle of sharks.' The story would engulf his presidency and almost take him under. 'The media looks like it's trying to create another Watergate,' admitted Reagan. That was because he had broken the law and might legitimately have been impeached. In the end, Reagan was saved by his decision to open everything up to scrutiny and a clever strategy to focus attention on the one aspect of the scandal that the president had known nothing about – turning over profits to the Contras from the sale of arms to Iran. The president would eventually escape with a congressional rap across the knuckles, but for a considerable period afterwards his popularity and credibility were shot through. He had been either culpable or asleep at the wheel. Neither state enhanced his reputation. Democrats could hardly believe their good fortune. Not only had they retaken Congress, but finally something had stuck to 'the Teflon president'. To many, it seemed as if this was the moment when the 'conservative revolution' had juddered to a halt.[62]

This was the context in which Margaret Thatcher faced questions from the press in Washington amid a frenzy of gossip and counter-gossip over the developing scandal.

Thatcher had first got wind of the US administration 'going rogue' the previous year. In December 1985, a few days after leaving his post as national security adviser, Bud McFarlane had flown to London to attend a meeting between an NSC aide, Lieutenant-Colonel Oliver North, and an Iranian arms dealer, Manucher Ghorbanifar. Had McFarlane still been national security adviser, then certain diplomatic niceties would have been afforded him. But with McFarlane now a private citizen, MI5 felt at liberty to bug his meeting at a Hilton hotel near Heathrow airport. Afterwards, a report was circulated to a small group of officials and ministers, including the prime minister.

Two months later, the incoming ambassador to the United States, Sir Antony Acland, accompanied by the prime minister's special adviser on foreign affairs, Sir Percy Cradock, used a courtesy call to John Poindexter at the White House to enquire gently whether America might be considering an arms-for-hostages deal in the Middle East. When they did not receive a denial, the British diplomats drew their own conclusions. Thereafter, ministers and officials steered well clear of the subject, presumably on the grounds that they did not want even the slightest association with a covert policy that could end in scandal. Even during the raid on Libya and at the G-7 summit in Tokyo at which terrorism was the first item on the agenda, the specific question of arms for hostages was not raised with the Americans. Certainly Thatcher did not tackle Reagan about it. Britain simply turned a blind eye, wanting neither a nod nor a wink on the subject from the White House.

When the story broke, with Thatcher in Washington, she followed a consistent line: play (up) the man, not the ball. This approach began in her first press conference. Thatcher made it clear that 'we pursue a policy of not delivering lethal weapons' to Iran. But for the president himself, there was unequivocal support. 'I believe implicitly,' she declared firmly, 'in the president's total integrity on that subject.'[63] It was an endorsement for which Reagan was grateful. 'Later in Wash. she did a press conference & went into bat for us,' he wrote in his diary. 'Most helpful.'[64]

Reagan recorded how he and Thatcher had discussed Iran-Contra at Camp David. This in fact was why they had met completely alone without note-takers. Reagan was not worried about a prime-ministerial tongue-lashing on Reykjavik. It was their discussion on the scandal that he did not want minuted. 'We cannot recall any previous meeting in which the president played such a direct role in the arrangements,' Peter Sommer noted to Poindexter. Thatcher had endured the Westland crisis only the previous year and might have had some practical advice to offer. No doubt she also helped to buck up the president's spirits with assurances of her personal support and regard. In truth, we cannot know what was said. But when she left the room, it was to come out fighting on behalf of the president.[65]

A few weeks after returning from Washington, by which time the Iran-Contra scandal was in full swing, Thatcher took the unusual step of writing a private note to the president in her own hand, which was delivered through back channels rather than the usual diplomatic route. It was among the most personal letters Thatcher ever wrote to him:

> The press and media are always so ready to criticise and get people down. I know what it's like. But your achievements in restoring America's pride and confidence and in giving the West the leadership it needs are far too substantial to suffer any lasting damage. The message I give to everyone is that anything which weakens you, weakens America; and anything that weakens America weakens the whole free world. Whatever happened over Iran is in the past and nothing can change it. I fervently believe that the message *now* should be that there is important work to be done and that YOU are going to do it. You will find great support for that over here in Europe – and I am sure in America too. If you would like to talk about the issues on which we need to press ahead, I hope that you will call me.[66]

It was an offer the president was happy to accept. 'A call to Margaret Thatcher to respond to her warm handwritten letter re our "Irangate",' Reagan wrote appreciatively in his diary after receiving the note. Thatcher's support had come at a very low moment for Reagan, when the president's appetite for being commander-in-chief seemed to have completely deserted him. 'I don't like Mondays,' he had written despondently that same week. Officials were so concerned at how withdrawn and confused Reagan often appeared that they quietly had papers drawn up to have him declared 'disoriented' and disabled under the Twenty-fifth Amendment.[67]

Shortly after the phone call from the White House, the prime minister's friend Woodrow Wyatt told her something that the former Labour leader, Hugh Gaitskell, had once said to him. 'Anybody can be loyal to me when I'm right,' Gaitskell had remarked. 'What I want is people who are loyal to me when I'm wrong.'[68] On this occasion it was a test Thatcher had passed in Washington.

10

A Thunderous Round of Applause

On 27 March 1987, with an election looming in Britain, Ronald Reagan got a glimpse of what life might be like without Margaret Thatcher in office. It would be fair to say that the alternative did not appeal. The twenty-minute visit to the Oval Office by the leader of the opposition, Neil Kinnock, immediately got off to a bad start when the president mistook one member of the Labour delegation for the British ambassador (they both had bushy eyebrows). This slip was an uncharacteristic discourtesy that transmitted broader contempt. 'It was a short meeting,' Reagan noted afterwards, 'but I managed to get in a lick or two about how counter productive "Labors" defense policy was in our dealings with the Soviets.'

'In all candor,' the president warned his visitors, 'Labor's position on defense issues would make it very difficult for any American administration to carry on as before.' Reagan was dishing out payback to Kinnock for a speech in New York beforehand that contained references to 'poodles', 'being led by the nose', and 'accepting the governorship of the 51st state.'

The Labour leader had gone to the White House hoping to burnish his global credentials. 'He, of course, wants his meeting with you to go well,' national security adviser Frank Carlucci advised the president, 'and to show that he, like Mrs Thatcher, is an important player in international affairs.' Secretary of State George Shultz concurred. 'What does Kinnock want?' he asked rhetorically of Reagan: 'To meet with the president as leader of the British Opposition and potential prime minister to demonstrate that he is a serious figure in international affairs.' Shultz advised 'an even handed approach' in order to 'deflect charges of favoritism and interference'. Nevertheless, it was vital that 'the British public understand' that Labour Party policy 'would involve serious consequences for the UK and the Alliance.'[1]

As the Labour delegation slunk out of the Oval Office, Reagan made sure to give them a kick for good measure. 'The President made clear that he had no intention of intervening in Britain's domestic affairs, but he said we disagree with Labor's defense policy,' the acting press secretary, Marlin Fitzwater, announced afterwards. For good measure, he repeated the president's language and pointed out that Labour's policy 'would undercut our negotiating position in Geneva.' In all, Kinnock's treatment in Washington was a noteworthy rebuke to the leader of a major political party of an important western European ally.[2]

Inevitably, the British press had a field day. Kinnock was reported to be 'stunned and dismayed' at the row in Washington. 'What happened there,' judged *The Times*, 'was that the administration, worried by any prospect of a British Government which sought to reverse the policies of nearly 40 years, deployed its big guns to answer back – in a manner which it thought might be permissible. Mr Kinnock has got his come-uppance in the process and one wonders if he should ever have expected less.'[3]

Much of the criticism of Kinnock came from newspapers that were ideologically unsympathetic to his party. But even Labour insiders recognised that the visit had been a disaster. 'One can admire Neil for his courage in going but not for his political judgement,' lamented a member of the shadow cabinet, Giles Radice. It constituted 'hardly the best backdrop for a general election.'[4]

For this was Reagan's *coup de grâce* on behalf of Thatcher: the gutting of her principal political opponent had come just weeks before the PM was widely expected to call a general election. Shultz had advised the president that he should use the opportunity to 'demonstrate publicly our respect for the democratic process in the UK'. In the end, however, Reagan acted in a manner that made his electoral preference as clear as if he had marched into a polling station in Finchley and personally marked his cross on the ballot paper next to 'Thatcher, Margaret Hilda – The Conservative Party candidate'.

Mixed motives drove Reagan's humiliation of the Labour Party leader. To a large degree, this was personal. Although he had often been irritated by Thatcher's hectoring style, the president had recently had good cause to be grateful for the PM's characteristic willingness to face down criticism. She had stood by Reagan over the Iran-Contra scandal, offering both public support and private words of comfort at this low point in his presidency. That had been followed up in February 1987 with a personal phone call to Reagan when the Tower Commission published its report into the affair.

The commission's conclusion – that Reagan had known nothing of the arms-for-hostages policy of his own administration – was as damaging in its own way to the president's reputation as any illegal act on his part. Reagan, it seemed, was not the master of his own White House. Years later, in 1994, when his Alzheimer's disease was announced, some would even ask if the early signs of that illness had contributed to this situation. 'I could not shake my feeling, though, that something was amiss,' recalled his son, Ron, after a day spent in the White House that year.[5]

Reagan had been uncharacteristically down during the crisis. 'It was the only time I really saw him low,' remembered one close friend, Senator Paul Laxalt. 'The Iran-Contra affair,' said Ron, 'its shady characters with murky motives, its architecture of internal betrayal – was a perfect example of the sort of mess Dad was ill suited, at any age, in any condition, to appreciate.'[6] Thatcher's expressions of personal regard therefore mattered a great deal. 'A morale boost,' the president noted on his official call sheet following a telephone chat with both Margaret and Denis Thatcher. 'People there are very high on us.' It was a nice sentiment by the Thatchers, but in reality it was one that few others in Britain seemed to share. Two weeks after the conversation, the US ambassador in London, Charles Price, would draw Washington's attention to data in UK opinion polls that showed 'a low regard' for the United States and its president.[7]

When Kinnock arrived in Washington in March 1987 casting

aspersions not just on the Anglo-American relationship but on Thatcher personally, it offended Reagan's sense of good manners and his feeling of obligation towards his closest ally. His response, delivered in the global Headmaster's office, had that feeling of a clip round the ear to a naughty schoolboy who had been cheeky to matron. No wonder that Kinnock went home making the admonished child's perennial complaint: 'It's not fair!'

Yet while personal likes and dislikes played an important part in this fiasco for Labour, there was policy calculation behind Reagan's criticism. The president's popularity had crashed during the Iran-Contra scandal. A *Washington Post* poll in January 1987 showed that two-thirds of respondents thought that Reagan was trying to hide something. Given that the last year of any presidency is usually a 'lame duck' period as the focus moves to the forthcoming general election, most people concluded that the Reagan presidency was effectively over.

In the end it was Gorbachev who gave Reagan a plausible way out. On the same day in February that Reagan spoke to Thatcher and her husband, the Soviet leader issued a statement saying that Moscow was prepared to negotiate a separate agreement with the United States on intermediate-range missiles in Europe. 'We are putting our proposals on the table of negotiations with the US in Geneva,' he said. After the brinkmanship of Reykjavik, Gorbachev had backed down: the Soviets were offering a deal without attaching any conditions on SDI. 'It looks good,' Reagan wrote in his diary, 'but we mustn't get too carried away . . .' In fact, it was the issue that would put Reagan's popularity back on an upward curve.[8]

It was hardly any wonder, then, that Neil Kinnock received a frosty welcome in the Oval Office. Labour's unilateralist nuclear policy threatened everything that Reagan hoped to achieve in his last year and a half in office. Frank Carlucci spelled this out for the president beforehand. A potential Labour government, he warned, 'weakens the Western bargaining position because it signals to the Soviets that, should they ever walk away from the table, Labor would still expel our nuclear missiles. The net result of a Labor government would be a "denuclearized" Britain and a drastic weakening of Western security.' The importance of this shift for the president was clear: 'We will not achieve arms reductions without Alliance solidarity.'[9] Given that this approach was now the principal focus of the administration, it was only to be expected that Reagan wanted 'to get in a lick or two' at this potential threat to his disarmament strategy.

Kinnock's humiliation by the president of the United States was a welcome bonus for Margaret Thatcher, whose pre-election strategy, like Harold Macmillan's in 1959, was to emphasise her credentials as an important global leader with a trip to the Soviet Union. While Kinnock was on his way back from the White House, the Iron Lady flew to Moscow for what would be a triumphant visit to see Gorbachev. There she wowed the Soviet crowds and British media alike with her glamorous black, fur-lined outfits from Aquascutum and her stinging public criticisms of the Soviet system. Yet what really caught the eye was Gorbachev's obvious respect. The two leaders had a staggering thirteen hours of direct talks. 'I cannot ever remember having spent so much time in discussion with another world leader,' an exultant Thatcher told reporters on the plane home. One Whitehall official described the talks as a 'philosophical bashing' ranging across every aspect of East–West relations. At one stage the two leaders argued about the merits of capitalism versus Communism, and Thatcher told him: 'We are all capitalists. The only difference is that for you it's the state that invests, while for us it's private individuals.' Gorbachev was momentarily flummoxed.[10]

Margaret Thatcher's excursion to Moscow was a personal triumph. Afterwards, she described it as the most fascinating and important foreign visit she had ever made. The trip had underlined a number of her central political points at home and abroad. In Britain, the head-to-head debates with Gorbachev and her rapturous reception on the streets of the Soviet Union had served to emphasise her place as an iconic leader of the West. As her supporters were quick to point out, she was the longest serving leader in the western alliance. Her economic policies were being emulated around the globe. She enjoyed a 'special relationship' with the leaders of the two superpowers. Even her European allies had come to recognise that on defence matters she was their most eloquent and persuasive spokesperson. 'The comparison with Mr Neil Kinnock's American trip could not be more stark,' concluded a leading article in the *Sunday Times*.[11]

Yet there was also a point to be made to the White House. Thatcher had demonstrated great personal loyalty to Reagan over the previous months, but she had neither forgiven nor forgotten that at Reykjavik the president had almost signed away Britain's nuclear deterrent. Just as in 1983 – when after the Grenada humiliation her fury with Reagan had manifested itself in a first trip to the Soviet Union and the 'discovery' of Gorbachev – so now after Reykjavik she took an opportunity to remind Reagan that she had her own relationship with the Soviet leader. This stopped short of being an awkward partner *à la française* for the Americans. But it was a shot across the bows to demonstrate that Thatcher was not an ally who could be taken for granted.

This fact was registered in Washington, and not without a little irritation. George Shultz was due to fly to Moscow a few weeks after Thatcher for crucial arms control negotiations. The State Department, fearing that their man had been upstaged by Thatcher, briefed dismissively that the prime minister's visit was 'a good warm up' for Shultz.[12] Warm-up or not, it would be Thatcher who would be given credit for the breakthrough with Gorbachev when the leaders of the G-7 met at the Venice summit in June. Shultz was among the most accomplished secretaries of state in modern US history, but on this occasion he was merely best supporting actor to Thatcher's leading lady.

Whatever irritations remained in Washington about Thatcher, there was never any question that the administration, particularly the president himself, wanted a Conservative victory at the polls. Indeed, their attitude was the international version of Reagan's famous Eleventh Commandment: 'Thou shalt not speak ill of any fellow Republican'. In this instance the Labour Party alternative was completely unpalatable. There was also a certain affection for Thatcher's 'handbagging' style, which had become an amusing feature of life in the White House. When she was thundering disagreement down the phone line from London, Reagan might hold up the telephone so that the rest of the room could hear her. 'Isn't she wonderful?' he would say, shaking his head ruefully.[13]

The president's enthusiasm for Thatcher over Kinnock in 1987 came close to diplomatic solipsism. At the end of May, halfway through the election campaign, Reagan all but admitted to European correspondents that he was looking forward to a Thatcher win. 'I have to tell you,' he said, 'I have great admiration for the manner in which Prime Minister Thatcher has handled not only the domestic affairs but the international affairs.' To rub salt into Labour's wounds, he also pointed out that if a government was elected in Britain on a ticket of unilateral disarmament and the removal of US bases, 'I would try with all my might to persuade that government not to make those grievous errors.' Horrified American officials immediately began to spin that of course the president remained neutral in the election and that the United States had 'survived labor governments before' and would do so again in the event. After all, the 'strength and closeness' of the Anglo-American relationship transcended party politics. However that 'line to take' was not helped by the decision of the defense secretary, Caspar Weinberger, to appear on a platform with Norman Tebbit, the Conservative Party chairman.[14]

By the time that Reagan and Thatcher arrived in Venice for the G-7 summit, it must have seemed to Labour as if the entire international calendar had been arranged as an extended party political broadcast for the incumbent prime minister. In fact, it was Thatcher, using a prime minister's prerogative to call an election whenever she liked, who had organised the electoral calendar to ensure that her international credentials were showcased to their best effect. The timing of the election so near the G-7 summit was no coincidence.

Three days before the polls opened, after a long working dinner on 8 June, the heads of government issued a joint statement on East–West relations that committed each country to 'maintaining a strong and credible defence' and reaffirmed 'the continuing importance of nuclear deterrence in preserving peace.' The point was not lost on the accompanying press pack. 'Whether all the other leaders intended it or not,' commented *The Times*'s correspondent, 'they had given Mrs Thatcher an important final trump card in the crucial election argument about defence.'[15]

The following morning, Reagan and Thatcher sat down for talks again in private. In the preceding six years they had met together like this scores of times. Even taking into account the inevitable wobbles of an election campaign, neither of them thought this would be their last meeting in office. The talks over, Reagan then gave Thatcher one last pre-election gift: a glorious photo opportunity as they travelled together in the presidential motorboat down the Grand Canal to San Giorgio Maggiore.

On 11 June 1987 the British electorate went to the polls and returned a Conservative government with a majority of 102. Margaret Thatcher became the only prime minister in the twentieth century, and only the second since Lord Liverpool in 1826, to win three consecutive general elections.[16]

'Mr President, are you pleased that Mrs Thatcher won?' shouted out reporters to Reagan as he prepared to fly back from Europe to Washington.

'Now I can say it?' he asked with a broad smile: 'Yes!'[17]

Elections and re-elections on both sides of the Atlantic over the previous six years had always prompted Margaret Thatcher to suggest an immediate visit to Washington in order to reassert the 'special relationship'. The year 1987 was no exception. Even before the election had taken place, Charles Powell from the prime minister's private office had tapped up the Americans at the G-7 summit. 'During Frank [Carlucci]'s discussion with Powell,' reported Assistant to the Secretary of Defense Marybel Batjer, 'Powell mentioned that PM Thatcher would like to come to Washington in July.' Her thirteen hours with Gorbachev notwithstanding, on this occasion 'the PM would like to spend 1 hour or 1½ hour with the Pres.'[18]

The day after her election victory, Thatcher pressed home the point in a telephone call with Reagan. It had been a busy day for the president. Only moments earlier he had delivered one of most remarkable speeches of his career. Standing in front of the Berlin Wall at the Brandenburg Gate in West Germany, Reagan had boldly declared: 'Mr. Gorbachev, tear down this wall!' That line had been used after intense debate within the administration, with Secretary of State George Shultz and the new chief of staff, Howard Baker, both advising the president to delete it as unnecessarily antagonistic. Reagan refused. He understood the importance of associating Gorbachev personally with the hated Berlin Wall. 'Among us speechwriters, I don't think there was any doubt at all about what the Gipper was up to,' remembered Peter Robinson, the principal author of the speech.[19]

The demand to 'tear down this wall' would be remembered as one of Reagan's best lines, but public reaction at the time was muted, leading Baker to ponder, 'Well damn, maybe it wasn't as important as I thought it was.' Later he changed his mind, reflecting that 'History has treated it very differently'. Indeed, it would provide grateful historians of all stripes with a key narrative plot point in the story of how the cold war ended. When the wall did come down two years later, Reagan was hailed by Europeans on the Communist side of the divide for his determination and vision. 'In the Europe of the 1980s, Ronald Reagan presented a vision,' recalled Lech Walesa, who would be elected president of Poland the following year. 'For us in Central and Eastern Europe, that meant freedom from the Soviets. Mr Reagan was no ostrich who hoped that problems might just go away. He thought that problems are there to be faced. This is exactly what he did.'[20]

Given that the Brandenburg Gate speech became so iconic in the story of how the cold war ended, it seems surprising now that Thatcher's reaction to it was so casual. 'Mrs. Thatcher,' noted the American memcon of 12 June, 'asked if the president was having a good day in Berlin.' Reagan explained how he had 'called for the wall to come down'. Thatcher said 'she had heard the crowd had roared its approval. She then moved on to ask after "Nancy" . . .'

Thatcher may not have recognised the important symbolism of the Berlin speech, but Reagan was quicker in appreciating her historic achievement in winning a third term. It had been a 'magnificent victory!' She in turn thanked him for handling everything 'beautifully'. And she so wanted to come to see him 'for a long talk' before his holiday in August. The president did not disappoint. Five days later, the White House press office announced that an invitation had been issued and accepted. The prime minister would be visiting the president on 17 July.[21]

Thatcher had been keen to underline her status as an international figure with an early visit to Washington, but the Reagan administration recognised she had another agenda. Naturally she would focus 'on our negotiations with the Soviets,' wrote George Shultz, 'but the occasion [provides] her as well with an opportunity to assess the president's mood and standing and at the same time to provide the support implicit in a visit from such an important head of government.'[22]

Thatcher's VC-10 touched down at Andrews Air Force Base late in the evening of 16 July. 'Our political fortunes at this time could not have been more different,' she later reflected of Reagan and this visit. 'I had just won an election with a decisive majority, enhancing my authority in international affairs. By contrast my old friend and his administration were reeling under the continuing "Irangate" revelations.' Everyone understood that this was perhaps the first time that Reagan needed Thatcher more than she needed him.[23]

Hours before meeting the president, the PM conducted four interviews with American television networks during which she was repeatedly pushed on the question of Reagan's competence. When Forrest Sawyer of CBS suggested that critics were saying no head of state could now take the president at his word, Thatcher pushed back hard. 'I'm astonished, absolutely astonished!' she fumed. 'I have dealt with the president for many, many years and I have absolute trust in him.' But surely, the interviewer asked, she must fear that the president 'trying to breathe some new life into his presidency could make concessions that you would not like?' Indeed, this was precisely what Thatcher feared, and what she would say to the president later that morning. But it was not something she was going to share with the American public. 'The United States is not trying to breathe new life into this presidency,' she told Sawyer firmly. 'President Reagan is president and will continue to be president, and is taking a very active role in these matters. I have seen it. It is one of the things I have come over to talk about – the next step.'[24]

Later that morning, at 11.30 am Reagan gave Thatcher a warm welcome in the Oval Office. As the two walked outside for a photo opportunity, the president thanked the prime minister for her support that morning, and explained why he had decided not to answer press questions on 'Irangate', preferring to wait until the congressional hearings were completed. Then it was back to the Oval Office for forty-five minutes of private conversation. Thatcher found the president hurt by what was unfolding. She reassured him that she was determined to do everything possible to help. This was not a matter of personal loyalty. Reagan had eighteen months still to serve as leader of the most powerful country in the world. 'It was in all our interests that his authority be undiminished,' she reflected.[25]

Thatcher was not above using Reagan's political difficulties as a means to gain extra leverage. When Reagan and Thatcher convened in the Old Family Dining Room alongside secretaries Shultz, Weinberger and James Baker, the prime minister did not hesitate to put the president on the spot. Her 'nervy' TV interviewers that morning had 'insisted the president knew everything and had made bad decisions,' she said, or otherwise insinuated that 'he was so detached that he made too few decisions.' She left that hanging for Reagan to answer, without any kind of obvious get-out.

Thatcher was good at extracting straight answers, but Reagan was the master of not giving them. His political instincts immediately kicked in, as he effortlessly deflected Thatcher's comment with an amusing anecdote. Many years earlier, he told her, when he was governor of California, he had given a speech at the Albert Hall in London. Lunch had come in a box: a lamb chop with some fruit – but no utensils. So Reagan had picked up his chop with his fingers and started eating. Immediately the press photographers snapped away, and sure enough the next day the story had been that the governor had eaten with his fingers because he didn't know which fork to use. 'You can't win with the press,' Reagan concluded. 'Lyndon Johnson often [said] that if he were seen walking across the Potomac river, the Washington press would criticize him the next morning for not knowing how to swim'.[26]

It was classic Reagan – funny, pointed, and diversionary – and symptomatic of his detached presidential style. Thatcher seemed to understand that, but knew it was a luxury that the adversarial British system did not allow. 'This makes one tough enough to stand up to almost anything,' she told Reagan. Certainly a few TV interviews were not going to rattle her.[27]

Having established that she was going to stand by the president, Thatcher attempted to push home her advantage on matters of substance. She had 'mixed feelings' about the Intermediate-Range Nuclear Forces (INF) Treaty that Reagan and Gorbachev were due to sign in December. The withdrawal of intermediate land-based missiles risked decoupling Europe from NATO, because it raised questions about whether in the last resort the United States would use nuclear weapons to deter a Soviet conventional attack on western European countries. It followed from the INF Treaty that NATO must have other nuclear weapons, modernised and strengthened, in order to retain a credible deterrent. In particular, she feared that the 'zero' on INF might lead to another 'zero' on short-range nuclear forces (SNF). It was a development she was determined to thwart at all costs.[28]

Face to face with the president, his secretaries of state and defense, the treasury and the national security adviser, Thatcher laid out in specific terms what she wanted: submarine-launched cruise missiles and additional F-111 aircraft under the control of NATO to compensate for the loss of land-based cruise and Pershing missiles; and the need to resist pressure from the disarmament-minded Germans for early discussion of reductions of SNF in Europe. As a subsidiary issue, Thatcher also raised the possibility of keeping the old German Pershing IA ballistic missiles for the remaining few years of their natural life and not including them in the INF Treaty. On this latter point, Thatcher found herself unable to convince the Americans, but she had greater success on the more substantive issue of strengthening SNF. 'The president and I saw eye to eye,' she wrote afterwards, satisfied at the progress made in the wake of the INF Treaty. She saw the future of SNF as the most crucial element in Britain's nuclear deterrence.[29]

Reagan seemed cheered by Thatcher's presence and resilience – 'in agreement about everything,' he noted – and the meeting ended in good humour with the president relating 'Soviet' jokes. The last of these told how soon after enacting a new law to curb speeding on the roads, Gorbachev found himself running late for a meeting. His driver wouldn't break the law, so the Soviet leader took over at the wheel. Further down the road, two policemen watched him speed past. One gave chase, stopped the car, but then returned to where the second officer was waiting. 'Why didn't you arrest him?' the second officer asked. 'He was too important,' replied the first officer. 'Who is this important person then?' asked the second officer. 'I don't know,' said his partner, 'but his driver was Gorbachev.'[30]

Even Thatcher, who famously lacked a sense of humour, got this joke. With gales of laughter still echoing round the room, Reagan whisked her out to the family quarters to say hello to Nancy. The relationship between the first lady and the prime minister had always been cordial rather than affectionate, but on this occasion Nancy Reagan seemed to give Thatcher a particularly warm welcome. The first lady had been following every line of analysis on 'Irangate', leaving her upset and badly bruised by the attacks on the president. Thatcher's resolute defence of Nancy's husband had not gone unnoticed.

In private, Thatcher worried that Nancy was making the president more depressed by repeating to him hostile media comments, but she was not going to give ammunition to the first lady's antagonists. Nancy was reviled by many for her abrasiveness and idiosyncratic habits, which included ensuring that the presidential timetable met with the approval of her personal astrologer. Nancy was fiercely loyal, however, and was known to see people in black and white as either friends or enemies. Thatcher had her own mildly eccentric husband upon whom she relied more than most people realised, so she understood how much Reagan leant on Nancy. The extent of that reliance during the current crisis would become painfully clear a few months later when Nancy was diagnosed with breast cancer. At the hospital where she had a mastectomy, wrote the couple's son, Ron, his father 'broke down, sobbing uncontrollably'. The thought of losing her was simply 'more than he could bear.'[31]

Back to business a short while later, both leaders paid glowing tributes to each other in statements at the diplomatic entrance to the White House.[32] No sooner had they finished speaking than journalists, ignoring what had been said, began firing questions at Reagan on Irangate. 'Press yelling Q's at me,' Reagan noted wearily in his diary, 'which I won't answer til the hearings are over.'[33]

Thatcher was shocked by the vehemence of the questioning, which may explain why later that day she ratcheted up her own defence of the president. Recording an interview with Leslie Stahl for *Face the Nation* on CBS, Thatcher condemned the American media, and even came close to rebuking the US Congress, for 'trying to discuss every single tiny little thing that happened' on Irangate. When Stahl asked Thatcher if she was 'saddened' by what had happened, the prime minister tore into her.

'No, I think you are taking far too downbeat a view,' Thatcher exclaimed. 'Now why are all you media taking a downbeat view? Cheer up! America is a strong country with a great President, a great people and a great future!' Stahl seemed taken aback. 'Lighten up – is that what you are telling us?' she asked. Thatcher, unsmiling, fixed her with a stare. 'Cheer up! Be more upbeat!' she ordered. Stahl tried again. 'I must say you are being a cheerleader about it, but we do hear that our influence has been greatly damaged; we hear that our credibility has been shredded; we hear that we have to take extraordinary steps to prove ourselves to . . .'

Thatcher cut her off midstream to deliver another broadside in favour of the president. 'Why are you doing your level best to put the worst foot forward? Why?' she demanded to know. America was 'a great country'. It had a people who were 'enterprising, self-reliant'. Even during 'this difficult period' the president was showing 'tremendous initiative' in tackling global problems. 'This is not a story of a person who has been deflected by one particular problem from dealing with the great matters which affect the world,' she thundered. 'I beg of you, you should have as much faith in America as I have!' When Stahl asked her final question – 'was the president down?' – Thatcher dismissed her out of hand. 'No. The President is fine!' she exclaimed. 'He is President of the United States!'[34]

It had been a forceful performance, one which displayed Thatcher's battling qualities that Americans so admired. Only a few hours earlier, she had been up on the Hill for tea in the Senate Leadership Offices, where she had amused her audience by browbeating a famously abrasive senator, Jesse Helms – a fierce critic of British action during the Falklands War – into uncharacteristic silence. Now she had taken a public sideswipe at the 'downbeat' American media for their protracted criticism of the president. It was daring, high-wire stuff, which reinforced her image as the fearless Iron Lady. One admiring senator noted that it was as if she had gone after them with a baseball bat for their impudence.

Another who was appreciative was the president of the United States. 'Margaret Thatcher on "Face the Nation" was absolutely magnificent,' he wrote in his diary at Camp David.[35] Reagan knew what it felt like to be on the receiving end of a Thatcher rebuke. On this occasion he was only too delighted to have it deployed on his behalf.

A few days afterwards, during a meeting of the cabinet, Reagan was interrupted by an aide to say that the prime minister was on the line returning an earlier call. Reagan, who was never one to stand on ceremony, offered to take the call in another room; the cabinet insisted that they should leave to allow him to speak to the prime minister. In the end, he took the call while the others remained. Reagan thanked Thatcher for her vigorous defence on *Face the Nation*, and then added, 'Well, I'm here with a bunch of my cabinet secretaries, and they'd all like to do the same and express their thanks for your support of our administration.' With that, Reagan held up the phone, and the members of cabinet, taking their cue from the president, gave Thatcher a thunderous round of applause so that she could hear their gratitude.

It was a telling moment – recognition that Thatcher, while often a difficult partner, had also been a loyal one. And not least at a time, said Reagan, when Washington was 'as hot as Hades.'[36]

RAF Brize Norton. 7 December 1987. The Russian Ilyushin aircraft touched down on English soil and taxied to an immaculate halt alongside the ceremonial red carpet. A few moments later, the door opened, and out stepped Mikhail Gorbachev. A broad grin spread across his face as he bounced down the steps, looking, said one reporter, 'more like an escaped dissident than the leader of the "evil empire".'[37] Waiting for him at the bottom of the stairs was Margaret Thatcher. They shook hands warmly, half-embraced and exchanged enthusiastic greetings. Then it was inside for two hours of talks: Gorbachev was on his way to Washington for a summit with Reagan and there was much to discuss.

For Thatcher, the stopoff by Gorbachev was a priceless public-relations coup that reinforced a sense of British pre-eminence in Europe not seen since the days of the wartime alliance. It was also an important opportunity to influence strategy and negotiations. In part, the talks suited both superpowers. Gorbachev hoped that Thatcher's noted scepticism about SDI could be deployed to Soviet advantage during the forthcoming meetings. And given her violent reaction to the talks at Reykjavik, it was also useful for Gorbachev to take the prime minister's temperature before seeing Reagan to get a sense of what America's European allies would, and would not, be prepared to accept. For Reagan, the calculation was even more straightforward. Aside from asking Thatcher to put Gorbachev on the back foot on human rights and Afghanistan, Reagan was glad to let loose her robust debating skills on the Soviet leader and to hear what kind of form he might be in.

Thatcher had her own agenda, too. Her strategy of getting involved in direct talks with the Soviets had begun after the humiliation of Grenada and the accompanying recognition that 'this is how large powers behave'. Those fears in 1983 had been more than realised three years later, when 'the earth shook' and she watched horrified as Reagan at Reykjavik came close to giving away western Europe's nuclear deterrent. For all her personal affection for Reagan and staunch defence of him during Irangate, Thatcher had never entirely trusted him after those betrayals. 'I never ceased to believe in the importance of nuclear weapons as a means of deterring conventional, not just nuclear, war,' she said after the Brize Norton meeting – 'the one issue on which I knew I could not take the Reagan administration's soundness for granted.' This was the reason why she was 'so delighted' when Gorbachev 'accepted my invitation to stop over at Brize Norton on his way to the United States to sign the INF Treaty.' Gorbachev had to hear from her own lips where western Europe stood. In this way, she concluded, 'I could exert beneficial influence' and avoid a repeat of the crisis in the western alliance that followed Reykjavik.

Afterwards, British officials confirmed that Thatcher and Gorbachev went at it 'hammer and tongs' in the discussions. The most robust exchanges came on nuclear weapons and what would happen after the INF Treaty was signed. Thatcher made clear 'my determination to keep nuclear weapons.' Gorbachev responded that the prime minister obviously preferred to 'sit on a powder keg rather than an easy chair.' Thatcher tartly reminded him of the very large powder keg the Soviets already had 'in conventional and chemical forces'.[38]

After two hours of 'frank, lively, and informal' talks, Gorbachev readied himself to leave, only to find that his wife Raisa was still not back from visiting a local primary school. Thatcher used the spare moment to ask him *sotto voce* whether he might consider allowing the family of the Soviet defector and double-agent Oleg Gordievsky to leave Moscow for Britain. 'He pursed his lips and said nothing,' Thatcher recalled – 'The answer was all too clear.' He was saved from further embarrassment by the return of Raisa. 'She wanted to know what he had been doing and then straightened his tie,' remembered an amused Kenneth Baker, the education secretary – 'It was clearly a working relationship'. Gorbachev, it seemed, enjoyed the company of strong women. Emerging again out onto the tarmac, he offered warm words of praise for Thatcher and talked of their 'unique personal relationship'. Then he was off, flying on to Washington and a meeting with President Reagan.[39]

While Gorbachev was in the air, the president came on the line to London, where Thatcher had returned to 10 Downing Street. 'She leaned on him on the negotiation & on human rights,' Reagan recorded afterwards. 'She was very encouraged by his attitude & his answers.' Reagan expected 'some tough sessions' with Gorbachev, but he was glad that the prime minister 'had clearly softened him up'.[40]

After Thatcher had put the phone down, she became another nervous bystander, waiting for the outcome of the summit in Washington and praying that it would not become another Reykjavik. Although she had done much to recreate the consultation of the wartime alliance of Roosevelt, Stalin and Churchill – 'the big two and a half' – this remained, for all her influence, a club from which Britain was ultimately excluded. 'I was only trying to use my influence to further something which could be properly furthered in accordance with my beliefs and the situation which I had outlined to Mr Gorbachev and which Ron Reagan also believed in,' she said afterwards. After Gorbachev left, all the junior partner could do was sit by the phone, waiting for 'Ron' to call again.[41]

The Washington summit meeting began on 8 December, when Gorbachev rolled up at the White House in an enormous limousine. 'That's bigger than anything we have,' complained Reagan. Talks between the two men were 'rousing'. They signed the INF Treaty, which, although it only affected 5 per cent of their nuclear warheads, represented the first time the superpowers had reduced their nuclear forces. The treaty also abolished an entire class of weapons, which included the cruise, Pershing and SS-20 missiles that had been the focus of such controversy in Europe in 1983. Underlying the treaty were new rules for verification, including unannounced on-site inspections of each other's nuclear weapons facilities – a practical application of Reagan's favourite phrase of 'trust but verify'.[42]

Gorbachev achieved the public-relations coup of the summit by instructing his driver to pull over several blocks from the White House and jumping out for a walkabout to meet astonished Washingtonians. It was perhaps a lesson he had learnt from Thatcher, who months earlier had done something similar in Moscow to popular acclaim. Gorbachev's own experience profoundly affected him. 'In Washington,' he told the Politburo afterwards, 'perhaps for the first time, we understood so clearly how important the human factor is in international politics.'[43]

For all the 'Gorbymania' that swept through the United States in December 1987, American officials remained pleased and even a little taken aback by how brilliantly the president performed. The Soviet leader was ten times more knowledgeable, vigorous and subtle. Yet, recalled the senior US arms negotiator, Kenneth Adelman, 'it was uncanny how Reagan, every time he got in the room with Gorbachev . . . took him to the cleaners. Not only that, but Gorbachev ended the summit knowing that Reagan had bettered him.'[44]

Reagan had his fund of lame jokes, which Gorbachev enjoyed through gritted teeth, but when it came to the key issues he had a directness that cut through everything. The situation in Afghanistan, which Thatcher had debated fiercely with Gorbachev, was one such example. The Soviets had invaded the country at the end of 1979, summarily executing the president, and installing a new puppet regime. For the USSR, this had been an action of last resort to protect their interests in the traditional 'great game' in the region. For America, on the other hand, it seemed the ultimate proof of Soviet aggressive intent. Jimmy Carter, then president, lamented that only at that moment had he appreciated the true ruthlessness of Communism. His successor understood it implicitly. 'Reagan got in the room with Gorbachev,' continues Adelman, 'and said, "Mike, you got 120,000 troops in Afghanistan? It's just genocide. They don't want to be there. You're killing kids. You're butchering the country. It's just genocide, Mike." Here's Gorbachev in his earphones, cannot imagine what he's hearing.'[45]

Lou Cannon, Reagan's long-term friend and biographer, had a folksy theory about Reagan's commanding performances at the summit with Gorbachev. Cannon had known a football player in his high school who was about average until someone hit him hard. Then he transformed into an all-star. Everyone in the league learnt to leave him alone. Reagan had that quality to his presidency. For much of the time, he was 'fine, mediocre in all kinds of performance.' But when it came to the important plays, 'then he turned spectacular'. Adelman, who watched Reagan at close hand in Geneva, Reykjavik and Washington, concurred, perhaps to his own surprise, that the president 'was a big-game player in a big game.'[46]

Reagan was thrilled with the success of the meeting with Gorbachev. Afterwards, he escaped to Camp David for a few days of rest, where he received positive new polling data. 'The summit was a big plus,' he wrote excitedly. His overall approval rating was 67 per cent. Approval for his handling of the Soviets was 81 per cent. These were the kind of figures that Reagan had enjoyed before Iran-Contra, and which would see him leave office a year later as one of America's more popular commanders-in-chief. 'It was a year marked by the worst foreign policy debacle of the

Reagan administration,' concluded David Broder in *The Washington Post*, 'yet it ended on a diplomatic high note'.[47]

From Camp David, Reagan 'phoned reports' to NATO allies on the summit with Gorbachev. This was the kind of consultation that he had promised Thatcher at Camp David in the aftermath of Reykjavik.

Reagan opened these conversations with 'a personal readout' of his meetings with Gorbachev. He had found the Soviet leader to be 'very confident' and – said apparently without irony – 'not at all like a political leader who was under fire'. Talks had been 'cordial', but they were 'also very candid', with positions 'firmly stated'. In particular on human rights and regional issues, such as Afghanistan, Gorbachev had taken 'a very tough line'. Undoubtedly, the INF Treaty had been 'the key summit event' and he had told Gorbachev that 'this was a precedent that needed to be set – toward reductions, not just limiting the expansion of nuclear weapons'. They had made 'real progress' towards reaching 50 per cent reductions of strategic offensive weapons. The president reiterated that progress on the strategic arms reduction treaty (START) had come 'without sacrificing SDI'. He also thought it was significant that Gorbachev expressed 'a strong desire' to achieve progress in other areas, especially on conventional force reductions and on chemical weapons. 'At least it is clear that Gorbachev wants to talk seriously about it,' Reagan concluded.

In each of his phone calls, Reagan finished by emphasising alliance solidarity. 'Our consulting so closely,' said the president, 'had made it clear to Gorbachev that he could not split the Alliance.' And for Thatcher there was an additional bouquet: while the other leaders received an almost identical briefing, Reagan began his phone call to the prime minister by waxing lyrical in his 'appreciation for pre-summit consultations'.[48]

The process of consultation with allies after the Washington summit was continued by Secretary of State George Shultz, who immediately embarked upon a six-nation briefing tour. He repeated the president's message that there was cause for optimism that the 'under-structures' of a superpower agreement on strategic offensive weapons were in place, but emphasised that 'deep differences' remained. In London, he showered Thatcher with praise, declaring that progress in the arms talks could not have come about without her 'courage, consistency and perseverance'. Without her and the deployment of cruise missiles in Britain, he went on, 'there would have been no treaty.' He had come to London, therefore, to declare his 'admiration' for the prime minister. It must have been a relief for the exhausted Shultz to be among 'friends', where his own achievement was hailed by the foreign secretary, Geoffrey Howe, as 'momentous' and offering 'hope for mankind'. It contrasted with his reception in France, where the foreign minister, Jean-Bernard Raimond, sniffily informed him that 'we will not know for twenty-five years' whether the INF Treaty was historic. 'How French,' reflected Shultz.[49]

For Thatcher, there was only relief that the Washington summit had not caused an earthquake under her feet in the manner of Reykjavik. Concerns remained about the American strategy – not least Reagan's ultimate desire to abandon nuclear weapons – but that was a battle for another day. As the year drew to a close, she could reflect that, like Reagan, her own poll ratings had shot up, and that around the world she was seen by politicians and press alike as a global figure of great stature, the only European leader who could command attention in both Moscow and Washington. 'Leading lady,' ran the headline in an admiring profile in Canada's *Globe & Mail*. 'Britain's Margaret Thatcher is clearly atop the political heap in Europe.'

Yet for all her dominance, Thatcher understood that the sands of international politics were shifting beneath her feet. The president was entering his final year in office. Already the question was being asked in London and elsewhere: would the lady's influence in Washington remain after Reagan's exit, stage right?

11

The Last Waltz

The last NATO summit of the Reagan-Thatcher era exemplified in so many ways the unusual relationship between the two main protagonists. Though the leaders of the Atlantic Alliance had convened on and off during the intervening period, the meeting on 2 March 1988 was the first formal NATO summit in six years and the first attended by a French president in more than twenty-two. They had gathered at Thatcher's instigation and she had set the agenda. 'It is the need to emphasise to the Soviet Union,' she told CBS News beforehand, 'that the President of the United States always consults his NATO allies and that he even comes to Europe to do so. We go to the United States to talk to him but he comes to Europe. It is to show that we are absolutely behind the President in the Intermediate Nuclear Weapons treaty and to show that we believe that what is now vital after the 50% reductions that are being negotiated, is the next stage and we want to give him our views about that.'[1]

Reagan had arrived in Brussels in typically positive spirits, declaring that he expected the summit to 'go well'. But despite his success at the Washington summit with Gorbachev and the promise of another summit in Moscow, there was an inevitable sense that the president was already a diminished figure. Primaries for the US presidential elections were well under way, with Vice-President George Bush predicted to sweep the board the following week on 'Super Tuesday' and assume the mantle from Reagan as leader of the Republican Party. For Thatcher, the summit was about charting the way forward by reiterating NATO's commitment to strong defence and nuclear deterrence. For Reagan, it was a farewell tour to celebrate the success of NATO solidarity over INF and to bring eight years of the Atlantic Alliance under his leadership to an upbeat conclusion.[2]

For much of the summit, Reagan seemed distracted and a little sentimental. In a touching gesture at the beginning of the meeting, he quietly swapped his nameplate with that of George Shultz so that he could sit next to Thatcher. While they were chatting, he commented that the room looked familiar, and seemed taken aback when Thatcher reminded him that they had met at that exact spot after the first summit with Gorbachev in 1985. Perhaps it was an early sign of the illness that would cloud Reagan's final years, although in truth he saw so many different venues in so many different countries, it was hardly surprising if they blurred into each other.

Throughout the summit, while Thatcher talked (and talked), Reagan sat looking on with visible admiration and affection. At other times, to the consternation of officials, he seemed to nod off. Later, in front of the media, he allowed Shultz to answer the lion's share of questions. He played no part in the discussions to draw up the final communiqué. At the last press conference of the summit, the president had to admit that he didn't know whether he had seen the final text of that draft communiqué, leaving Howard Baker, his new chief of staff, hastily to confirm that naturally the president had signed off on the final wording.[3]

Thatcher in contrast was on fire. At an early stage in the proceedings, with the president apparently asleep and the other leaders trotting out self-satisfied platitudes on the glory of NATO, Thatcher cut in to speak without waiting for her turn. 'I am going to introduce common sense,' she bluntly told Lord Carrington, NATO's secretary-general and her former foreign secretary. Taking the floor, she launched into a blood-curdling analysis of the Soviet Union's military potential. NATO should not be seduced by Gorbachev, whose goal, she warned, was to divide western Europe from the United States, to denuclearise the Europeans and leave them at the mercy of superior Soviet conventional forces. Of course praise should be given where it was due: Gorbachev was bold, courageous, intent on introducing more freedom into the Soviet Union, and was ready to take his troops out of Afghanistan. But this did not mean that the West could let down its guard. A modernised conventional and nuclear capability remained essential to western freedom and security. Afterwards, she briefed journalists in her most withering tones that there was not the slightest inconsistency in breathing blood and thunder in one breath, and offering Gorbachev her personal seal of approval in the next. After all, she had done the talent-spotting in the first place.[4]

Thatcher's warnings about Gorbachev were rooted in her fears about his seduction of western opinion. The Soviet leader had by this stage become an iconic figure throughout the West. He was deluged with fan mail, and was the subject of innumerable profiles, academic studies and popular books, which tended to range in tone from complimentary and admiring to fawning. To criticise 'Gorby' was to be in the minority. Not only was he a 'peacemaker', but he seemed to be a genuinely 'nice guy'. 'He had clearly caught the world's imagination, symbolising as he did the departure from the scene of the Bolshevik monster,' wrote Dmitri Volkogonov, later a defence adviser to the Russian government. 'When he spoke – which he did a great deal – people no longer felt the old fear.'[5]

Thatcher, however, did still feel the old fear, and believed herself vindicated in that opinion eighteen months later when a Soviet scientist, Vladimir Pasechnik, defected to Britain. 'The fact that Vladimir defected was one of the key acts of the entire ending of the Soviet Union and the end of the cold war,' recalled Christopher Davis from the Defence Intelligence Staff. 'It was the greatest breakthrough we ever had.' What Davis learnt on debriefing Pasechnik revealed a new, sinister dimension to Soviet defence: a strategic biological weapons programme. Not only did this include battlefield weapons, but it focused primarily on long-range strategic weapons using plague and smallpox. The Soviets were also working towards developing a new biological warfare agent totally resistant to treatment. 'You do not choose plague to put on a battlefield,' said Davis. 'You choose plague because you're going to take out the other person's country. Full stop.'

Pasechnik detailed how Foreign Minister Eduard Shevardnadze had attended high-level briefings on the programme in 1988. If Shevardnadze knew, Pasechnik said, Gorbachev must have known as well. When Thatcher got her first briefing note on the defection from the Joint Intelligence Committee it confirmed her instincts, expressed at the NATO summit, about the need for caution with Gorbachev. 'Was this a man they could do business with,' David Hoffman of *The Washington Post* later asked, 'or was he the leader of a country and a system that created – and was still creating – the most destructive biological weapons mankind had ever known, in violation of all treaty promises?'[6]

Back at the NATO summit, Thatcher's performance was hailed as magisterial, displaying both her sense of wider strategy and a formidable command of detail. 'It was a summit that was transformed by the force and doggedness of Thatcher, who dominated proceedings that normally revolve around an American leader's program,' judged the *Post*. 'It was Thatcher who assumed command,' agreed the *Sunday Times*. 'She was at her most forceful, overshadowing the president as the most outspoken leader at the summit. For the first time in its 40-year history, the alliance was not being led by the Americans.'[7]

Yet for all Thatcher's dominance in debate, it was the president who stole the show. As the summit drew to a close, Reagan delivered a final peroration that none, including Thatcher, could match. 'I'm going to wing it,' the president had told Shultz, as the secretary of state passed him the cue cards. For just under ten minutes, Reagan held his audience bewitched. Having seemed so distracted, he now spoke with passion and commitment about what NATO meant for freedom in every country represented in that room. In the past, they had fought wars against each other, but after the Second World War, these countries had said 'enough' and forged a new alliance to keep the peace. All they had to do, Reagan said, was stay together and keep their obligations to each other. That offered the surest path to peace.

Sitting beside Reagan, Thatcher nodded her approval and appeared visibly moved. 'It was corny,' said one British official, 'but because the old boy quite clearly meant every word, it was very telling.' Even George Shultz, for whom lack of public emotion had become an admired trademark, brimmed with feeling about 'a wonderful experience'. For Reagan, there was satisfaction that yet again he had put in another show-stopping performance. 'I ad libbed one that was hailed by all,' he recorded with satisfaction in his diary.[8]

The NATO summit in March 1988 set the valedictory and emotional tone to Reagan's final year, which included a last 'grand tour' as leader of the free world. It was also the beginning of a subtle change in the dynamic of the president's relationship with Margaret Thatcher. Despite the fondness for Thatcher personally and respect for her professionally, there had always been a hard-headedness about Reagan's attitude towards the British prime minister. He was always prepared to give her time, but when her interests conflicted with his own, as over Grenada or at Reykjavik, he barely gave her a second thought. As this final year went on, however, as well as letting the PM take the lead at the NATO summit, Reagan also began to think of her as an essential part of his legacy.

With the presidential race heating up in the spring and early summer of 1988, the Democrats found a competent, technocratic candidate in Michael Dukakis of Massachusetts, who was polling well ahead of George Bush. Whatever concerns Reagan may have had about being succeeded by a north-eastern liberal Democrat, the thought of Bush did not fill him with enthusiasm. Despite having challenged Reagan for the nomination in 1980, Bush had been a loyal and self-effacing vice-president. Reagan felt that Bush had earned his right to run, and when he was subsequently elected, Reagan took considerable care never to criticise him. Yet their relationship was always more cooperative than warm. There was never any sense that the managerial Bush was part of the 'Reagan revolution'. Later, this difference would manifest itself in tension between the outgoing and incoming teams during the transition in 1988–9. 'The Bush people, when George was elected, did not treat the Reagan people well,' remembers Senator Paul Laxalt. 'Oh they were so rude . . . It was just brutal . . . It was get-even time.'[9]

Reagan endorsed Bush at a Republican fund-raiser in May 1988 that pulled in $5 million for the campaign. But such was the president's perceived lack of enthusiasm for the candidate that he was forced to issue a statement the next day. 'George has been a partner in all we have accomplished, and he should be elected,' Reagan said. 'He has my full confidence and my total support. I will campaign actively on his behalf.' Reagan confessed to 'surprise' that his endorsement had been seen as 'lukewarm'. Yet the contrast with his endorsement of Thatcher a few weeks afterwards could hardly have been clearer. He arrived in London on 2 June 1988 as part of the return journey from Moscow. The official agenda showed that the president would be reporting on his summit talks with Mikhail Gorbachev, but, noted the *New York Times*, the meeting 'was more important as a historical marker in the Reagan-Thatcher relationship than a meeting of substance.'[10] On both sides, there seemed a determination to show just how 'special' that relationship between the two leaders and their respective countries really was.

On this occasion it was symbolism that mattered most. Reagan had come to see Thatcher personally; the other NATO allies were left with a briefing from George Shultz in Brussels. Thatcher pulled out every available stop for the president. His visit began with tea at Buckingham Palace with the Queen. 'Are you happy to see the Queen instead of Mrs Gorbachev?' shouted an American reporter (breaking Palace protocol) to the first lady during the photo call. 'I'm happy to see the Queen at all times,' Nancy mischievously replied, making no effort to keep the grin off her face.[11]

From the Palace, Reagan travelled up the Mall and on to meet Thatcher at the Foreign Office, where a guard of honour of the Welsh Guards had been drawn up in the quadrangle for his inspection. She then escorted him along a red carpet through the Foreign Office into Downing Street.

Inside No. 10, Thatcher invited photographers into the famous cabinet room to capture the image, thought to be unique, of a foreign leader sitting at the cabinet table. After dinner, the Reagans and the Thatchers from an upstairs window overlooking Horse Guards Parade watched the massed bands of the Household Division during the annual Beating Retreat, a ceremony dating back to the seventeenth century when the parading of Post Guards with drums heralded the closing of camp gates and the lowering of flags at the end of the day. It was the kind of pageantry that the British did so well – a magnificent sight of 406 men and 61 horses drawn from the Household Cavalry and the Foot Guards, in a blaze of scarlet and blue tunics, plumed brass helmets and the iconic bearskin hats worn since the Battle of Waterloo.[12]

In forty-five minutes of substantive talks between the PM and the president, there was none of the drama that had characterised previous post-summit talks. British officials afterwards briefed that Thatcher was satisfied that the president had avoided a repeat of 'the disaster of Reykjavik'. Certainly there had been nervous moments before the president's trip to Moscow, when Reagan had spoken in Helsinki of his dream of a nuclear-free world. Now Thatcher was reassured to hear that he would not be rushed into a new strategic arms reductions treaty on the back of summit euphoria. That enabled her to offer warm congratulations to Reagan on his summit success, particularly the way in which he had spoken out on human rights and for his efforts to make direct contact with the Soviet people.[13]

For Reagan, substance and symbolism came together when he issued an invitation to Thatcher to visit him at the White House shortly after the election in November to meet his successor, whoever that might be. Thatcher was thrilled by the offer and accepted immediately. Afterwards, American officials briefed that the invitation was unprecedented recognition of the close personal relationship that had developed between the two leaders, adding, 'It's been a pretty special one.' Marlin Fitzwater, the White House spokesman, pointed out that it would be the twentieth one-on-one meeting between the president and the prime minister during the eight years they had shared in office. The gesture was intended to underline the strength of the Anglo-American relationship. But it was also much more than that, as would become clear the following day at a speech by the president in the City of London.

Against the spectacular medieval backdrop of the Guildhall, Reagan delivered an encomium on Thatcher and the special relationship that left many observers almost embarrassed by its force and directness. The president declared that they were all living through 'momentous events':

> And that's why, although history will duly note that we, too, heard voices of denial and doubt, it is those who spoke with hope and strength who will be best remembered. And here I want to say that through all the troubles of the last decade, one such firm, eloquent voice, a voice that proclaimed proudly the cause of the Western alliance and human freedom, has been heard. A voice that never sacrificed its anticommunist credentials or its realistic appraisal of change in the Soviet Union, but because it came from the longest-serving leader in the alliance, it did become one of the first to suggest that we could 'do business' with Mr. Gorbachev. So, let me discharge my first official duty here today. Prime Minister, the achievements of the Moscow summit as well as the Geneva and Washington summits say much about your valor and strength and, by virtue of the office you hold, that of the British people. So let me say, simply: At this hour in history, Prime Minister, the entire world salutes you.[14]

Reagan's elevated rhetoric, taken alongside his invitation to meet the new president at the end of the year, demonstrated that he was casting Thatcher in a leading role for that 'newer world' without him. As *The Times* said in its leader the following day, the consensus afterwards had been that 'Mr Reagan wishes Mrs Thatcher to carry his baton into the future and that he particularly hopes she can influence his successor to take it up.' The contrast with the president's 'lukewarm' endorsement of Vice-President George Bush was stark. If there was to be an 'heir' to the Reagan revolution, and a keystone to East–West relations and the Atlantic Alliance, the president seemed to be giving his blessing to Margaret Thatcher.

The prime minister, in a white hat, sat impassive as Reagan laid on the compliments. But when her turn came, she did not disappoint. The president had made America 'strong and confident again'. He had been 'a staunch and loyal ally'. He had 'changed attitudes and perceptions about what is possible' by 'standing firm in your own beliefs'. From that 'strong fortress of conviction' he had enlarged 'freedom the world over': his personal courage, gentle humour and spirit of optimism were 'all part of the special quality' he had brought to the presidency. Reagan had 'restored faith in the American dream.' In doing so he had done 'the greatest possible service not only to your own people but to free people everywhere.' For that legacy and so much more, concluded Thatcher: 'Thank you, Mr. President! Thank you for your presidency, thank you for your testament of belief, and God Bless America!'[15]

These extravagant tributes by Reagan and Thatcher in such a grand, historic setting were the culmination of a long public love-in between the two leaders. From the outset of their relationship, each had taken care to make a pronounced fuss of the other in front of any audience, including the press. This attitude, first struck in the 1970s when Governor Reagan visited London, had been put on another level when President Reagan took the unconventional step of dining at the British Embassy during Thatcher's first visit to Washington in 1981. Thereafter, the level of showy affection had been ratcheted up at every opportunity. Even when the two were at loggerheads, both leaders took care to maintain an impeccable *bonhomie* during their public appearances. The Guildhall tributes Reagan and Thatcher paid to each other in 1988 took the visible appreciation levels into the stratosphere. Off-the-record briefings reinforced the positive message. 'It's philosophically rooted,' one US official told the *New York Times*, 'and they will miss each other. Both sides have gotten, in baldest terms, support on the major crucial security issues as they've proceeded, whether it's the Falklands or Libya. When the chips are down, she's been prepared to stand with us and vice versa.'[16]

Sentimentality had begun to seep in, and with it an inevitable rewriting of history. On Reagan's side, friends and officials began to wax lyrical about the affection the president had for 'Maggie'. 'I just think they literally loved one another, politically as well as otherwise,' said Paul Laxalt. 'They had a great relationship. She just adored Ron in every way, and he thought she was the lady. This was not only political, it was personal.'[17] Even Thatcher, in an attitude that would solidify as time went by, developed an analysis that departed from the hardheaded realism of her early years. Then she had recognised that a close relationship with the American president was important because it allowed her, the leader of a medium-sized country, to speak truth to power in the furtherance of British interests. Now she had come dangerously close to seeing that relationship as an absolute good in itself.

On one level, Thatcher seemed to recognise this herself. A few weeks later, at the Toronto G-7 summit, the prime minister effortlessly fielded media questions about whether a change of president would affect the Anglo-American relationship and her place on the world stage. 'I was here when President Reagan joined us,' she firmly told Jon Snow of ITN, 'because I was here in 1979 . . . and my role hasn't changed, and won't. I shall just go on preaching and practising the things that I believe in.'[18]

Yet many within her circle remained concerned. Geoffrey Howe confessed to a growing anxiety that Margaret was 'carrying the "special" relationship perhaps one bridge too far.' And a few weeks after Reagan's visit, at a No. 10 garden party, one adviser was 'taken aback' by the way in which Thatcher spoke about the president. 'She dilated with enthusiasm on Reagan's visit to Britain,' noted George Urban in his diary. 'He has clearly become her hero.' Thatcher told stories about the Reagans in the prime-ministerial flat, where he had cracked jokes and sung along to tunes played by the Guards Band. 'President Reagan,' she enthused, 'is a warm person, very informal, witty to a degree and intellectually much underrated.' Urban bit his tongue – it was a garden party, after all – but reflected afterwards: 'This fawning praise was just a little too much for me. Why "President" Reagan all the time? Our no-nonsense prime minister, so ready with her tongue in parliament and *vis-à-vis* Europeans, has been overawed by the charm and power of the American.' For Urban, who previously had advised her to get close to the president, now to judge that 'the Anglo-American "special relationship" was becoming one-sided to the point of embarrassment,' raised questions about whether Thatcher, in contrast to her hardheaded assessment of Gorbachev, had been seduced by her own rhetoric.[19]

The fears of 'pro-Europeans' would soon be confirmed as the combative drafting process began for an address by the PM to the College of Europe in Bruges in September 1988. It was a battle the Foreign Office lost. 'Practically every suggestion that the Foreign Office have made has been rejected,' noted the trade minister, Alan Clark, in his diary. 'They were foolish, because by their interference and provocation they have turned a relatively minor ceremonial chore into what could now well be a milestone in redefining our policy towards the Community.'[20]

The Bruges speech, delivered on 20 September 1988, laid down a transatlantic vision for Europe that went beyond the European Community, which 'is *one* manifestation of that European identity, but it is not the only one.' This wider vision was based on enterprise and global free trade. It included European nations east of the Iron Curtain, where 'people who once enjoyed a full share of European culture, freedom and identity have been cut off from their roots.' And it looked across the Atlantic, where 'European values have helped to make the United States of America into the valiant defender of freedom which she has become', not least through NATO, which underpinned European security. Thatcher's final words proclaimed her belief in the primacy of this Atlantic world. 'Let us have a Europe which plays its full part in the wider world, which looks outward not inward,' she declared, 'and which preserves that Atlantic community – that Europe on both sides of the Atlantic – which is our noblest inheritance and our greatest strength!'[21]

The forthrightness of Thatcher's Bruges speech provoked strong headlines in Europe. 'Elephant in the China Shop of Europe,' blared the Italian newspaper *La Stampa*. Officials in Brussels complained that Thatcher had revealed her true anti-European colours. Then there was her tone. 'Not all that she says is objectionable,' sniffed one Eurocrat; 'it's the way that she says it.' Reactions within Europe tended to focus on Thatcher's analysis of the 'nightmare' of ever closer European union rather than the renewed vision for the Atlantic community. However, White House officials noted these transatlantic sections of the speech with great enthusiasm. A briefing memo for the president by national security adviser Colin Powell explained that 'Prime minister Thatcher's assertiveness in advancing her vision . . . generates hostility from our European allies.' Her image as 'autocratic and uncompromising' had been 'reinforced' by the Bruges speech, but her points were 'all welcomed by us'. Particularly important, noted Powell, was Thatcher's 'warning that in moving toward further reductions in trade barriers within Europe, the European Community should not encase Europe in a barrier of protectionism . . . and insistence that Europe shoulder a great burden for defense.'

George Shultz concurred with this analysis. Thatcher, he reminded the president, 'has often used her position within NATO and the European Economic Community to explain and defend our common interests.' Every attempt should be made 'to encourage Mrs Thatcher in her efforts in the EC to assure that steps to establish a single internal market by 1992 do not result in increased external trade barriers.'[22]

It was a telling prelude to Thatcher's trip to Washington in November. So often in the past, the prospect of a visit by the Iron Lady had filled members of the administration with trepidation. Now as they prepared for her final visit, the stage was set for a sentimental, collegial farewell.

The White House. 16 November 1988. In the end, Reagan and Thatcher went out as they had come in: with ruffles and flourishes. Union flags lined the route as the prime minister's limousine made its way to 1600 Pennsylvania Avenue. Thatcher emerged from the car, regal in a red-lined, houndstooth-check cape, to be greeted warmly by Reagan as his last 'official visitor' to the White House. On the South Lawn, the autumnal weather that morning of mists, falling leaves and watery sunshine provided a photogenic backdrop to this political swansong. Hovering in the background, looking 'awkward again, wimpy even', said one observer, was the president-elect, George H. W. Bush.[23] Thatcher would be meeting him for breakfast the following morning, but today was all about her and Reagan. A 19-gun salute resounded across the Potomac. An honour guard was inspected. National anthems were played, with Thatcher placing her hand across her heart during 'The Star-Spangled Banner'.

The speeches were affectionate and sweeping. 'Her speech was a eulogy to me & our admin,' Reagan recorded in his diary. 'She praised me as having changed the whole world.' The president for his part was no less laudatory. When they came together in 1981, they had faced 'a crisis of faith, a crisis of will among the democracies', he said now. There were many who had questioned whether 'democratic institutions could survive, whether the modern world had made them obsolete.' Eight years later, 'change, extraordinary change' had come upon the world. Thatcher had played a 'special role' in achieving this remarkable turn of events. 'It was my privilege, last June,' continued the president, 'to note in a speech at Guildhall your extraordinary role in the revitalization of freedom. Today, in welcoming you to these shores, I and the American people again restate our gratitude. In the critical hour, Margaret Thatcher and the people of Great Britain stood fast in freedom's defense and upheld all the noblest of your island nation's traditions; yours was the part of courage and resolve and vision . . . We can hope today that in meeting those dangers we have transformed this decade into a turning point, a turning point for our age and for all time.'[24]

Inside the Oval Office, Reagan and Thatcher embarked on their last private conversation as president and prime minister. There were no great issues to discuss, but there were certainly compliments to be paid. 'We have accomplished much,' Reagan told Thatcher. 'We, together, have been the driving force for change over the last eight years!' They discussed Gorbachev and disarmament talks in general terms, with Reagan reassuring Thatcher that 'The approach and the goals we have worked out together will remain crucial'.[25] In the past, Thatcher had valued these precious moments alone with the president to bend his ear about some point of particular significance. Indeed, Colin Powell had warned the president about this beforehand. 'The purpose of her visit is not just to exchange accolades on the relationship,' he suggested, 'but to continue to build on it. She will be armed with an agenda, which she will want to pursue with you.' In fact, today, this seemed not to be the case. She was happy to reminisce a little with Reagan and to hear his thoughts on Gorbachev and the new president. She may even have been uncharacteristically emotional, choking up at one point in the Oval Office and unable to speak. But she also had a heavy cold, so it was difficult to tell.[26]

After ten minutes or so, others including the president-elect and the secretary of state were invited to join the leaders in the Oval Office for a plenary session. They discussed disarmament in more detail, with Reagan thanking Thatcher for 'your strong support for SNF modernization.' These points, he said, had been stressed to the West German chancellor, Helmut Kohl. There was some discussion of the Middle East. And most gratifying of all for Thatcher were Reagan's compliments for the Bruges speech – 'You are right on the mark!' – with the president praising her determination 'that Europe should not embrace protectionism' through the Single European Act, which aimed to create a free-trade area within the European Community by 1992. There was only one issue that in retrospect looked like a departing word of warning: as they discussed arms control and defence issues, Reagan advised Thatcher it would be important to take into account 'the political realities' regarding Germany. It was the first intimation of what would become a serious shift of emphasis in the foreign policy of the incoming administration, which put a higher premium on Germany than Britain as the regional power in Europe.[27]

Meanwhile in the Green Room, while the leaders talked, Nancy Reagan was entertaining Denis Thatcher, whose company she had always seemed to enjoy. 'Come visit us in California,' she told him warmly, adding that they couldn't wait 'to show you some of our favourite California sights.' It confirmed something on which both the Thatchers agreed as they came away from the White House that morning. 'Reagan seemed to be quite pleased at going underneath, and so did Nancy,' Mrs Thatcher said afterwards. 'They were very relaxed about it, and obviously thought they had had enough and it was time for him to have a rest.'[28]

After the plenary session in the Oval Office, events moved into a more public and whimsical phase. Thatcher went from the White House to the State Department, where George Shultz had laid on a dinner in her honour. Beforehand he had disconcerted Charles Price, US ambassador to London, by inquiring whether Thatcher had a sense of humour. Uneasily, the ambassador had asked the secretary what he had mind. 'What I don't have in mind,' replied Shultz waspishly, 'is offering to seat her and then pulling the chair out from under her.'

In fact, Shultz had judged the victim of a mild 'roasting' down to a tee, bestowing upon Thatcher 'the first and only Grand Order of the Handbag'. He explained that the order was in recognition of the important role that Thatcher's bag had played in international diplomacy. When compromise proved impossible, or communiqués were mired in obscure and tepid prose, said Shultz, 'that is when Prime Minister Thatcher produces her handbag and pulls out of it, almost like a rabbit out of a hat, a statement which invariably becomes the statement we adopt.' To increasing laughter, he observed that it seemed fitting that Thatcher should be given a new bag, since her role in the Atlantic Alliance had inspired a new addition to NATO vocabulary: 'Handbag, verb transitive, bag, bagging; 1. to inspire through leadership, energy and special powers of persuasion, agreement on alliance programs and priorities that advance the achievement of the Western cause; 2. to employ a unique diplomatic satchel; 3. to bag is generally considered to be more desirable than to be bagged.'

Before presenting the black patent bag, Shultz theatrically noted that he wanted to check the contents. Sure enough, there were papers inside, what he called some 'Margaret Thatcherisms' taken from her past speeches and statements. 'It's well known that you speak in a clear voice and never carry an empty bag!' concluded Shultz, as Thatcher looked on beaming.[29]

The secretary's gesture was a touching one, but it was rooted in respect for Thatcher's abilities both as an ally and an adversary. Much of the pleasure of his joke was in the self-deprecating way it acknowledged that he himself had on more than one occasion been the victim of a 'handbagging'. Yet, as he made clear in a note to the president, Thatcher had been an important alliance partner. 'The US-UK "Special Relationship" is as strong as ever,' he told Reagan privately, 'and remains of fundamental importance to the foreign policy of both nations.' The visit would be an opportunity 'to thank the prime minister for her support of administration policies.'[30]

Where the secretary of state's tribute had been tongue-in-cheek, what followed later was full-on emotion bordering on the saccharine. Inside the White House, the Washington elite gathered for the last state banquet of the Reagan era. When it came to the toasts, Reagan shot the works in praise of Thatcher and their achievements together. 'She is a leader with vision and the courage to stay the course until the battles are won,' he proclaimed. He had been 'fortunate' to enjoy such a 'personal rapport and a genuine friendship with Margaret Thatcher.' Their relationship had 'added to the great stream of Anglo-American history and helped strengthen the tradition of a special relationship between the leaders of our two nations.' There was no question that 'the impact of Mrs Thatcher's leadership at home and abroad secures her place in history,' enthused Reagan. 'She's a world leader in every meaning of the word. And Nancy and I are proud to claim the Thatchers as our friends, just as America is proud to claim the United Kingdom as a friend and ally.'

Thatcher's reply was no less fulsome. 'You have been more than a staunch ally and wise counsellor,' she told him. 'You have also been a wonderful friend to me and my country . . . I can do no better, Mr President, than repeat your own favourite verdict on a film script. "That story", Sam Goldwyn once said, "is wonderful; it is magnificent; it is prolific!" So, too, Mr President, have been the Reagan Years!' As the audience thundered its approval, Nancy Reagan was seen to wipe away a tear. 'I'm feeling very sentimental, nostalgic,' the first lady said afterwards.[31]

Then, as the band struck up 'Shall We Dance?', Reagan swept Thatcher, resplendent in pink, onto the dance floor to twirl their remarkable relationship into history.

'There was an air of nostalgia,' Reagan wrote in his diary that night. 'Our final state dinner etc.

'She really is a great stateswoman.'[32]

Amid the kudos and mutual back-slapping, there was one last tragedy to give Reagan and Thatcher pause for thought. A few weeks after the prime minister's visit to the Reagan White House, a Pan Am jumbo jet bound for New York exploded and crashed into the town of Lockerbie in Scotland. In total, 259 people on board the flight and 11 on the ground died in the crash. Debris from the aircraft was scattered across 845 square miles and the impact reached 1.6 on the Richter scale. In due course, evidence of a bomb would be found. In January 2001, after an eighty-four-day trial held in the Netherlands under Scottish law, Abdelbaset Ali Mohmed al-Megrahi was given a life sentence. He was believed to be a Libyan intelligence agent.[33]

Thatcher immediately visited the scene of the crash to see for herself and to comfort mourners. 'Those of us who saw it will just never never forget the experience,' she told David Frost in a television interview afterwards. A few hours after she returned from Lockerbie, Reagan phoned. 'I want to thank you for your expression of sorrow on the Pan Am 103 tragedy,' he told her. 'On behalf of the American people, I also want to thank the rescue workers who responded so quickly and courageously. Our thoughts and prayers are with the victims of this accident, both the passengers on the plane and the villagers in Scotland and with their loved ones.'[34]

What neither seemed to consider was whether the attack on Pan Am 103 was part of a spiral of 'tit for tat' attacks, in this case a Libyan state-sponsored act of retaliation for the US bombing of Libya in 1986, which had killed 101 people, including Gaddafi's adopted daughter, and landed Thatcher in such trouble domestically. That attack in turn had been a response to the Libyan state-sponsored terrorist attack on a discothèque in West Berlin a few weeks beforehand. In his memoirs, Reagan did not mention Lockerbie, but he did claim that by the end of his presidency, 'our air attack on Libya had silenced some of the state-sponsored terrorism directed from Tripoli.' Thatcher in her memoirs, published in 1993, wrote of her support for the US attack on Libya that 'It turned out to be a more decisive blow against Libyan-sponsored terrorism than I could ever have imagined . . . Gaddafi had not been destroyed but he had been humbled. There was a marked decline in Libyan-sponsored terrorism in succeeding years.' When Thatcher published *Statecraft* in 2002, by which time the verdict on Megrahi had been handed down, she was forced to concede that 'Libya was clearly behind the bombing in 1988 of a Pan American aircraft over Lockerbie'. Yet she was still able to write that Libya had 'sponsored a series of terrorist actions against America and its allies – until with my strong support, President Reagan taught Gaddafi a lesson in the US raid of 1986'.

Certainly it was a lesson that Reagan and Thatcher had administered; the single worst terrorist attack on British soil that followed suggests it was not one without consequences.[35]

Lockerbie was a depressing coda to the Reagan–Thatcher years, but it was not one upon which either chose to dwell. In a glowing article for *National Review* ('Reagan's Leadership, America's Recovery'), published to coincide with the president's departure from office, Thatcher praised his 'success in the continuing battle against terrorism.' Her conclusion on the Reagan years was unambiguous. 'The results of that strong leadership are all around us,' Thatcher declared. 'President Reagan departs the political scene leaving America stronger and more confident, and the West more united than ever before.'[36]

In a private note to Reagan in the days before he left office, she was, if anything, even more effusive. 'As you leave office, I wanted to say thank you,' she wrote. 'You have been a great president, one of the greatest, because you stood for all that is best in America. Your beliefs, your convictions, your faith shone through everything you did. And your unassuming courtesy was the hallmark of the true and perfect gentleman. You have been an example and an inspiration to us all.'[37]

Sitting in the Oval Office on his last evening as president, Ronald Reagan was moved enough by Thatcher's letter to make one last gesture of solidarity towards her. There was a folder of letters and photographs to be signed. Included among them was a note of farewell to Thatcher. 'For the past eight years,' it read,

> our partnership has strengthened the ability and the resolve of the Western alliance to defend itself and the cause of freedom everywhere. The world's improving prospects for peace and security are the ideas we cherish – ideas you began planting in Britain a decade ago. You have been an invaluable ally, but more than that, you are a great friend. It has been an honor to work with you since 1981.[38]

Reagan read over the letter approvingly, and then put it to one side. He worked through all his other letters, before returning again to Thatcher's and signing 'Ron' for one final time.

It was the last official letter of his presidency.

With that, Reagan left the Oval Office for the family residence to write his diary and get an early night.

'Tomorrow,' he wrote, 'I stop being President.'[39]

Epilogue

'Lead me into the sunset . . .'

Ronald Reagan Presidential Library, Simi Valley, California. 6 February 1993. Celebrations to mark the former president's eighty-second birthday had been meticulously crafted. Showbiz razzmatazz abounded with TV host Merv Griffin as a colourful master of ceremonies. Money was on show too for a black-tie gala dinner of the kind that habitually raised millions for the library. But there was also an unequivocal message. Margaret Thatcher's presence at the top table was a symbol of the historical narrative that had emerged from the 1980s: here sat the two leaders who had taken on the Soviet Union and won. To put this achievement into an historic context, the presidential library had mounted an exhibition for guests to enjoy – *The Art and Treasures of Winston Churchill*. The point could not have been made more clearly. Reagan and Thatcher stood alongside Roosevelt and Churchill as global titans who had acted together to defend democracy and vanquish tyranny.[1]

Except that the evening did not quite work out like that. This occasion would not be remembered as an evening of triumph and congratulation. Instead, it would become the marker for personal tragedy.

Everything started well, with a rousing tribute to Reagan from Thatcher, who praised the president's courage and vision. The American responded with characteristic humour and modesty. 'I don't think I really deserve such a fuss,' he quipped, 'but as George Burns once said, I have arthritis and I don't deserve that either.'

Then Reagan proposed a toast to Thatcher as his closest friend and ally. The audience stood to clink their glasses and applaud, before resuming their seats. When the guests had quietened down, Reagan began to speak again. Only to everyone's horror, he repeated with identical words and gestures the salute to Thatcher he had given moments earlier. For a second everybody in the room froze, until a palpable and gracious collective decision was made simply to ignore the repetition. Up onto their feet came the audience to acknowledge Thatcher once again. The audience then held its breath, waiting and hoping, only relaxing when Reagan moved on to another subject.[2]

It was easy to put the former president's lapse down to an octogenarian muddle. These things happened. The press did not report the mistake; guests, in an era before Twitter, did not circulate the gossip to a cannibalistic blogosphere. In fact it was more like the days of Churchill, when news of this kind simply never reached the ears of the general public.[3] Yet by the time Margaret Thatcher returned to the United States the following year for Reagan's eighty-third birthday, it was clear that muddle had turned into something more fateful. 'I remember we met beforehand to do all the photographs which we usually do,' she recalled. 'And he was very quiet and not very communicative at all. Nancy had to lead him to the platform holding him by the hand. And when she put up her hand to wave, immediately she said to Ron, "Wave", and he did. I had thought that he was probably very tired.'[4]

Nancy Reagan knew better. When the couple got back to their hotel that night, she had John Hutton, physician to the president, come up to the room. 'I'm a little confused,' the former commander-in-chief admitted. 'I don't know where I am.' Later that year, the Mayo Clinic in Minnesota confirmed to President Reagan that he had early-stage Alzheimer's disease. He announced the news to the American public in a moving and uplifting letter:

> Let me thank you, the American people, for giving me the great honor of allowing me to serve as your President. When the Lord calls me home, whenever that may be, I will leave with the greatest love for this country of ours and eternal

optimism for its future. I now begin the journey that will lead me into the sunset of my life. I know that for America there will always be a bright dawn ahead.[5]

And with that Reagan was gone – exiting the public stage for the last time.

The announcement of Reagan's illness and his departure from public life were choreographed with a grace and dignity that were not granted to Margaret Thatcher. When Thatcher's daughter, Carol, casually revealed in a memoir in 2008 that her mother had dementia, it drew a stinging rebuke from Ron Reagan, the youngest son of the former president. Carol's revelation and the worldwide headlines it caused, said Reagan, were 'in monumentally bad taste and unnecessary.'[6] Others were even more brutal. 'My question is why did Carol think it right to reveal her mother's plight, especially when none of her political friends had ever done so even in their political books?' asked Kelvin McKenzie, editor of *The Sun,* Britain's bestselling tabloid during Thatcher's heyday. 'I can only conclude it was done for money. I hope she feels proud of herself.'[7]

Thatcher's illness was in many ways characteristic of this later period in her life, which had been dominated by sadness and disappointment. For the most part, that was the result of the ruthless way in which she was dispatched from power. Ronald Reagan had enjoyed a farewell world tour and the ceremonial of the new president's Inauguration Day. Thatcher's exit was more painful – literally a tearful farewell in Downing Street. Unlike the US Constitution, with its term limits enshrined in the Twenty-second Amendment, the British system seems almost designed to end unhappily for holders of the office of prime minister. Most leave because they have lost a general election. Some go because they no longer command the confidence of their party or Parliament. Few exit because they've had enough and want to go.

In 1989, the year that Reagan left office, Margaret Thatcher celebrated ten years as prime minister. Many, including her husband Denis, had urged her to use this anniversary as an opportunity to bow out on a high note. Instead, Thatcher began talking of beating Lord Liverpool's record of fourteen years in office. 'We might even break Walpole's record!' she told a startled journalist in September 1989.[8] The prospect of twenty years of Thatcher as PM was too much for one patrician Tory backbencher, Sir Anthony Meyer, who promptly challenged her for the party leadership. Thatcher won easily, but Meyer was a stalking horse for a much stronger candidate the following year – her long-term rival and former defence secretary, Michael Heseltine.

In the leadership election of November 1990, Heseltine did enough in the first round to provoke a cabinet coup against Thatcher. They abandoned her, each saying that she would lose the second-round vote. 'I was sick at heart,' she later wrote. 'I could have resisted [opponents] and potential rivals and even respected them for it; but what grieved me was the desertion of those I had always considered friends and allies and the weasel words whereby they had transmuted their betrayal into frank advice and concern for my fate.'[9] It was a lesson not lost on Alan Clark, one of the few members of the government who remained loyal to her. 'There are no true friends in politics,' he reflected in his diary. 'We are all sharks circling, and waiting, for traces of blood to appear in the water.'[10]

Margaret Thatcher resigned on 22 November 1990 after 11 years and 209 days as prime minister. Many factors accounted for her fall, including a new 'community charge' system of local taxation that prompted riots and marches throughout the country; an attitude towards Europe that alienated senior members of her cabinet; the perception of a 'bunker' mentality in Downing Street; and, perhaps most important of all, a slew of opinion polls which suggested the Conservatives would lose the next general election. Each made an important contribution to a more straightforward political reality: after more than a decade, people by and large felt it was time for change. As Thatcher made it clear that she wanted to go 'on and on', a graceful exit ceased to be an option. Instead, she became the victim of one of the most brutal defenestrations in modern British politics. As if to prove the point that people just fancied a change, the Conservative Party and then the electorate voted for a new prime minister as far removed in character from Margaret Thatcher as it was possible to imagine – the mild-mannered John Major, whose *Spitting Image* TV puppet cast him entirely in grey. The sense of betrayal that continued to surround Thatcher's removal would overshadow Major's premiership and poison the well of Conservative politics for a generation.

Thatcher herself was never reconciled to the manner of her departure. 'I miss it,' she told George H.W. Bush a decade afterwards. 'I wish I were still there.'[11]

Reagan was characteristically gracious to Thatcher during this difficult transition. Just two weeks after Thatcher's resignation as prime minister, the former president found himself in London on a four-day visit. Arrangements had been made earlier in the year for him to see Thatcher in Downing Street. Now the two met at Claridge's Hotel in Mayfair, where Reagan privately consoled Thatcher on the brutality of political life and publicly declared, 'I salute you!' while they posed for the waiting media.[12] He immediately invited her to speak at his birthday celebrations the following February. This generous act, repeated each year until his withdrawal from public life, would become an important element of Thatcher's life after power.

Less than a month before Reagan wrote to the American people to announce his Alzheimer's disease, he sent Thatcher a birthday greeting that offered her both valedictory thanks and one last lesson in how to count your blessings. 'What a wonderful opportunity to celebrate you and your lifetime of accomplishments and tell you how much you have meant to us through the years,' he told her movingly. 'How blessed I have been to celebrate so many of life's special moments with you.' Then at the end, for the first time, he signed off 'Fondly, Ron'.[13]

It was an affectionate final touch to a relationship that at one time had been among the most analysed and discussed in the world.

The personal sadness of these twilight years, and the gentle affection that now existed between Reagan and Thatcher, helped gloss over just how difficult the relationship had been.

During eight years together in power, these two leaders had fought and disagreed over almost every major international decision that they had confronted: imposing sanctions on the Soviet gas pipeline; the Falklands crisis, when Thatcher had been 'horrified' by the president's ambivalence and irresolution; Grenada, when Reagan felt the same about Thatcher's lack of conviction; arms control and the abolition of nuclear weapons; the Strategic Defense Initiative; the Middle East, notably Lebanon and Libya; the relationship with Gorbachev, not least at Reykjavik, where Thatcher believed Reagan had come within an inch of betraying the entire western alliance.

These constant skirmishes and conflicts were far removed from the popular myth of Reagan and Thatcher in a loving 'political marriage'. Yet their alliance was of first-rank importance, albeit not for the reasons that many, including even the principal actors themselves, stated at the time.

The stature of that relationship can be illustrated by events that took place just a few months after Reagan left the White House in 1989, as Thatcher celebrated the landmark of ten years in office. That summer, Ronald Reagan made London the venue for his first overseas trip since leaving the White House. His arrival, noted the *New York Times*, 'was welcomed almost as visiting nobility.' At the Guildhall, Reagan was greeted by liveried heralds with sounding trumpets. There was an emotional return to Downing Street to dine with Thatcher. And at Buckingham Palace the Queen entertained the Reagans to lunch, after which the Palace announced that Her Majesty had been pleased to confer a knighthood on the former president. 'I can't say how proud I am,' Reagan told waiting reporters afterwards, beaming as he displayed the regalia of the Order of the Bath. 'Don't drop them!' the Queen joshed him in a rare public display of humour.[14]

Amid the pageantry, fanfares and honours, there was also political substance. In the Gothic splendour of the Guildhall, where Reagan had spoken the previous year during his final visit to Britain as president, he now delivered a powerful speech on the communications revolution that he believed had begun an unstoppable march towards global democracy. This was especially timely coming days after a military crackdown by the Chinese government against protesters in Tiananmen Square. 'You cannot massacre an idea,' Reagan declared. The seeds of democracy had been planted. It might take 'years or even decades', but one day 'the people of these countries [will] sit in the shade of democracy.' Totalitarian states were increasingly helpless against the communications technology that facilitated the spread of information – the 'oxygen of the modern age'. The knowledge it delivered 'seeps through the walls topped with barbed wire and wafts across the electrified, booby-trapped borders'. Ultimately, totalitarian regimes would be powerless to resist. 'The Goliath of totalitarianism will be brought down by the David of the microchip,' he promised. 'I believe more than armies, more than diplomacy, more than the best intentions of democratic nations, the communications revolution will be the greatest force for the advancement of human freedom the world has ever seen.'[15]

Reagan's continuing star quality and his ability to articulate big ideas – arguably *the* big idea of the coming century – were in marked contrast for Thatcher with the recent visit of President George H.W. Bush, who had been in London just two weeks earlier. That trip, Bush's first to Europe as commander-in-chief, had been a difficult one for the prime minister. The new president was coming to mark the fortieth anniversary of NATO at a conference in Brussels. Thatcher had suggested London as the venue, but had been turned down flat. Instead, the president's stay in the UK was tacked on at the end of his European tour – a day trip before returning to his Kennebunkport retreat in Maine to play golf. An expedition outside London was cancelled. In contrast to Bonn, where he stayed for two days and made a keynote address, there was no major speech in London. 'There is nothing of substance here and little of color,' lamented Larry O'Rourke, who wrote the press pool copy for Bush's visit to No. 10.[16]

The president's dismissive attitude, rooted in his annoyance at Thatcher's apparent intransigence on European security issues, seemed to many a conscious snub of the prime minister. At the NATO conference and again in London there was an undercurrent of American irritation with her. As the two emerged from dinner at No. 10, both leaders endured awkward questioning about the state of the alliance. 'We have had a marvellous day!' Thatcher lied, trying to make the best of things. 'It is so easy to talk to George Bush because, of course, we have been talking over the years and we have the same views.' When Bush was asked to comment, he ducked the question. 'I tell you what, I am awful busy,' he blathered. 'I have got to get home and go to bed real fast. No, I cannot do it!' Finally, with Thatcher looking on aghast, the president recovered enough poise to sound a pro forma note of thanks. 'It was a wonderful trip,' he said, 'and we, of course, have great respect for the Prime Minister; our relationship with the UK is strong.' Closer to the truth was the judgement of one US official, who briefed the *New York Times*: 'We've heard one lecture too many from her.'[17]

These two visits to London in quick succession by the fortieth and forty-first presidents of the United States reveal three important aspects of the broader relationship between Ronald Reagan and Margaret Thatcher.

First, more than either would have liked to admit, they illustrate the significance of Palmerston's comment, repeated to Thatcher by Gorbachev in 1984, that 'Nations have no permanent friends or allies, they only have permanent interests.' Historically, it was an assertion that was at least half true for Britain and America. They were on the winning side together in the three major conflicts of the twentieth century. If not permanent, the alliance was at least something like a habit or even a pattern.[18] Yet just as in the era of Roosevelt and Churchill, the relationship between Reagan and Thatcher was characterised as much by constant manoeuvring for advantage as instinctive cooperation. Theirs was less a friendship between 'soulmates' than an exacting diplomatic engagement between the leaders of two sovereign, independent states of vastly different strengths and interests. Undoubtedly it had its own unique qualities. Their encounters rested not on some inevitable cultural unity between two 'English-speaking peoples', as Thatcher (echoing Churchill) often claimed, but on geopolitical and ideological interests that sometimes overlapped but at other times sharply diverged. Their contrasting personalities would not naturally have made them friends. Thatcher's position as a major European ally, with close intelligence and defence ties, always guaranteed her a hearing at the White House. But once there, she had to argue her case issue by issue. No year was the same as another. Success in one set of circumstances did not guarantee it in another. When the faces at the top table changed, as they did when Bush replaced Reagan, so too did the dynamic within the relationship.[19]

Second, both Reagan and Thatcher understood that statecraft was a war of ideas. For both, this battleground was primarily about the articulation of beliefs. Reagan's speech in London in June 1989 was a classic of its type: unsparing of totalitarianism yet expressing an unquenchable optimism about the future. Reagan outlined a powerful *idea* in that speech – that the communications revolution would advance freedom 'more than armies, more than diplomacy, more than the best intentions of democratic nations' – but it was prefaced by two words that gave that idea personal authority: *I believe*. This emphasis on the power and possibilities of belief itself was something that had been there from the outset of Reagan's presidency; in his first inaugural address he had called on Americans 'to believe in ourselves and to believe in our capacity to perform great deeds, to believe that together with God's help we can and will resolve the problems which now confront us.'[20] This emphasis was not simply rhetorical. It extended to Reagan's policy making, whether shaping cold-war strategy around a belief that the Soviet Union was doomed to the ash heap of history, trusting his instinct that Gorbachev was a man of goodwill, or defying his entire national security team about total nuclear disarmament on the grounds that the concept of mutually assured destruction was a moral abomination. This approach was all summed up in one of Reagan's favourite and often repeated quotations, Tom Paine's 'We have it in our power to begin the world over again.' It was the belief – hardly conservative – on which Reagan built his entire grand strategy.

Thatcher, like Reagan, was a conviction politician, whose statecraft was often based on instinct. Indeed, her intellectual mentor in the 1970s, Alfred Sherman, judged Thatcher to be a practical illustration of that distinction drawn by the Spanish political philosopher José Ortega y Gasset: 'She was a woman of beliefs, and not ideas (beliefs, in his view, being the more important).'[21] Yet Thatcher more than Reagan put far greater emphasis on testing these beliefs against ideas. She revelled in the adversarial combat of policy discussion. Her fierce debates with Gorbachev were among the most intellectually thrilling episodes of her political life. At key moments in her premiership – for example, her first meeting with Reagan; the decision to reach out to younger Soviet leaders; the implications of SDI – she convened expert seminars to develop and challenge her thinking. And she read voraciously – not just her official boxes, but the constant stream of books and papers sent to her by academic friends at think tanks such as the Centre for Policy Studies. Thatcher's rhetoric was less obviously visionary than Reagan's, but she became a force on the world stage in part because she had the ability to articulate her beliefs in a way that was formidable in its clarity. This was the imposing statecraft of the 'Iron Lady', the only person, according to his chief of staff, 'who could intimidate Ronald Reagan.'[22]

Third, the clearness of vision provided by the Reagan–Thatcher axis never seemed more obvious or valuable than after it had gone. When George Bush made that first trip to Europe in 1989, it was conducted amid widespread criticism at home and abroad about his passivity and lack of ambition. Bush was a cautious realist at heart. On entering office, he had commissioned a general review of US foreign policy without giving any sense either of direction or objective. Then he sat back waiting for 'something' to happen. This led to grave doubts about the new president's ability to inspire and lead the western alliance. The contrast with what – or rather, who – had come before was not lost on Thatcher and other European leaders. 'The Bush administration is passive, reactive, unimaginative,' complained Gianni De Michelis, Italy's deputy prime minister, at the NATO summit. 'It is incredible, but Ronald Reagan seems to understand what's going on better than Bush does.'[23]

Everyone by 1989 recognised that they were living in extraordinary times. Some even claimed that year we had reached 'the end of history'.[24] It was not that Bush and his team failed to understand that something big was happening. This was 'one of those rare moments of historical transition from one era to another,' acknowledged Marlin Fitzwater, the White House spokesman.[25] The problem was that President Bush didn't have a vision for how to deal with it. He was hostile to giving Thatcher a prominent role in debating a blueprint for the post-cold-war world, but his own vision did not extend much beyond 'wait and see'. In fact, his managerial approach to leadership would gel far better with that of Thatcher's successor, John Major, with whom Bush enjoyed a much easier relationship. As Maureen Dowd, the *New York Times* columnist, would observe during the 1997 British general election: 'Just as George Bush seemed to shrink around Ronald Reagan, so Mr Major fades to gray when the gloriously mad Margaret Thatcher steams into view, clutching her famous clarity and her famous handbag.'[26]

'Fades to gray' was never a criticism that could be levelled at either Reagan or Thatcher – or indeed Mikhail Gorbachev. Reagan would modestly judge that he had simply 'been dropped into a grand historical moment.'[27] Yet both leaders displayed – and sometimes even shared – a political and strategic vision. For good or ill, each at a crucial moment in history actively sought to remake the world in which they lived. The managerial leadership that followed them ensured that an important opportunity was missed.

After the Second World War, Roosevelt and Churchill had been followed by the likes of Truman, Bevin, Keynes, Marshall and Kennan, who within five years had rebuilt the western alliance and created a new world order that would last throughout the cold-war era. In contrast, policy makers in the immediate post-cold-war world bobbed along on a sea of prosperity and self-congratulation. When the Twin Towers in New York were attacked on 9/11, the traumatised West had to find a strategy and a world-view in a hurry. The one it turned to was the 'War on Terror', which served not to unite the western alliance or the international community, but to divide it. The previous decade – that valuable moment when the West might have tested a vision to facilitate the movement from one world order to another – had been time squandered. Not only had there been few ideas. It had been a brief post-ideological age in government. 'With former supporters accusing you of "dithering" and longing for the clarity of purpose of your strong-willed predecessor – who would you be?' asked the American conservative commentator

William Safire in 1992. 'You would be either the post-Reagan President of the United States or the post-Thatcher Prime Minister of Britain.' It was a judgement that spoke for the decade.[28]

Reagan and Thatcher in the 1990s quickly passed out of the orbit of day-to-day politics. When Bill Clinton arranged to see Reagan in 1992, the president-elect kept the former commander-in-chief waiting almost an hour. When Thatcher wrote several times to Clinton in the mid-1990s, she didn't even get a reply.[29]

The attention of history has been more emphatic. The partnership between Reagan and Thatcher may not have been the mushy, love-struck political marriage of contemporary myth. They fought hard with each other, taking on difficult issues one by one. When today British and American forces are committed in difficult conflicts around the world, it is worth remembering that some of the most vicious rows of the 1980s came at times when one leader was trying to keep the other out of military engagements. These ferocious debates, along with the decisions that came from them, were important not because Reagan and Thatcher agreed on everything. Indeed, they often seemed to agree on very little. No, their leadership mattered because both understood themselves to be engaged together in the service of an Atlantic enterprise that stretched back across the century and beyond. The dynamics and success of that project shaped the twentieth century and the world in which we live today.

That legacy of Reagan and Thatcher continues to engage the political imagination of those who have succeeded them. 'Both of us came of age during the 1980s,' wrote Democratic president Barack Obama and Conservative prime minister David Cameron during the forty-fourth president's state visit to Britain in May 2011.

> Like so many others, we recall a turbulent decade that began with armies confronting each other across a divided Europe and ended with the Berlin Wall coming down, millions freed from the shackles of communism and human dignity extended across the continent. The Cold War reached this conclusion because of the actions of many brave individuals and many strong nations, but we saw how the bond between

> our two countries – and our two leaders at the time – proved such a vital catalyst for change. It reminded us that when the United States and Britain stand together, our people and people around the world can become more secure and more prosperous.[30]

Ronald Reagan and Margaret Thatcher would have said 'Amen' to that.

Acknowledgements

For help in a variety of ways, I wish to thank: Bertie Ahern, Judith Brett, Ted Bromund, Kathleen Burk, Peter Clarke, Karina Daly, Steve Ellis, Patrick Geoghegan, Jonathan Hallett, Adrian Hardiman, Eoghan Harris, Andrew Heyn, George Hook, Catherine Hynes, Cynthia Koch, Phillipa Levine, Mark Little, Brian Murphy, Denis O'Brien, Fintan O'Toole, Susan Pedersen, Niamh Puirseil, Andrew Roberts, Declan Ryan, Jay Sexton, Mark Simpson, Peter Strafford, Miles Taylor, Caroline Walsh, Stuart Ward, Sean Wilentz, and Garry Wills; Robert Brigham and his colleagues in the History Department at Vassar; the President, Hugh Brady, and former colleagues at University College Dublin, especially Kate Breslin, Maurice Bric, James McGuire, Michael Staunton and Harry White; Jenny Mandel, Suzy Zoumbaris and Steve Branch at the Ronald Reagan Library for their speedy attention to my endless enquiries; the Margaret Thatcher Foundation, especially Christopher Collins; and Andrew Riley at the Churchill Archives Centre, who has been a cheerful and expert guide throughout and even allowed me to see (but not touch!) Lady Thatcher's iconic handbag.

Thanks to my colleagues at Bard College, particularly the President, Leon Botstein, members of the History Program – Mayra Armstead, Christian Crouch, Rob Culp, Jennifer Derr, Carolyn Dewald, Tabetha Ewing, Cecile Kuznitz, Mark Lytle, Greg Moynahan, Joel Perlmann, James Romm, Gennady Shkliarevsky, Alice Stroup, and David Woolner – along with Jonathan Becker and Jonathan Cristol at the Bard Globalization and International

Affairs Program, Roger Berkowitz and Wyatt Mason at the Hannah Arendt Center for Politics and the Humanities, Dean of the College Michele Dominy, Karen Sullivan, Felicia Keesing, Laurie Nash, Leslie Clockel, Joe Luzzi and Helena Baillie, Eric Trudel, Jane Smith, and Bruce and Odile Chilton. Special thanks go to Deirdre d'Albertis and Peter 'Mr Arsenal' Gadsby. A conversation with Ellen Condliffe Lagemann was crucial in writing the epilogue. Walter Russell Mead helped me think about the broader strategic issues. Bard students, as well as being a delight to teach, continue to push and press at ideas in class to my great benefit.

I owe an enormous debt to Kathryn Aldous, Simon Ball, Mark Lytle, Andrew Riley and Richard Vinen, each of whom took valuable time away from their own work to read and improve mine. David Reynolds, Alvin Jackson, Sir David Cannadine and Linda Colley are always incredibly generous with their time and encouragement.

This book is the third that I have had the great pleasure of working on with Tony Whittome, who remains as wise and influential a presence as ever. I am also extremely grateful to Tom Mayer in New York for his careful and challenging reading of the text. Georgina Capel at Capel & Land continues to make my life so much easier. Thanks also to Jocasta Hamilton, Caroline Gascoigne, Paulette Hearn and Robert Weil.

The battered armchair in Mark Lytle's office at Bard has proved a most congenial place to sit and talk about history, politics and many other things besides. Stephen Graham is a warm and gracious presence both in college and around the Aldous family kitchen table. Simon Ball has been a constant source of ideas, provocation and amusement for more than twenty years since we met at Cambridge. My late father, John Aldous, would I hope have enjoyed this book set in the era when he taught me to engage with the political world around us. I could not have written the book without the support of my family: my wife, Kathryn Aldous, our daughter, Elizabeth Aldous, and my mother, Patricia Aldous. In true Eighties fashion, it is to this 'A-Team' that *Reagan and Thatcher* is dedicated with love and gratitude.

Richard Aldous
Annandale-on-Hudson, NY

Notes

PROLOGUE

1 *New York Times*, 12 June 2004. 'Eulogy for President Reagan': Margaret Thatcher Foundation online archive <http://www.margaretthatcher.org> docid=110360 (accessed 22 Mar. 2011). The Margaret Thatcher Foundation archive (cited hereafter as MTF) represents a unique historical resource. This remarkable project, devised and expertly run by Christopher Collins, provides a vast range of archival material relating to Margaret Thatcher that is constantly updated as documents are released into the public record. Historians of contemporary Britain owe Mr Collins and the Thatcher Foundation a profound debt of gratitude. URLs at http://www.margaretthatcher.org/ are stable; the six-digit ID number provides a stable route to any particular document. The online archive also involves a partnership between the Thatcher Foundation and the Churchill College Archives Centre, which houses the private papers of Baroness Thatcher. I am grateful to Andrew Riley, curator of the Thatcher Papers, for his advice and encouragement.
2 See primarily the Ronald Reagan Oral Histories (cited hereafter as RROH) at the Miller Center, University of Virginia <http://millercenter.org/president/reagan> and the British Diplomatic Oral History Programme (cited hereafter as BDOHP) at the Churchill College Archives Centre <http://www.chu.cam.ac.uk/archives/collections/BDOHP>.

3 Sarah Brown, *Behind the Black Door* (London, 2011), p. 209.
4 Tony Benn, *Free at Last: Diaries, 1991–2001* (London, 2002), p. 211.

CHAPTER ONE

1 Nicholas Henderson, *Mandarin: The diaries of Nicholas Henderson* (cited hereafter as *Diaries*) (London, 1994), pp. 384–5.
2 Memo, Al Haig to the President, 18 Feb. 1981: Folder 'Department of State briefing book re: the visit of British prime minister Thatcher' (1 of 3), Box 91434, Ronald Reagan Presidential Library, Simi Valley, CA. Obituary of Nicholas Henderson, *Guardian*, 17 Mar. 2009.
3 Interview with Sir Oliver Wright: BDOHP. Henderson, *Diaries*, pp. 372–6.
4 Interview with Richard Allen, 28 Dec. 2002: RROH.
5 Henderson, *Diaries*, pp. 372–82. Memo, Al Haig to the President, 18 Feb. 1981: Folder 'Department of State briefing book re: the visit of British prime minister Thatcher'. Reagan did however attend a state dinner at the Soviet Embassy in December 1987 hosted by Mikhail Gorbachev.
6 Margaret Thatcher, *The Downing Street Years* (London, 1993), p. 158. Memo, Presidential interview with BBC, 7 Jan. 1984: Office of the President, Presidential briefing papers, File, 21 Jan. 1981, Ronald Reagan Library. Thatcher to Reagan, 20 Jan. 1981: MTF, docid=104553 (accessed 27 July 2007).
7 Memo, Brzezinski to Carter, 12 May 1979: MTF, docid=110467 (accessed 2 Feb. 2010). Jimmy Carter, *White House Diary* (New York, 2010), p. 97.
8 Thatcher, *Downing Street Years*, pp. 68–9.
9 Telegram, Henderson to FO, 20 Dec. 1979: MTF, docid=112144 (accessed 2 Feb. 2010). Carter, *White House Diary*, p. 337. Telephone conversation between Thatcher and Carter, 28 Dec. 1979: MTF, docid=112219 (accessed 5 Jan. 2011). Carter to Thatcher, 10 Feb. 1980: MTF, docid=112689 (accessed 26 Mar. 2011).
10 Remarks on becoming prime minister, 3 May 1979: MTF, docid=104078 (accessed 6 Jan. 2011). Margaret Thatcher, *The Path to Power* (London, 1995), p. 118.

11 David Reynolds, 'A "Special Relationship"? America, Britain and the International Order since the Second World War', *International Affairs* (Royal Institute of International Affairs), vol. 62, no. 1 (Winter 1985–6), pp. 1–20; http://www.jstor.org/stable/2618063. Nigel J. Ashton, 'Anglo-American Relations from World War to Cold War', *Journal of Contemporary History*, vol. 39, no. 1 (January 2004), pp. 117–25; http://www.jstor.org/stable/3180673.

12 Speeches at the White House, 16 Nov. 1988: MTF, docid=107384 (accessed 13 Oct. 2010).

13 Alex Danchev, *On Specialness: Essays in Anglo-American relations* (London, 1998), pp. 2–3.

14 See Christopher Thorne, *Allies of a Kind: The United States, Britain and the war against Japan, 1941–45* (London, 1978), p. 150; and Reynolds, 'A "Special Relationship"?'

15 David Reynolds, *The Creation of the Anglo-American Alliance, 1937–41: A study in competitive co-operation* (London, 1981).

16 Walter Russell Mead, *God and Gold: Britain, America and the making of the modern world* (London, 2007), p. XIII. More generally on FDR and Churchill, see also 'Roosevelt, Churchill and the wartime Anglo-American alliance, 1939–45: Towards a new synthesis', in Hedley Bull and William Roger Louis (eds.), *The Special Relationship: Anglo-American relations since 1945* (Oxford, 1986), pp. 17–41.

17 A phrase coined in this context by David Reynolds in his seminal study: *The Creation of the Anglo-American Alliance, 1937–41: A study in competitive co-operation.*

18 Richard Aldous, *Macmillan, Eisenhower and the Cold War* (Dublin, 2005), pp. 168–71; Nigel Ashton, *Kennedy, Macmillan and the Cold War: The irony of interdependence* (London, 2002); Arthur Schlesinger, *A Thousand Days: John F. Kennedy in the White House* (London, 1965), pp. 339–41. Jonathan Colman, *A 'Special Relationship'?: Harold Wilson, Lyndon B. Johnson and Anglo-American relations 'at the summit', 1964–68* (Manchester, 2004). Catherine Hynes, *The Year that Never Was: Heath, the Nixon administration and the Year of Europe* (Dublin, 2009).

19 Reagan's visits in 1975 and 1978 are described in Thatcher, *Path to Power*, p. 372; Ronald Reagan, *The Autobiography: An*

American Life (London, 1990), p. 204; Geoffrey Smith, *Reagan and Thatcher* (New York, 1991), pp. 2–10; and Nicholas Wapshot, *Ronald Reagan and Margaret Thatcher: A political marriage* (New York, 2007), pp. 85–92. See also Roy Hattersley, *Who Goes Home? Scenes from a political life* (London, 1995), p. 132.

20 Hattersley, *Who Goes Home*?, p. 132.

21 Hugo Young, *One of Us* (London, 1989), p. 250. Richard Cockett, *Thinking the Unthinkable: Think tanks and the economic counter revolution, 1931–1983* (London, 1994), p. 281.

22 Thatcher, *Path to Power*, p. 372; Speech given by Governor Reagan of California, 'The new noblesse oblige', to the Institute of Directors' annual conference, Royal Albert Hall, London, 1969. This speech is listed among Thatcher's personal papers: THCR 1/9, Churchill Archives Centre; *Wall Street Journal*, 5 Nov. 2009. 'Margaret Thatcher interviewed about Ronald Reagan', 8 Jan. 1990: MTF, docid=109324 (accessed 5 May 2011).

23 Interview with Peter Hannaford, 10 Jan. 2003: RROH.

24 Iain Dale (ed.), *Memories of Maggie* (London, 2000), pp. 122–3.

25 Reagan to Thatcher, 30 Apr. 1975: MTF, docid=110357 (accessed 25 July 2007). Interview with Peter Hannaford, 10 Jan. 2003: RROH. Kiron Skinner, Annelise Anderson, and Martin Anderson (eds.), *Reagan: A life in letters* (New York, 2003), p. 724.

26 Interview with Richard Allen, 28 Dec. 2002: RROH. Ion Trewin (ed.), *The Hugo Young Papers: Thirty years of British politics off the record* (London, 2008), p. 123.

27 Thatcher, *Path to Power*, p. 372.

28 Address by Reagan, Los Angeles, 14 Dec. 1978: MTF, docid=111687 (accessed 4 Feb. 2010).

29 Darren Dochuk, *From Bible Belt to Sun Belt* (New York, 2011), pp. 392–3. Garry Wills, *Reagan's America: Innocents at home*, 2nd edn (New York, 2000,) pp. 21–2.

30 Thatcher, *Path to Power*, p. 5. John Cambell, *Margaret Thatcher. Vol.1: The Grocer's Daughter* (London, 2000), pp. 15–18.

CHAPTER TWO

1 Thatcher, *Path to Power*, p. 372.
2 Campbell, *Grocer's Daughter*, p. 3. I follow Campbell on Thatcher's early life. See also Peter Clarke's perceptive essay, 'The Rise and Fall of Thatcherism', *London Review of Books*, vol. 20, no. 24, 10 Dec. 1998.
3 Campbell, *Grocer's Daughter*, p. 25.
4 Ibid., p. 50.
5 Thatcher, *Path to Power*, p. 95. Long after Thatcher's retirement, these early travails were dramatised in a clever and amusing TV play by Tony Sain, *The Long Road to Finchley* (2008). The young Thatcher was played with sassy charm by Andrea Riseborough. Geoffrey Palmer played the dyspeptic Sir John Crowder.
6 Clarke, 'The Rise and Fall of Thatcherism', *London Review of Books*, 10 Dec. 1998.
7 Young, *One of Us*, pp. 47, 55–6.
8 Cockett, *Thinking the Unthinkable*, pp. 237–9. Interview with John Coles, BDOHP.
9 Peter Clarke, *Hope and Glory: Britain, 1900–1990* (London, 1996), pp. 351–2.
10 John Ranelagh, *Thatcher's People* (London, 1992), p. ix.
11 Francis Fukuyama, 'Big-Government Skeptic', *New York Times Book Review*, 8 May 2011.
12 Thatcher, *Path to Power*, p. 50. Cockett, *Thinking the Unthinkable*, p. 266. Hugo Young and Anne Sloman, *The Thatcher Phenomenon* (London, 1985), pp. 60–1.
13 Young and Sloman, *Thatcher Phenomenon*, p. 64.
14 Record of a meeting between the prime minister and members of the US Congress at the US Senate, 17 Dec. 1979: MTF, docid =112139 (accessed 9 Feb. 2010).
15 *Sunday Telegraph*, 7 Feb. 2010.
16 Bernard Donoughue, *Downing Street Diary*, Vol. 2 (2008); 'Jim's Lessons', http://www.newstatesman.com/uk-politics/2008/09/callaghan-government-cabinet. Thatcher, *Downing Street Years*, p. 18.
17 Cockett, *Thinking the Unthinkable*, p. 281.
18 Andrew Adonis and Tim Hames, *A Conservative Revolution?*

The Thatcher-Reagan decade in perspective (Manchester, 1994), pp. 220–1.

19 Interview with Kenneth Adelman, 30 Sept. 2003: RROH. Thomas W. Evans, *The Education of Ronald Reagan: The General Electric Years and the untold story of his conversion to Conservatism* (New York, 2006), p. 9.

20 Martin Anderson and Annelise Anderson, *Reagan's Secret War: The untold story of his fight to save the world from nuclear disaster* (New York, 2009), p. 12. Interview with Howard Baker, 24 Aug. 2004: RROH.

21 Interview with Howard Baker, 24 Aug. 2004: RROH.

22 Interview with Martin Anderson, 11–12 Dec. 2001: RROH. Anderson and Anderson, *Reagan's Secret War*, p. 1.

23 Evans, *The Education of Ronald Reagan*, pp. 167–9. Text of the speech: Ronald Reagan Library <http://www.reagan.utexas.edu/archives/reference/timechoosing.html>.

24 Philip Jenkins, *Decade of Nightmares: The end of the sixties and the making of eighties America* (New York, 2006), pp. 8, 93–5.

25 Interview with Stuart Spencer, 15–16 Nov. 2001: RROH. Reagan, *An American Life*, p. 19.

26 Interview with Caspar Weinberger, 19 Nov. 2002: RROH.

27 On Reagan's early life, see James T. Patterson, *Restless Giant: The United States from Watergate to Bush v. Gore* (New York, 2005), pp. 129–30. See also Thomas W. Evans, *The Education of Ronald Reagan* (New York, 2007), and Lou Cannon, *President Reagan: The role of a lifetime* (New York, 1991), pp. 33–87.

28 Reagan, *An American Life*, p. 28.

29 Evans, *The Education of Ronald Reagan*, p. 10.

30 Reagan, *An American Life*, p. 89. Wills, *Reagan's America*, pp. 294–7. Evans, *The Education of Ronald Reagan*, p. 139.

31 Reagan's time at GE is detailed in Thomas W. Evans's thought-provoking study, *The Education of Ronald Reagan.*

32 Knott and Chidester, *At Reagan's Side*, p. 68.

33 Thatcher to Reagan, 5 Nov. 1980: MTF, docid=104216 (accessed 25 July 2007).

34 Thatcher, *Path to Power*, p. 372.

35 The phrase is Disraeli's.

CHAPTER THREE

1 Remarks arriving at the White House, 26 Feb. 1981: MTF, docid=104576 (accessed 31 Aug. 2008). The prime minister's files for the US visit – PREM19/600 and PREM19/601 – are available at MTF, http://www.margaretthatcher.org/archive/1981_PREM19.asp (accessed 2 January, 2012).
2 Allen to Reagan, undated: Folder, United Kingdom Prime Minister Thatcher visit, Box 91434, Executive Secretariat files (VIP visits), Ronald Reagan Library.
3 Alan Clark, *Diaries, 1972–1982: Into politics* (cited hereafter as *Diaries: Into politics*) (London, 2000), p. 204.
4 E. H. H. Green, *Thatcher* (London, 2006), pp. 55–82. *Time*, 16 Feb. 1981.
5 Thatcher, *Downing Street Years*, p. 159.
6 George Urban, *Diplomacy and Disillusion at the Court of Margaret Thatcher: An insider's view* (London, 1996), pp. 20–21. Trewin (ed.), *Hugo Young Papers*, p. 155. *The Sun*, 30 Dec. 2010.
7 Urban, *Diplomacy and Disillusion*, p. 27.
8 UK National Archives, PREM 19/227, 4 June 1980: http://www.nationalarchives.gov.uk/news/december2010-files.htm (accessed 11 Jan. 2011). Urban, *Diplomacy and Disillusion*, p. 25. Green, *Thatcher*, pp.175–6.
9 Michael Carver, *Tightrope Walking: British defence policy since 1945* (London, 1992), pp. 120–1.
10 Paul Bremer to Richard Allen, Thatcher visit, post-meeting briefing, 18 Feb. 1981; James Rentschler to Richard Allen, 20 Feb. 1981: Folder UK Prime Minister Thatcher visit 1981, Box 91434, Executive Secretariat files (VIP visits), Ronald Reagan Library. Remarks by the President, 26 Feb. 1981: MTF, docid=104576 (accessed 31 Aug. 2008).
11 John Lewis Gaddis, *Strategies of Containment*, rev. edn (Oxford, 2005), p. 354.
12 Henderson, *Diaries*, p. 387.
13 Speeches at the British Embassy dinner for President Reagan, 27 Feb. 1981: MTF, docid=104581 (accessed 31 Aug. 2008).
14 Ibid. Douglas Brinkley (ed.), *The Reagan Diaries* (New York, 2007), p. 5. Henderson, *Diaries*, p. 390.

15 Private meeting with Prime Minister Thatcher of Great Britain, 28 Feb. 1981: Office of the President, Folder 'Feb. 27, 1981', Box 1, Ronald Reagan Library. Brinkley (ed.), *Reagan Diaries*, p. 5.
16 Knott and Chidester, *At Reagan's Side*, p. 206.
17 House of Commons statement by the prime minister (American Visit), 2 Mar. 1981: MTF, docid=104585 (accessed 31 Aug. 2007). Henderson, *Diaries*, p. 390.
18 Thatcher to Reagan, 5 Mar. 1981: MTF, docid=109286 (accessed 31 Aug. 2007).
19 Wills, *Reagan's America*, p. 2.
20 Thatcher to Reagan, 30 Mar. 1981: MTF, docid=109228 (accessed 31 Aug. 2008).
21 Interview with Lyn Nofziger, 6 Mar. 2003: RROH.
22 Thatcher, *Downing Street Years*, pp. 782–3.
23 Reagan to Thatcher, 27 Apr. 1981: National Security Affairs, Assistant to the President, Head of State file, Folder UK PM Thatcher cables (1), Box 34, Ronald Reagan Library.
24 Interview with Max Friedersdorf, 24–25 Oct. 2002: RROH. Andrew Roberts, *A History of the English Speaking Peoples since 1900* (London, 2006), p. 523. See also Sean Wilentz, *The Age of Reagan* (New York, 2008), pp. 277–8. Richard Rhodes, *Arsenals of Folly: The making of the nuclear arms race* (London, 2008), p. 149.
25 Skinner, Anderson, and Anderson (eds.), *Reagan: A life in letters*, p. 739.
26 Anderson and Anderson, *Reagan's Secret War*, pp. 50–5.
27 Interview with Martin Anderson, 11–12 Dec. 2001: RROH.
28 Thatcher, *Downing Street Years*, p. 164.
29 Mitterrand, however, did have one ace to play with Reagan at Montebello. He revealed that the French had recruited a high-level defector in place in Moscow and offered to share the intelligence with the Americans: David Hoffman, *The Dead Hand: The untold story of the cold war arms race and its dangerous legacy* (New York, 2009), p. 34. Reagan, *An American Life*, pp. 351–3. Brinkley (ed.), *Reagan Diaries*, p. 31.
30 *New York Times*, 6 Nov. 1980. Jentleson, *Pipeline Politcs*, p. 184.
31 Pierre Trudeau, *Memoirs* (Toronto, 1994), p. 222.
32 Brinkley (ed.), *Reagan Diaries*, p. 3.
33 Ibid., p. 32.

34 Richard Vinen, *Thatcher's Britain: The politics and social upheaval of the 1980s* (London, 2009), pp. 108–13. See also Nigel Lawson, *The View from No. 11: Memoirs of a Tory radical* (London, 1992), pp. 44–5.
35 Told in John Nott, *Here Today, Gone Tomorrow* (London, 2002), p. 198. Vinen, *Thatcher's Britain*, pp. 112–15. John Campbell, *Margaret Thatcher.* Vol. 2: *The iron lady* (London, 2003), p. 113. Green, *Thatcher*, pp. 69–70.
36 The minister quoting Churchill was Ian Gilmour. Young, *One of Us*, pp. 218–19. Vinen, *Thatcher's Britain*, p. 131.
37 Clark, *Diaries: Into politics*, p. 251.
38 Ferdinand Mount, *Cold Cream: My early life and other mistakes* (London, 2008), p. 238. Vinen, *Thatcher's Britain*, p. 115. Young, *One of Us*, p. 223.
39 Allen to Reagan, 31 July 1981: MTF, docid=110522 (accessed 31 Aug. 2007).
40 Pew Research Center: http://pewresearch.org/pubs/1818/reagan-recession-public-opinion-very-negative (accessed 6 May 2011). Jenkins, *Decade of Nightmares*, pp. 166–7, 180–1. Patterson, *Restless Giant*, pp. 154–5.
41 Knott and Chidester, *At Reagan's Side*, p. 87.
42 Interview with Max Friedersdorf, 24–25 Oct. 2002: RROH.
43 Patterson, *Restless Giant*, pp. 110–11, 151–2. John Aloysius Farrell, *Tip O'Neill and the Democratic Century* (Boston, 2001), pp. 554–62. *New York Times*, 11 Mar. 2001.
44 Nott, *Here Today, Gone Tomorrow*, p. 20.
45 Young, *One of Us*, p. 241.
46 Allen to Reagan, 31 July 1981: MTF, docid=110522 (accessed 31 Aug. 2007). Reagan to Thatcher, 11 Aug. 1981: National Security Affairs, Assistant to the President, Head of State file, Folder UK PM Thatcher cables (1), Box 34, Ronald Reagan Library.
47 Thatcher to Reagan, 20 Aug. and 1 Oct 1981: MTF, docid=109290, 109291 (accessed 31 Aug. 2008).
48 Michael Dockrill, *British Defence since 1945* (Oxford, 1988), pp. 113–14. John Baylis, *Anglo-American Defence Relations*, 2nd edn (London, 1984).
49 John Dumbrell, *A Special Relationship: Anglo-American relations from the cold war to Iraq* (London, 2006), pp. 55, 166–8. Baylis, *Anglo-American Defence Relations, 1939–1984*, p. 87.

50 Thatcher to Reagan, 19 Oct. 1981: MTF, docid=109293 (accessed 31 Aug. 2007).
51 Wilentz, *The Age of Reagan*, p. 151.
52 Robert Jervis, review of *The Zero Option* by Thomas Risse-Kappen, *Political Science Quarterly*, vol. 104, no. 2 (Summer 1989), pp. 336–7, <http://www.jstor.org/stable/2151588>. Christoph Bluth, review of *The Zero Option* in *International Affairs*, vol. 65, no. 3 (Summer 1989), p. 554, <http://www.jstor.org/stable/2621771>.
53 Anderson and Anderson, *Reagan's Secret War*, pp. 67–8.
54 Ibid., p. 71.
55 Remarks to members of the National Press Club, 18 Nov. 1981, <http://reagan2020.us/speeches/arms_reduction_and_nuclear_weapons.asp> (accessed 5 Jan 2011).
56 *New York Times*, 19 Nov. 1981.
57 House of Commons, PMQs, 19 Nov. 1981: MTF, docid=104745 (accessed 31 Aug. 2008).
58 Allen to Reagan, 9 Nov. 1981; Weinberger note of meeting with Thatcher, 11 Dec. 1981: MTF, docid=110524,110635 (accessed 31 Aug. 2007).
59 Hoffman, *The Dead Hand*, p. 33.
60 Bernard Wasserstein, *Barbarism and Civilization: A history of Europe in our time* (London, 2007), pp. 619–20.
61 Brinkley (ed.), *Reagan Diaries*, p. 57. List of sanctions, Paul Kengor, *The Crusader: Ronald Reagan and the fall of communism* (New York, 2006), p. 107.
62 Brinkley (ed.), *Reagan Diaries*, p. 57. NSC minutes, 22 Dec. 1981: MTF, docid=110968 (accessed 31 Aug. 2007).
63 Thatcher, *Downing Street Years*, pp. 253–4.
64 Haig telegram to Reagan: MTF, docid=109312 (accessed 31 Aug. 2007).
65 Ibid.
66 Cover sheet to Haig telegram to Reagan: MTF, docid=109312 (accessed 31 Aug. 2007). Brinkley (ed.), *Reagan Diaries*, p. 65.
67 Thatcher, *Downing Street Years*, pp. 251, 256.
68 George Walden, *Lucky George: Memoirs of an anti-politician* (London, 1999), p. 213.
69 See, e.g., both sides of the argument outlined in David

Pryce-Jones, *The War that Never Was: The fall of the Soviet Empire, 1985–1991* (London, 1995), pp. 105–6.
70 Mark H. Lytle, 'Reviewed Work: Pipeline Politics, by Bruce Jentleson', *Journal of American History*, vol. 74, no. 3 (December 1987), pp. 1103–4. James Mann, *The Rebellion of Ronald Reagan: A history of the end of the cold war* (New York, 2009), p. 30.
71 Hoffman, *The Dead Hand*, pp. 34–5. Weiss's account of the 'Farewell Dossier': <https://www.cia.gov/library/center-for-the-study-of-intelligence/csi-publications/csi-studies/studies/96unclass/farewell.htm#ft6> (accessed 28 Oct. 2010). *New York Times*, 2 Feb. 2004.
72 Kengor, *The Crusader*, p. 122.
73 Minutes of NSC meeting, 16 Oct. 1981: MTF, docid=110939 (accessed 31 Aug. 2007). Kengor, *The Crusader*, p. 126.
74 Paul Kengor and Patricia Clark Doerner, *The Judge: William P. Clark, Ronald Reagan's top hand* (San Francisco, 2007), p. 165.
75 Odd Arne Westad, *The Global Cold War* (Cambridge, 2005), p. 337. Kengor, *The Crusader*, pp. 126–7, and more generally on NSDD 2–120.
76 Kengor and Doerner, *The Judge*, p. 167. <http://www.heritage.org/research/lecture/ronald-reagan-and-the-fall-of-communism>.
77 Jentleson, *Pipeline Politics*, pp. 184–5; 194.
78 Ibid., pp. 195–8.

CHAPTER FOUR

1 Clark, *Diaries: Into politics*, pp. 310–11.
2 Hurd, *Memoirs*, p. 311.
3 Richard Aldous, *The Lion and the Unicorn: Gladstone vs. Disraeli* (London, 2006), pp. 65–6.
4 Sir Lawrence Freedman, *The Official History of the Falklands Campaign* (cited hereafter as *Falklands*), Vol. II (London, 2005), p. 17. The outstanding contemporary account of the conflict, blending political analysis and war reportage, is Max Hastings and Simon Jenkins, *The Battle for the Falkland Isles* (London, 1983).
5 Dockrill, *British Defence since 1945*, p. 115.

6 Nicholas Ridley to Ian Gow, 11 June 1980:MTF, docid=112678; 'Britain puts forward four options on Falklands' (Ridley visit & leaseback), MTF, docid=112605 (accessed 31 Mar. 2011). Gerald W. Hopple, 'Intelligence and Warning: Implications and Lessons of the Falkland Islands War', *World Politics*, vol. 36, no. 3 (April 1984), pp. 339–61. Stable URL: http://www.jstor.org/stable/2010378. Peter J. Beck, review article, 'The Conflict Potential of the "Dots on the Map"', *International History Review*, vol. 13, no. 1 (February 1991), pp. 124–33. Stable URL: http://www.jstor.org/stable/40106326. Denzil Dunnett, 'Self-Determination and the Falklands', *International Affairs* vol. 59, no. 3 (Summer 1983), pp. 415–28. Stable URL: http://www.jstor.org/stable/2618795.

7 *Independent*, 23 Feb. 2010.

8 Richard C. Thornton, *The Falklands Sting: Reagan, Thatcher and Argentina's bomb* (Dulles, VA, 1998), pp. xiv–xvi.

9 Ibid., p. 74. Guillermo A. Makin, 'Argentine Approaches to the Falklands/Malvinas: Was the resort to violence foreseeable?', *International Affairs*, vol. 59, no. 3 (Summer 1983), pp. 391–403 Stable URL: http://www.jstor.org/stable/2618793.

10 Reagan, *An American Life*, p. 358.

11 Statement by the Prime Minister, House of Commons, 3 Apr. 1981: MTF, docid=104910 (accessed 31 Aug. 2007). Campbell, *The Iron Lady*, p. 133.

12 Hansard, 3 Apr. 1982, http://hansard.millbanksystems.com/commons/1982/apr/03/falkland-islands (accessed 30 May 2011).

13 Lord Carrington, *Reflect on Things Past* (London, 1998), pp. 370–1.

14 Interview with Robert Wade-Gery: BDOHP.

15 Interview with John Coles: BDOHP.

16 Thatcher, *Downing Street Years*, p. 179.

17 Reagan to Thatcher, 1 Apr. 1982: MTF, docid=109265 (accessed 31 Aug. 2007).

18 Ibid.

19 Interview with Peter Hall: BDOHP. James Rentschler's Falklands Diary, 1 April–25 June 1982, p. 2: MTF, 'The Falklands War 1982', http://www.margaretthatcher.org/archive/1982_falklands.asp (accessed 5 Mar. 2010). Rentschler's diary is a fascinating and invaluable source for US policy making during the

war. He advised Reagan inside the White House and travelled with Haig during the latter's 'shuttle diplomacy'. Moreover, Rentschler writes in such a vivid and direct fashion that his diary brings the reader right into the room.

20 Henderson, *Diaries*, pp. 349–50. W. Michael Reisman, 'The Struggle for the Falklands', *Yale Law Journal*, vol. 93, no. 2 (December, 1983), pp. 287–317. Stable URL: http://www.jstor.org/stable/796308.

21 Interview with John Coles: BDOHP.

22 George C. Herring, *From Colony to Superpower: US foreign relations since 1776* (New York, 2008), pp. 556–7.

23 Ibid., pp. 884–5.

24 John Ranelagh, *The Agency: The rise and decline of the CIA* (New York, 1986). Thornton, *The Falklands Sting*, pp. 62–7.

25 James Rentschler's Falklands Diary, 1 April–25 June 1982, p. 3: MTF, 'The Falklands War 1982' (accessed 5 Mar. 2010).

26 Interview with John Coles: BDOHP.

27 James Rentschler's Falklands Diary, 1 April–25 June 1982, p. 4: MTF, 'The Falklands War 1982' (accessed 5 Mar. 2010).

28 Ibid.

29 Haig to Reagan, 9 Apr. 1981: MTF, docid=109216 (accessed 31 Aug. 2007).

30 Reagan to Haig, 9 Apr. 1981: MTF, docid=109219 (accessed 31 Aug. 2007).

31 Talking points, Galtieri: Denis Blair files, Folder UK 1982 (03/01–04/30), Box 90233, Ronald Reagan Library.

32 Talking points, Thatcher: Denis Blair files, Folder UK 1982 (03/01–04/30), Box 90233, Ronald Reagan Library. James Rentschler's Falklands Diary, 1 April–25 June 1982, p. 9: MTF, 'The Falklands War 1982' (accessed 5 Mar. 2010). Dumbrell, *A Special Relationship*, p. 198.

33 Nott, *Here Today, Gone Tomorrow*, p. 291. Thatcher, *Downing Street Years*, p. 199. James Rentschler's Falklands Diary, 1 April–25 June 1982, p. 10: MTF, 'The Falklands War 1982' (accessed 5 Mar. 2010).

34 Thatcher, *Downing Street Years*, p. 199. (Brinkley (ed.), *Reagan Diaries*, vol. 1, p. 123.

35 James Rentschler's Falklands Diary, 1 April–25 June 1982, p. 9: MTF, 'The Falklands War 1982' (accessed 5 Mar. 2010).

36 Ibid. Thatcher, *Downing Street Years*, p. 199. Douglas Brinkley (ed.), *The Reagan Diaries*, vol. I, abridged edn (New York, 2009), p. 123.
37 Statement to the House of Commons: MTF, docid=104918 (accessed 8 Mar. 2010).
38 Tony Benn, *The Benn Diaries, 1940–1990* (London, 1995), p. 533.
39 James Rentschler's Falklands Diary, 1 April–25 June 1982, p. 9: MTF, 'The Falklands War 1982' (accessed 5 Mar. 2010). Freedman, *Falklands*, Vol. II, p. 157.
40 Ibid.
41 Enders to Haig, 'Your meeting with the president, 20 April 1982': Denis Blair files, Folder UK 1982 (03/01–04/30), Box 90233, Ronald Reagan Library. Brinkley (ed.), *Reagan Diaries* (abridged), p. 81.
42 Freedman, *Falklands*, Vol. II, p. 170.
43 Francis Pym, *The Politics of Consent* (London, 1984), p. 1.
44 Thatcher, *Downing Street Years*, pp. 205–6.
45 Nott, *Here Today, Gone Tomorrow*, p. 293.
46 Freedman, *Falklands*, Vol. II, pp. 177–8.
47 James Rentschler's Falklands Diary, 1 April–25 June 1982, p. 9: MTF, 'The Falklands War 1982' (accessed 5 Mar. 2010). The Falklands Roundtable, 2003: RROH. Dumbrell, *A Special Relationship*, p. 199.
48 Thatcher, *Downing Street Years*, p. 211. Brinkley (ed.), *Reagan Diaries*, p. 80.
49 Freedman, *Falklands*, Vol. II, pp. 177–8.
50 Remarks on the recapture of South Georgia ('Rejoice'), 25 Apr. 1982: MTF, docid=104923 (accessed 26 July 2011). Thatcher, *Downing Street Years*, p. 212.
51 Interview with Sir Anthony Parsons: BDOHP.
52 Henderson, *Diaries*, p. 454.
53 The Falklands Roundtable, 2003: RROH.
54 Description of US military and intelligence support: Henderson, *Diaries*, pp. 442–4.
55 Brinkley (ed.), *Reagan Diaries*, p. 79.
56 James Chace, 'The turbulent tenure of Alexander Haig', *New York Times*, 22 Apr. 1984.
57 Reagan, *An American Life*, p. 359.

CHAPTER FIVE

1 For a description of the sinking of HMS *Sheffield*, see Sandy Woodward, *One Hundred Days: The memoirs of the Falklands battle group commander* (London, 1992), pp. 1–22; Lawrence Freedman and Virginia Gamba-Stonehouse, *Signals of War: The Falklands conflict of 1982* (London, 1990), p. 289.
2 Nott, *Here Today, Gone Tomorrow*, p. 309.
3 *The Falkland Islands: What Now? What Next?*, 4 May 1982: James Rentschler's Falklands Diary, 1 April–25 June 1982, pp. 27–8: MTF, 'The Falklands War 1982' (accessed 5 Mar. 2010).
4 Bremmer to Clark, 4 May 1982: Denis Blair files, Folder UK 1982 (05/01–07/31), Box 90223, Ronald Reagan Library.
5 Thatcher, *Downing Street Years*, p. 217. Freedman, *Falklands*, Vol. II, p. 328.
6 Brinkley (ed.), *Reagan Diaries*, p. 84.
7 Thatcher, *Downing Street Years*, p. 221.
8 Ibid.
9 Wapshott, *Ronald Reagan and Margaret Thatcher*, p. 178.
10 *Sunday Times*, 20 Nov. 2005: MTF, docid=110663 (accessed 14 Jan. 2011).
11 Interview with John Coles: BDOHP.
12 Nott, *Here Today, Gone Tomorrow*, p. 305.
13 *Sunday Times*, 20 Nov. 2005: MTF, docid=110663 (accessed 14 Jan. 2011).
14 Ibid.
15 *Daily Telegraph*, 13 Mar. 2002.
16 Patterson, *Restless Giant*, p. 200. 'The Use of Military Power', 28 Nov. 1984, <http://www.airforcemagazine.com/Magazine Archive/Pages/2004/January%202004/0104kee per.aspx> (accessed 24 Mar. 2011).
17 'UK-Argentine War', undated: Denis Blair files, Folder UK 1982 (05/01–07/31), Box 90223, Ronald Reagan Library. Freedman, *Falklands*, Vol. II, p. 511.
18 Herring, *From Colony to Superpower*, pp. 884–5.
19 'Falklands Strategy on the eve of British invasion', undated: Denis Blair files, Folder UK 1982 (05/01–07/31), Box 90223, Ronald Reagan Library.

20 Henderson, *Diaries*, p. 466.
21 Conversation reconstructed from 'Reagan phone call to Thatcher (urges ceasefire)', 31 May 1982; *The Times*, 8 Mar. 1992: MTF, docid=110526 (accessed 31 Aug. 2007). See also James Rentschler's Falklands Diary, 1 April–25 June 1982, p. 34: MTF, 'The Falklands War 1982' (accessed 5 Mar. 2010).
22 Henderson's conversations with Thatcher and Haig: Henderson, *Diaries*, pp. 466–7.
23 James Rentschler's Falklands Diary, 1 April–25 June 1982, p. 34: MTF, 'The Falklands War 1982' (accessed 5 Mar. 2010).
24 Ibid.
25 Talking Points for Reagan/Thatcher meeting, 3 June 1982: James Rentschler's Falklands Diary, 1 April–25 June 1982, pp. 34–5: MTF, 'The Falklands War 1982' (accessed 5 Mar. 2010).
26 Henderson, *Diaries*, pp. 469–70.
27 Unsually there were no note-takers present, although both leaders said afterwards that they had stuck closely to their talking points. Talking Points for Reagan/Thatcher meeting, 2 June 1982: James Rentschler's Falklands Diary, 1 April–25 June 1982, pp. 34–5: MTF, 'The Falklands War 1982' (accessed 5 Mar. 2010).
28 Freedman, *Falklands*, Vol. II, pp. 530–1.
29 Nott, *Here Today, Gone Tomorrow*, p. 291. Freedman, *Falklands*, Vol. II, pp. 531–2.
30 UN vote: Freedman, *Falklands*, Vol. II, p. 528–30.
31 Thatcher, *Downing Street Years*, p. 232. Henderson, *Diaries*, p. 471.
32 Kitty Kelley, *Nancy Reagan* (London, 1991), pp. 303–5. Henderson, *Diaries*, p. 434.
33 Henderson, *Diaries*, p. 435.
34 Interview with James Kuhn, 7 Mar. 2003: RROH. Tony Benn, *The End of an Era: Diaries, 1980–1990* (London, 1992), p. 227.
35 Frank Prochaska, *The Eagle and the Crown: Americans and the British monarchy* (New Haven, 2008), pp. xii, 182–3.
36 Ibid., pp. xiv, 184. Nigel Hamilton, *American Caesars: Lives of the US presidents from Franklin D. Roosevelt to George W. Bush* (London, 2010), p. 352.
37 Campbell, *The Iron Lady*, pp. 25–7. Thatcher, *Downing Street Years*, pp. 21–23. *Time*, 15 Aug. 1977. 'The Secret World of

Whitehall: Behind the black door', BBC 4, broadcast 23 Mar. 2011. Aldous, *The Lion and the Unicorn*, p. 190. An amusing spoof on life inside the flat at No. 10 can be found in *Yes Prime Minister*, episode 1, series 1, broadcast on 9 Jan. 1986 while Thatcher was PM. Thatcher enjoyed the series and had previously appeared as herself in *Yes Minister* in 1984.

38 *Independent*, 5 Sept. 2010. Thatcher, *Downing Street Years*, p. 41.

39 Reagan speech, Royal Gallery, Westminister, 8 June 1982: MTF, docid=109421 (accessed 31 Aug. 2007).

40 Robert C. Rowland and John M. Jones, *Reagan at Westminster* (College Station, TX, 2010), pp. 39–46, 87.

41 Lou Cannon quoted in Kengor, *The Crusader*, p. 143. Rowland and Jones, *Reagan at Westminster*, pp. 90–5, 105. Henderson, *Diaries*, p. 473.

42 Thatcher, *Downing Street Years*, p. 233.

43 Henderson, *Diaries*, p. 472.

44 *Guardian*, 15 June 1982, <http://www.raf.mod.uk/falklands/rollofhonour.html> (accessed 17 Feb. 2011).

45 Clark, *Diaries: Into politics*, p. 333.

46 PMQs, 17 June 1982: MTF, docid=104970 (accessed 24 Mar. 2010).

47 Reagan to Thatcher, 18 June 1982: MTF, docid=109363 (accessed 31 Aug. 2007).

48 Henderson, *Diaries*, pp. 476–9.

49 Interview with John Coles: BDOHP.

50 Kengor, *The Crusader*, p. 150.

51 Brinkley (ed.), *Reagan Diaries*, p. 89.

52 Brief for Thatcher/Reagan meeting, 22 June 1982: MTF, docid=110520 (accessed 31 Aug. 2007).

53 A vivid account of the meeting in the White House is given in Henderson, *Diaries*, p. 479.

54 Interview with BBC, 1 Sept. 1982: MTF, docid=104815 (accessed 25 Mar. 2010). Henderson, *Diaries*, p. 479.

55 Kengor, *The Crusader*, pp. 152–3.

56 Jentleson, *Pipeline Politics*, pp. 176–7.

57 Interview with BBC, 1 Sept. 1982: MTF, docid=104815 (accessed 25 Mar. 2010).

58 Louis to Secretary of State, July 1982: Denis Blair files, Folder

UK 1982 (05/01–07/31), Box 90233, Ronald Reagan Library.
59 Memorandum of conversation between Weinberger and Thatcher, Office of the Secretary of Defense, 8 Sept. 1982: MTF, docid=110636 (accessed 10 Aug. 2011).
60 Kengor, *The Crusader*, pp. 161, 184–5.
61 Bremer to Clark, 30 Oct. 1982: MTF, docid=109269 (accessed 29 Mar. 2010). In 2010, General Bignone was sentenced to twenty-five years in prison for crimes committed during the 'dirty war' – *New York Times*, 20 Apr. 2010.
62 Reagan to Thatcher, 2 Nov. 1982: MTF, docid=109269 (accessed 29 Mar. 2010).
63 George Shultz, *Turmoil and Triumph: My years as secretary of state* (New York, 1993), pp. 152–3.
64 Ibid.

CHAPTER SIX

1 'The Queen makes a royal splash': *Time* magazine, 14 Mar. 1983. Interview with James Kuhn, 7 Mar. 2003: RROH.
2 Interview with James Kuhn, 7 Mar. 2003: RROH.
3 Smith, *Reagan and Thatcher*, p. 107.
4 Knott and Chidester, *At Reagan's Side*, p. 95.
5 Ibid.
6 Reagan SDI speech, 23 Mar. 1982, <http://www.reagan.utexas.edu/archives/speeches/1983/32383d.htm> (accessed 30 Mar. 2010).
7 Brinkley (ed.), *Reagan Diaries*, p. 140.
8 Frances FitzGerald, *Way Out There in the Blue: Reagan, Star Wars and the end of the cold war* (New York, 2000), pp. 241–8.
9 Interview with Kenneth Adelman, 30 Sept. 2003: RROH.
10 Jack Matlock, *Reagan and Gorbachev* (New York, 2004), p. 61.
11 Rhodes, *Arsenals of Folly*, p. 158. FitzGerald, *Way Out There in the Blue*, pp. 256–7.
12 Ibid.
13 Address by Edward M. Kennedy, Brown University, 4 Jun. 1983, <http://tedkennedy.org/ownwords/event/cold_war> (accessed 22 May 2011).

14 Interview with Sir Oliver Wright: BDOHP. Thatcher, *Downing Street Years*, p. 463.
15 Thatcher, *Downing Street Years*, p. 463.
16 Description of SS-20 and Pershing II missiles: See Hoffman, *The Dead Hand: The untold story of the cold war arms race and its dangerous legacy*, pp. 60–1.
17 Reagan to Thatcher, 16 Feb. 1983: Assistant to the President for National Security Affairs, Head of State File, Folder: United Kingdom, Prime Minister Thatcher – cables 1, Box 34, Ronald Reagan Library.
18 Ibid.
19 Brinkley (ed.), *Reagan Diaries*, p. 156. Shultz, *Turmoil and Triumph*, pp. 355–6.
20 Shultz, *Turmoil and Triumph*, p. 356. Brinkley (ed.), *Reagan Diaries*, p. 156. Frederic Bozo, *Mitterrand, the End of the Cold War, and German Reunification* (New York, 2009), p. 4. Declaration on security, Williamsburg summit, 1983, <http://www.g7.utoronto.ca/summit/1983williamsburg/security.html> (accessed 1 Apr. 2010).
21 Thatcher interview, 8 Jan. 1990: MTF, docid=109324 (accessed 18 June. 2010). Smith, *Reagan and Thatcher*, pp. 107–11.
22 Douglas Brinkley, *The Reagan Diaries* (unabridged), Vol. I (New York, 2009), pp. 230, 347. Shultz, *Turmoil and Triumph*, p. 353. Thatcher to Reagan, 29 May 1983: MTF, docid=110963 (accessed 31 Aug. 2007). Interview with George Shultz, 18 Dec. 2002: RROH.
23 Thatcher to Reagan, 2 June 1983: MTF, docid=109329 (accessed 31 Aug. 2007). Thatcher, *Downing Street Years*, pp. 300–1.
24 On Thatcher's election victory, see Richard Vinen, *Thatcher's Britain*, pp. 126–33; 151–3.
25 Thatcher, *Downing Street Years*, p. 299.
26 Reagan to Thatcher, 15, 16 and 20 June 1983: MTF, docid=109273; 109330; 109331 (accessed 31 Aug. 2007).
27 Louis to Shultz, 15 Sept. 1983: MTF, docid=109408. Clark to Reagan, 19 Sept. 1983: MTF, docid=11602 (accessed 31 Aug. 2007).
28 Thatcher to Reagan, 15 Sept. 1983: MTF, docid=109227 (accessed 27 Jan. 2011). Rhodes, *Arsenals of Folly*, pp. 162–3.

29 Howe, *Conflict of Loyalty*, pp. 316–17. Thatcher, *Downing Street Years*, p. 452. Hoffman, *The Dead Hand*, pp. 88–9.
30 Urban, *Diplomacy and Disillusion*, pp. 39–40.
31 NSC briefing for the president (visit of PM Thatcher), 19 Sept. 1983: MTF, docid=110602 (accessed 31 Aug. 2008). Thatcher, *Downing Street Years*, pp. 323–4.
32 Jentleson, *Pipeline Politics*, pp. 220–1.
33 Thatcher, *Downing Street Years*, pp. 323–4.
34 Shultz, *Turmoil and Triumph*, p. 372.
35 Brinkley (ed.), *Reagan Diaries*, Vol. I, p. 278.
36 Kengor, *The Crusader*, pp. 191–2. Westad, *The Global Cold War*, pp. 339, 344–5.
37 Howe, *Conflict of Loyalty*, p. 324.
38 Denis Healey, *The Time of My Life* (London, 2006), p. 508. Howe, *Conflict of Loyalty*, p. 328. Hansard, 24 Oct. 1983, <http://hansard.millbanksystems.com/commons/1983/oct/24/grenada> (accessed 14 Apr. 2010).
39 Reagan to Thatcher, 24 Oct. 1983: MTF, docid=109428 (accessed 31 Aug. 2007).
40 Thatcher, *Downing Street Years*, p. 331.
41 Reagan to Thatcher, 24 Oct. 1983: MTF, docid=109429 (accessed 31 Aug. 2007).
42 Michael Heseltine, *Life in the Jungle* (London, 2000), p. 259. Howe, *Conflict of Loyalty*, p. 329.
43 Thatcher, *Downing Street Years*, p. 331.
44 Interview with Howard Baker, 24 Aug. 2004: RROH. Brinkley (ed.), *Reagan Diaries*, Vol. I, p. 279.
45 Reagan to Thatcher, 25 Oct. 1983: MTF, docid=109430 (accessed 31 Aug. 2007).
46 Hansard, 25 Oct. 1983, <http://hansard.millbanksystems.com/commons/1983/oct/25/grenada> (accessed 14 Apr. 2010).
47 Tony Thorndike, 'The Grenada Crisis', *The World Today*, vol. 39, no. 12 (December 1983), pp. 468–76. Stable URL: http://www.jstor.org/stable/40395465. John Quigley, 'The United States Invasion of Grenada: Stranger than Fiction', *University of Miami Inter-American Law Review*, vol. 18, no. 2 (Winter 1986–7), pp. 271–352. Stable URL: http://www.jstor.org/stable/40176207.
48 Thatcher, *Downing Street Years*, p. 332. Hansard, 25 Oct. 1983,

<http://hansard.millbanksystems.com/commons/1983/oct/25/engagements> (accessed 14 Apr. 2010).
49 Westad, *Global Cold War*, pp. 339, 345. Mann, *The Rebellion of Ronald Reagan*. Eldon Kenworthy, 'Grenada as Theater', *World Policy Journal*, vol. 1, no. 3 (Spring 1984), pp. 635–51.Stable URL: http://www.jstor.org/stable/40208958.
50 Hill to McFarlane, 2 Nov. 1983: MTF, docid=110647 (accessed 31 Aug. 2007).
51 Thatcher, *Downing Street Years*, p. 332.
52 Reagan phone call to Thatcher (record of conversation), 26 Oct. 1983: MTF, docid=109426 (accessed 31 Aug. 2007).
53 Shultz, *Turmoil and Triumph*, p. 336.
54 Interview with Kenneth Adelman, 30 Sept. 2003: RROH. Smith, *Reagan and Thatcher*, p. 126. Shultz, *Turmoil and Triumph*, p. 340.

CHAPTER SEVEN

1 Urban, *Diplomacy and Disillusion*, pp. 64–5.
2 Howe, *Conflict of Loyalty*, pp. 336–7.
3 Campbell, *The Iron Lady*, p. 278.
4 Roberts, *A History of the English-Speaking Peoples since 1900*, p. 540. Brinkley (ed.), *Reagan Diaries*, Vol. I, p. 278.
5 Reagan to Thatcher, 23 Oct. 1983: MTF, docid=109278 (accessed 31 Aug. 2007).
6 Summary of Reagan/Thatcher correspondence: Hill to McFarlane, 4 Nov. 1983: MTF, docid=109364 (accessed 31 Aug. 2007). Thatcher, *Downing Street Years*, p. 333.
7 Interview with Richard Allen, 28 Dec. 2002: RROH. Thatcher, *Downing Street Years*, p. 334.
8 <http://www.rand.org/pubs/conf_proceedings/CF129/> Thatcher, *Downing Street Years*, p. 334. Herring, *From Colony to Superpower*, p. 875.
9 Reagan to Thatcher, 8 Feb. 1983: MTF, docid=109342 (accessed 19 Apr. 2010). Kemp to McFarlane, 8 Feb. 1984: Folder, United Kingdom Prime Minister Thatcher (8305659–8306168), Box 35, Assistant to the President for National Security Affairs, Head of State file, Ronald Reagan Library.

10 Ibid.
11 Gordon S. Barrass, *The Great Cold War: A journey through the hall of mirrors* (Stanford, CA, 2009), pp. 303–5.
12 Richard J. Aldrich, *The Hidden Hand: Britain, America and cold war secret intelligence* (London, 2001). Barrass, *The Great Cold War*, p. 305.
13 Thatcher, *Downing Street Years*, pp. 457–8.
14 *Economist*, 3 and 10 Mar. 1984; *US News & World Report*, 19 Mar. 1984.
15 *Economist*, 31 Mar. 1984.
16 Wick to McFarlane, 21 Mar. 1983: MTF, docid=110641 (accessed 31 Aug. 2007). Shultz to Reagan, 14 May 1984: Folder, The President's Trip to Europe, Box 91427, Executive Secretariat, NSC, Trip file, Ronald Reagan Library.
17 Briefing Book, 'United Kingdom': Folder, The President's Trip to Europe, Box 91429, Executive Secretariat, NSC, Trip file, Ronald Reagan Library. Smith, *Reagan and Thatcher*, pp. 139–40.
18 Briefing Book, 'Working dinner hosted by Prime Minister Thatcher': Folder, The President's Trip to Europe, Box 91429, Executive Secretariat, NSC, Trip file, Ronald Reagan Library. John O'Sullivan, *The President, the Pope and the Prime Minister: Three who changed the world* (New York, 2006), pp. 247–8.
19 Brinkley (ed.), *Reagan Diaries*, Vol. I, pp. 354–5.
20 Reagan, *An American Life*, p. 354.
21 Reagan to Thatcher, 19 June 1984: MTF, docid=109345 (accessed 31 Aug. 2007).
22 *New York Times*, 10 June 1984.
23 Reagan to Thatcher, 18 July 1984: Folder, United Kingdom Prime Minister Thatcher (8305659–8306168), Box 35, Assistant to the President for National Security Affairs, Head of State file, Ronald Reagan Library.
24 Fielding to Reagan, 16 Aug. 1984: Folder, United Kingdom Prime Minister Thatcher (8305659–8306168), Box 35, Assistant to the President for National Security Affairs, Head of State file, Ronald Reagan Library.
25 Campbell, *The Iron Lady*, pp. 430–1. 'On this day', 12 October 1984, <http://news.bbc.co.uk/onthisday/hi/dates/stories/october/12/newsid_2531000/2531583.stm> (accessed 27 Apr. 2010).

26 Brinkley (ed.), *Reagan Diaries*, Vol. I, p. 390. Reagan call to Thatcher, 12 Oct. 1984: MTF, docid=109352 (accessed 31 Aug. 2007).
27 Reagan to Thatcher, 12 Oct. 1984: MTF, docid=109351 (accessed 31 Aug. 2007).
28 Reagan to Thatcher, 26 Oct. 1984: Folder, United Kingdom Prime Minister Thatcher (8290407–8390524), NSC Executive Secretariat, Head of State file, Ronald Reagan Library.
29 Thatcher to Reagan, 7 Nov. 1984: MTF, docid=109368 (accessed 31 Aug. 2010).
30 Urban, *Diplomacy and Disillusion*, p. 86.
31 Reagan to Thatcher, 13 Nov. 1984: Folder, United Kingdom Prime Minister Thatcher (8290407–8390524), NSC Executive Secretariat, Head of State file, Ronald Reagan Library.
32 Thatcher to Reagan, 29 Mar. 1983: MTF, docid=109327 (accessed 31 Aug. 2010).
33 Vinen, *Thatcher's Britain*, pp. 193, 199–200.
34 Briefing Book, 'United Kingdom': Folder, The President's Trip to Europe, Box 91429, Executive Secretariat, NSC, Trip file, Ronald Reagan Library. Reagan to Thatcher, 6 Apr. 1983; Clark to Reagan, 28 Mar. 1983: MTF, docid=109328 (accessed 29 Apr. 2010).
35 Department of State briefing paper, 'US-UK aviation relations': Folder, UK Prime Minister official visit Dec. 1984, Box 91440, VIP visits, NSC Executive Secretariat, Ronald Reagan Library. Brinkley (ed.), *Reagan Diaries*, Vol. I, p. 397. *Financial Times*, 19 Jan. 1985; Edmund Dell, 'Interdependence and the judges: Civil aviation and antitrust', *International Affairs*, vol. 61, no. 3 (1985), p. 367. James Patrick Hanlon, *Global Airlines* (Oxford, 1999), p. 213.
36 Price to Reagan; Sommer to McFarlane, 20 Dec. 1984: Folder, UK Prime Minister official visit Dec. 1984, Box 91440, VIP visits, NSC Executive Secretariat, Ronald Reagan Library.
37 As Sir Nicholas Henderson made clear to Tony Benn – Benn, *Diaries, 1991–2001*, p. 211.
38 Barrass, *The Great Cold War*, pp. 313–15.
39 Interview with Charles Powell, BDOHP. Thatcher, *Downing Street Years*, pp. 459–61. Interview with Mikhail Gorbachev, 23 Apr. 2001, PBS, *Commanding Heights*: http://www.pbs.org/wgbh/

commandingheights/shared/minitextlo/int_mikhailgorbachev.html (accessed 18 May 2011).

40 Howe, *Conflict of Loyalty*, pp. 358–9. BBC interview, 17 Dec. 1984: MTF, docid=105592 (accessed 31 Aug. 2007). Barrass, *The Great Cold War*, p. 314.

41 Interview with Charles Powell, BDOHP, Michael Lucas, 'SDI and Europe', *World Policy Journal*, vol. 3, no. 2 (Spring 1986), pp. 219–49. Stable URL: http://www.jstor.org/stable/4020901. Anderson and Anderson, *Reagan's Secret War*, p. 191. Smith, *Reagan and Thatcher*, p. 149.

42 Anderson and Anderson, *Reagan's Secret War*, pp. 186–9. Brinkley, (ed.), *Reagan Diaries*, Vol. I, p. 409.

43 Campbell, *The Iron Lady*, pp. 288–9.

44 Geoffrey Smith, a member of the travelling press corps, provides a wonderful description of Thatcher's plane journey and visit to Camp David in his *Reagan and Thatcher*, pp. 151ff.

45 United Press International, 22 Dec. 1984. Report by Norman Sandler. Bernard Ingham, *Kill the Messenger* (London, 1991), p. 260.

46 McFarlane to Reagan, 21 Dec. 1984: Folder, UK Prime Minister official visit Dec. 1984, Box 91440, VIP visits, NSC Executive Secretariat, Ronald Reagan Library.

47 Shultz to Reagan, 20 Dec. 1984; McFarlane to Reagan, 21 Dec. 1984: Folder, UK Prime Minister official visit Dec. 1984, Box 91440, VIP visits, NSC Executive Secretariat, Ronald Reagan Library.

48 Sommer to Kimmitt, 3 Dec. 1984: folder, UK Prime Minister official visit Dec. 1984, Box 91440, VIP visits, NSC Executive Secretariat, Ronald Reagan Library.

49 Meeting with Prime Minister Thatcher, Camp David, 22 Dec. 1984: MTF, docid=109185 (accessed 31 Aug. 2007).

50 Thatcher, *Downing Street Years*, p. 462.

51 Anderson and Anderson, *Reagan's Secret War*, p. 193.

52 Barrass, *The Great Cold War*, p. 305.

53 McFarlane to Reagan, 21 Dec. 1984: Folder, UK Prime Minister official visit Dec. 1984, Box 91440, VIP visits, NSC Executive Secretariat, Ronald Reagan Library.

54 Brinkley (ed.), *Reagan Diaries*, Vol. I, p. 411. Interview with Charles Powell, BDOHP.

CHAPTER EIGHT

1 Brinkley (ed.), *Reagan Diaries* (unabridged), Vol. I, p. 418. Edmund Morris, *Dutch: A memoir of Ronald Reagan* (London, 2000), pp. 510–11.
2 Reagan's second inaugural address: <http://avalon.law.yale.edu/20th_century/reagan2.asp> (accessed 10 May 2010).
3 Lawrence Freedman, *The Evolution of Nuclear Strategy* (London, 2003), p. 395.
4 Thatcher to Reagan, 14 Jan. 2010: MTF, docid=109361 (accessed 31 Aug. 2010).
5 McFarlane to Deaver, 31 Jan. 1985: MTF, docid=110541 (accessed 31 Aug. 2007).
6 Weinberger to Thatcher, undated [29 Jan. 1985]: MTF, docid=109362 (accessed 31 Aug. 2007). Harold Brown, 'Is SDI Technically Feasible?', *Foreign Affairs*, vol. 64, no. 3, *America and the World 1985* (1985), pp. 435–54. Stable URL: http://www.jstor.org/stable/20042669. FitzGerald, *Way Out There in the Blue*, pp. 371–2.
7 Interview with Charles Powell: BDOHP. Reagan's second inaugural address: <http://avalon.law.yale.edu/20th_century/reagan2.asp> (accessed 10 May 2010).
8 'Endorsing Mrs. Thatcher's desire to address Congress', McFarlane to Reagan, 10 Jan. 1985: MTF, docid=110542 (accessed 31 Aug. 2007).
9 Urban, *Diplomacy and Disillusion*, p. 91. Thatcher, *Downing Street Years*, p. 468.
10 Interview with George Shultz, 18 Dec. 2002: RROH
11 Thatcher, *Downing Street Years*, p. 468.
12 Speech to Congress, 20 Feb. 1985: MTF, docid=105968 (accessed 12 Sept. 2009).
13 Heseltine, *Life in the Jungle*, p. 255.
14 Talking points for the president's meeting with prime minister Thatcher: Folder, UK Prime Minister official visit 02/1985, Box 91440, VIP visits, NSC Executive Secretariat, Ronald Reagan Library.
15 Heseltine, *Life in the Jungle*, p. 255. Thatcher, *Downing Street Years*, p. 469.

16 Thatcher to Reagan, 22 Feb. 1985: MTF, docid=109370 (accessed 12 Sept. 2007).
17 Talking points for the president's meeting with prime minister Thatcher: Folder, UK Prime Minister official visit 02/1985, Box 91440, VIP visits, NSC Executive Secretariat, Ronald Reagan Library. Campbell, *The Iron Lady*, p. 291.
18 An account of the speech is found in Howe, *Conflict of Loyalty*, pp. 391–3. For the broader context of European concerns, see *Daedalus*, vol. 114, no. 3, *Weapons in Space*, Vol. II: *Implications for Security* (Summer 1985), pp. 297–313. Healey: Hansard, 14 June 1978 <http://hansard.millbanksystems.com/commons/1978/jun/14/economic-situation> (accessed 24 Feb. 2011).
19 *Washington Post*, 21 Mar. 1985.
20 FitzGerald, *Way Out There in the Blue*, p. 176.
21 *Washington Post*, 21 Mar. 1985.
22 Ibid. Knott and Chidester, *At Reagan's Side* p. 108.
23 Interview with Charles Powell: BDOHP. Howe, *Conflict of Loyalty*, p. 396.
24 Campbell, *The Iron Lady*, p. 292.
25 Interview with Kenneth Adelman, 30 Sept. 2003: RROH.
26 Ibid. Interview with James Kuhn, 7 Mar. 2003: RROH.
27 Thatcher to McFarlane, 29 July 1985: MTF, docid=110637 (accessed 12 Sept. 2007); McFarlane to Thatcher, 15 Aug. 1985: MTF, docid=110638 (accessed 12 Sept. 2007). Smith, *Reagan and Thatcher*, p. 167. Thatcher interview, 8 Jan. 1990: MTF, docid=109324 (accessed 18 June 2010).
28 Sommer to McFarlane, 15 Aug. 1985: MTF, docid=110638 (accessed 12 Sept. 2007).
29 *Daily Mail*, 14 May 2010. Michael Lucas, 'SDI and Europe', *World Policy Journal*, vol. 3, no. 2 (Spring 1986), pp. 219–49. Stable URL: http://www.jstor.org/stable/40209013. David Dimbleby and David Reynolds, *An Ocean Apart* (London, 1988), p. 322.
30 Interview with Kenneth Adelman, 30 Sept. 2003: RROH.
31 Jim Kuhn, *Ronald Reagan in Private* (New York, 2006), p. 164.
32 David Reynolds, *Summits* (London, 2007), pp. 340–1.
33 Interview with Kenneth Adelman, 30 Sept. 2003: RROH.
34 Reagan, *An American Life*, p. 635.
35 Reynolds, *Summits*, p. 344.

36 Philip D. Stewart, 'Gorbachev and Obstacles Toward Détente', *Political Science Quarterly*, vol. 101, no. 1 (1986), pp. 1–22. Stable URL: http://www.jstor.org/stable/2151441. Reynolds, *Summits*, p. 347. David Reynolds, 'Summitry as International Communication', *International Affairs*, vol. 85, no. 1 (London, 2009), p. 123.
37 Matlock, *Reagan and Gorbachev*, pp. 165–6. Reynolds, *Summits*, p. 353.
38 Memorandum of conversation, special session of NATO, 21 Nov. 1985: MTF, docid=109315 (accessed 13 Sept. 2007).
39 Report to meeting of NATO leaders, 21 Nov. 1985: MTF, docid=109315 (accessed 25 Feb. 2011).

CHAPTER NINE

1 House of Commons Statement, 27 Jan. 1986: MTF, docid=106318 (accessed 26 July 2011). Alan Clark, *Diaries* (London, 1993), p. 133.
2 Sarah Curtis (ed.), *The Journals of Woodrow Wyatt*, Vol. 1 (London, 1998), p. 74.
3 Campbell, *The Iron Lady*, p. 493. Douglas Brinkley (ed.), *The Reagan Diaries* (New York, 2009), Vol. II, p. 565.
4 Dimbleby and Reynolds, *An Ocean Apart*, pp. 322–3.
5 Thatcher was briefed by Sir John Cuckney, chairman of Westland, using Woodrow Wyatt as a go-between: See Curtis (ed.), *Wyatt Journals*, Vol. 1, p. 46.
6 Sommer to McFarlane, 27 Sept. 1985: File, UK PM Thatcher 851142, Head of State file, NSC Executive Secretariat, Ronald Reagan Library. Cobb to McFarlane, undated [September 1985]: File, UK PM Thatcher 851142, Head of State file, NSC Executive Secretariat, Ronald Reagan Library.
7 McFarlane to Reagan, 30 Aug. 1985; Reagan to Thatcher, 4 Nov. 1985: File, UK PM Thatcher 851142, Head of State file, NSC Executive Secretariat, Ronald Reagan Library.
8 *The Times*, 30 Nov. 1985.
9 BBC, 'On this day', 27 Dec. 1985, <http://news.bbc.co.uk/onthisday/low/dates/stories/december/27/newsid_2545000/2545949.stm> (accessed 21 May 2010).

10 Chronology of US-Libya relations: <http://www.america.gov/st/texttrans-english/2008/September/20080909135234eaifaso.9841425.html&distid=ucs> (accessed 21 May 2010). Knott and Chidester, *At Reagan's Side*, p. 117. Brinkley (ed.), *Reagan Diaries*, Vol. II, p. 557. Reagan, *An American Life*, p. 518.

11 Poindexter to Reagan, undated: File folder 8600439, System files records, NSC Executive Secretariat, Ronald Reagan Library.

12 Press conference for American correspondents, 10 Jan. 1986: MTF, docid=106300 (accessed 13 Sept. 2007).

13 Sommers to Poindexter, undated [16 Jan. 1986]: File folder 8600439, System files records, NSC Executive Secretariat, Ronald Reagan Library.

14 Pearson to Poindexter, 21 Jan. 1986: File folder 8600439, System files records, NSC Executive Secretariat, Ronald Reagan Library.

15 Reagan to Thatcher, undated: File folder 8600439, System files records, NSC Executive Secretariat, Ronald Reagan Library.

16 Pearson to Sommers, undated: File folder 8600439, System files records, NSC Executive Secretariat, Ronald Reagan Library. Poindexter to Reagan, undated: File folder 8600439, System files records, NSC Executive Secretariat, Ronald Reagan Library. Similar arguments were replayed in 2003 during the planning and early stages of the war in Iraq, when the example of US intervention in Libya in 1986 was often cited. See 'Fire Power', *Washington Post*, 23 July. 2003.

17 Shultz, *Turmoil and Triumph*, p. 678.

18 'Libya', Issue Brief for Congress, 10 April 2002, p. 10. Congressional Research Service, Library of Congress (accessed 10 Mar. 2011). Brinkley (ed.), *Reagan Diaires*, Vol. II, p. 586.

19 Thatcher, *Downing Street Years*, p. 443; *The Times*, 12 Apr. 1986.

20 Howe, *Conflict of Loyalty*, p. 505; Thatcher, *Downing Street Years*, p. 445.

21 Howe, *Conflict of Loyalty*, pp. 505–6; Thatcher, *Downing Street Years*, p. 446; Dimbleby and Reynolds, *An Ocean Apart*, p. 346.

22 *New York Times*, 15 Apr. 1986. Reports initially said that eighteen

F-111 planes had taken off from the UK; the USAF later confirmed that the number was more than forty. Ed Moloney, *A Secret History of the IRA* (New York, 2002), p. 14. Michael Brecher and Jonathan Wilkenfeld, *A Study of Crisis* (Ann Arbor, MI, 1997), p. 93.

23 Thatcher, *Downing Street Years*, p. 447.

24 Ibid.

25 Baker, *The Turbulent Years*, p. 269.

26 Curtis (ed.), *Wyatt Journals*, Vol. 1, p. 124.

27 *New York Times*, 20 Apr. 1986; *Guardian*, 16 Apr. 1986.

28 House of Commons statement (US bombing of Libya), 16 Apr. 1986: MTF, docid=106363 (accessed 13 Sept. 2007).

29 *The Times*, 16 Apr. 1986.

30 Edward Heath, *The Course of my Life* (London, 1998), p. 619.

31 David Owen, *Time to Declare* (London, 1991), p. 642.

32 *New York Times*, 26 Apr. 1986; Brinkley (ed), *Reagan Diaries*, Vol. II, p. 590.

33 Interview with Caspar Weinberger, 19 Nov. 2002: RROH. *Time* magazine, 28 Apr. 1986.

34 *Washington Post*, 25 Apr. 1986; Shultz, *Turmoil and Triumph*, p. 687.

35 *Washington Post*, 22 Apr. 1986.

36 *The Times*, 24 Apr. 1986.

37 Reagan to Thatcher, 14 Mar. 1986: File folder 8600439, System files records, NSC Executive Secretariat, Ronald Reagan Library. Brinkley, (ed), *Reagan Diaries*, Vol. II, p. 619.

38 Press conference after Tokyo G-7, 5 May 1986: MTF, docid=106385 (accessed 13 Sept. 2007).

39 For a summary of the Rekjavik summit, see Reynolds, *Summits*, pp. 358–63. Rhodes, *Arsenals of Folly*, pp. 236–70. Transcripts of the summit: MTF, docid=109177, 109178, 109179, 109180, 109181.

40 Hoffman, *The Dead Hand*, p. 262. Rhodes, *Arsenals of Folly*, pp. 271–2.

41 Kengor, *The Crusader*, p. 261.

42 Reykjavik summit, memcon, 12 Oct. 1986: MTF, docid=110621 (accessed 28 May 2010).

43 Shultz, *Turmoil and Triumph*, p. 773.

44 Interview with James Kuhn, 7 Mar. 2003: RROH.
45 Ibid.
46 *New York Times*, 15 and 19 Oct. 1986.
47 Mann, *The Rebellion of Ronald Reagan*, p. 46. Matlock, *Reagan and Gorbachev*, p. 239. Michael Mandelbaum and Strobe Talbott, 'Reykjavik and Beyond', *Foreign Affairs*, vol. 65, no. 2 (Winter 1986), pp. 215–35. Stable URL: http://www.jstor.org/stable/20042975.
48 Pryce-Jones, *The Fall of the Soviet Empire, 1985–1991*, p. 122. Mann, *The Rebellion of Ronald Reagan*, p. 48. For Perle's commentary at the time, see Richard Perle, 'Reykjavik as a Watershed in U.S.-Soviet Arms Control', *International Security*, vol. 12, no. 1 (Summer 1987), pp. 175–8. Stable URL: http://www.jstor.org/stable/2538922.
49 *Washington Post*, 30 Oct. 1986. Interview with Kenneth Adelman, 30 Sept. 2003: RROH. Reynolds, *Summits*, p. 363. Rhodes, *Arsenals of Folly*, pp. 271–2. Dmitri Volkogonov, *The Rise and Fall of the Soviet Empire* (London, 1999), p. 495. Clare Berlinski, *There is No Alternative: Why Margaret Thatcher matters* (New York, 2008), p. 293.
50 Thatcher, *Downing Street Years*, p. 471; Dale, *Memories of Maggie*, p. 144; Howe, *Conflict of Loyalty*, p. 523.
51 Thatcher, *Downing Street Years*, p. 472; McFarlane to Reagan, 30 Aug. 1985; Withdrawal sheet 'summary of telephone conversation, Reagan/Thatcher, 13 Oct. 1986': File, System files, Records, NSC Executive Secretariat, Ronald Reagan Library. Jane M. O. Sharp, 'After Reykjavik: Arms Control and the Allies', *International Affairs*, vol. 63, no. 2 (Spring 1987), pp. 239–57. Stable URL: http://www.jstor.org/stable/3025423.
52 Berlinski, *There is No Alternative*, p. 293.
53 Poindexter to Reagan, 12 Nov. 1986: File folder: Thatcher visit November 15 (2), Box 90902, NSC European & Soviet Affairs Directorate, Ronald Reagan Library.
54 Ibid.
55 Shultz to Reagan, 12 Nov. 1986: File folder: Thatcher visit November 15 (2), Box 90902, NSC European & Soviet Affairs Directorate, Ronald Reagan Library.

56 'Possible common press points': File folder: Thatcher visit November 15 (2), Box 90902, NSC European & Soviet Affairs Directorate, Ronald Reagan Library. Smith, *Reagan and Thatcher*, p. 221. Ridgway to Shultz, 5 Nov. 1986: File folder: Thatcher visit November 15 (2), Box 90902, NSC European & Soviet Affairs Directorate, Ronald Reagan Library.

57 Interview with James Kuhn, 7 Mar. 2003: RROH.

58 Tillman to Poindexter, 23 Oct. 1986; President's talking points: File folder: Thatcher visit November 15 (2), Box 90902, NSC European & Soviet Affairs Directorate, Ronald Reagan Library.

59 Press conference after Camp David talks, 15 Nov. 1986: MTF, docid=106514 (accessed 14 Sept. 2007).

60 *Sunday Times*, 16 Nov. 1986; Thatcher, *Downing Street Years*, pp. 473, 772.

61 Press conference after Camp David talks, 15 Nov. 1986: MTF, docid=106514 (accessed 14 Sept. 2007).

62 Anderson and Anderson, *Reagan's Secret War*, pp. 318–22; Stephen F. Hayward, *The Age of Reagan* (New York, 2009), pp. 529, 532. Brinckley (ed.), *Reagan Diaries*, Vol. II, p. 661. Patterson, *Restless Giant*, pp. 206–13.

63 Press conference after Camp David talks, 15 Nov. 1986: MTF, docid=106514 (accessed 14 Sept. 2007). Smith, *Reagan and Thatcher*, pp. 204–13.

64 Brinkley (ed.), *Reagan Diaries*, Vol. II, p. 658.

65 Sommer/Lavin to Poindexter, 10 Nov. 1986: File folder: Thatcher visit November 15 (2), Box 90902, NSC European & Soviet Affairs Directorate, Ronald Reagan Library.

66 Thatcher to Reagan, 4 Dec. 1986: MTF, docid=109432 (accessed 2 June 2010).

67 Brinkley (ed.), *Reagan Diaries*, Vol. II, p. 667. *Newsweek*, 23 Jan. 2011.

68 Curtis (ed.), *Wyatt Journals*, Vol. 1, p. 370.

CHAPTER TEN

1 Meeting with Neil Kinnock, briefing and background papers for the President, 27 Mar. 1987: MTF, docid=110648 (accessed 13 Oct. 2007). Brinkley (ed.), *Reagan Diaries*, Vol. II, p. 705. Obituary of Oliver Wright, *The Times*, 9 Sept. 2009; Healey, *The Time of my Life*, p. 535. It was not the first time that Healey had been discomforted in such a way. As he entered the room to meet Chernenko in Moscow in October 1984, the Soviet leader could be heard loudly asking his advisers, 'Healey, Healey? Who's he?' – *The Times*, 30 Mar. 1987.
2 *New York Times*, 28 Mar. 1987.
3 *The Times*, 30 Mar. 1987.
4 Giles Radice, *Diaries, 1980–2001* (London, 2004), p. 157.
5 Ron Reagan, *My Father at 100: A memoir* (New York, 2011), p. 216.
6 Interview with Paul Laxalt, 9 Oct. 2001: RROH. Reagan, *My Father at 100*, p. 216.
7 Recommended Telephone Call, 28 Feb. 1987: MTF, docid=109434 (accessed 13 Oct. 2007). *The Times*, 25 Mar. 1987.
8 Anderson and Anderson, *Reagan's Secret War*, pp. 335–7.
9 Reagan meeting with Neil Kinnock, briefing and background papers, 27 Mar. 1987: MTF, docid=110648 (accessed 13 Oct. 2007).
10 *Sunday Times*, 5 Apr. 1987; Smith, *Reagan and Thatcher*, p. 229. Thatcher interview, 8 Jan. 1990: MTF, docid=109324 (accessed 18 June 2010).
11 *Sunday Times*, 29 Mar. 1987.
12 *Sunday Times*, 5 Apr. 1987.
13 *Weekly Standard*, 15 Jan. 2007.
14 *The Times*, 28 May 1987; *Guardian*, 5 June 1987.
15 *The Times*, 10 June 1987.
16 Tony Blair would repeat the trick in 1997, 2001 and 2005.
17 *Guardian*, 13 June 1987.
18 Batjer to Colin Powell, 9 Jun. 1987: MTF, docid=110639 (accessed 13 Oct. 2007).
19 Kengor, *The Crusador*, p. 264.

20 Interview with Howard Baker, 24 Aug. 2004: RROH. *Wall Street Journal*, 11 June 2004.
21 Memcon, Reagan and Thatcher, 12 June 1987: MTF, docid=110335 (accessed 13 Oct. 2007); Press release, 17 June 1987: MTF, docid=110639 (accessed 13 Oct. 2007).
22 Shultz, *Turmoil and Triumph*, p. 909.
23 Thatcher, *Downing Street Years*, p. 770.
24 CBS News interview, 17 July 1987: MTF, docid=106913 (accessed 13 Oct. 2007).
25 Memcon, Reagan and Thatcher meeting at the White House, 17 July 1987: Folder UK (June–July 1987), Box 92271, Thomas E. McNamara Files, Ronald Reagan Library. Thatcher, *Downing Street Years*, pp. 770–1.
26 Memcon, Reagan and Thatcher meeting at the White House, 17 July 1987: Folder UK (June–July 1987), Box 92271, Thomas E. McNamara Files, Ronald Reagan Library.
27 Ibid.
28 Thatcher interview, 8 Jan. 1990: MTF, docid=109324 (accessed 18 June 2010). Thatcher, *Downing Street Years*, p. 771.
29 Thatcher, *Downing Street Years*, pp. 771–2.
30 Drawn from Memcon, Reagan and Thatcher meeting at the White House, 17 July 1987: Folder UK (June–July 1987), Box 92271, Thomas E. McNamara Files, Ronald Reagan Library. Brinkley (ed.), *Reagan Diaries*, Vol. I, p. 751.
31 Thatcher, *Downing Street Years*, p. 770. Reynolds, *Summits*, p. 329. Reagan, *My Father at 100*, p. 217. http://www.nytimes.com/1987/10/18/us/surgeons-remove-cancerous-breast-of-nancy-reagan.html (accessed 21 Mar. 2011).
32 Statement after meeting President Reagan, 17 Jul. 1987: MTF, docid=106914 (accessed 13 Oct. 2007).
33 Brinkley (ed.), *Reagan Diaries*, Vol. II, p. 751.
34 Interview, CBS, *Face the Nation*, 17 July 1987: MTF, docid=106915 (accessed 13 Oct. 2007).
35 Brinkley (ed.), *Reagan Diaries*, Vol. II, p. 751.
36 Ibid. Smith, *Reagan and Thatcher*, p. 213. Thatcher interview, 8 Jan. 1990: MTF, docid=109324 (accessed 18 June 2010).
37 *Sunday Times*, 13 Dec. 1987.

38 *Sunday Times*, 13 Dec. 1987. Thatcher, *Downing Street Years*, p. 773.
39 *Sunday Times*, 13 Dec. 1987; Baker, *The Turbulent Years*, p. 353. Thatcher, *Downing Street Years*, p. 773.
40 Brinkley (ed.), *Reagan Diaries*, Vol. II, p. 809. Thatcher, *Downing Street Years*, p. 774.
41 Thatcher interview, 8 Jan. 1990: MTF, docid=109324 (accessed 18 June 2010).
42 Brinkley (ed.), *Reagan Diaries*, Vol II, p. 809. The summary of the INF Treaty and the Washington summit is drawn from David Reynolds, *Summits*, pp. 364–5.
43 Ibid.
44 Barbara Farnham, 'Reagan and the Gorbachev Revolution: Perceiving the End of the Threat,' *Political Science Quarterly*, vol. 116, no. 2 (2001), pp. 225–52. Interview with Kenneth Adelman, 30 Sept. 2003: RROH.
45 Ibid. Pryce-Jones, *The Fall of the Soviet Empire, 1985–1991*, p. 20. Westad, *The Global Cold War*, p. 322.
46 Interview with Kenneth Adelman, 30 Sept. 2003: RROH.
47 Brinkley (ed.), *Reagan Diairies*, Vol. II, p. 811; *Washington Post*, 20 Dec. 1987.
48 Paul Schott Stevens to Melvyn Levitsky, 18 Dec. 1987, Memcons, Reagan with Thatcher, Kohl, Takeshita and Mitterrand: File 8709130, System files, Records, NSC Executive Secretariat, Ronald Reagan Library; Presidential talking points for conversation with Thatcher, 11 ec. 1987: MTF, docid=110583 (accessed 13 Oct. 2007).
49 *Guardian*, 17 Dec. 1987.

CHAPTER ELEVEN

1 Thatcher TV interview with CBS, 22 Jan. 1988: MTF, docid=107153 (accessed 13 Oct. 2007).
2 *Washington Post*, 2 Mar. 1988; *The Times*, 2 Mar. 1988.
3 *Guardian*, 4 Mar. 1988; *New York Times*, 4 Mar. 1988.
4 *Guardian*, 5 Mar. 1988.
5 Volkogonov, *The Rise and Fall of the Soviet Empire*, p. 489.

6 Hoffman, *The Dead Hand*, pp. 333–6. Christopher Andrew, 'Red Alert', *Literary Review* (February 2011), p. 9.
7 *Washington Post*, 4 Mar. 1988; *Sunday Times*, 6 Mar. 1988.
8 *Sunday Times*, 6 Mar. 1988. Brinkley (ed.), *Reagan Diaries*, Vol. II, p. 848.
9 Interview with Paul Laxalt, 9 Oct. 2001: RROH.
10 *New York Times*, 2 June 1988.
11 *Washington Post*, 3 June 1988.
12 *The Times*, 2 June 1988.
13 *New York Times*, 2 June 1988; *Guardian*, 3 June 1988; *The Times*, 3 June 1988.
14 Public Papers of Ronald Reagan, 3 June 1988: <http://www.reagan.utcxas.edu/archives/speeches/1988/060388a.htm> (accessed 24 June 2010).
15 Reply to Reagan's speech at Guildhall, 3 June 1988: MTF, docid=107253 (accessed 13 Oct. 2007).
16 *New York Times*, 2 June 1988.
17 Interview with Paul Laxalt, 9 Oct. 2001: RROH.
18 TV interview for ITN: MTF, docid=107267 (accessed 13 Oct. 2007).
19 Urban, *Diplomacy and Disillusion*, pp. 95–7; Howe, *Conflict of Loyalty*, p. 508.
20 Wall to Kerr, 29 June 1988: MTF, docid=111778 (accessed 25 Jun. 2010). Clark, *Diaries*, p. 227.
21 The Bruges Speech, 20 Sept. 2010: MTF, docid=107332 (accessed 13 Oct. 2007).
22 Powell to Reagan, 15 Nov. 1988: MTF, docid=110574 (accessed 25 June 2010). Shultz to Reagan, 4 Nov. 1988: MTF, docid=110569 (accessed 13 Oct. 2007). Paul Sharp, *Thatcher's Diplomacy: The revival of British foreign policy* (London, 1997), pp. 168–70. *Sunday Times*, 25 Sept. 1988.
23 *Guardian*, 17 Nov. 1988.
24 Brinkley (ed.), *Reagan Diaries*, Vol. II, p. 979; Speeches at White House arrival ceremony, 16 Nov. 1988: MTF, docid=107381 (accessed 13 Oct. 2007).
25 Quotes from Reagan's speaking cards, 16 Nov. 1988: MTF, docid=110572 (accessed 13 Oct. 2007).

26 Powell to Reagan, 15 Nov. 1988: MTF, docid=110574 (accessed 25 June 2007).

27 Quotes from Reagan's speaking cards, 16 Nov. 1988: MTF, docid=110572 (accessed 13 Oct. 1988).

28 Talking Points for Mrs Reagan's coffee with Denis Thatcher, 16 Nov. 1988: Folder, Margaret Thatcher, 11/16/1988, Box 92450, NSC Coordination Office Records, Ronald Reagan Library. Curtis (ed.), *Wyatt Journals*, Vol. 1, p. 669.

29 *Washington Post*, 17 Nov. 1988.

30 Shultz briefing for Reagan, Thatcher visit, 4 Nov. 1988: MTF, docid=110569 (accessed 13 Oct. 2007).

31 Speeches at the White House state banquet, 16 Nov. 1988: MTF, docid=107384 (accessed 13 Oct. 2007); *Washington Post*, 7 Nov. 1988.

32 Brinkley (ed.), *Reagan Diaries*, Vol. II, p. 979.

33 BBC, 'On this day', 21 Dec. 1988 <http://news.bbc.co.uk/onthisday/hi/dates/stories/december/21/newsid_2539000/2539447.stm> (accessed 30 Jun. 2010). Abdelbaset al-Megrahi was controversially released from a Scottish prison on compassionate grounds in 2009.

34 TV interview for TV-Am, 30 Dec. 1988: MTF, docid=107022; Reagan call to Thatcher, 22 Dec. 1988: MTF, docid=109435 (accessed 30 June 2010).

35 Reagan, *An American Life*, p. 704; Thatcher, *Downing Street Years*, pp. 448–9; Margaret Thatcher, *Statecraft* (London, 2002), p. 232. *Sunday Telegraph*, 5 Sept. 2009.

36 Article for *National Review*, 30 Dec. 1988: MTF, docid=107425 (accessed 13 Oct. 2007).

37 Thatcher to Reagan, 19 Jan. 1988: MTF, docid=110359 (accessed 13 Oct. 2007).

38 Reagan to Thatcher, 19 Jan. 1988: MTF, docid=110358 (accessed 13 Oct. 2007).

39 Brinkley (ed.), *Reagan Diaries*, Vol. II, p. 1011.

EPILOGUE

1 *Los Angeles Times*, 29 Jan. 1993; 7 Feb. 1993.
2 Cannon, *President Reagan: The role of a lifetime*, preface to rev. edn, 2000. *Newsweek*, 23 Jan. 2011.
3 When Churchill had a severe stroke in 1953, it went unreported in the newspapers. The prime minister was said to be tired and in need of rest. He did not appear in public for several months.
4 PBS, *American Experience: Reagan*. Transcript: http://www.pbs.org/wgbh/americanexperience/features/transcript/reagan-transcript/ (accessed 14 Apr. 2011).
5 Ibid.
6 Carol Thatcher, *A Swim-on Part in the Goldfish Bowl* (London, 2008), pp. 255ff.
7 *New York Times*, 2 Sept. 2008.
8 Interview, *Dundee Courier*, 7 Sept. 1989: MTF, docid=107755 (accessed 15 Apr. 2011).
9 Thatcher, *Downing Street Years*, pp. 851–5.
10 Clark, *Diaries*, p. 373.
11 Thatcher, *Swim-on Part*, p. 257. *Daily Mail*, 15 Feb. 2007.
12 *Wilmington Star-News*, 7 Dec. 1990.
13 Skinner, Anderson, and Anderson (eds.), *Reagan: A life in letters*, p. 727.
14 *New York Times*, 13, 14 June 1989.
15 *New York Times*, 13 June 1989.
16 US pool report of Thatcher/Bush meeting, 1 June 1989: MTF, docid=110748 (accessed 22 Apr. 2011).
17 Joint press conference outside No. 10, 1 June 1989: MTF, docid=107687 (accessed 22 Apr. 2011). *New York Times*, 26 May; 1–2 June 1989.
18 Mead, *God and Gold: Britain, America and the making of the modern world*, pp. 5, 13.
19 Reynolds, 'Rethinking Anglo-American Relations', *International Affairs*, vol. 65, no. 1 (Winter 1988–9), pp. 89–111. Stable URL: http://www.jstor.org/stable/2620984. Reynolds, 'A "Special Relationship"? America, Britain and the International Order since the Second World War' in *International Affairs*, vol. 62, No. 1 (winter, 1985–1986), pp. 1–20: http://jstor.org/stahle/2618063

20 Daniel T. Rodgers, *Age of Fracture* (Cambridge, MA, 2011), pp. 24–5.
21 Alfred Sherman, *Paradoxes of Power: Reflections on the Thatcher interlude* (Exeter, 2005), p. 25.
22 Interview with Howard Baker, 24 Aug. 2004: RROH.
23 *New York Times*, 26 and 29 May 1989. Campbell Craig and Fredrik Logevall, *America's Cold War* (Cambridge, MA, 2009), pp. 338–9.
24 Fukuyama, 'The End of History?', *The National Interest*, (Summer 1989).
25 *New York Times*, 29 May 1989.
26 *New York Times,* 26 Apr. 1997.
27 Craig and Logevall, *America's Cold War*, p. 345.
28 *New York Times*, 16 Mar. 1992.
29 Knott and Chidester, *At Reagan's Side*, p. 218. Arthur Schlesinger, *Journals, 1952–2000* (New York, 2007), p. 768.
30 *The Times*, 23 May 2011.

Index